False Prophets and Preachers

False Prophets
AND Preachers

Henry Gresbeck's Account of the
Anabaptist Kingdom of Münster

CHRISTOPHER S. MACKAY

Early Modern Studies 18
Truman State University Press
Kirksville, Missouri

tsup.truman.edu

Cover art: Johann Karl Ulrich Bähr, *Jan van Leiden tauft ein Mädchen*. Oil on canvas, 1840. Westphalian State Museum of Art and Cultural History.
Cover design: Teresa Wheeler

Library of Congress Cataloging-in-Publication Data

Names: Gresbeck, Heinrich, active 1540. | Mackay, Christopher S., 1962–
Title: False prophets and preachers : Henry Gresbeck's account of the
    Anabaptist kingdom of Münster / [translated and annotated by] Christopher
    Mackay.
Other titles: Berichte der Augenzeugen über das münsterische
    Wiedertäuferreich. English
Description: Kirksville, Missouri : Truman State University Press, 2016. |
    Series: Early modern studies ; 18 | Includes bibliographical references.
Identifiers: LCCN 2015042883 (print) | LCCN 2016006745 (ebook) | ISBN
    9781612481418 (library binding : alkaline paper) | ISBN 9781612481425 ()
Subjects: LCSH: Gresbeck, Heinrich, active 1540. |
    Anabaptists—Germany—Münster in Westfalen—History—16th century. |
    Münster in Westfalen (Germany)—Church history—16th century. | Münster
    in Westfalen (Germany)—History—16th century. |
    Germany—History—1517-1648.
Classification: LCC BX4933.G3 G7413 2016 (print) | LCC BX4933.G3 (ebook) |
    DDC 943/.5614031—dc23
LC record available at http://lccn.loc.gov/2015042883

Kelliae carissimae ac de me optime merenti,
cuius ocelli, siquid desit meis, supplent!

Contents

Illustrations

Introduction

The Radical Reformation in Münster

Late one night in late May 1535, five men warily snuck out of the besieged city of Münster. One man became separated from the group. He wandered in the dark, trying to avoid the enemy troops in the trenches, but eventually decided to give himself up and hope for the best. This man, Henry Gresbeck, was to play a major part in the recapture of the city from the Anabaptists. He would also write the only eyewitness account of what had gone on in the city for the preceding fifteen months. Gresbeck addressed his account to the prince-bishop, possibly to explain his role in the Anabaptist rebellion and his importance to the eventual capture of the city. Gresbeck's original manuscript seems to have disappeared into the prince-bishop's archive (eventually turning up in the archives in Cologne). His account had no effect on the sixteenth-century treatments of the events in Münster; it was only rediscovered in the mid-nineteenth century. That account is here translated into English for the first time.

The best-known surviving source for the events in Münster was written a generation later by the schoolmaster Herman von Kerssenbrock, who was a boy at the time of the Anabaptist regime and fled the city. He wrote his history in Latin a generation later (in the 1560s), partly using archival information but mostly by borrowing from earlier historians. Kerssenbrock's magisterial work eclipsed not only the influence of earlier historians, but also the knowledge of Gresbeck's eyewitness account.

It was only with the 1853 publication of Gresbeck's account in a collection of documents edited by C. A. Cornelius that his involvement in the fall of the city came to be generally known. Cornelius based his edition of the Low German on two derivative manuscripts. One was a heavily edited copy of Gresbeck's account from the ducal library in Darmstadt and the other a copy that was edited and converted into High German from a library in Meiningen. Cornelius was unable to consult another manuscript of Gresbeck that was located in Cologne. I have used a copy of the original manuscript that Gresbeck submitted to the prince-bishop to prepare a much better edition of the original text, and that text is the basis of the following translation. The Cologne manuscript appears to be the original manuscript Gresbeck had submitted to the prince-bishop. The translation presented in this volume is based on that early copy.

The narrative presented in Gresbeck's retrospective account is not without its own difficulties, but not only does it give us the perspective of a common man on very unusual events, it is also the only account written by a man who actually witnessed these events with his own eyes. To judge by his account, Gresbeck was a keen observer of events around him, and he presents his story with verve and humor.

1. The Münster Rebellion

The Anabaptist regime in Münster was brief—from February 1534 to June 1535—and the fact that the city was under siege resulted from one of the most remarkable events of the early Reformation in Germany.[1] In the years before 1533, the city of Münster was gripped with reforming fervor, which was adopted in part by the dignitaries of the local city council. The city was under the control, however, of the prince-bishop of Münster, who held both religious and secular powers. The city council had extorted wide-ranging privileges that amounted to autonomy from the newly appointed Bishop Francis of Waldeck in 1533, but these would prove to be short-lived. The Reformers were intent on going much further in their religious innovations

---

1. For a short (generally narrative) introduction to the events in Münster, see Klötzer, "Melchiorites and Münster." For the general history of the city in the late medieval and early modern period, see Lutterbach, *Der Weg in das Täuferreich.* Arthur, *Tailor-King,* is an unreliable popularizing treatment. Due to disputes with the city council of Münster at the time, Kerssenbrock was unable to get his work published, and it remained in manuscript form until the Latin text was finally published in 1899, edited by Detmer on the basis of one particularly good manuscript. (I've been informed by Berndt Thier of the Stadtmuseum Münster that other good early witnesses [i.e., other versions] to the Kerssenbrock text have come to light, but the new textual information provided by them has not been published.) The only modern translation of Kerssenbrock's work is my own: Kerssenbrock, *Narrative of the Anabaptist Madness,* ed. Mackay.

than the Lutheran-inspired members of the city council were willing to go. One particularly noteworthy element in the Reformers' beliefs was the rejection of infant baptism. They believed that baptism had to be voluntarily undertaken by responsible adults. Since at that time pretty much everybody would have received baptism as an infant, anyone who underwent a new baptism as an adult was a rebaptizer, or Anabaptist (*Wiedertäufer* in modern High German, the literal translation of the Latinate *anabaptista*).

At this time, there were throughout the areas to the west and north of Münster (the Low Countries and Frisia) many followers of Melchior Hofman, who held religious views of a distinctly radical nature, including a belief that the apocalypse was close at hand. Hofman himself was under arrest in Strasburg, but the radical adherents of his views took control of the Münster council during the regular elections in February 1534, and soon moved to expel from the city all those who did not actively support their agenda. The result of this was that many men fled the city, leaving their wives behind to guard the family property. The radical Anabaptists were now in firm control of the city.

The radicals' leader was a huge, charismatic man from Holland named John Mathias. Under his leadership, the inhabitants organized a military force to defend themselves and undertook raids against neighboring towns. After Mathias died in one such raid around Easter, control of the city was assumed by a biblically inspired council of twelve elders. During this early period of Anabaptist rule, a sort of communal form of ownership was dictated for the city. On the grounds that it was wrong for one Christian to have more than another or to take advantage of a fellow Christian through shady dealing, coins and precious metals (gold and silver) were confiscated; food and clothing were added to the list of items to be held in common and doled out to the populace on an as-needed basis by public officials.

The prince-bishop responded to what he took to be disobedience on the part of his subjects by gathering an army. He stationed his troops outside the city, hoping for an opportunity to retake the city. A major assault in May failed because some of the troops attacked prematurely. Another assault in late August came to grief in the face of stiff resistance from the defense. The prince-bishop's finances were now exhausted, and he sought the assistance of neighboring princes. They agreed to fund the military campaign against the city, but took over command of the operation, which they placed in the hands of Count Wirich of Falkenstein. In the fall, the expensive steps were finally taken to fully surround the city with a complete circuit of manned trenches, eventually cutting it off from the outside world.

Meanwhile, their seemingly miraculous success in driving back the assault on the city in August led to exaltation among the Anabaptists in Münster. In the aftermath of John Mathias's death, John of Leiden, a one-time tailor, had assumed leadership of the radicals. He was seen as the instrument of God's expected victory over his foes, and he soon instituted a full regal court. A prominent figure in the court was Bernard Knipperdolling, a member of the traditional ruling class of Münster who had taken the radicals' side in the religious disputes of previous years. Both John of Leiden and Knipperdolling used state violence to suppress opposition to the Anabaptist regime.

The radicals did not face resistance only from outside. The radicals caused widespread discontent in July 1534 when they abolished traditional monogamous marriage and replaced it with a polygamous scheme based on Old Testament precedents. A more practical reason for the innovation may have been the large excess of adult females compared to males. This surprising move was bitterly opposed by many and produced a revolt in the city, which the Anabaptists managed to put down only with difficulty.

In the fall, before the city was put under a tight siege, embassies were sent out to neighboring communities to stir up revolt. These embassies were uniformly unsuccessful, and the envoys put to death. By the winter of 1535, things were looking bad for the Anabaptists. Their king hoped to stir up revolution among sympathizers in the Low Countries, but these expectations proved to be as illusory as the efforts to convert the towns around Münster. By the springtime, while the king's court was still living rather comfortably on the confiscated provisions of the community, the regular populace was beginning to suffer from starvation and there was widespread discontent. The king resorted to appointing "dukes" who were supposed to rule the earth in the king's name after the final victory of the Anabaptists. In practice, their purpose was apparently to keep the growing dissatisfaction with the king's rule under control. It was under these circumstances of desperation and suppression that the five men mentioned above were driven to flee the city.

Two of these men had plans to capture the city: Henry Gresbeck, a local cabinetmaker, and Little Hans of Longstreet (Henseken van der Langenstraten), a renegade soldier from the prince-bishop's army who had fled to the city but later regretted his decision. After the men became separated,

Gresbeck revealed his plan to the officers in the pay of the neighboring princes, while Little Hans was eventually put in touch with the prince-bishop by his former commander. Both Gresbeck and Little Hans collaborated in preparations for the attempt to seize the city through a secret nighttime assault on the city's massive defenses, but only Little Hans took an active role in implementing the plan, leading the troops into the city. At first, the closing of a gate locked the first wave of troops in the city, and a battle raged throughout the final hours of the night. Eventually, however, additional troops from outside gained entry, and the Anabaptists surrendered. Many were slaughtered at the time of the town's capture, and after three days of plunder by the victorious troops, the Anabaptists' property was confiscated. John of Leiden, Knipperdolling, and one other of the king's main supporters were put to death in February 1536.

Little Hans was hailed by the prince-bishop for his role in the city's capture, and he figures prominently in the surviving accounts written by the Anabaptists' enemies. Gresbeck, on the other hand, is entirely ignored in these accounts. In order (it would seem) to vindicate his role in the city's capture (and presumably to gain restitution for his confiscated property), Gresbeck wrote his long account of the Anabaptist episode in Münster.

2. Religious Background

Though there were certainly some challenges to its claims, the Latin-speaking Roman Catholic Church of the later Middle Ages was dominant throughout Western Europe until the Augustinian monk and theology professor Martin Luther began in 1517 a series of attacks on practices and doctrines that quickly developed into the widespread rejection of the traditional church and the establishment in many places in northern Europe of new forms of ecclesiastic organization.[2] Although the Anabaptists shared many ideas with the earlier Reformers, their distinctive interpretations set the radical reformers of Münster at odds with the more conservative Lutherans.[3]

---

2. For a good general introduction to the state of the medieval church on the eve of the Reformation, see MacCulloch, *Reformation*, 3–52. For the medieval church in general, see Logan, *History of the Church*. See Duffy, *Siege Warfare*, for an extensive (if biased) discussion of the sorts of popular piety that the Reformers objected to (the treatment is, of course, of English practices and beliefs, but these wouldn't have been greatly different from those in Germany).

3. For the classic treatment of the "radical" reformation, see Williams, *Radical Reformation*. For a

The immediate issue that Luther raised was that of indulgences (remission from punishment in purgatory as a "reward" for meritorious behavior). Luther denied that the pope had the power to "obligate" God to do anything, and this argument quickly resulted in a rejection of the church's ability to make innovations by its own authority (ultimately based in Catholic thought on the "power of the keys" granted by Christ to St. Peter). The Anabaptists certainly agreed with Luther in the rejection of papal authority and of the validity of "medieval accretions" (practices not based on the New Testament). Luther's followers made a concerted effort to set up a new organization of their own, and tried on numerous occasions to win the radical Anabaptists over to their new conception. The Anabaptists refused to join the Lutherans, but all parties took for granted the need for some sort of ecclesiastical organization.

An important difference between the Anabaptists and the Lutherans was their views on baptism. Luther considered baptism part of the mechanism by which God distributed his grace to Christians. Since God's grace was entirely dependent upon his omnipotent goodness, human activity had nothing to do with the granting of grace, and so Luther saw nothing wrong with infant baptism. In effect, since God's grace was freely available to all Christians, there was no need for the individual's will to be involved in the acquisition of it, so grace could just as well be given to infants. In fact, it made more sense for baptism—as a symbol of God's universal grace—to be bestowed at the start of life. The Anabaptists, however, would have a quite different interpretation of the biblical institution. For them, baptism represented the active conversion of an adult fully aware of the significance and consequences of the act.

The two groups also disagreed on the subject of the Eucharist. In the traditional Catholic interpretation (transubstantiation), during the Eucharist, the ceremony commemorating the Last Supper (for the New Testament evidence, see Matthew 6:17–30, Mark 14:12–26, Luke 22:7–38, John 13–17), the wine and bread were literally converted into the blood and flesh of Christ (with the consumption of the former reserved for the officiants). Luther retained the Eucharist, feeling that this sacrament was another vehicle by which the word of God was made available to Christians; but Luther not only made the wine available to the congregants but also somewhat

---

more succinct treatment, see Goertz, "Radical Religiosity in the German Reformation," 70–85. For a solid introduction to Luther's life and thought, see Oberman, *Luther*.

reconfigured the traditional notion of transubstantiation. In his view, while there was a union of the physical wine and bread with the blood and flesh of Christ, it was the case both that the materials retained their original composition and that the blood and flesh were also there. He famously compared the result to an iron heated in a fire: it retains characteristics of both iron and fire. This view is traditionally termed "consubstantiation," though some Lutherans are adamant that consubstantiation is a different concept and Luther's idea should be called sacramental union. Regardless of the terminology and the exact details of Luther's view, while he rejected the complete conversion of the wine and bread, he nonetheless did feel that in some way the blood and flesh were also present in the sacramental food and drink. This was an interpretation the Anabaptists would reject. For them, the Last Supper was symbolically commemorated in a communal meal in which the bread and the wine had no mystical power, but retained their regular nature.

For Luther, infant baptism signified that all the baptized Christians in the community belonged to the recognized church. That is, he took it for granted that all nominal Christians belonged to the church, whatever their personal failings. The radicals of Münster adopted a much higher standard for acceptance as a "true" Christian. Only those who properly lived the Christian life (as they understood it) and who overtly manifested their resolve to do so through adult baptism were considered Christians, and all others were enemies of the true faith. Loyalty to God was taken to have priority over any other considerations, and in the final analysis the Anabaptists agreed with the medieval view that there was a unity between secular and religious authority. Whereas for Lutherans, the state consisted of all valid Christians within its territories, the radicals' exclusivist understanding of the Christian community would lead them to either forcibly convert or drive out those who rejected their teachings.

2.1 Origins of Anabaptism

All baptisms recorded in the New Testament involved adults. The Gospel of Mark describes John the Baptist as proclaiming "a baptism of repentance for the remission of sins" (1:4), and Jesus himself states, "Whoever believes and is baptized shall be saved" (Mark 16:16).[4] It is hard to see,

---

4. Of course, the absence of any text after Mark 16:9 in the manuscript Sinaiticus (also called Aleph), the best witness to the ancient text of the New Testament, shows that this verse is a later

the Anabaptists argued, how an infant could believe, and even if one is inclined to disjoin the notions of belief and baptism in the second passage (contrary to the surface sense of the passage), an infant can hardly repent.[5] On this basis, the doctrine arose in the 1520s that baptism is a rite that should be undergone by an adult in full knowledge of the tenets of the faith, and the term for this sort of baptism is "believer's baptism." In the context of the sixteenth century, when everyone who adopted the new rite would perforce have previously received traditional baptism as infants, such believer's baptism would be a second baptism or rebaptism, and the term Anabaptist (from the Greek for "rebaptizer") arose to characterize them. (Gresbeck uses the German version of this, *wedderdopper* in his Low German, the equivalent of the High German *Wiedertäufer*.) Naturally, since the radicals rejected the validity of the initial infant baptism, there could be no "re"-baptism for them, and the term is in origin one of hostility. Nonetheless, the term is useful to describe those who adhered to the doctrine of believer's baptism, especially because in the absence of "Anabaptism," there is no common term to define this (rather variegated) strain of Protestant thought. The theological disputes about the nature of baptism began in the early to mid-1520s in southern Germany, and the radical interpretation spread rapidly.

2.2 Melchior Hofman

In his attack on the traditional church's monopoly of access to God, Luther had criticized the separation of the priesthood from the full body of believers. He argued that every Christian was in effect a priest, though only those who had been called upon by the community or authority to exercise this function in a formal manner were proper priests. Although a number of radical religious leaders were, like Luther, renegade Catholic priests (Ulrich Zwingli, Balthasar Hübmaier, Menno Simons), others had no formal religious training before embarking on the propagation of the new faith as they saw it. One such man was Melchior Hofman, whose brand of Anabaptism was to be the ultimate inspiration for the remarkable turn of affairs in

---

addition to the text. No one in the sixteenth century knew this, and the English here is simply a translation of Luther's rendering of the text.

    5. The traditional explanation of the remark about the remission of sins in connection with baptism is that this refers to original sin. Even if one grants this theoretical possibility, the specification of repentance ought to exclude such an explanation.

Münster.[6] Born in about 1495 in Swäbisch Hall in southwestern Germany, Hofman was a furrier by trade, and he eventually ended up in Livonia on the Baltic in 1522. Already an adherent of Luther, he got into trouble as a preacher in assorted German towns along the eastern shore of the Baltic (at one point his preaching resulted in an iconoclastic riot), and by 1526 he held a position as preacher in Stockholm. In 1527, his preaching yet again caused rioting, and he had to flee. He took up residence in the Baltic port city of Lübeck, but once the municipal authorities became aware of the radical nature of his preaching, they too sent him packing. He then sought to establish himself in Denmark, where the king was attempting a reformation. Hofman soon became embroiled in doctrinal disputes with the Lutheran preachers, and he traveled to Wittenberg to get a letter of commendation from Luther. Hofman had gained Luther's approval back in 1525 by concealing his doctrinal differences, but now Luther repudiated him.

What separated Hofman from Luther was not only his iconoclasm and allegorical interpretation of the Eucharist but also his apocalyptic eschatology. Already, in a work of 1526, Hofman predicted that the cataclysmic war between God's chosen and the godless as foretold in the book of Apocalypse (also called Revelation) would take place seven years later, in 1533.[7] The only element lacking for the program that would cause such turmoil in Münster was the doctrine of believer's baptism. A disputation was set up in the duchy of Schleswig (controlled by the Danish king) in 1529 to "test" Hofman's views, but it was clearly intended to provide an authoritative venue in which to reject them. In April, Hofman was ordered to recant or leave; he refused to recant and was duly banished. He moved to East Frisia (a German area on the North Sea coast to the southwest of Denmark to the eastern shore of the estuary of the River Ems), which was then in religious foment under the influence of Zwinglian ideas, and there he collaborated with Andreas Karlstadt, Luther's erstwhile colleague who was now his radical opponent.[8] Once more, Hofman ran into trouble with the Lutherans, and in June he moved to the city of Strasburg, one of the great centers of Reformation thought.

6. For a full analysis of Hofman's views (though a chronologically confusing biography), see Deppermann, *Melchior Hoffman*.
7. The figure of seven years was apparently reached by adding the forty-two months assigned to the two witnesses in Apocalypse 11:3 to the similar figure given to the Beast in 13:5.
8. For a discussion of Karlstadt's influence on Hofman (plus an extensive treatment of Hofman in his own right), see Pater, *Karlstadt as the Father*, 173–253.

Hofman was at first welcomed in Strasburg, but his doctrine had become even more radical, and he soon earned the enmity of local Zwinglian religious leaders. He saw himself as a prophet of God, and added to his apocalyptic views a conviction of the validity of believer's baptism. (Exactly when or under what circumstances this happened is unknown; perhaps Karlstadt had recently influenced him.) Swiss Anabaptists had arrived in Strasburg back in 1526, and although Wolfgang Capito had a certain amount of sympathy for them, the other Reform leaders in the city were implacably opposed to their teachings. After being rejected by the religious authorities, Hofman consorted with the so-called Strasburg prophets, a group of lower-class individuals who claimed to receive visions from God. Hofman was completely convinced of the validity of these prophecies and even published a book about them. Despite the city's rejection of him, however, Hofman officially declared that Strasburg would be the New Jerusalem mentioned in the book of Apocalypse and would form the center of resistance against the godless in the impending cataclysm that would mark the end of the world in 1533.

In April 1530, Hofman rashly asked the Strasburg city council to grant the Anabaptists a church, and for his efforts he was duly expelled. By the next month he was back in East Frisia, where he now began to spread his apocalyptic version of the doctrine of Anabaptism. He acquired several hundred followers in this area, which was riven with strife between Lutherans, Sacramentarians, and Catholics, but he was first forced to withdraw from Emden, the main city, in May, and he had to leave the entire territory in the fall. Apart from a visit to Strasburg in December 1531, Hofman's movements between there and his final arrival in Strasburg in 1533 are somewhat obscure, but he seems to have been successful in spreading his apocalyptic beliefs in the Low Countries and Frisia. In the Low Countries, the Sacramentarian movement, which rejected the actual presence of Christ in the bread and wine of the Eucharist, was widespread, and it was tolerated by the local magistrates, who were reluctant to uphold the repressive orders of the central government (the regency was held in the name of the absent Emperor Charles V by his aunt Margaret and then by his sister Mary after Margaret's death in November 1530).[9] Hofman's doctrines were propagat-

9. For the Sacramentarian setting in the Low Countries, see Williams, *Radical Reformation*, 528–35. The term "Sacramentarian" is in origin a hostile one used by Luther to denigrate the more radical

ed in Sacramentarian circles, and it was the prohibited practice of adult baptism that attracted the attention of the (reluctant) local authorities.

A change in Hofman's policy on encouraging adult (re)baptism was brought about by the actions of one of his followers. John Voelkerts had been baptized by Hofman in Emden, and began to act as his emissary in Amsterdam. (Among the first to be baptized by Voelkerts was Bartholomew Boekbinder, who would later spread the good word to Münster.) Initially the authorities were tolerant of Voelkerts's activities, but Voelkerts wished a martyr's death. Even though, when he was first arrested, the authorities all but invited him to escape, he not only refused to do so, but even revealed the names of those he had baptized. Eventually nine others were arrested, and on December 5, 1531, they were beheaded in The Hague. This news shocked Hofman, who thought it pointless to court a martyr's death, and he ordered a halt to adult baptism until the end of 1533.[10] For the next year, the temporary suspension (*Stillstand* or "standstill") of adult baptism brought a virtual halt to the execution of Melchiorites (as Hofman's followers may be termed). This makes it hard to track the exact spread of Hofman's sect in this period, but it would seem that its message of impending doom proved attractive to Sacramentarians.

In March 1533, Hofman returned from his peregrinations (most recently in East Frisia) to Strasburg, the city that he was sure would be the salvation of mankind in the last days. The city council, which had recently been taking a turn towards Lutheranism, was not at all pleased with his faith in their city; when he was accused in May of plotting rebellion, the council ordered his arrest. Hofman welcomed this as part of the apocalyptic last days, as he had been predicting since 1526 that a great council would imprison one of the two witnesses mentioned in Apocalypse 11; as it turned out, this was himself. When he was brought to trial before the city's synod in June, the charge of plotting rebellion was dropped and he was tried for his views on various technical theological points. Since there was no proof of any plot to stir up rebellion, there was no cause to execute him, yet he had large numbers

---

reformers who refused to accept his comparatively conservative views about the Eucharist. It is nonetheless a convenient one (and it is hard to see what to use in its place); for the origin and modern usage of the word, see ibid., 85, 95–96.

10. Since Hofman predicted that the apocalyptic end of the world would take place in 1533, the rebaptism could wait until then. In any case, he justified his action by analogy with the two-year suspension of the rebuilding of the great temple in Jerusalem that is recorded in Ezra 4:24.

of followers, and his unshakable faith in his prophecy of the world's demise made him dangerous. He would remain in close and isolated detention until his death (under obscure circumstances, apparently in 1543).

2.3 The Melchiorites

As the end of 1533 approached, and the time predicted for the apocalypse came ever nearer, the prohibition against believer's baptism began to chafe among the Melchiorites of the Low Countries, because they believed that such "real" baptism was the equivalent of the seal that distinguished the pious from the godless in Apocalypse 7:3 and 9:4. There was nothing the imprisoned Hofman could do, so John Mathias (or Matthys) took advantage of this discontent to replace Hofman as the direct leader of the Melchiorites.[11] A baker by trade, Mathias had long been involved in the Sacramentarian movement, and for his views, he had been sentenced to having his tongue pierced in 1528. He now proclaimed that he was Enoch, the second of the two witnesses mentioned in Apocalypse 11 as the leaders of the godly in the last days. The Melchiorites continued to view Hofman as the new Elijah, but previously the role of Enoch had been bestowed upon Cornelius Polderman, another of Hofman's followers.[12] On All Saints' Day (November 1), Mathias lifted the prohibition against adult baptism, and the same day he met and baptized John Bockelson of Leiden, who would eventually succeed Mathias as the Anabaptist leader in Münster and be crowned its king. At that time, Mathias also decided to abandon his previous wife, and took as his new "spiritual" wife the beautiful young Diewer, whom John of Leiden would in turn marry upon Mathias's death in battle. Mathias sent emissaries (including John) to various Melchiorite communities in the Low Countries to assert his authority, and his leadership was generally accepted once he managed to overawe the Melchiorites of Amsterdam, who included some of Hofman's earlier adherents, such as Bartholomew Boekbinder and William de Cuiper. At year's end, with his leadership now generally recognized, Mathias sent off further emissaries, who were not only to proclaim the resumption of adult

---

11. For Mathias's usurpation of authority among the Melchiorites, see Deppermann, *Melchior Hoffman*, 333–39.

12. Strictly speaking, the two witnesses are not named in Apocalypse, but in popular medieval eschatology these two were identified as Old Testament figures Enoch and Elijah. For the sixteenth-century context in general, see Petersen, *Preaching in the Last Days*; for the broader context in medieval eschatology, see Cohn, *Pursuit of the Millennium*, 145.

baptism but to bid the faithful to assemble, as they would constitute the 144,000 pious people who were to oppose the Antichrist according to Apocalypse 7:4 and 14:1. Boekbinder and de Cuiper were first sent to Leeuwarden, and after delivering their message there, they continued on to Münster. There, on January 5, 1534, they baptized Bernard Rothman and the other radical preachers, who were dominant in the city and would soon take over the city. Eight days later, another pair of Mathias's emissaries, John of Leiden and Gerard de Cuiper, appeared in Münster, and in early February, Mathias himself arrived. These Melchiorites would take advantage of the religious discord within Münster to establish that city (rather than Strasburg) as the New Jerusalem that would witness the final conflict predicted in Apocalypse.

Modern scholars debate whether the men who seized control of Münster were the "legitimate" heirs of Melchior Hofman. The very question is prejudicial, in that it implies that Hofman had some sort of copyright on his ideas, and those who "infringed" this control through misinterpretation are inherently wrong and misguided. It is preferable to consider the question from the point of view of the internal logic of ideas. The men in Münster seem to have genuinely believed that the last days would begin in 1533, and that events would unfold just as related in the book of Apocalypse. Both Hofman and Mathias shared this belief, but differed on the stance that they, as the prophets who would lead the pious in the coming conflict, should adopt towards this conflict. Hofman took a rather more passive attitude and thought that God should be left to implement the conflict without human intervention. Mathias, on the other hand, decided that it was necessary to prepare the faithful to take an active role in the events foretold for them. If words like "delusional" are to be used of Mathias, Bockelson, Knipperdolling, and other leaders of the radicals in Münster (and this judgmental tone is still frequently used of them), then it should be pointed out that they were no more deluded than Hofman. They simply acted upon their beliefs, whereas Hofman waited for events to take place of their own accord while he languished in his prison cell.

2.4 Radical Views of the Münster Melchiorites

The Münster radicals' views on theology and other aspects of religion were unique in several respects.[13] Given the Sacramentarian background of so

---

13. For a general discussion of the policies of the Münster regime, see Klötzer, *Die Täuferschaft*

many of the radicals from the Low Countries, it's not surprising that they rejected the traditional belief in transubstantiation (as well as Luther's modified consubstantiation), which saw a real transformation of the Eucharist bread and wine into Christ's flesh and blood. (For more on this, see folio 29r in Gresbeck's account and note 149 in the translation.[14])

The nature of the relationship between Christ as the Son of God and God himself—a concept that caused much dispute in antiquity but was generally uncontroversial during the Middle Ages—again became a matter of great dispute at the time of the Reformation. The notion that had been accepted as orthodox since antiquity held that the three "persons" of God (Father, Son, and Holy Spirit) were seen as manifestations of a single God, and this threefold conception of God is called the Trinity. A different line of thought in antiquity known as Monophysitism held that the divine nature of Christ supplanted the humanity of the fetus of Jesus that was conceived in Mary; Hofman adhered to a similar idea that arose in the 1520s (he famously compared the birth of Christ through Mary to the passage of water through a pipe). In his final days after his capture, John Bockelson of Leiden (the erstwhile king of the Anabaptist kingdom) showed himself willing to recant a number of his views, but he balked at the notion that God was born of a human.[15] One interesting side effect of the emphasis on the divinity of Christ was that they had a tendency to assimilate Christ to God the Father. A notable aspect of the Münster radicals' conception of God is their constant invocation of "The Father," which for them meant the vengeful and jealous God of the Old Testament.

Hofman's doctrine included a strong belief in divine inspiration. He went so far as to publish the prophetic dreams of some of his followers, and it was such a dream that led him to return to Strasburg, where he was arrested. Such divinely inspired prophets were not uncommon among the more radically minded (e.g., the "Zwickau prophets" whose visions threatened the social order in 1522). Although the established church of the Middle Ages did what it could to suppress or at least check such spontaneous revelations

---

von Münster.

14. Folio numbers from the original Low German manuscript on which the present translation is based are given within the translation, placed in square brackets before the first word on the page, with the numeral indicating the sheet (folio) and "r" and "v" indicating the recto (front) and verso (back) of the sheet. For more on the pagination of the manuscript, see note 60 below.

15. See Kerssenbrock, *Anabaptistici furoris*, ed. Detmer, 872.

from people who were not in holy orders, it is not surprising that in their careful reading of the Bible, some reformers were led by Acts 2:1–21 to think that God would again speak directly to the common man. It is noteworthy that Acts 2:38 connects (seemingly adult) baptism for the remission of sins with the reception of "the gift of the Holy Spirit." The radicals of Münster would not infrequently invoke this "spirit of the baptizer" (fols. 66v, 73r, 100v).

The Münster radicals often referred to the Reformation notion that biblical precedent was necessary for any ecclesiastical practice to be considered valid (they often professed to be willing to admit to error if it could be demonstrated through citation of the Bible), and they concomitantly rejected any practices that could not be validated in this way. The latter brings with it the notion that any papist practices from the past that do not pass muster by the standard of the New Testament are mere human accretions that had to be eradicated.

A very specific form of rejection of the traditional forms of worship is the destruction of the religious art that adorned the churches. Of course, a prohibition against the worship of images is one of the Ten Commandments (Exodus 20:3–4; Deuteronomy 5:8), and in both the Old Testament and the works of the early church fathers, idolatry was associated with the worship of false gods. Hence, hostility to traditional religious art was a prominent feature of the early rejection of the Roman Church. Karlstadt had disagreed with Luther over the issue, and Hofman was forced to leave first Dorpat in Livonia and then Stockholm after his preaching resulted in iconoclastic rioting. A notable aspect of the Münsterite Anabaptists was their destruction of the city's churches and their art, which Gresbeck describes at length (fols. 111r–114v).

The events of Münster are incomprehensible without a clear understanding that the main driving force behind the radical leaders was the belief that the events portrayed in the book of Apocalypse were about to come to pass and that they would play a prominent role as the 144,000 who would do battle with the forces of the Antichrist.[16]

In the early books of the Old Testament, God promises the Israelites that if they worship him properly, he will assure them of success as a people in the secular world (the *locus classicus* is Deuteronomy 28). But this does not

---

16. For a quick overview of the Münsterites' apocalyptic views and the origins of these in the ideas of Hofman, see Kirchhoff, "Die Endzeiterwartung der Täufergemeinde," 20–24.

in fact result in military triumph. This failure works itself out in two related ways. First, the history of the Israelites is portrayed in the Old Testament (especially in Kings and Chronicles) as a recurring cycle in which the Israelites renege on their end of the bargain by worshipping the pagan gods of their neighbors and God, in retaliation, withdraws his support, causing them to suffer military defeat at the hands of their enemies. The Israelites would then repent, God would restore his favor, and the pattern would repeat again and again. Second, the prophets, who claimed to be speaking for God, came forth with various visions and dreams in which they described (often in rather obscure "mystical" language) the ultimate humiliation of the Lord's (and the Israelites') enemies and the triumph of his chosen people. The one text from early Christianity written in this tradition that made it into the canon of the New Testament is the book of Apocalypse, whose author calls himself John. This author was identified in antiquity with the evangelist John, though the identification was disputed even then and is unlikely to be correct.[17] In any case, the bizarre imagery of the book, with all its beasts and swords and its gripping (if surreal) depiction of a final war between the forces of good and evil, had a strong influence on the mystically inclined throughout the Middle Ages.[18] The vision in Apocalypse of the struggle between the pious and the wicked could be associated with various statements of Jesus in the Gospels, which express hostility towards the wealthy (e.g., Matthew 19:23–24, Mark 10:23–25, Luke 18:24–25) and indicate an eventual inversion of the social order when people will be judged according to their religious merits (Matthew 19:30, Mark 10:31, Luke 13:30).

Though the book of Apocalypse stands on its own as a Christian work, its imagery calls to mind works of the Old Testament which either inspired that book or were written under the inspiration of the same models, and the radicals informed their interpretation of Apocalypse with such texts as

17. Some of the earliest "Christians" still felt themselves to be close to the Jewish tradition; that strain of Christianity is represented by the Gospel of Matthew and Apocalypse. Other Greek-speaking Christians distanced themselves from Jesus's Jewish background and were receptive to Greek culture, notably the Gospels of Luke (this tendency is also noticeable in Acts) and John. The obscure allegory of the book of Apocalypse is hardly compatible with the influence of Greek philosophical thought in the Gospel according to John, which sets it apart from the other three canonical gospels.

18. The classic treatment is Cohn, *Pursuit of the Millennium*; although really a sociological study of the cultural settings that favored millenarian ideas and behavior, Cohn discusses the development of millenarian thought. For a treatment of the apocalyptic strain in the radical strain of Reformation thought, see Klaassen, *Living at the End of Ages*. The book of Apocalypse did not appeal to more rationally inclined religious thinkers such as Erasmus and Luther, though their dislike of the work was based on rather different reasons; see Backus, *Reformation Readings of the Apocalypse*, 3–11.

Daniel 7, Ezekiel 9, and 2 Esdras 4. These violent images of a relentless and savage God (the Father) who protects his chosen people against their (and his) far more numerous (and wicked) foes had recently inspired Thomas Müntzer in his support of peasant attacks on the social order back in the Peasants' War, and the same spirit infused the radicals of Münster.

As good reformers who wished to return the church to the pristine state of the apostolic age, the radicals naturally found much inspiration in both the Old and the New Testaments. To some extent, this is a variant on the point about accepting as valid only those practices that could be justified in the text of the Bible. In this case, however, the point is not to vet current practice against the apparent usage of the Bible, but to attempt to recreate the state of affairs that the Reformers thought was laid out in the text. Acts 4 seemed to validate direct inspiration of men through the Holy Spirit; verses 32 through 37 were taken to mean that the followers of Christ should share their goods communally, and the radicals' confiscation of the property of the faithful in Münster was one of the more shocking events to sixteenth-century (and later) sensibilities.[19]

Inspiration based on the New Testament was not out of the ordinary at a time when the cry *ad fontes* led to various efforts to recapture the spirit of the primitive church (however interpreted). What is rather distinctive in the thought of the Münster radicals is the extent to which their emphasis on the apocalypse caused them to dwell upon the Old Testament. This is perfectly understandable given that the book of Apocalypse overtly harkens back to the Old Testament by referring to the pious as being raised from the twelve tribes of Israel (7:4–8) and describes the city that will descend from heaven after the final triumph over the godless as the New Jerusalem (21:2). The fact that Apocalypse was written after the model of various prophetic visions from the Old Testament contributed to a natural inclination to interpret the events it predicted in terms of the Old Testament story of the Israelites.

The radicals seem to have taken to its logical conclusion both the association of the pious in Apocalypse with the Israelites and their assumption

---

19. And the fallacious notion that this religiously inspired attempt to establish a community without personal wealth was a precursor of modern communism led to much scholarly misinterpretation in East Germany (similar strains in the thought of Müntzer were handled in the same vein). For a treatment of the theoretical underpinning of the policy of communal property in Münster, see Stayer, *German Peasants' War*, 123–38.

that they were themselves the pious by conceiving of themselves as the modern embodiment of the ancient Israelites. While it might be reasonable enough for Christians to view themselves as being comparable to the ancient Israelites by virtue of the fact that both are portrayed as having a special bond with God, the radicals took the comparison quite literally. One woman attempted to recreate the biblical story in which Judith saved a besieged Jewish town through the crafty murder of the enemy commander by sneaking out of besieged Münster in order to give the prince-bishop a poisoned garment (fols. 29v–30r). The Münsterite King John also conceived of himself as a new King David and divided the defenders of the city into the "twelve tribes."[20] The cathedral yard was named Mt. Zion (cf. Apocalypse 14:1). John of Leiden gave out names for newborns on the basis of the nomenclature of the Old Testament patriarchs (fol. 110r). The use of music and banners in the military was justified by the practice of the Israelites (fol. 35v). The "dukes" chosen by the Anabaptists towards the end of the siege were overtly equated with the leaders of the twelve tribes of Israel who led the Israelites to triumph in the book of Judges (fol. 134r).

There was one more element of biblical imitation that undoubtedly went the furthest in branding the radicals as unredeemed perverts in the eyes of their contemporaries, and this was polygamy.[21] The introduction of the practice may have been motivated by the circumstance that there were far more women than men in the besieged city, and in contemporary thought a woman needed a man to look after her. In any case, the radicals justified it by the example of the Old Testament patriarchs (fol. 38v).

3. The Historical Context

To understand the geographical setting of the events that took place in Münster, it is necessary to erase the borders of the modern (nation-) states of the Netherlands, Belgium, Luxemburg, and Germany. All of these territories were regions within the Holy Roman Empire, and while the circumstances that would eventually lead to their establishment as autonomous states already existed at the time of the events in Münster,

---

20. Kerssenbrock, *Anabaptistici furoris*, ed. Detmer, 773, with notes.
21. Kerssenbrock routinely portrays John of Leiden as a libertine satyr, as if the institution of polygamy were a fraud concocted to satisfy his lust.

they were certainly not autonomous at the time. First, all of these were areas in which Germanic dialectics were spoken (with the exception of French-speaking Wallonia at the south of Flanders, in modern Belgium). The low-lying territory along the North Sea and (very roughly speaking) to the west of the rivers Rhine and Ems may be neutrally described as the Low Countries.[22] This region achieved some sort of conceptual unity in the fifteenth century when the dukes of Burgundy (a branch of the French royal family) acquired control over various counties and duchies. In 1477, the rash Duke Charles the Bold was killed in battle, leaving his many territories to his daughter Mary. Most of the Burgundian territory in what is now eastern France was lost in war, but Mary's husband Maximilian, the son and heir of the Habsburg Holy Roman Emperor Frederick III, retained control of the Burgundian holdings in the Low Countries. Though these territories remained distinct, there had been attempts to impose centralized oversight of the various territories under the rule of the dukes of Burgundy, and this inchoate unity was strengthened when the area remained loyal to Mary. In 1515, Maximilian's grandson Charles (soon to become the Holy Roman Emperor) entered his majority in the Low Countries. Upon Charles's abdication in 1555, his Low Country territories passed to his son Philip II of Spain. The effects of the Reformation were strong in the north and the territories, faced with a Catholic ruler, revolted and established a Calvinist republic in 1588. The south meanwhile remained under Habsburg control (first Spanish, then Austrian) until 1794. Thus, the historical accident of Habsburg control of the southern area led to the establishment of a separate identity for that region. If not for that fact, these areas speaking a dialectical variety of German might today simply be regions of a German state without a distinct literary language of their own.

But at the time of the Anabaptist kingdom, all of these developments lay in the distant future. Gresbeck's world consisted mainly of the northwest of modern-day Germany. The broader area is known as Westphalia, a subdivision of the old dukedom of Lower Saxony (so called to distinguish it

---

22. This is basically an English version of the French term *pays bas*. "Netherlands" is the English equivalent of the Dutch "Nederlands," which has become restricted in application to the Dutch Republic/Kingdom. The fact that the name of the province of Holland (only the most prominent of the provinces that constituted the new republic) was adopted in English as a popular designation of the Dutch Republic shows that there had not previously existed any self-evident term for the area.

from the later kingdom of Saxony to the southwest), and one region of this was the Münsterland, whose major city was Münster and which was under the jurisdiction of the bishop of Münster.

Use of the term "German language" causes difficulties in understanding the linguistic situation in the region around Münster in the sixteenth century. The ancient West Germanic language group consisted of a number of related dialects spoken in central and northern Europe. Eventually, a form of southern (High) German became the accepted literary language of all Germany, and all the other varieties were relegated to the status of socially inferior dialects, which are now mostly in the lamentable process of dying out. In the early sixteenth century, High German was beginning to gain its predominant position; this was the dialect of eastern central Germany, and had already begun to gain wide currency elsewhere in German-speaking territory, when Luther's use of it for his influential biblical translations and for his other writings gave it additional prestige in the Protestant north. But there was still a lively literary form of northern German known as Low German (*Niederdeutsch* or *Plattdeutsch*), which was spoken (and written) all along the North Sea and the Baltic from the area of the northern Low Countries as far to the east as the German towns of Livonia, where Melchior Hofman began his preaching. Already at this time, written Low German began to adopt High German forms, and by the middle of the seventeenth century, it had been supplanted by High German as the language of the educated elite. Gresbeck's own language (Low German) gives clear evidence of High German influence.[23] One of the dialects of this area was Westphalian, the form of German used in the Münsterland. The modern Dutch language is the descendant of Old Low Franconian (Franconian is the name for the dialects of central Germany). This Franconian dialect intruded to the northwest into the Low Countries, and displaced Frisian (a variety of Low German). Although Dutch had a slightly different origin from the Low German dialect of Westphalia, the Low Franconian language adopted certain characteristics of Low German, and in any case, unlike the other Franconian dialects, it did not participate in the so-called second (or High) German consonant shift, which is the primary distinction between the Low and the High German dialects.

23. Though his language is clearly Low German, he does admit High German forms like *essen* alongside the Low German form *eten*, and he even occasionally uses the High German pronoun *er* in place of the Low German *he* (just like English).

While there were perceptible differences between the Westphalian dialect of Münster and the language of the Low Countries directly to the east, these were comparatively minor, and it is anachronistic to think that the present-day border between Germany and the Netherlands had any significance in the early sixteenth century. To people of the time, there would have been no absolute distinction between "German" speakers in the Münsterland and "Dutch" speakers to the immediate west. Nonetheless, regional loyalties and rivalries did exist, and Gresbeck clearly had a bad attitude about Hollanders (fol. 93r). The future histories of the Netherlands and Belgium lay far in the future, and the notion of the Dutch language as an independent language would have been meaningless.[24] This is not to say that the Low Countries did not have certain peculiarities of their own. They were culturally far more subject to French influence, and the Sacramentarian tendencies of the 1520s were to some extent at least the result of various pietistic movements that were characteristic of the fifteenth century. Nonetheless, in the early sixteenth century, the various territories that constituted the Habsburg possessions in the Low Countries were simply another part of the empire, and this very similarity would contribute to the ease with which the Melchiorite movement of the Low Countries was so readily received in neighboring Münster.

3.1 Political Authority in the Holy Roman Empire

The events of Münster played themselves out against the background of the political decentralization of the Holy Roman Empire. In the budding nation-states of England and France and in the kingdoms of the Spanish peninsula, the monarchy had certainly suffered setbacks along the way, but by the early sixteenth century, the central authority had established its control over the anarchic forces of local feudal territories. In Germany, the prolonged struggle of the house of Hohenstaufen against the papacy had

24. The eventual development of Dutch as a national language of education and literature has led to the designation of its late medieval ancestor as Middle Dutch rather than Middle Low Franconian. If the Habsburg association had not led to the distinctive and independent development of the Low Countries, Low Franconian would simply be one more "dialect" of German that would now be in the process of being driven into extinction by High German. (Note that the English term *Dutch* is simply a deformation of *deutsch*, the German word for "German," and in the Netherlands the language is known rather neutrally as *nederlandisch*.) Naturally, none of this talk of what would have happened if the Low Countries had not gone their own way should be taken as a disparagement of the present-day countries or their sometimes complicated linguistic situations. The point is that the present independent status of these regions should not be read back into the early sixteenth century.

resulted not simply in the destruction of the dynasty but also in the collapse of central control over the vast number of territories—large and small, hereditary and ecclesiastical—into which the empire was divided. These local authorities assumed responsibility for such government as was exercised, and the emperor had no direct control except to the extent that he himself was a territorial magnate (Charles V held the most expansive collection of territories within the empire). Although the emperor could issue edicts on his own and preside over the imperial diet (the assembly of the princes and cities who were directly subordinate to him) and pass laws through it, he had no ability to enforce such laws without the cooperation of the local powers. It was this situation that first allowed the Lutherans to establish themselves in various territories, and it also contributed to the unique circumstances that allowed the Melchiorite takeover of Münster.

One organ for local cooperation consisted of the imperial circles (*Reichskreisen*) into which the empire was divided in 1500. Soon numbering ten, these units were more or less contiguous blocks of local authorities directly subject to the empire. Among other administrative functions, the circles, which met in a local assembly known as a *Landtag*, were responsible for maintaining public order within their territory, and the prince-bishop of Münster, whose lands fell within the Upper-Rhenish/Westphalian circle, would eventually turn to the other members of the circle for assistance in suppressing the Anabaptist takeover of his see.

One of the peculiarities of Germany was the large number of prelates who controlled extensive territories. In the distant past, emperors had exercised power through bishops and other prelates appointed by them, and this practice had led to the prolonged Investiture Conflict in which the emperors opposed the papal claim to the exclusive right to bestow episcopal positions. The emperors had long since lost control of episcopal appointments, and in the case of Münster, the chapter (a college of clerics) of the cathedral had the right to appoint the new bishop, who then had to secure confirmation from the pope (at a high price, which had to be paid by his temporal subjects). The cathedral chapter (the members of the chapters are known as canons; the vernacular term in Münster was *Domherren* or "cathedral lords") was controlled by members of the local nobility, and they would elect someone of the high noble rank as the bishop, who was known as a prince-bishop by virtue of his control over both secular and ecclesiastical jurisdiction. Thus, not only was the central ecclesiastical administration controlled by noblemen, but the prince-bishop himself did not even have to be a priest. Francis of Waldeck did not get around to being consecrated as a priest until 1543, eleven years after his election by the cathedral chapter.

Although the story of the Anabaptist radicals centers around the city of Münster, from the point of view of the prince-bishop, it involved his entire diocese. The wealth and fortifications of the city allowed it to stand up to the prince-bishop in a way that was not feasible for the smaller towns, but the latter were affected by the religious turmoil of the times and did show a certain inclination to reform (though this was suppressed without too much difficulty). In any case, the bishop in his capacity as secular ruler had to deal with the estates of the diocese, that is, with those entities who had traditional claims to direct interaction with their overlord—apart from the diocesan capital in Münster and the other recognized towns, the nobility of the diocese acted as a corporate body in relation to the prince-bishop—and these groups met as separate estates in the diet (assembly) of the diocese. For the most part, the nobility (who had a vested interest in the traditional order through their control of the cathedral chapter) supported the prince-bishop in his efforts to bring the city to heel.

Like the population of any late medieval and early modern city, the residents of Münster were divided into a number of distinct status groups, mostly hereditary.[25] At the top were the knights of the bishopric.[26] Their main residences were on their rural estates, but they also had elaborate houses in the bishopric's main city. The knights were exempt from the city's jurisdiction.

The residents of the city who held political rights were divided into two subgroups.[27] At the top were the patricians.[28] These men belonged to families that had been wealthy in the past and had established a hereditary claim to political leadership of the city. Over time, however, the patricians wished to become assimilated to the knighthood and so withdrew from participation in the city government. Most patricians would side with the

---

25. Kerssenbrock discusses the city government in chapter 8 of his introduction.

26. Kerssenbrock, *Anabaptistici furoris*, ed. Detmer, 104–5.

27. For a general discussion of Münster's citizen body, see Lutterbach, *Der Weg in das Täuferreich*, 46–51.

28. Kerssenbrock, *Anabaptistici furoris*, ed. Detmer, 107–8, 108–9. For a modern discussion, see Lahrkamp, "Das Patriziat in Münster." They lost their dominance within the city as a result of the civil strife of the 1450s (on which see Lutterbach, *Der Weg in das Täuferreich*, 54–57), and their refusal to accept outsiders into their ranks and insistence on marrying among themselves meant that the number of patrician families gradually shrank through natural extinction, which further undermined their control of the city.

prince-bishop after the Anabaptist takeover of the city, but some, like Knipperdolling and Gerard Kibbenbrock, were themselves adherents of Anabaptism and would become prominent leaders in the new regime (much to Gresbeck's retrospective outrage).

The main body of citizens of the city was the burghers (High German *Bürger*). This group consisted of all the residents of the city who had the right to vote in municipal elections but didn't belong to a patrician family. This status wasn't exactly hereditary, but in practice the present burghers were the children of past ones. This group was divided into two. Certain particularly wealthy families of non-patrician status routinely held office on the city council.[29] These families were distinguished from the general mass of the citizenry, to which Gresbeck belonged. Even if he was not of a prominent family, Gresbeck is obviously proud of his status as a burgher, referring to himself throughout his third-person account of his flight from the city and participation in its capture as "de borger" and specifying his status as a burgher in his signature at the end of both his letter to his previous employers (appendix, document 2) and his narrative of the Anabaptist regime (fol. 156v).

In addition to these citizen residents, the city was home to a number of people excluded from participation in its government. These were mostly serfs (people who were in the possession, after a fashion, of rural landowners) and freemen (people who were of serf origin but whose ancestors had acquired a certain independence from their lords without becoming entirely free).[30] There would no doubt have also been immigrants of varying wealth but mostly of lowly status who came to the city from other places. Gresbeck makes no reference to such people as such, but presumably his phrases like "the poor people" ("dat arme voelck," "de armen lude") largely encompasses such people at the bottom of the socioeconomic hierarchy who were carried along by the events around them. (See also the discussion of Gresbeck's attitude towards the "simple" people in section 5.1.)

The city's electoral system and form of government do not enter into the narrative except to the extent that the Anabaptists won the election of 1534 and then promptly abolished the old system. Still, it may be useful to give a brief overview of the system that everyone in the city would have been famil-

---

29. For these prominent non-patrician families, see Lahrkamp, "Das Patriziat in Münster," 199.
30. Kerssenbrock, *Anabaptistici furoris*, ed. Detmer, 109.

iar with.[31] The city was divided into six electoral wards, which were the same as the city's regular parishes.[32] The voters of each district voted for electors who would do the actual voting for the members of the city council.[33] Four parishes (St. Lambert's, St. Ludger's, St. Martin's, St. Tilgen's/Giles's) chose two electors each, and two (The Jews' Field/St. Servatius's and the Parish-Across-the-Water/Our Dear Lady's) had one each, for a total of ten. These ten electors then chose the twenty-four members of the city council. The elections took place on the first Monday in Lent. Once elected, the council members distributed the various offices of municipal government among themselves. The most important of these were the two burgher masters (the rest exercised various administrative and judicial functions).

There were two further elements in the deliberations of the council. First, there were two aldermen who were elected to represent the entire citizenry.[34] Next, the heads of the sixteen guilds (the professional organizations for the important crafts of the city) could also give their views to the council.[35] Because of their ability to give voice to the immediate concerns of important segments of the city's population (the skilled workers and the general populace), the guild masters and aldermen could have a decisive influence on the council's decisions.

3.2 Early Modern Warfare

One aspect of public life of sixteenth-century Germany that may seem puzzling is the right of the local ruler to raise troops on his own authority. By virtue of this authority, the prince-bishop of Münster would gather an army against the rebels in the city. The later fifteenth and early sixteenth centuries saw a swift development in military organization, as the spread of small firearms led to semiprofessional infantry armies (in place of the knighthood and ad hoc feudal levies of the previous period).[36] The

31. Ibid., 105–7.
32. Strictly speaking, there were seven parishes, but St. James's Church, which was located by the cathedral, was for the use of canons rather than the general populace (ibid., 46).
33. Such a system was designed to thwart any troublemaking tendencies among the broad group of voters by entrusting the final selection to the presumably more prudent electors selected by them. This presupposition lies behind the electoral college used for selecting the president of the United States, though in practice the electors very quickly gave up any independent deliberation and became bound by the popular voting of their states.
34. Ibid., 112.
35. Ibid., 111–12.
36. For an evaluation of the thesis of a military revolution (i.e., a revolutionary change in military

extensive use of mercenaries began when the highly effective infantrymen of Switzerland began selling their services in the later fifteenth century; soon similar troops were raised in Germany, and these were known as *Landsknechte* (termed simply *milites*, or "soldiers," by Kerssenbrock).[37] These freebooting soldiers were hired by private contractors (who also served as their colonels) to fight for a particular political authority. The prince-bishop incurred huge expenses maintaining his army (the spiraling costs of military activity proved to be an ongoing headache for earlier modern rulers), and he was soon forced to seek the financial support of neighboring princes, who thereby gained control over the operation against the city.[38]

The field tactics of such armies required that the soldiers be trained in field maneuvers. At first, the Anabaptists of Münster showed hostility to this sort of training and organization, but practical realities soon forced them to give way to regular military usage in those areas (fol. 35v). Though Gresbeck writes often of military training in the city, as things turned out, there was to be little opportunity to practice maneuvering in open formation since the Anabaptists remained hemmed in, in the city.

A notable development in military technology during the late fifteenth and early sixteen centuries was increasing prominence taken by firearms. By the end of the fifteenth century, armies tended to have equal numbers of pikemen (soldiers armed with a long pole known as a pike and fitted at the end with a sharp metal tip) and arquebusiers (soldiers armed with a somewhat cumbersome handheld firearm known as an arquebus).

For centuries, the use of artillery had been restricted to sieges. It was only in the fifteenth century that armies began to frequently use mobile field artillery, and it was only in the early sixteenth century that the wide varieties of artillery began to be regularized. This regularization increased the efficiency of the guns, since previously each gun had to have its own peculiar size of ammunition. Although Gresbeck seems to be quite clear

---

practice) during this period, see Black, *European Warfare*, 32–54.

37. The classic treatment of the independent officers who raised such troops on behalf of sovereigns who pay them for this service is Redlich, *German Military Enterpriser*. For a handy (if dated) treatment of the Landsknechts in our period, see Oman, *History of the Art of War*, 74–88; and for a colorful (if not exactly academic) treatment, see Miller, *Landsknecht*; and Richards, *Landsknecht Soldier*. For extensive treatments in German, see Blau, *Die Deutschen Landsknechte*; and Baumann, *Landsknechte*.

38. Kirchhoff, "Die Belagerung und Eroberung Münsters," discusses at length the often tiresome arrangements between the prince-bishop and the other princes.

about the different varieties of guns, these cannot be precisely determined in terms of length or caliber; only the general nature of the guns can be given.[39] Whereas two of the Low German terms directly correspond to the translations "falconet" and "serpentine," the word "slange" is a general term for "gun," but here it almost certainly corresponds to the English term "culverin." Though other terms were used, among the various varieties of mobile artillery, culverins were the largest (firing shot of perhaps twelve pounds up to just under twenty pounds), falcons were in the middle range, and the smallest major pieces were falconets (shot in the range of three to five pounds). The culverins were commonly divided into a larger regular version and a somewhat smaller variety called "demi." As Gresbeck indicates, there were often oversized culverins of unusually large size, which he calls a "field gun [*slange*]." Seemingly, Gresbeck is here using "falconet" for the variety often called "falcon," and "demi-falconet" for "falcon." At any rate, it would seem that "demi-falconet" is not a commonly used term. As for "serpentine," this was the term for the smallest sort of artillery (rather than infantryman's firearm), which was a breech-loading piece made of iron (as opposed to the bronze used for casting larger pieces); as a breechloader, it is also known in English as a "chamber cannon."

As it turned out, the Anabaptists' use of their new field army was rather limited. In the early days of their regime, they would march out on raids and would sometimes exchange volleys (*schuetgefar* or "exchange of fire") with the besiegers, but these raids were soon given up. At the start of the siege, the prince-bishop's troops set up a loose system of fortifications outside the city. Undoubtedly, the prince-bishop hardly expected that the Anabaptists in the city would be able to hold out for long against a professional army. But hold out they did, and the besiegers responded by trying, in turn, two methods of taking a heavily defended position: the direct assault on the city walls, and the slow starvation of the city.[40]

The direct method of attempting to end a siege was an assault on the walls. The besiegers launched two assaults against the city's walls, and both failed. Eighty years earlier, the mighty walls of Constantinople had

---

39. For a quick discussion of the varieties of cannon, see Arnold, *Renaissance at War*, 30; for a fuller treatment, Egg, "From Mariagnano to the Thirty Years' War."

40. For a somewhat disjointed discussion of siege warfare in this period, see Duffy, *Stripping of the Altars*. For a more succinct treatment, see Black, *European Warfare*, 84–88.

been breached by the huge artillery train of the Ottoman emperor, but in fact, the use of artillery against fixed fortifications was still in its infancy, and the theoretical study of how to defend and defeat fixed fortifications would continue from the late fifteenth century until the eighteenth century. The city of Münster had very elaborate fortifications (fols. 127v–128r), which included walls, artillery placements, and an elaborate moat system designed to deny the besiegers access to the walls.[41] The two stormings of the walls involved the use of ladders to try and climb over the walls, but the defenders were able to defeat these efforts. The Anabaptists were apparently clever in their use and improvement of the city's fortifications. Even their religiously motivated destruction of the city's churches was tempered by the need to maintain suitable platforms for their artillery (fol. 112r). The besiegers too used their artillery against the city's fortifications, but even the prolonged bombardment carried out for several days before the second assault failed to make much of a dent (as it were) in the city's defenses (fol. 52r), and even this damage was soon made good by the defenders (fol. 53r).

Another method of taking a fortified position was through starvation. After failing to take the city by storm, the besieging armies established a tight siege, with a full system of trenches dug around the city and elaborate blockhouses for the stationing of the besieging troops. This costly effort was intended to cut off the city's communications with the outside world and to eventually starve out the defenders. These siegeworks were built in the fall of 1534, and by the spring of 1535 the general population in Münster was starving (though not the Anabaptist leadership, much to Gresbeck's retrospective outrage). Yet, there was no particular sign that the Anabaptists were ready to surrender when Gresbeck and Little Hans of Longstreet escaped from the city in late May and separately offered similar plans to take the city by subterfuge, taking advantage of the slackened diligence of the defenders to sneak a force into the city at night. No doubt one reason why the besiegers were so keen to implement this plan was the desire to end the costs of the prolonged siege through a coup de main. And so the city fell.

41. For Kerssenbrock's discussion of the city's fortifications, see his introductory chapter 4 (Kerssenbrock, *Anabaptistici furoris*, ed. Detmer, 18–26). Kerssenbrock was to be criticized by the city council for divulging this information; see Kerssenbrock, *Narrative of Anabaptist Madness*, ed. Mackay, 40, 43.

4. Henry Gresbeck

Apart from two letters written right after the capture of the city that discuss Henry Gresbeck's role in that capture (appendix, documents 3 and 4), our knowledge of Gresbeck's life mostly derives from two texts, both written by the man himself.[42] The first is a letter (appendix, document 2) that he tried to smuggle out of the city towards the end of the siege to his old patrons and employers, a pair of local squires and their mother. The other source is his account of the Anabaptist regime. These two sources provide rather limited information about Gresbeck's life. Gresbeck was a "young man" at the time of the city's capture (fols. 142v–143r). While there is no way to tell exactly what this means, it is hard to see how he could have been much older than twenty-five, which would place his birth about 1510 to 1515. He had at some time served for an unknown period of time as a landsknecht (fol. 142v), and had after that gone on to acquire the profession of cabinetmaker (fol. 156v). The time necessary for this seems to put him in the upper range of possible age. He was a burgher of the city of Münster (fol. 156v), though according to his letter he was employed outside the city at the time of the Anabaptist takeover in February 1534, being in the employ of two local squires. He claims in the letter that he went to the city at that time to look after his mother's property, which suggests that at the time his father was dead. He also indicates that he got married in the besieged city. His mother died in 1542, leaving him her house because of his merit in the city's capture. Perhaps, this last detail indicates that he had siblings whose exclusion from the inheritance had to be justified. In any event, at the time he lived in the neighboring bishop's see of Osnabrück.[43] Nothing seems to be known of his later fate.

If Gresbeck served outside of the Münsterland, his parochialism gives no sign of it. While he mentions several small towns around Münster, he exhibits little knowledge of or interest in the broader world. Once he speaks rather vaguely of the wide world that might be infected by the spread of Anabaptism as the "High or Low Countries" (fol. 95r), which signifies upper and lower Germany. He refers to the prospect of help coming from

---

42. According to Kirchhoff, *Die Täufer in Münster*, 222, Gresbeck also used "Averdinck" as his last name, but there's no evidence for this in our texts. His letter (appendix, document 2) gives the spelling "Gresbeckke." He spells his given name "Hynryk."

43. For the details, see Kirchhoff, *Die Täufer in Münster*, 222, 223.

Holland (fol. 75r), and knows some details about an abortive uprising there (fol. 86r). When indicating the origins of the various groups of people who occupied the monasteries in Münster, he names a number of specific towns from the Münsterland, but lumps everyone else under the broad designation "foreign folk" (fol. 118r).[44] For whatever reason, Gresbeck decided to latch onto the hated Hollanders and Frisians as the fanatical backbone of the Anabaptists in Münster, but paid little heed to the geographic origins of the other Anabaptists who came to Münster.

It would appear that Gresbeck is less than forthright about his own involvement with the Anabaptist regime. Despite being so willing to speak of his departure from the city and his role in the capture, Gresbeck says nothing about his activities during the first fifteen months. There is reason to conclude that Gresbeck was accepted as a reputable member of the Anabaptist community. He was apparently present (fol. 71v) at the meeting when the missionaries to other cities were chosen in October 1534, and he held a military position right to the end. He speaks in detail of one anecdote that took place at all the gates of the city by describing what happened at the gate where we know he was assigned, and then he says briefly that the same went on elsewhere (fol. 136r).[45] Clearly, he was considered a soldier like any other. He also mentions that once his departure was noted in the city while he was still milling around outside, his friends from the city called to him to return (fol. 142v). That's hardly how they would have treated someone they didn't consider one of their own. Furthermore, given his willingness to talk about his role at the end of the siege, his complete silence about any early activities of his own has to raise the suspicion that whatever he had done before would not look creditable to the prince-bishop. Presumably, he had supported the Anabaptist regime during the months before his escape and was considered a member in good standing of the Anabaptist community until his flight from the city.

The last portion of his account details his flight from the city and his role in its capture (fols. 141v–151r), so there's no need to recount this portion of his life here. In the coda of the work, Gresbeck contrasts the lack

---

44. Gresbeck was not unaware of the origin of individuals from places other than Holland and Frisia. He refers to one man as coming from Brabant (fol. 121r) and another from Jülich (fol. 141r).

45. Cf. the procedure in describing the parody mass, with the second performance (fols. 104v–106v) being described with much more detail than the first one (fol. 104r). Presumably, Gresbeck attended only the second performance.

of greed as a motive on his own part with Little Hans's purely mercenary motivation in proposing a plan for the city's capture, noting that in fact Gresbeck's own property had been confiscated along with that of other Anabaptists (and an attempt to regain this property may well have been responsible for the writing of the work). Nothing more is known of Gresbeck's life.

The likelihood that Gresbeck wrote in his own clear book hand (see section 6 of the introduction) both the letter and the clean copy of the account indicates that he had had a certain amount of formal learning. Certainly, the very composition of the work (whatever its flaws) is indicative of a fertile mind. On the other hand, Gresbeck frequently mangles the spelling of Latinate words that appear in the account, which suggests that his education was merely a practical one in the vernacular.[46]

Gresbeck does give some clues as to his earlier religious views. One element of the Anabaptist community that seems to have particularly struck his fancy was the abolition of money and the attempt to establish an apostolic community of property on the basis of the Acts of the Apostles. In retrospect, Gresbeck is rather bitter about this (fols. 21v, 23v, 48v, 117r, 124v, 138r, 154r). He speaks positively of the idea in the abstract (fol. 22v), but constantly disparages the fact that eventually the general populace was reduced to starvation, while the king and his court continued to live in luxury (fols. 57r, 96v, 126v, 137r, 139v). He pointedly notes how people couldn't get back the provisions and money they had voluntarily surrendered for the common good (fols. 45r, 125r). Of course, one can't say for sure what inspired him at the start, but his stance in the later account suggests that he had been positively impressed by the notion of social equality of Christians.

The other aspect of the Anabaptist regime that he discusses at length is polygamy. This he is uniformly hostile to, ascribing it to lust (fols. 39r, 47v) and comparing it to "living like cats and dogs" (fol. 46v). Since it was instituted only in the late summer of 1534, long after Gresbeck had been stuck in the city, it couldn't have had any influence on his initial decision to stay.

---

46. Mostly, these instances involve a spelling reflective of a colloquial pronunciation that ignores the etymological origin of the word: "knoeynkesye" (fols. 2v, line 13, and 10v, line 31) for "canonickesei"; "ordennansee" (fol. 3v, line 6) and "ardenanssie" (fol. 40r, line 6) for "ordenantie"; "koer" for choir (fol. 17r, line 9, 120v, line 11); "instrament" for "instrument" (fol. 37v, line 2); "kuenkebynen" for "concubinen" (fol. 54r, line 24); "argelyest" for "organist" (fol. 66v, line 7); "akermente" for "sacramente" (fol. 71r, line 14); "tyespessassie" for "disputatie" (fol. 97v, line 21); "septtor" for "scepter" and "pentencie" for "penitencie" (fol. 103v, line 13); "artychker" for "artychkel" (fol. 117r, line 8); "sellen" for "cellen" (fol. 155v, line 16); "prynssepall" for "principal" (fol. 156r, line 25).

Certainly, in his letter he states that he acquired a single wife in Münster, and there's no evidence that he took on a second one. To some extent, this issue has to be left undecided, since after the downfall of the Anabaptists, he could hardly have said anything except how bad polygamy was.

Gresbeck expresses negative views about various other notable aspects of the Anabaptists and their practices. He's rather derisive about the habit of the Anabaptists to "bear witness" loudly and to invoke their God as "the Father" (de Vader) (fols. 45v, 52v–53r, 65v, 87r, 114r, 117v). He likewise has little regard for the prophesying and divine inspiration that is such a notable element of the Anabaptists' religious experience (fols. 13v–14r, 15v–16r, 20r, 66v, 73r, 99v–100r), overtly accusing the prophet Henricus Graes of lying about his purported revelations (61r–61v) and derisively parodying the "baptizer's spirit" that came upon Anabaptist leadership (fols. 26r, 66v, 73r, 99v) as a "fool's spirit" (fol. 65v). Given the failure of so many of their prophecies to come to fruition, such retrospective disparagement is hardly unexpected. Gresbeck also speaks unfavorably of the Anabaptist destruction of art and architecture, which he describes at length (fols. 111r–114v). And of course he mentions the fact that people were compelled to submit to adult baptism or pay the consequences (fols. 11v–12v). He says nothing about his own baptism, but given his apparent good standing among the Anabaptists down to the time of his flight, it's hard to see how he could not have undergone rebaptism.

All those elements are very public manifestations of the Anabaptist regime that could hardly have failed to impress someone before whose eyes they had taken place. On the other hand, he has a list of "articles" in which he attempts to lay out the Anabaptists' beliefs (fols. 115r–117r). This is a confused mixture of actual beliefs and of negative characterization of their behavior by a hostile observer. At the end, he ingenuously remarks that there were a number of other beliefs, but he could not remember them. Seemingly, abstract theological doctrines were not an issue of great concern to him.

One is left with the impression that Gresbeck was an enthusiastic supporter of the idea that a community of socially and economically equal Christians was to be established in Münster. In his letter to his old employers (appendix, document 2), he claims that his sole concern was to protect property, but the letter pointedly asks them to forgive him if he had angered them. Clearly, he needed to apologize for his presence in the city, and so could not have admitted to having favored the most prominent aspect of the Anabaptists' religious deviance.

5. Gresbeck's Account

There is no introduction or dedication to the work. It launches directly
into a general discussion of the background of the narrative, which pretty
much begins with the Anabaptist takeover in February 1534. Conceivably,
the overall conception and purpose of the work were explained in a cover
letter that accompanied it when it was presented to its recipient. But there
is one indication within the text of whom it was meant for. At the end
of one paragraph (fol. 34v), appear the words "myen genedege her van
moenſter" (my gracious lord of Münster). In his 1853 edition of Gresbeck's
work, Cornelius didn't know what to make of the words and omitted them
as an error. But presumably they're a vocative. In this case, Gresbeck was
addressing himself to the prince-bishop, to whom the work must have been
dedicated.

Why did Gresbeck do this? To answer this question, we have to consider the last quarter or so of the work, which treats his flight from the city
and the aftermath of his capture. Down to his description of his flight from
the city, Gresbeck has not written a word in the work about himself, and
he tells us nothing about the planning that led him to escape the city. All
he tells us is that one night in the late spring of 1534, desperation in the
starving city led him to try and sneak out with four companions whom he
didn't particularly trust. Since the fall of 1534, the city had been cut off
from the outside world by a continuous circuit of trenches, and the men
had to make their way through these trenches without being caught and executed. Milling around tentatively in the darkness, Gresbeck and one other
man set off on their own, and towards dawn, after losing sight of the other
man, Gresbeck surrendered to some troops. They took pity on him because
of his youth—they normally shot all their male captives to death—and he
asked them to take him to their captain, as he had important information.
What he had was a plan for the capture of the city.

Meanwhile, one of his other companions, a man named Little Hans of
Longstreet, managed to make good his escape through the trenches when
the drumming at the changing of the guard created a commotion. This
man was a renegade from the besieging army (fol. 141v) who had defected to the Anabaptists. Eventually, he regretted this decision, and had to
avoid falling directly into the hands of the besieging army, since he would
be executed as a traitor (fol. 144r). Instead, he hurried off to the town of
Hamm, where a retired old commander of his resided. This commander

then asked for a safe conduct for Little Hans from the prince-bishop. This was eventually granted, because Little Hans also had a plan for capturing the city. Gresbeck and Little Hans were soon put together to sort out the details. While Little Hans actually led the assault on the city, Gresbeck was left on the outside during the attack, because he was still viewed with some suspicion as an Anabaptist (though Gresbeck tries to fudge this). While Little Hans would be richly rewarded for his role in the city's capture, Gresbeck not only received nothing for his contribution to the capture but also suffered the confiscation of his own property (as did all of the rebels).[47]

To understand the varying treatment of the two men, one has to take into account the command structure of the besieging army. In the late summer of 1534, after the second failure to capture the city by storm, the prince-bishop basically ran out of money. He turned with hat in hand to neighboring princes, who agreed to foot the bill but took over command of the army, putting Count Wirich of Falkenstein in charge.[48] This was the man to whom Gresbeck eventually laid out his version of the plan for the city's capture. Yet, all the subsequent credit for the plan went to Little Hans of Longstreet. For whatever reason, the bishop gave no recognition to Gresbeck, who is entirely unmentioned in any of the sixteenth-century histories of the Anabaptist kingdom. The supposition is close at hand that the bishop included Gresbeck in the resentment he felt against those who had taken over the siege of his city. Presumably, Gresbeck was associated in the prince-bishop's eyes with the people who had taken his army from him, and he preferred to give sole credit for the plan to the man associated with himself. Hence, the fundamental purpose of Gresbeck's account could well have been to gain credit from the prince-bishop for his role in the city's capture and perhaps also secure the return of his confiscated property.

There is no overt indication of when Gresbeck wrote his account. The account ends with a few events that took place in the immediate aftermath of the city's capture (fols. 154v–156r). He doesn't refer directly to the execution in January 1536 of John of Leiden, Knipperdolling, and Krechting, but he does allude (fol. 145r) to the fact that Krechting's body would hang alongside those of the other two, in cages suspended from the tower of St.

---

47. For a discussion of the extent of the confiscations and their disposal, see Hsia, *Society and Religion in Münster*, 9–10.

48. Kerssenbrock, *Anabaptistici furoris*, ed. Detmer, 747.

Lambert's parish church.[49] The work must have been composed at some later date. There's no way to be more specific, but if Gresbeck's purpose were to help get his property restored to him, one would imagine that the work was written sooner rather than later.[50]

There is no indication that Gresbeck consulted any written material in composing his work. Furthermore, he uses the phrase "not retained in memory" four times in relation to names and concepts he can't recall (Anabaptist preachers, fol. 3r; collaborating ex-burgher masters, fol. 3r; "articles" of the Anabaptists, fol. 117r; names of collaborating burghers, fol. 120r). Clearly, he did not ask anybody to help out with even such a rudimentary fact as the names of prominent men who cooperated with the Anabaptists.[51] It is also noteworthy that he apparently had forgotten the name of John Dusentschuer, referring to him generically as the "limping preacher" (fols. 62r–73r). Considering how prominent a role this man plays in the narrative, it's remarkable that Gresbeck obviously has both forgotten the man's name and done nothing to find it out. Note also the Lutheran clergyman whose efforts to undermine the Anabaptists are mentioned at some length (fol. 8r). Several times Gresbeck refers to him vaguely as the "Hessian," presumably because he either never knew or had forgotten the man's name.[52] Perhaps he was a less important figure than Duesenschuer, but also a less controversial one in the aftermath of the city's fall. Surely, Gresbeck would have had no trouble in finding somebody to tell him the man's name if he'd had any outside informants. Gresbeck knows the name of two of the three "officiants" in a parody mass, but of the third he remarks that the man was Knipperdolling's servant whose name was "unknown to

49. The cages in which the bodies were displayed were left as a permanent warning and are still there today (the decayed original cages had to be replaced with replicas in the nineteenth century).

50. Cornelius, *Berichte der augenzeugen*, lxxii n28 thinks that Gresbeck's discussion (fol. 7r–v) of whether or not the people who brought Anabaptism to the city were still alive shows that Gresbeck composed his text some time later than the events he describes. However, since Gresbeck also thinks that very few people survived the capture of the city (fol. 127v), the factor of time doesn't seem relevant. In any event, Gresbeck is clearly thinking in that passage of those responsible for the debacle, and comparatively few of these men (as opposed to the general mass of Anabaptists) survived the capture of the city (see fol. 152v for the general carnage of the Anabaptists in the aftermath of the capture).

51. Note also his confusion (fols. 4r, 5r) of Eric of Brunswick-Grubenhagen (bishop of Münster, 1532) with his predecessor, Eric of Saxony (bishop, 1508–22). The confusion of the ephemeral later bishop with his much longer serving predecessor is explicable enough, but it would seem that nobody was in a position to correct this error of memory on Gresbeck's part.

52. Conceivably, Gresbeck had less interest in this foreign figure. At any rate, he had no trouble with the name of the local clergyman (Master Tynen) who got into an altercation with Rothman (fol. 3r–v).

me" (fol. 105r). Apparently, Gresbeck had no recourse to make good this ignorance on his part.

Given the care for the task that seems to be implied by the effort to carry it out, it seems unlikely that sheer laziness or indifference was to blame for this procedure. Could it be that for whatever reason Gresbeck felt it best to keep the project secret until the work was ready for presentation to its intended recipient and so felt constrained from asking for anyone's assistance, even with such a seemingly innocuous question as the name of the preacher? On the other hand, Gresbeck notes that virtually no male Anabaptists survived the fall of the city (fol. 127v), and so, since his account mostly relates to events he witnessed himself, perhaps he wasn't in contact with anybody who would be in a position to give him any substantive help with such matters.[53]

5.1 Structure and Themes

The basic structure of Gresbeck's account is chronological. That is, the overall course of the narrative is from the start to the beginning, but there is a tendency for specific stories of a thematic nature to be inserted into a certain stretch of the narrative without strict chronological ordering. For instance, the later permission for divorce is confusingly inserted into a discussion of the problems caused by the initial introduction of polygamy (fol. 79r–v), and the section on the Anabaptist reaction to the revelation of Henricus Graes's betrayal (fol. 76r–76v) includes a number of tangential thoughts. First comes the taunting letter that Graes subsequently sent to the city (fol. 77r). Discussion of Rothman's way of handling this letter leads to a notice about how Rothman similarly treated a letter sent by Landgrave Philip of Hesse, which in turn leads to a discussion of the theological issue referred to in the letter (fol. 77r–v). This sort of association caused a major failure in the chronology. When he discussed the failure, in the fall of 1534, of Rothman's book *Restitution* to bring about efforts in the Netherlands to

---

53. It is true that in fol. 20r, Gresbeck notes in passing that a man who had witnessed some strange behavior on the part of John of Leiden survived the fall of the city, receiving pardon under unspecified circumstances. He also notes emphatically in a later passage (fol. 120r) that some of the people that he had just listed as Anabaptist collaborators were still alive, and specifically cites the man who was chosen as the duke assigned to the Cross Gate as one of those who managed to escape from the far side of the city at the time of its capture. He even overtly notes that the survivors are still astonished at what they saw (fol. 127v). Hence, there were some men available for Gresbeck to consult, but perhaps it would have been safer for him to avoid the company of such people.

relieve the siege, Gresbeck recalled an incident of the time when the king carried out an execution and said that people should do the same if relief didn't arrive by Easter (fol. 78r). Gresbeck proceeds to discuss how the king dealt with this situation the subsequent spring (i.e., March 1535) when the relief did not in fact appear. The subsequent narrative is thrown off when he goes on to treat events that took place later in 1534 as if they took place after Easter.[54] This failure was presumably caused by Gresbeck's reliance on his own memory without any outside assistance.

The work is divided into distinct sections that generally cover a single topic. With one exception (the section on matrimony, starting at fol. 38v) there is no overt indication of the subject of these sections. Some consist of just a few sentences (e.g., the one about Knipperdolling's arrest on fol. 3v or the one about new plans on fol. 134v), and a few can be quite long (e.g., the one about the special meal on fols. 104r–107r or the one about a day's entertainment on fols. 87v–90v) but most cover a page or so.

Gresbeck's sensibilities often seem to have a sort of cinematographic feel about them. Instead of analyzing a concept like the Anabaptists' derision of traditional practices, he narrates one striking illustration of this (the parody mass described on fols. 104r–106v). He tends to show rather than tell.

Gresbeck is pretty much uniformly hostile to John of Leiden, whom he characterizes as a mercurial tyrant and who he says was possessed by a devil (fol. 100v, also fols. 43r, 65r, 73r; Knipperdolling also had a devil, fol. 99v; the "Father" to whom the Anabaptists so often appealed was also a devil, fol. 117v). One particularly remarkable aspect of his account is the drawn-out effort to shift the blame for the events in Münster to outside elements. As we have seen, he clearly refers to himself as a burgher of the city, and he repeatedly speaks of the evil effects of what he calls "the Hollanders and the Frisians (the criminals)," a phrase that is a constant refrain (fols. 2v, 23v, 29v, 47r, 48r, 52v, 67v, 81r, 118v, 119r, 122r; the epithet "criminal" is also used of the Anabaptists in general, fols. 86r, 107r, 114v, and of their leadership,

---

54. Events that are narrated later but took place prior to Easter include the extended confrontation between Knipperdolling and the king (fols. 98r–103v), which apparently took place in October (see also note 502 to the translation), the parody mass (fols. 104r–106v), which seems to have taken place on Christmas (see also note 528 to the translation), the renaming of the gates (fol. 107r–v), which was already going on in December (see also note 538 to the translation), and the destruction of the churches, which actually began at the time of the Anabaptist takeover but was resumed with a vengeance in late January 1535 (see also note 564 to the translation).

fols. 33v, 126v). Seemingly, he can't refer to them without making their culpability for the criminal acts overt. He's also very bitter about the cooperation of the local notable Bernard Knipperdolling with the outsiders. He notes at the beginning that the Anabaptist leadership consisted of Hollanders and Frisians, but among them there were also locals like the ex-burgher masters Knipperdolling and Gerard Kibbenbrock (fols. 2v–3r). At one point when the natives are close to rising against the king, he bitterly notes how Knipperdolling's failure to rally the opposition meant its failure (fol. 140r). Furthermore, it was Knipperdolling, Kibbenbrock, and other burghers who supported the Anabaptist movement who were ultimately responsible for allowing the foreign elements to seize control of the city (fol. 153v; see also fol. 122r). Fundamentally, if Gresbeck's immediate purpose was to gain credit for his role in the city's capture and to avoid any association with its excesses, from a civic point of view, he wanted to exculpate the city's population for the Anabaptist excesses by shifting responsibility to these outside elements.

While Gresbeck generally equates the foreign Hollanders and Frisians with the "real rebaptizers" (fols. 26v, 35r, 39r, 57r, 67r, 73v; cf. 48v),[55] he also distinguishes the category of the "real baptizers" (fols. 14v, 23v, 24r, 35r, 87r, 99r, 117r, 122r) from those who were carried along by enthusiasm but were not really committed. Not only does the latter category encompass the burgers of Münster who were compelled by the Anabaptists, but also "foreigners" who abandoned their lives at home to follow the "false prophets," much to their later regret (fols. 33v, 45v–46r).

Gresbeck devotes an entire section to the eloquence of Anabaptist preaching (fols. 45v–46r). Here he relates this eloquence to persuading foreigners to abandon their property and families and come to Münster, a decision that he says they would come to regret. Presumably, this power of persuasion also applies to the adherence of local burghers to Anabaptism, though he does not make this connection himself. Though he generally tries to contrast the city and its residents in the abstract from the Anabaptism (that is, it is imposed on the city), he nonetheless notes that there was a substantial local element that helped keep the Anabaptists in power (fol. 81r), and he even has a list of collaborators whose names he can remember (fols. 119r–120r), noting that these men were an integral

---

55. Note that the "real" rebaptizers were even physically distinguishable by the unnatural paleness of their complexion and expression (fols. 98v–99r).

part of the king's court and played a key role in keeping the population under control (fol. 120r).

In speaking of the Anabaptists in Münster, Gresbeck makes a recurrent distinction between the "simple people" who "knew no better" because they did not have the mental capacity to perceive how misguided the "real" Anabaptists and their teaching were (fols. 60r, 75r, 95r, 99r) on the one hand, and those on the other who "knew better" but were unable to say anything because of the intimidation imposed on them by the real Anabaptists through their use of violence. A recurrent theme is the extent to which the Anabaptists maintained their regime through force, in both a passive and an active sense. This force (Low German "dwang," translated as "duress") was used initially to intimidate the population into acquiescing in their domination (fol. 17r). The ongoing threat of such violence kept the population restrained from actively opposing the Anabaptists (fols. 22v, 25r, 25v, 119r, 120r, 130r, 133r, 134r, 145r), kept people from fleeing the city at the end of the siege (fol. 122v), and restrained people who felt reservations about the Anabaptist regime from speaking their minds (fols. 125v, 129v, 136v). This force also drove them to carry out actions that they otherwise wouldn't have done, such as tear down churches (fol. 7v) and submit to polygamous marriage (fols. 46v, 50r). On this basis, Gresbeck distinguishes those who were "truly guilty" (as he characterizes John of Leiden and Knipperdolling) from those who got caught up in a situation that they had at first sought out or acquiesced in but would eventually come to bitterly regret (fols. 12v, 33v, 40v–41r), as well as those (such as himself?) who were simply caught up in circumstances not of their own making (fol. 46v). He makes a related distinction between simple people who weren't in a position to know any better and those who did know better but were compelled to keep their misgivings to themselves (fols. 95r, 99v).

5.2 Gresbeck's Reliability

Gresbeck's account is literally unique in that nobody else who had actually lived under the Anabaptist regime in Münster wrote an account. Kerssenbrock (and others) did write accounts on the basis of information that ultimately derives (in part) from those who were themselves eyewitnesses, but such information is of course at least secondhand. In any event, what Gresbeck says can, to some extent, be checked through comparison with the external sources. Certainly, two contemporary accounts of the capture of the siege (see documents 3 and 4 in the appendix) amply attest to the accuracy of Gresbeck's account of his role in the city's capture. Hence, in this regard, Gresbeck stands vindicated in the face of Kerssenbrock's version, which is completely unaware of Gresbeck and ascribes exclusive credit for the city's capture to Little Hans of Longstreet.

For the earlier part of the story, Kerssenbrock and Gresbeck are in general agreement, though, as indicated in the notes, there are numerous discrepancies over details. In these matters, there's no fixed procedure for resolving who is right. Kerssenbrock is of course writing at a much later date on the basis of earlier accounts, but those accounts may well have preserved an accurate record. Gresbeck, on the other hand, was writing within a year or so of city's fall, but on the basis purely of his own memory without, it would seem, any external assistance. It should not be surprising if his memory at times failed him, especially in matters of detail and chronology.[56]

One point in favor of Gresbeck's reliability is not so much what he does say as what he doesn't. He chooses not to say anything about his activities before the fall of the city. As noted above, this presumably means that these activities would not have reflected well on him, so he thought it best to say nothing. And yet who could have gainsaid him if he undertook to portray himself in a favorable light? Few adult male Anabaptists survived the city's fall, and they presumably would have had little opportunity or motive to contest Gresbeck if he had shown himself acting in some way hostile to the Anabaptist regime. And even if he considered such a presentation of himself potentially dangerous, what would have prevented him from talking about his own supposed mental reservations, including himself overtly among those who "knew better" (fol. 103v) but were forced to keep silent (fols. 125v, 129v, 136v) because of the Anabaptists' intimidation? Yet, even under such circumstances, Gresbeck preferred to equivocate by simply remaining silent rather than fabricate a self-serving story that nobody would have been in a position to refute.

As a retrospective account that is clearly meant to please the sentiments of the Anabaptists' enemies and that could hardly have failed to be

56. A major example of chronological confusion is the error in dating the expectations of relief from outside (see also section 5.1). Errors of detail would be represented by Gresbeck's ascription of leadership of the Anabaptists during the uprising of July 1534 to Tilbeck rather than Radeker (fol. 49r and also note 252 to the translation) and his failure to note the "limping prophet" (Dusentschuer's) role in the proclamation of John of Leiden as king (fol. 62r with note 342 to the translation).

influenced by the disastrous outcome of the Anabaptist regime, Gresbeck's version of the affairs of the city during this tumultuous period obviously cannot be taken at face value, particularly in terms of his evaluation of facts as opposed to the events themselves, and even those "facts" are clearly subject to the uncertainty of his ability to recall events that took place under stressful circumstances a year or two in the past. But he was just as obviously an intelligent man with keen powers of observation, and within the parameters of the reservations laid out, there's no reason to consider his account to be anything but a mostly accurate presentation of his experiences.

As for his negative assessment of the Anabaptists and their leaders, this is a reflection of his disenchantment with a religious and social movement that presumably fired his imagination at the start, but soon developed a very dark aspect, and eventually resulted in death for many of its followers, ruination for Gresbeck's beloved Münster, and personal catastrophe for himself. What we have is a guarded but sincere account written by a common but intelligent man who lived through very uncommon times.

6. Basis of This Translation

Gresbeck's work was first published by C. A. Cornelius in 1853 in an antiquarian collection of documents relating to the Anabaptist takeover of Münster. Cornelius based his text on two manuscripts, the first substantially more important than the second.[57] The former was Handschrift 105 in the ducal library in Darmstadt, which is now housed with the same number in the Universitäts- und Landesbibliothek Darmstadt.[58] This manuscript was written in the 1560s for Eberhard Graf zu Solms und Herr zu Münzenberg, who was a descendant of one of the commanders of the besieging army. It retains the Low German of the original version, but with substantial deviations. It routinely changes the orthography of the text and also mostly incorporates the editorial changes made on the original manuscript (these are discussed below). The second manuscript Cornelius used is preserved in the Herzogische Bibliothek in Meiningen (now in the Thüringisches Staatsarchiv Meiningen) and was a conversion

---

57. For a full discussion of the various manuscripts and their relationship to one another, see section 1 of the German edition.

58. For a discussion of this manuscript (by Berndt Thier) plus a few illustrations of artwork contained in it, see Albrecht, *Das Königreich der Täufer*, 111–12.

of the text into High German (and likewise includes the editorial changes). For this reason, the Meiningen manuscript was used by Cornelius
only to restore the text in passages where the Darmstadt manuscript was
clearly defective.

In his preface, Cornelius mentions that after mostly completing his text
on the basis of the two manuscripts already described, he found a better one
in Cologne. Unable to consult it fully at the time, he states his intention to
report at a later date on the relationship of the Cologne manuscript to the
ones he used.[59] As far as I know, he never fulfilled this promise. The text
translated here is based on this third manuscript, which belongs to the City
Archive (Stadt-Archiv) of Cologne. Pagination shows that the manuscript
was originally conceived as a single text, and the coda at the end shows that
the manuscript is complete.[60] At an unknown date, the manuscript was
bound tightly into a manuscript, and a new pagination was added. The Cologne manuscript is also the basis of the edition of Gresbeck's Low German
text that is a companion volume to the present one. The pagination from
the original manuscript is included in both the translation and the Low
German text to facilitate comparison between the two.

In March 2009, the building housing Cologne's City Archive collapsed, seemingly as the result of improperly conducted excavations being
carried out underneath it for a new subway tunnel. This disaster caused the
old archives in which the Gresbeck manuscript was housed to be buried in
rubble and perhaps damaged by water. The great majority of the archival
material was rescued and freeze-dried to prevent further water damage, but
the project of attempting to recover the material preserved in this state may
take decades. At any rate, the state of the Gresbeck manuscript is unknown
at this stage, and it's impossible to know when, if ever, it will become available again for study.

Luckily, I secured a digital copy of the manuscript in 2007. Only
after the collapse of the archive did I discover that three folios had been
inadvertently omitted from this digitized copy. At that point, it was of

<hr>

59. Cornelius, *Berichte*, lxiii n2.

60. Throughout the manuscript, pairs of folios are numbered consecutively with Roman numbers
starting with the second pair. That is, the fifth page (the recto side of the third folio, which marks the
start of the second pair of folios) is marked with the number "ij" (=2), and the seventh page (the start
of the third pair of folios) is marked with "iij" and so on throughout the manuscript. This peculiar
notation is then used sporadically to mark tens of folios (i.e., the numbers 20, 30, 40, 50, 60, 70, 80,
90, 110, and 120 are marked, mostly in Roman but occasionally in Arabic numbers).

course impossible to have the overlooked pages digitized, but the error could be made good by a feeble microfilm that was taken of the manuscript around 1970. This microfilm copy is close to illegible, but with the use of Cornelius's text and a familiarity with Gresbeck's orthographic practices, it's possible to make sense of the microfilm text to recover the manuscript's text.

The Cologne manuscript may well be Gresbeck's clean copy of his account, written in his own hand, to judge by a comparison of its handwriting with the handwriting in the letter Gresbeck sent out of besieged Münster in the spring of 1535 (appendix, document 2). That letter must have been written by Gresbeck himself, for the following reasons.

a. He tells at some length of the adverse consequences when someone in the city shared his intention to defect from the city with someone he considered his friend, and that person betrayed the plan to the king (fols. 123r–123v). This event most likely took place before Gresbeck sent the letter out of the city. It clearly impressed itself on his memory at the time, and under such circumstances he ought to have been very leery of sharing his plan for escape with anyone else.

b. The letter itself shows Gresbeck's wariness by specifying that any response shouted back to him from outside the city was to be addressed to a pseudonym lest his identity be revealed.

c. Gresbeck was very circumspect in dealing with his companions in defecting from the city (fol. 141v).

Given these circumstances, one would imagine that he would be unlikely to entrust the task of writing the letter revealing his intentions to anybody else. And even if he did, the likelihood that such a person would survive the capture of the city and remain available to copy over Gresbeck's account is remote. It is thus almost certain that Gresbeck wrote both the letter and the Cologne manuscript with his own hand.

The handwriting of the letter is somewhat tidier and squarer than that of the historical account, but perhaps the difference is due to the clearly different nib of the pen used for the letter and an attempt to write the comparatively short letter in as tidy a manner as possible, whereas the account, being much longer, was written in a somewhat more flowing and careless manner. In any event, the two documents share a number of orthographic quirks (like dotting the letter "y" and using a symbol that resembles "66" for the vowel in the pronoun "ju"), though it is true that the two documents do diverge in some regards (for instance, the letter uses the letter form "w" in word-initial position, whereas the account regularly uses "v" for both the sounds /v/ and /w/). Perhaps Gresbeck tried to improve his spelling in preparation for writing down his account for presentation to the prince-bishop. In any event, the orthography of the two texts is very similar, and even if the Cologne manuscript was written by another person, that person was not only copying a draft written by Gresbeck but introduced into the text corrections that must have been composed by Gresbeck.

The Cologne manuscript has a number of corrections on it. A large number of these were written over by the original scribe (most likely Gresbeck himself) as he was copying the text over in this final version. Sometimes these edits take the form of marginal additions and changes to the text. At other times, a sentence was started, then words were struck out and the text continues with a variant version of the same sentence. In these instances, Gresbeck apparently decided to rewrite the text while he was copying it. There's no way to tell when the marginal edits were made, though it's perhaps more likely that they were made on a paragraph-by-paragraph basis rather than forming part of a complete revision made after the whole manuscript was written. For the most part, these corrections are simply additions for the sake of clarifying some perceived ambiguity in the text as written. At one point (marginal insertion at fol. 120r, line 21), a similar sort of correction is made by a noticeably different hand (presumably for some reason Gresbeck had someone else write in his own correction). This second hand is boxier and more angular than Gresbeck's but still has a formal appearance.

In addition to these improvements made by the original scribe, there is a separate set of corrections made to the completed text by a subsequent editor or editors in the early modern period. These editorial corrections fall into two related but clearly distinct categories. First, a small number of notes are written in Latin in a clear, formal humanist hand; some of these comments pertain to content with some special interest to an ecclesiastic. They include a large heading about the destruction of the churches (top of fol. 111r), and a point where some comment had been made that seems to have related to the issue of the rebaptism of adults, but this was struck out heavily and can no longer be read (start of the new section on fol. 47r).[61] There are also a number of instances where a picture of a hand with extended index finger points to noteworthy text (often further specified with a line drawn along the margin). More frequently, however, this ecclesiastical commenter expresses his disapprobation of what he takes to be repetitiveness in Gresbeck's account, this sentiment often being expressed in mordent terms. At times, large amounts of text are struck out on these grounds.[62]

The other early modern editor writes in German. He uses a shoddy, brown ink that's clearly distinguishable from the still-black ink of the original text (and seemingly of the Latin comments). In addition, this editor's corrections are distinguishable by his much sloppier and more cursive Gothic hand . This editor made certain orthographic changes (for example, Gresbeck's frequent use of "v" for /v/ is frequently modified into "w" with the addition of a stroke at the start of the letter), but he was mostly concerned with the style of the text. He changes a lot of words, seemingly simply on the grounds of rejecting Gresbeck's vocabulary (sometimes replacing a Low German word, like "warde," with its High German equivalent, like "Wahrheit"), and he sometimes rewrites the text from a stylistic point of view. In particular, he couldn't abide Gresbeck's quirk of beginning a sentence with the odd phrase "so den lesten" ("eventually," "in the end," with the Low German preposition "tho" apparently confused with the adverb "so" and perhaps also the High German "zu"), which he very frequently strikes out, mostly replacing it with some other connective expression.

The stylistic concerns of the German editor seem to be rather similar to the views expressed by the Latin editor, and remarkably the German editor at one point actually replaces the German "vorrede" with the Latin term "aduocatus" (fol. 59v, line 22). It would certainly be easiest to assume that

---

61. Above the section on the small number of survivors that starts at the top of 127r, the editor writes as if a heading "infantes subiungi possint" ("the infants could be added below"). The exact sense of this comment is unclear.

62. Text is marked for excision in fol. 93r, line 26, to 93v, line 6, with the words "ante dictum est, propterea excludatur" ("it's been said before, so let it be cut out"). The text at the end of the supposed articles of the Anabaptists seems to have been particularly annoying to the editor, earning three comments: "eadem habes fere in principio horum gestorum" ("you have pretty much the same material in the beginning of this account), "quere et inuenies eadem in precedentibus" ("look and you'll find the same material in what precedes"), and "et hec predicta sunt" ("this material too has been said before"). A very long excision from 127v, line 5, to 128v, line 16, is accompanied with the words "eandem semper cantilenam canere vitio datur, propterea hec omissa sunt" ("Always singing the same song is considered a fault, so this passage has been omitted"). A final excision from fol. 156r, line 28, to fol. 156v, line 7, has no comment.

the same man was responsible for both the Latin and the German comments, and simply used a sloppier hand when writing in the vernacular. It should be noted, however, that the excision indicated for fol. 165r, line 28, through fol. 156v, line 7, was made on top of text that had already been annotated with the addition of parentheses, and it would seem that the immediately following deletion of "so dem leften" is also by a different hand. This suggests that the large excision was marked by a second reader, though it is also possible that a single man first went through the text, making corrections, and subsequently marked out large amounts of the text for excision.

In addition, there are instances where the original text has been struck out without being replaced. The most remarkable instances of these involve John of Leiden's court. In Gresbeck's long list of committed Anabaptists (fol. 119r–v), certain names have been struck out. This calls to mind the trouble that Kerssenbrock landed himself in when he related in his history of the Anabaptist events the roles of certain people whose important descendants objected to his attempt to preserve activities that the descendants would prefer to be forgotten (conflict over this matter was one of the factors that thwarted his efforts to get his work published in his own lifetime).[63] In addition, a reference to Little Hans of Longstreet's services with the king are struck out (fol. 94r–v), which perhaps suggests that this was done by someone associated with the prince-bishop, who wished to delete information that reflected poorly on Little Hans (though it should be noted that a later reference to his service with the king is left alone in fol. 147r). Whoever struck out the names and Little Hans's role presumably had some specific motives in selecting the names to be excised from the account. On the whole, the names don't appear as significant figures in Kerssenbrock's account or in Kirchhoff's list of known Anabaptists, and I leave for others the task of attempting to divine the reason for the excisions.

7. The Translation

Gresbeck writes in a charmingly unaffected style that clearly reflects a spoken idiom rather than the more stilted syntax characteristic of literary German (and this difference may have contributed to the annoyance that the ecclesiastical editor clearly felt in reading the text). In rendering this into

---

63. For this rather flimsy charge, see Mackay, *Narrative of the Anabaptist Madness*, 41–42, 44.

English, I have tried to retain the colloquial feeling, which leads not only to the use of simple vocabulary but the occasional retention of constructions that are not, strictly speaking, logical in a written context, especially the use of fronted nominal subjects that are recapitulated with a pronoun.[64]

Names can cause a problem, as some individuals are variously known by High German, Low German, and Dutch forms of their names. Following the practice of my translation of Kerssenbrock's history, I've routinely rendered given names in their English form (for instance, the "king" is known as "John" rather than "Jan" or even "Johann"). Apart from any other considerations, since all the names have English versions, this practice makes the characters seem less alien.

64. An example in English of a fronted subject in English would be "my brother, he's a doctor." Such phrases are standard in some languages (e.g., the famous "l'état, c'est moi"), but are not standard in English and virtually never seen in print, though common enough in colloquial speech.

Origin and Narrative of the Rebaptism at Münster in Westphalia That Took Place in the Year 1535

Overview of the work[1]

This is the beginning of the rebaptizing at Münster in Westphalia: how the burghers opposed one another, how those burghers who accepted rebaptism ruled together with a priest called Bernard Rothman[2]

---

1. Though the original manuscript is clearly divided into distinct sections with one exception (fol. 38v), no headings are given. To make the overall flow of the account clearer, headings have been added by the editor. These appear in bold to indicate their status as an addition to the original text.

2. For Rothman's early history, see Kerssenbrock, *Anabaptistici furoris*, ed. Detmer, 160–64; for the extensive corpus of his writings, see Stupperich, *Die Schriften B. Rothmanns*; for a general treatment of his role in the early stages of religious strife in Münster, see Lutterbach, *Der Weg in das Täuferreich*, 67–89. Of comparatively humble origin (his father was a blacksmith), Rothman enjoyed the support of a relative who was a vicar of the college of St. Maurice's. After serving as a schoolmaster in Warendorf (a small town east of Münster), he got a university education at Mainz, and in 1524 was appointed as priest at St. Maurice's outside the city. He was sent off to Cologne to strengthen his already dubious orthodoxy (the university there was a model of conservative rectitude), but instead he went to various centers of reform thought such as Wittenberg and Strasburg. In July 1531, he returned to St. Maurice's and in January 1532, was installed in St. Lambert's in the city (Kerssenbrock, *Anabaptistici furoris*, ed. Detmer, 192). From then on, his radical preaching became a constant source of friction between the prince-bishop, who wished to curb his incitements to reject orthodoxy, and the city council, which wished to protect him (or at least was compelled by Rothman's popularity to adopt this position). He increasingly fell under the influence of the Anabaptist ferment, and in January 1534 had himself rebaptized by emissaries of John Mathias. He then became a major leader in the Anabaptist regime in Münster. Although Rothman was supported by a number of other radical preachers, he clearly made the strongest impression on Gresbeck, being the only preacher to appear throughout in his account. His

(Stutenberent[3]), and Knipperdolling,[4] and some other burghers and all his [Knipperdolling's] adherents, how the other burghers and the clergy were opposed to this and had to depart from them, abandoning everything that they had, and how they [the rebaptizers] eventually chased the other burghers from them on a Friday, and how their own lord, the bishop of Münster, Osnabrück, etc., Count Francis of Waldeck,[5] besieged the city with cavalry and landsknechts[6] in order to take the city of Münster and to punish the rebaptizers, and how there were Hollanders and Frisians in Münster, who made themselves out to be prophets (John of Leiden[7] was a tailor and made himself out to be a prophet, and he was eventually chosen as king by the rebaptizers; John Mathias[8] was another Hollander who made

---

fate at the time of the capture of the city is unclear (the literary sources uniformly claim that he changed into military gear at the time of the final assault on the city and died in combat, but his body was never found and efforts were made in the years after the city's fall to track him down; see ibid., 842n1). See also Kirchhoff, *Die Täufer in Münster*, 585.

3. For the derivation of the nickname, see Kerssenbrock, *Anabaptistici furoris*, ed. Detmer, 422. The first half of the name comes from a Low German word (*stuten*) for "white bread." As part of the rejection of traditional practice, he would give out pieces of this bread in place of the normal communion wafers, and he was happy to take pieces of it to people who had been unable to attend the informal Anabaptist ceremony that replaced the traditional mass. The second half is simply the Low German form of the name "Bernard." Hence, the name means something like "White Bread Bernie." Given the derivation, the name must have been meant to be disparaging, and it obviously struck Gresbeck's fancy, as he normally uses it when referring to Rothman.

4. Bernard Knipperdolling was a prominent member of the patrician class that dominated the city council of Münster, and had long had radical religious inclinations (Kerssenbrock, *Anabaptistici furoris*, ed. Detmer, 323). He was an elector in the selection of the city council in 1533 (ibid., 392), and was made burgher master of the Anabaptist city council chosen on February 23, 1534. He was a prominent supporter of the Anabaptists in general and of John of Leiden's regime in particular. He is a particular focus of Gresbeck's animosity, as he views Knipperdolling as the leader of the local supporters of the Anabaptist government and a major impediment to the supposed efforts of the locals to overthrow the Anabaptist control of the city. See also Kirchhoff, *Die Täufer in Münster*, 335.

5. Francis of Waldeck (1491–1553), a younger son of the count of Waldeck, was intended from youth to pursue an ecclesiastical career. Already bishop of Minden, he was elected bishop of Münster by the cathedral chapter in 1532, but (as noted below) had a hard time asserting his authority in the bishopric. He was a vague supporter of reform, but certainly was not going to allow it to threaten his traditional prerogatives as the secular and ecclesiastical head of his bishopric.

6. For the sense of "Landsknecht," see introduction, section 3.2. In this case, the landsknechts were hired for the service of prince-bishop Francis in his siege of Münster.

7. John of Leiden is one of the central figures in Gresbeck's tale. The illegitimate son of a judge, he pursued a number of careers early in life, including teaching oratory and acting as a tailor (for his early life, see Kerssenbrock, *Anabaptistici furoris*, ed. Detmer, 640–46). He became a trusted lieutenant of John Mathias, and visited Münster in the fall of 1533. He returned on January 13, 1534, and continued to serve Mathias. Upon Mathias's death, John of Leiden took over his leadership (as well as his wife), and in the late summer became the king of the besieged town.

8. John Mathias (Matthias, Matthijs) was a baker of Haarlem in Holland who became a major figure in the Melchiorite ferment in the Low Countries. There, Mathias gradually usurped the authority of the absent Hofman (in 1533, Hofman was arrested in Strasburg, remaining in prison until his death) among his followers, and asserted that the overthrow of the godless and the establishment of the millenarian regime on earth was at hand (see Deppermann, *Melchior Hoffman*, 333–39). In Jan-

himself out to be a prophet; and some of the other Hollanders and Frisians who made themselves out to be preachers), and how these men in Münster ruled and how they eventually dealt with the common people, and what they intended with the baptism, and how they betrayed the common people, doing away with their lives and property and everything that they had, and that they destroyed the churches and monasteries.

Opponents of Anabaptism flee the city

At first, when the baptizing first started at Münster, some of the burghers and women straightway got ready to get [1v] out of the city and take along what they could drive and carry away. Eventually, no one could have anything driven or carried out. The rebaptizers sat every day at the city gates and examined what people were leaving the city at the gates and what they were taking with them. If they had with them more than just what was on them, they took away what the people had from them.[9] They cut off the golden hooks from the women's collars and the buttons from their sleeves, and they couldn't take with them more than just what they had on.

Burial of an Anabapist

They buried a dead man outside the city gate in the countryside. This dead man didn't deserve to lie in the churchyard among godless people since he was a rebaptizer.[10] When it happened that they buried the dead man in the countryside, the burghers and the women withdrew from the city, and things began to be ready for the rebaptizers to hold the city by themselves.[11]

---

uary 1534, emissaries of Mathias baptized Rothman, and from then on the Anabaptists had become increasingly assertive in Münster. In early February 1534, Mathias himself arrived in the city and then led the Anabaptists until his death in April (see 25v–27r). Note that chronologically Mathias should appear before John of Leiden, but here Gresbeck introduces the latter first as the more prominent figure in his account.

9. See Kerssenbrock, *Anabaptistici furoris*, ed. Detmer, 503–4, for a description of similar treatment of those who left the city starting on February 12, 1534, in the aftermath of the temporary settlement between the Anabaptists and their opponents (9r–v). Presumably, Gresbeck has the same period in mind. He apparently just launches *in medias res* with the Anabaptists dominant in the city in early February 1534.

10. This sentence reflects the thinking of the Anabaptists.

11. This seemingly insignificant incident appears to serve the purpose of conveying Anabaptist attitudes in the period prior to their takeover of the city government in late February 1534.

Anabaptists' mania and their seizure of the city council

When it began to get dark in the evenings, the rebaptizers would run through the streets and shout, "Confess and repent! God is going to punish you!" and "Improve yourselves!" They shouted, "Father, Father, grant, stamp out, stamp out the godless! God will punish them!" As it was, God punished and stamped out *them*. Some people in the city would say [2r] that the rebaptizers had hired the criers to cry this way through the streets in the evenings and nights so that they would terrify the people and lead them astray. They would also preach at night in houses. They would gather together at night, and wouldn't preach during the day. For they didn't yet have possession of the city, but they did have sufficient possession of it.[12] They had the keys to all the city gates, and every night they closed off all the streets and lanes with iron chains.[13] They kept on with this closing until they chased away their opposition, which they eventually did. As soon as they'd chased away the burghers and clergy, both young and old, they no longer closed off any streets at night. Then they were a single people and were lords of the city of Münster. Whoever didn't wish to remain had to depart from the city or they would have killed them. They would certainly have driven out their opposition before the Friday, but they didn't wish to do this before they'd chosen a new council. In Münster, the new council was chosen on the first Monday in Lent, and they wanted to wait until then. When this Monday in Lent arrived, they dissolved the old council and chose a new one. These men were on the side of the other rebaptizers. Knipperdolling and Kibbenbrock[14] as burgher masters and the other councilors belonging to the rebaptizing were chosen in the same way as a council is chosen in the cities.[15]

12. In this not terribly clearly expressed thought, Gresbeck seems to distinguish the period starting on February 23, when they took over the city council, from the immediately preceding period when they were strong enough to throw their weight around but hadn't yet taken official control of the city.

13. This is also mentioned in Kerssenbrock, *Anabaptistici furoris*, ed. Detmer, 477.

14. Gerard Kibbenbrock was another patrician of radical religious inclinations and was considered one of the leading Anabaptists (Kerssenbrock, *Anabaptistici furoris*, ed. Detmer, 323). He was an elector for the selection of the city council in 1532 (ibid., 271), a member of the council in 1533 (ibid., 392), and became burgher master in the Anabaptist council elected on February 23, 1534 (ibid., 519). He served as building superintendent (*Baumeister*) under the regime of the twelve elders (ibid., 585), but his stock seems to have fallen once John of Leiden became king, as he was merely the king's food taster (ibid., 648). He was killed at the time of the city's capture (ibid., 850). He had two wives (ibid., 626n3). See also Kirchhoff, *Die Täufer in Münster*, 330.

15. For the election, see Kerssenbrock, *Anabaptistici furoris*, ed. Detmer, 519–20. The new coun-

Stutenberent is the cause of the strife

[2v] One time, the burghers of Münster made a raid from the city. This marching out took place three years or so earlier, before the baptizing took place in the city.[16] They captured a councilor of My Gracious Lord of Münster's, some canons, and some noblemen who resided in Münster and were burghers in the city.[17] They hauled them at night from a town called Telgte, which lies one mile from Münster.[18] I can't say anything more about what the situation was with this.[19] But at that time the priest Stutenberent was outside the city, and would preach in a village called St. Maurice's, which was a benefice of the cathedral chapter and lay two shots' distance from Münster.[20] When this priest would preach, the people in Münster would come out from the city and hear him preach. Eventually, the priest came into the city and preached, as you'll eventually hear. This business was introduced over time in this way, and it happened so quickly that things couldn't be set back again. That such a very great disagreement arose in the city of Münster among the council and among the burghers and clergy was caused by this priest with his preaching. So this priest is the real reason why such a disagreement arose in Münster.

Foreign Anabaptists come to Münster, and their prominent local supporters

The Hollanders and Frisians then arrived. These criminals from other lands who couldn't remain anywhere else moved to Münster and gathered there, so that a sinister faction came together from all lands. The leaders of the

---

cil was chosen on February 23, 1534, and the offices were assigned the next day.

16. For this raid, which took place during the early hours of December 26, 1532, see Kerssenbrock, *Anabaptistici furoris*, ed. Detmer, 339–43. As a result of the capture of highborn hostages by the city council of Münster in this treacherous act, the prince-bishop (the newly installed Francis of Waldeck) came to an agreement on February 14, 1533, with the Lutheran-dominated city council that granted the city virtual autonomy (for the terms, see ibid., 374–78). This agreement was abrogated with the Anabaptist takeover and the prince-bishop's subsequent capture of the city by force. As for Gresbeck's statement that this took place "about three years" before the baptism, this is perhaps just a mistake of copying, the text's Latin numeral *iij* being an error for *ij*.

17. For the list of men captured, see Kerssenbrock, *Anabaptistici furoris*, ed. Detmer, 342.

18. A "common German mile" was much larger than the corresponding English unit, equaling 4.6 of the latter (and 7.42 kilometers).

19. Seemingly, this raid is mentioned only to illustrate the strife that Rothman is held to be responsible for.

20. According to Kerssenbrock (*Anabaptistici furoris*, ed. Detmer, 73), the exact distance was 93 paces!

rebaptizers in Münster were the Hollanders [3r] and Frisians and some burghers in Münster: John Mathias (a prophet), John of Leiden (a prophet), Henricus the Hollander,[21] Schlachtschap,[22] Klopriss,[23] Stutenberent. These men were preachers, and there were even more preachers, but their names are not retained in memory.[24] Among the burghers the chief ones in Münster were Knipperdolling, Kibbenbrock, and some others whose names are also no longer retained in memory. The priest (Stutenberent) was a preacher in the city along with the others. You'll presently hear how this priest came into the city.

Stutenberent's early career

This man Stutenberent preached in the city three or four years before the arrival of the other preachers that I mentioned before (as well as after that). The longer things went on with this priest, the more innovation there was. He preached in St. Lambert's church, which is a parish church, preaching against the council and against the clergy in the city of Münster. One time, this priest stood up and preached in St. Lambert's church, and he preached something that was not pleasing to the pastor in the church.[25] The pastor went to stand

21. Apparently, Henricus Roll. An ex-Carmelite friar and Sacramentarian who was actually from Grave in Brabant rather than Holland proper, he became one of the so-called Wassenberg preachers who would play an important role in Münster. From 1528 on, Werner of Pallant, who was the bailiff of Wassenberg in the duchy of Cleves-Jülich (to the southwest of Münster), gave refuge to radical reformers who were persecuted elsewhere. Pressure from the duke eventually forced the bailiff to expel his protégés in 1533, but Roll had left before then and in August 1532 he was appointed as a reformer cleric at St. Giles's parish church by the city council. Roll was an important associate of Rothman's in advocating radical doctrine. He left the city in November 1533, when there was an attempt to suppress radical preaching, and he traveled through Frisia and Holland. In January 1534, he returned to Münster and was baptized by the emissaries of John Mathias. In February, he left the city to drum up support, and in August arrived in Maastricht, where he was soon arrested and burned at the stake.

22. Henry Schlachtschap of Tongres and Maastricht, a former cleric and another of the Wassenberg preachers. Kerssenbrock (*Anabaptistici furoris*, ed. Detmer, 541) preserves the letter from Rothman inviting Schlachtschap to come to Münster in early 1534. He was one of the preachers who were later sent out as apostles to Soest (ibid., 705; cf. 109v–110r), and was executed after being captured.

23. John Klopriss was yet another one of the Wassenberg preachers, coming to Münster after being expelled by the duke of Cleves-Jülich in 1534. He was sent as one of the apostles to Warendorf (Kerssenbrock, *Anabaptistici furoris*, ed. Detmer, 706), and was duly executed after capture. For a short summary of his life, see ibid., 707.

24. By "retained," Gresbeck means in his own memory. Some names quickly suggest themselves as important radical preachers: Herman Staprade, Godfrey Stralen, Dionysius Vinne, Henry Graes, John Dusentschuer. These were not obscure figures (Gresbeck himself treats the last two at some length), and Gresbeck's failure to recall their names here suggests that he didn't consult any oral sources, much less written ones, in composing his account.

25. This is the only passage where Gresbeck uses the term "pastor." Seemingly, the point is that the man in question is designated by "pastor" (equivalent to the modern German *Pfarrer* or "curate") because he's the person who actually carries out the pastoral duties in the church (as opposed, for

by Stutenberent in the pulpit, and he too began to preach. The two priests wanted to preach at the same time and quarreled with each other, so that there was laughter in the church. This pastor was named Master Timen, and he acted as rector[26] in the cathedral at Münster.[27] This priest had bought [3v] the church from another priest in the city, and for this reason, they were so opposed to the pastor that they preached in the church and carried out their business inside.[28] In Münster, there was a respectable council consisting of burgher masters, councilmen and aldermen, and of guilds, and there was good order in the city.[29] But as soon as this priest Stutenberent began to preach outside the city and in it, one burgher began to oppose the other, and some priests began to oppose the others, so that they weren't harmonious in the city of Münster, with each person all opposed to the other.

Knipperdolling's arrest by Frederick of Wied

At this time, the bishop of Münster was the brother of the bishop of Cologne, named Frederick of Wied.[30] This bishop of Münster, Frederick of Wied, had one time arrested Knipperdolling because he had forfeited his life by stirring up an uproar among the burghers and using violence, so that Knipperdolling

---

instance, to the situation in which the person in charge—the "rector"—is a mere benefice-holder who delegates his pastoral functions to a hired vicar). That is, although both he and Rothman are priests, the pastor is recognized (by Gresbeck) as the legitimate curate for the parish, and on this basis he disputes Rothman's right to speak in his church.

26. The title "rector" has a wide variety of meanings, but here it may designate the person appointed by the bishop to look after the day-to-day operations of the cathedral in his name.

27. Gresbeck's account here of the dispute between Rothman and Timen Kemner is somewhat vague in chronology. Rothman's supporters took control of St. Lambert's by force in February 1532, deposing the incumbent priest, Timen Kemner, and replacing him with Rothman (see Kerssenbrock, *Anabaptistici furoris*, ed. Detmer, 192). Kemner had been a long-standing opponent of religious reform (see ibid., 140–41, for such activities in 1525), and was a natural object of the radicals' outrage. Though there is no evidence to my knowledge that Rothman had previously intruded himself into the services at St. Ludger's, the mention below of his banishment would seem to imply that the events narrated here took place before his installation (that is, presumably in the fall of 1531 or very early 1532). The next sentence seems to indicate that Kemner's acquisition of his position through simony (see next note) made him a lightning rod of radical disapproval, and the anecdote here suggests that prior to the seizure of the church, the radicals actually barged into his church, where Rothman gave some sort of unofficial sermon. This earlier altercation may explain why it was later decided to install Rothman in this church in particular.

28. "Simony" is the term for the illegal but nonetheless widespread practice of acquiring ecclesiastical appointments through purchase (a custom strongly censured by the reformers). According to Kerssenbrock (*Anabaptistici furoris*, ed. Detmer, 192), the installation by force of Rothman as preacher of St. Lambert's was followed by the radical takeover of the other parish churches in Münster, which Gresbeck alludes to rather vaguely here.

29. For the role of the aldermen and guild masters in the city's government, see introduction, section 3.1.

30. Bishop from November 6, 1522, to March 22, 1532.

forfeited his life. Eventually, Knipperdolling was interceded for,[31] so that he received mercy, his release being purchased by his brothers.[32]

Frederick tries to drive out Stutenberent

Frederick of Wied, the bishop of Münster, banned this priest (Stutenberent) from the bishopric, the priest being ordered to leave the territory, so that he should no longer preach outside the city.[33] There were some burghers who brought him into the city, as I mentioned before. Thus, the bishop could [4r] not ban him from the city, though he had banned him from the territory.

Eric of Saxony becomes the prince-bishop

During the time that Bishop Frederick of Münster was lord in the bishopric of Münster, they couldn't come to an agreement with him, and they were all opposed to one another, and would not recognize His Grace. So the bishop of Münster (Frederick) set to it and transferred the bishopric of Münster to the bishop of Osnabrück and Paderborn, named Eric of Saxony, so that he would be lord over the bishopric and rule the territory.[34] The city of Münster and some of the other cities were unwilling to allow Bishop Frederick to transfer the territory in this way. But if Bishop Frederick had wished to give it up and wished the bishopric of Münster to be free and independent, in which case they would have been without a lord, the city of Münster would have let this happen, and they would then have made anew a selection of whomever they wished. Only the city of Münster, as well as some of the other cities in the bishopric, wanted to do this. The chapter, the knighthood, and the estates (some of them) were in agreement

---

31. For the procedure of intercession, see how the rebels who weren't executed produced witnesses to attest to their conduct (50r).

32. For the arrest of Knipperdolling in 1527, see Kerssenbrock, *Anabaptistici furoris*, ed. Detmer, 155–56.

33. The banishment was issued on January 7, 1532 (Kerssenbrock, *Anabaptistici furoris*, ed. Detmer, 173). It was the result of an extended series of suspensions from preaching that the prince-bishop issued and that Rothman duly ignored (see ibid., 168–72, for a wearisome collection of letters on the topic, with ibid., 169n1, for a discussion of Kerssenbrock's chronological confusion on this topic).

34. Gresbeck has confused Frederick's successor, Eric of Brunswick-Grubenhagen (1532), with his predecessor, Eric of Saxony (1508–22). (Given the identity of their given names and the much longer tenure of the predecessor, it's hardly surprising that his name stuck in Gresbeck's mind.) This confusion would bedevil the composition of 5v (see also note 43). For Frederick's decision to resign, see Kerssenbrock, *Anabaptistici furoris*, ed. Detmer, 193; and for the election of Eric, see ibid., 195.

with Bishop Frederick of Münster and with the bishop of Osnabrück and Paderborn that the latter should be the bishop of Münster. But there was much to do before it was sanctioned that the bishop of Osnabrück should be bishop of Münster.

Anti-monastic agitation

[4v] It also happened in Münster during the time of Bishop Frederick that some young fellows had gathered, and that there were also some burghers in the city, and they made a disturbance and ran into all the monasteries in the city of Münster.[35] In each monastery they had soup ladled out for them, and they ate it to spite the monasteries. They didn't know what sort of buffoonery they would do. There was much talk in the city of Münster of these "soup eaters," so that they all gradually began to make a start of it in this way.

Anticlerical agitation

They all committed much buffoonery in the city, all against the canons and the clergy. One Shrove Tuesday, they dressed up young fellows—some burghers, journeymen, craftsmen, and students—and these men drove the plough.[36] In front of it, they yoked priests and monks and beguines,[37] who pulled the plough through the city.[38] Some of the fellows who had dressed

35. This event of 1525 is mentioned without any detail by Kerssenbrock, *Anabaptistici furoris*, ed. Detmer, 127–28.

36. Following as it does directly after an event from 1525, this incident seemingly falls in the same year, but in fact it dates to 1534. The same event is clearly described by Kerssenbrock, *Anabaptistici furoris*, ed. Detmer, 518, where he tells the story directly before an event that he dates to February 21, while Gresbeck tells us that his story took place on Shrove Tuesday. Because the municipal elections set for the first Monday in Lent took place on February 23, 1534, the preceding Tuesday fell on February 17, which precisely corresponds with the implied date in Kerssenbrock.

37. "Beguine" is the term for laywomen who adopted an overtly religious way of life and lived in convents but did not take formal vows as nuns. The movement may have had earlier origins but became prominent in the Low Countries in the thirteenth century. In the next century, adherents became increasingly mystical, and to some extent the movement then fell under the suspicion of being heretical. Some elements were absorbed into more traditional monastic institutions, but the movement continued into the sixteenth century, when it was largely swept aside by the strife between Catholics and Protestants. In any case, Kerssenbrock makes no mention of their participation in the parody of Catholic rites (see also note 38).

38. Gresbeck has somewhat garbled the details, at least to judge by Kerssenbrock's account. According to him, there was a wagon in which a fool, who pretended to be a priest, rode. This wagon was pulled by three pairs of men imitating various orders of monks and friars (Franciscans, Teutonic Knights, Knights of St. John), and the driver was dressed up like the bishop. As they drove around, the sham priests made fun of Catholic ritual. The plough was a separate piece of fun, with a tall blacksmith

up, they went and threw holy water onto the streets.[39] They carried the relic in the city just as the lords of the relic do. In this way, they committed so much buffoonery in the city that over the course of time they made a start of it with their buffoonery.[40] Not all the burghers in the city of Münster did this, just a few good-for-nothings who never have any regard at all either for God or for men.[41] If the parish priests did have some guilt in the city, this could certainly have been punished so that they wouldn't have raved like this. For they do want to say that it was the priests' fault.[42]

Francis of Waldeck becomes prince-bishop

[5r] So Bishop Frederick of Wied handed the bishopric of Münster, with all its castles and strongholds, over to the bishop of Osnabrück and Paderborn, named Eric of Saxony, except Münster, along with some cities in the bishopric of Münster that adhered to Münster, wouldn't admit him. The bishop of Osnabrück and Paderborn retained the bishopric of Münster for seven weeks. Then this bishop (Eric of Saxony) died. Then Count Francis of Waldeck, bishop of Minden, was harmoniously chosen as bishop of Münster by the cathedral chapter and the knighthood and by the estates (cities).[43] In this way, the chapter, knighthood, estates (cities) in the bishopric

---

named Hupert Ruesscher dressed up as a Dominican and acting as the horse that was whipped to pull the plough along. This act must have been a piece of street drama that was to illustrate how the supposedly useless monks were to be forced to engage in real work. For a later parody of Catholic rites on the part of the Anabaptists, see 104r–106v.

39. According to Kerssenbrock, the sham priest wielded an aspergillum (instrument for scattering holy water). He also pretended to wear glasses and read out fake Latin from a book.

40. This sentence shows that Gresbeck thinks that the sort of derision of traditional ecclesiastical ritual that is exemplified in the events of Shrove Tuesday was the culmination of the sort of anticlerical activity that began back in 1525. Thus, Gresbeck implicitly connects the Anabaptist upheavals with the Lutheran rejection of the ceremonials of the traditional church a decade earlier.

41. Note how Gresbeck tries to minimize the culpability of the city as a whole by ascribing the blasphemous agitation for reform to a limited group of malcontents.

42. After the capture of the city by the besiegers, the argument was apparently made that it was the failings of the church hierarchy that caused the popular discontent against the church (see 165r–v). That is, this hostility was legitimate, and if anyone was to blame for the later excesses of the Anabaptists, it was the church itself. This was no doubt a response to the Catholic view that Lutherans were not simply wrong in their views but also discredited for having opened the door to the Anabaptist takeover. For the reflection of this perspective in Kerssenbrock's work, see *Anabaptistici furoris*, ed. Detmer, 56–57.

43. Eric died on May 14, 1532, and Francis, who had been bishop of Minden since February 1530, was elected on June 1, 1532. He was then chosen as Eric's successor as bishop of Osnabrück on June 11. Gresbeck's confusion of this Eric (really Eric of Brunswick-Grubenhagen) with the previous Eric (of Saxony) may have been the cause of confusion in the composition in the text. Before this sentence, the Cologne manuscript has a sentence that reads, "Then the brother of the bishop of Cologne, Count Frederick of Wied, was harmoniously chosen by chapter and by knighthood and estates of cities, who harmoniously chose the bishop of Minden, Francis of Waldeck." This was scratched out by

of Osnabrück chose Count Francis of Waldeck, bishop of Minden, so that they were all harmoniously satisfied together.[44] As for my writing this, the reason I do this is that the priest Stutenberent ruled like this over the course of time in Münster and outside in St. Maurice's Church, having made such a disagreement with Bishop Frederick of Wied and with Bishop Eric of Saxony, bishop of Osnabrück and Paderborn, and with Bishop Francis of Waldeck, bishop of Münster, Osnabrück, and Minden, that this priest was the first cause that dissension arose in Münster in this way.

Knipperdolling's resentment

[5v] It is certainly also to be both noted and believed that, up to the end, Knipperdolling kept it in his memory about Bishop Frederick of Wied, bishop of Münster, that he had once arrested him, so that Knipperdolling remembered his imprisonment and injury, and intended to get back at the bishop of Münster. So I certainly believe that Knipperdolling harbored this resentment. He was a bold and proud man, daring and bold was he in mind. Bishop Francis of Waldeck hadn't arrested him, and I hold that he had to pay for his anger as well.[45] But in the end, when the rebaptizers couldn't get away, they would certainly have let in Bishop Frederick of Wied if he'd been willing to release them, however angry Knipperdolling would otherwise have been.[46]

---

the original scribe, and the present sentence was slightly modified to fit in with its new context. Since Frederick of Wied succeeded the real Eric of Saxony back in 1522, seemingly Gresbeck at first got himself confused about which succession he was dealing with, and the text was modified (seemingly as the Cologne manuscript was being copied, since both the erroneous sentence and the present one were already written out when the mistake was realized and corrected). No effort was made to give short-lived Bishop Eric his correct name, however.

44. Gresbeck is wrong to say that the estates of the bishopric elected the new bishop. The canons of the cathedral (the so-called main clergy) had the exclusive right to select the bishop (Kerssenbrock, *Anabaptistici furoris*, ed. Detmer, 95–97). The estates of the bishopric (consisting of the clergy, the nobility, and representatives of Münster and the other important towns) would be called into session by the bishop, but they played no role in his selection. Presumably, Gresbeck chose to present the selection as he does in order to leave no doubt as to Francis's legitimacy as bishop, and, implicitly, as to the illegitimacy of his opposition.

45. Gresbeck means that even though Francis wasn't the bishop who had had Knipperdolling arrested (see 3v for this), Knipperdolling's motive in acting against the present prince-bishop Francis (through supporting the Anabaptists) was the desire to avenge himself for his mistreatment at the hands of Francis's predecessor (Frederick). The doubtful introductory phrase, "I hold," indicates that this is merely a conjecture on Gresbeck's part.

46. The point is that even though Knipperdolling supposedly hated Francis vicariously because of his treatment by Frederick, nonetheless, in their desperate straits at the final stage of the siege, the other Anabaptists would have turned the city over to Frederick (not to mention Francis) if he had been willing to be merciful. This conception contradicts Gresbeck's later assertion that the Anabaptists were

Stutenberent continues his agitation despite the city council's disapproval

Now that this Stutenberent was staying in the city, the council of Münster issued an edict ordering that no one in the city of Münster should be so bold as to lodge (offer dwelling to) this priest (Stutenberent).[47] This priest went into the city, and no one dared to lodge (place in their dwelling) this priest (Stutenberent). The peddlers in the city had a house, and it was owned by the peddlers' guild.[48] They gave this house to the priest, and he lived there against the will of the council, the aldermen and guild masters, and of [6r] some of the burghers in the city, who wished to have nothing to do with the fact that some burghers were keeping him in the city by force like this. The priest preached in the city all the same, and they all had to put up with this from him. The council and aldermen of Münster imagined that they would thwart this eventually, but when they tolerated this priest, so that he got a church in the city and the common man in the city went in and heard him preaching in it, things had gone too far. At this point, they couldn't prevent it and the commons got the upper hand, so that they became too powerful for the council. When this priest now had his rule like this in the city, there was already rebaptizing in Holland and Frisia, and they began to baptize and to gather there, just as the black peasants did.[49] These rebaptizers in Holland and Frisia and in

---

unwilling to surrender the city under any circumstances (see fols. 87r, 137r, 140r, 156r).

47. Here Gresbeck is mistaken. The city council never actually banished Rothman. Although there was a faction on the council that wished to curb his radicalism, his supporters prevented any substantive action against him, and the council was compelled by Rothman's supporters to spend a great deal of time and effort trying to justify to the prince-bishop their failure to do anything against him. Gresbeck's misrepresentation fits in with his general effort to exculpate the city of Münster as a whole and to shift the blame for the city's behavior to the foreign interlopers and their local collaborators (led by Knipperdolling).

48. Kerssenbrock (*Anabaptistici furoris*, ed. Detmer, 169n1) associates this grant of a house by the peddlers' guild with the incident in January 1532 when Rothman was sheltered in the city in violation of the bishop's banishment of him (the banishment mentioned above on 3v).

49. The phrase "black peasants" signifies participants in the great series of rural uprisings known as the Peasants' War of 1524–25 (for an overview, see Blickle, *Revolution of 1525*; Scott, "Peasants' War," 56–69). These rebellions are at heart a reflection of discontent among the peasantry at their treatment by the landowners, but the movement also became connected with the expectations of liberation aroused by Luther's railings against the faults of the traditional ecclesiastical establishment (and implicitly the secular order supported by the church). After showing some initial support, Luther (for various reasons) became extremely hostile to the peasants' movement and lent frenzied support to the at times draconian efforts to restore order. One reason for Luther's adversarial attitude was that certain religious leaders of a radical persuasion became spokesmen of the movement, most notably Thomas Müntzer. This support was based on the same sort of millenarian expectations that were to be a major element in

Münster had a more iniquitous intention with their faith than the black peasants did with theirs.

Anabaptists flock to Münster from Holland and Frisia

When there was now baptizing in Holland and Frisia, the Hollanders and Frisians learned that there was such a preacher in Münster in Westphalia and that he had control of the city with his preaching, and that there was such discord [6v] in the city between the burghers and the clergy. So the Frisians and Hollanders (rebaptizers) set out for this preacher in Münster.[50] When these Hollanders (rebaptizers) arrived in Münster, they went to this priest in his house. When they came to his house, they bid him peace, just as preachers were to do who were sent from the city of Münster to Warendorf, Coesfeld, and Osnabrück and were to bid peace there too.[51] If these cities wouldn't accept the peace, they were to sink down on the spot.[52] In this way, the Hollanders and Frisians first came to the priest (Stutenberent) in Münster and bid him peace. In this way, Stutenberent accepted the peace from them, and they were then of one mind about the baptizing.

Anabaptism spreads in the city

This priest Stutenberent took to himself Knipperdolling with his fellows, and they secretly baptized each other, until a company of the rebaptizers began to come into existence. At this point they baptized themselves in the city, and every day rebaptizers came to the city from other lands, so that

---

the Melchiorite disturbance in Münster, and perhaps it's this similarity that led Gresbeck to compare the two movements. Another, broader point of similarity is of course the fact that both movements sought to overthrow the established government.

50. As 1533 progressed, Rothman fell under the influence of the millenarian ferment of the Melchiorite movement, and his views became increasingly radical. John Mathias sent two emissaries (Bartholomew Boekbinder and William de Cuiper) to Münster, and they rebaptized Rothman (and other radicals such as Henricus Roll) on January 5, 1534. Gresbeck is rather vague here, but the Anabaptists who come to visit Rothman are presumably these emissaries.

51. This "bidding of peace" was a characteristic greeting of the Anabaptists, as noted directly below (7r; see also 26r, 29r, 62v, 67r, 74v, 98v, 103r, 134v); for its specific use as a way of inviting foreign communities to join the Anabaptist movement (as alluded to here), see 107v–109v, 110v. The implication of this association with the later attempts at "spreading the word" is that the Anabaptist movement in Münster was just as much a foreign imposition as were the later efforts at imposing Anabaptism in the smaller towns of the bishopric.

52. For the later prophecy that the cities not accepting the offer of peace would sink down to hell, see 71v–72r.

they then began to be powerful in the city. The priest first of all performed the baptism secretly, and he would also preach secretly in his house, baptizing many people (men, women, and maidens). In this way, the number of rebaptizers in the city grew to be so large that they began to openly baptize [7r] anyone who wished to have himself baptized. At this point, things in the city had gone so far with the rebaptizing that they carried out their business alone with their prophets and preachers. The rebaptizers had a secret token among themselves for men and women.[53] They wished to be very saintly and were unwilling to address the other burghers and women. Be it mother or father, they were unwilling to address anyone. When men met each other on the street, they gave each other their hand and kissed each other on the mouth, saying, "Dear brother, God's peace be with you." The other answered, "Amen." The womenfolk who'd been baptized also had a secret token among themselves. They would go around without any head scarf. They went around in a wimpel, and this wimpel had a covering over the head. The wimpel was their secret token, and you could recognize female rebaptizers by it. These rebaptizers and female rebaptizers would treat each other like brothers and sisters, so great was the love that they had among themselves. This is how the priest held his rule over the city. The burgher masters and council would have been happy to see him leave the city in good time, but the common man was all opposed to this. Many remained in the city and many left it. There were many people that they chased out on that Friday, and there were many who stayed on that day who were not culpable for the rebaptizing and were forced to it, while others in the city had to leave. I'll write no more of these people. I'm thinking instead of those who brought the priest into the city and maintained the preachers. In part, [7v] they're dead, but it's still my view that they aren't all dead.[54]

Anabaptists prophesy doom

The prophets and preachers (as named by me before) then came to the city. They preached throughout the city, and informed the nuns in the monasteries that the monasteries would sink down and that they should have

53. See Kerssenbrock, *Anabaptistici furoris*, ed. Detmer, 476, for special signs for gaining access to houses in which Anabaptist activities took place in January 1534.
54. Gresbeck notes elsewhere (127v) that very few people survived the capture of the city. In any event, he is clearly thinking here specifically of those responsible for the debacle (see 152v for the general carnage of the Anabaptists in the aftermath of the capture).

themselves baptized.[55] Some of the nuns left the monasteries and had themselves baptized, allowing themselves to be convinced by the false prophets and preachers in the way that many a person in Münster did. The preachers preached a lot like this about the monasteries, saying that they would sink down, since God was so angry about the monasteries that they would sink down. They convinced the people with their preaching, so that the people went and stood there and looked at the monasteries and churches. They were in expectation of this, wishing to see the great miracle and wondering when the monasteries and churches would sink down.[56] Oh, what they told the poor people, who didn't know that they themselves were to tear down the churches, that they were yet to come under such duress! The monasteries and churches remained standing, however, and did not sink down. After everyone had looked long enough, they could go back home. At this point, the rebaptizers were so powerful in the city that the other burghers who were unwilling to give themselves over for baptism had to leave the city.

A Hessian preacher opposes Anabaptism in the city

[8r] There was another preacher in the city, and he was opposed to the baptizing.[57] This preacher was a Hessian, and he would preach against the rebaptizing and tell the people what the preachers intended with rebaptism. Things eventually turned out just as this preacher said. The Hessian would preach that whoever wished to leave the rebaptizing should come to him and he would remove them from it. This was reported to the other preachers, and they drove him out of the city.

He came once more to the city and requested safe conduct from John of Leiden (he was already chosen as king at that time).[58] I hold that the

55. For the problems of the Convent Across-the-Water in January 1534, see Kerssenbrock, *Anabaptistici furoris*, ed. Detmer, 472–74.

56. See Kerssenbrock, *Anabaptistici furoris*, ed. Detmer, 481–83, for Rothman's seizure of the Convent Across-the-Water on February 6, 1534, and his false prophecy that the buildings and any nuns who remained within them would collapse on midnight of the following day. Here, Gresbeck is generalizing on the basis of this one event, which took place directly before his arrival in Münster, presumably under the influence of the later general attempts to destroy all ecclesiastical buildings (111r–114v, 118r–v, 136r).

57. The Lutheran clergyman Derek Fabricius came to Münster in the fall of 1533, sent by the reforming Philip I, Landgrave of Hesse, as part of his effort to win the city over for the Lutheran cause and to induce the radicals to give up their doctrine. Fabricius attempted to undermine the Anabaptists' leadership (Kerssenbrock, *Anabaptistici furoris*, ed. Detmer, 452–68) until he was finally forced from the city during the general expulsion of all non-Anabaptists on February 27, 1534 (ibid., 538).

58. For Fabricius's second mission to Münster, see Kerssenbrock, *Anabaptistici furoris*, ed.

Hessian came to the city on behalf of the landgrave and brought a letter.[59] Eventually, the Hessian left the city again, but John of Leiden and Knipperdolling stuck to their Father and their faith. The Hessian couldn't make them budge.

Prince-bishop's abortive attempt to seize control of the city

My Gracious Lord of Münster saw that they wouldn't let themselves be counseled. For he wished to be a gracious lord to them. But the rebaptizers in the city were unwilling to let themselves be counseled and paid no attention to the bishop's Grace. My Gracious Lord of Münster then set to it and reached an agreement with the council in the city of Münster and some of the burghers who didn't adhere to the baptizing [8v] that they were to open two of the city gates (the Gate of Our Dear Lady and the Jew Fields Gate) for the bishop.[60] The gates were opened to the bishop, so that he got two or three thousand peasants and some cavalrymen on horseback into the city, so that My Gracious Lord of Münster was now in possession of the city. The rebaptizers were in control of the marketplace, and they stood there in

---

Detmer, 762, where Kerssenbrock erroneously places the event in early 1535. In fact, it took place in November 1534 (see ibid., 762n1).

59. Discussed below (77r–v).

60. Gresbeck somewhat misrepresents the situation. He speaks as if there were a prearranged attempt to betray the city to the prince-bishop's forces, but things were rather more complicated than this (Gresbeck's version once again fits in with his efforts to exculpate the city as a whole for responsibility for the Anabaptist takeover). In early February 1534, the prince-bishop began to muster forces with the intention of seizing the troublemakers in the city, and rumors about these plans impelled the Anabaptists to seize the marketplace in the city with about five hundred supporters on February 9. In response, their opponents occupied the Parish Across-the-Water on the other side of the river Aa that flows through the city. According to Kerssenbrock, Tilbeck the burgher master had a letter from the prince-bishop requesting permission to bring his troops into the city and promising to respect the city's liberties. Tilbeck, however, was a prevaricator of radical leanings and suppressed the letter. During the night, large numbers of peasants and some cavalrymen were assembled outside the city under the authority of Derek of Merfeld, the bailiff of Wolbeck, and in the morning these were brought into the city by the two gates mentioned by Gresbeck (this detail is confirmed by a later account written by Bernard Rothman; see Kerssenbrock, *Anabaptistici furoris*, ed. Detmer, 496n1). The Anabaptists' opponents felt that the shedding of domestic blood in civil war was unacceptable and that the use of the prince-bishop's help to suppress the Anabaptists would undermine the city's traditional liberties and privileges; this sentiment was played upon during negotiations by the local Anabaptist leaders. The upshot was that a reconciliation was arranged the next day, at the instigation of Tilbeck and presumably with the consent of Derek of Merfeld, who was apparently in the city. As part of the agreement, the prince-bishop's forces withdrew. At what point exactly this happened and when the truce came into effect as a result of the exchange of hostages is not made clear by the unsatisfactory evidence. The troops may have withdrawn before negotiations started as a precondition, and the truce may not have started until February 11. For a much more detailed account, see ibid., 487–99.

their battle order, shouting and singing and jumping up and down.[61] Some were in the muck and ate the muck from the streets. They shouted to their Father and said what a great fire they saw in the air. This fire was positioned over the peasants and cavalrymen that My Gracious Lord of Münster had in the city. These peasants and cavalrymen were in possession of the Parish of Our Dear Lady, which is separated by the water that flows through the city. Over this water there were bridges, but these the rebaptizers had thrown down, so that this water lay between them like this. The peasants and cavalrymen had captured Knipperdolling and five or six other burghers who were rebaptizers and had placed them in the church tower of Our Dear Lady's. Knipperdolling was in the tower and shouted just as oxen do. They shouted, "O Father, Father, grant, grant! Punish the godless!" Eventually, they heard more cavalrymen riding up the streets, and then they fell silent in the tower and no longer shouted, thinking that My Gracious Lord of Münster had himself entered the city. [9r] If My Gracious Lord of Münster had come into the city, His Grace would have been in control of it.

Anabaptists thwart the prince-bishop's plan to seize control of the city

Eventually, the rebaptizers had a meeting with the officers who were with the peasants and landsknechts, and on both sides they promised hostages to guarantee that they would separate in friendship and love by the grace of My Lord of Münster (Tilbeck,[62] along with some other people on the council, reached such an agreement in the meanwhile), and that the rebaptizers promised hostages so that the peasants and cavalrymen withdrew from the

61. For the enthusiastic attitude of the Anabaptists, see Kerssenbrock, *Anabaptistici furoris*, ed. Detmer, 494–95 (Kerssenbrock dwells mainly on the behavior of the women). The details here are similar to Kerssenbrock's description of the Anabaptist victory celebrations (ibid., 500).

62. Herman Tilbeck was burgher master in 1533 (Kerssenbrock, *Anabaptistici furoris*, ed. Detmer, 392), and at the time when the Anabaptists began to seize control of the city in the winter of 1534, he remained in the city while his colleague as burgher master Caspar Judefeld departed to take the prince-bishop's side in the dispute, and he played a pivotal role in subverting the anti-Anabaptist movement in February. He wasn't elected to the Anabaptist council selected on February 23, 1534, but he did become one of the twelve elders who soon replaced the city council (ibid., 576). Though apparently he was still somewhat suspected by the Anabaptists soon after their takeover of the city (20r), he was instrumental in taking up leadership of the Anabaptists after the other leaders had been arrested during the abortive July uprising (48r–v). He also had two wives (ibid., 626n3) and served as John of Leiden's master of the court (*Hofmeister*), so there can be no doubt about his radical sensibilities. He was killed during the capture of the city (ibid., 850). See also Kirchhoff, *Die Täufer in Münster*, 700.

city.[63] The master wasn't at home there.[64] If they'd also taken Tilbeck, Knip-perdolling, Kibbenbrock, and some others, or if they'd kept possession of the city until My Lord of Münster had come into the city, then I would certainly believe that they would have separated in friendship and love by the grace of My Lord of Münster. As soon as the peasants and knights were out of the city, the rebaptizers immediately began to rage, and they closed all the city gates and took possession of the city.[65] The fire that they were supposed to have seen in the air was hellfire.[66] All the peasants and cavalry-men would supposedly have been burned up in it if they hadn't withdrawn from the city. The rebaptizers said that if the peasants had remained a half hour longer in the city, they would have been burned up in that fire and sunk into the abyss of hell. They informed the common folk in the city that God would have made so great a sign over [9v] the peasants and cavalry-men if they hadn't come out of the city. With such cleverness and deftness they got the peasants and cavalrymen out of the city by promising these hostages. The rebaptizers then laid the blame on the bishop, saying that he hadn't kept his word to them, and so they wouldn't keep theirs. It was all buffoonery, what they were engaged in (Knipperdolling and his company).

Prince-bishop's reaction to the failure of his plan

My Gracious Lord of Münster was on his way and would have entered Münster when the peasants and cavalrymen were in the city. When the peasants and cavalrymen came to meet him, My Gracious Lord of Mün-ster asked why they'd moved out of the city. When they answered that they'd promised hostages and would separate from His Grace in friend-ship, My Lord's Grace was not pleased. He became angry and said, "Then the devil must have been controlling you all," because the peasants and cavalrymen hadn't remained in the city until his Grace came in.[67] For

---

63. Gresbeck gives the impression that the negotiations were conducted between the Anabaptists and the prince-bishop's forces, but Kerssenbrock makes it clear that the burghers on both sides were the driving force. Presumably, Gresbeck emphasizes the participation of the prince-bishop's representatives because he once again wishes to reduce the city's responsibility for the later course of events.

64. This has the sound of an adage, referring to the lack of control on the part of the bishop.

65. So, too, Kerssenbrock, *Anabaptistici furoris*, ed. Detmer, 500–501.

66. See Kerssenbrock, *Anabaptistici furoris*, ed. Detmer, 501, for a similar description (based on the confession of a captured Anabaptist) of a fiery vision at this time (it involved an armed knight riding above the fire and threatening destruction).

67. According to Kerssenbrock, *Anabaptistici furoris*, ed. Detmer, 499, the prince-bishop merely wept. One wonders how Gresbeck could have known otherwise.

if His Grace had come into the city, the situation with the rebaptizers would never have gone so far.

Anabaptists identify their opponents

Once the peasants and cavalrymen had moved out of the city and the rebaptizers had taken possession of it, they guarded themselves. [10r] They also learned who would not have himself baptized and who was opposed to them. They learned this in the following way. When the peasants and cavalrymen were in the city and had possession of it, the opposition, who were unwilling to have themselves baptized, had hung straw wreaths on their doors, so that the peasants and cavalrymen would do no harm to these people.[68] The rebaptizers had hung no straw wreaths on their doors and were so brazen that they had no regard for the bishop, peasants, and cavalrymen, but dextrously got them back out of the city.

Anabaptists solidify their control of the city

So when the rebaptizers again had possession of the city by themselves, and the peasants and cavalrymen were gone, they preached in the city how God had struck the peasants in the heart, what a fire they'd seen in the air, and how they would have burned up in that fire. They then baptized many men and women. They also sent letters to Holland and Frisia describing what a great miracle had happened in Münster, how God had struck the peasants in the heart and thus they withdrew from the city of their own accord, and what a fire they'd seen in the air. Hence, the Frisians and Hollanders came to Münster, and they came from all lands.[69]

Anabaptists take control of the cathedral

[10v] So, the rebaptizers then got their way in the city of Münster. They ran to the cathedral and plundered it, chasing out all the priests.[70] They took the keys from the sextons and locked the cathedral on all sides. They

68. So, too, Kerssenbrock, *Anabaptistici furoris*, ed. Detmer, 493.
69. The last clause is a somewhat clumsy way of referring to the foreign Anabaptists who came from places other than Holland and Frisia.
70. For the attack on the cathedral, which started on February 24, 1534, see Kerssenbrock, *Anabaptistici furoris*, ed. Detmer, 521–23.

smashed apart the chests and cupboards.[71] They stayed inside for two or three days, singing and jumping. They smashed apart all the saints and burned them up.[72] Day and night they stayed in the cathedral and drank. There was a great rumor in the city that they were in the cathedral like this, smashing everything, and that the one was opposed to the other. The lords of the cathedral[73] and the other priests didn't return to the cathedral until the city was captured.

Anabaptists take over the city council and their opponents are downcast

So the first Monday in Lent arrived, and the rebaptizers dissolved the old council and chose a new one.[74] They appointed Knipperdolling and Kibbenbrock as burgher masters, and the men they put on the new council were all on the rebaptizers' side, since they wished to be people of a single sort. Once they'd chosen the council, they marched out in force and burned a village with its church.[75] It lies two shots' distance from the city and is called St. Maurice's, which was a benefice of the cathedral chapter.[76] [11r] At that time, there was many a downcast person in the city of Münster, and they said among themselves that no good would come of it now or ever, which eventually turned out to be the case. This was said by the burghers who had nothing to do with the rebaptizers, and also didn't help burn the village, and remained in the city until the end. Eventually, however, they had to leave the city together, as you'll presently hear. After the rebaptizers had burned the village, they marched back to the city,

71. The terms signify smaller and larger receptacles for valuables. Under the circumstances, Gresbeck must have in mind the containers for the safekeeping of the various items necessary for liturgical needs like the priests' vestments and the accoutrements for the mass.

72. Kerssenbrock (*Anabaptistici furoris*, ed. Detmer, 522–23) deplores at length the destruction of specific works of religious art (the term "saints" here signifies artistic representations of saints). Given the lack of any such details in Gresbeck's discussion of subsequent attacks on the parish churches (111r–114v), where he speaks mainly of the destruction of the physical fabric of the buildings rather than the artworks within them, it would seem that Gresbeck didn't have much interest in art. At any rate, he passes over in silence the remarkable insult (ibid., 522) by which the Anabaptists drilled a hole through a diptych portraying the Virgin Mary and John the Baptist and used it as flooring in a latrine for the guards on the city wall (see also note 575).

73. I.e., canons.

74. February 23, 1534 (see Kerssenbrock, *Anabaptistici furoris*, ed. Detmer, 519–21). Gresbeck makes it sound as if this was some special act of the Anabaptists, but this was the regular day for the annual selection of the new council.

75. February 27, 1534 (see Kerssenbrock, *Anabaptistici furoris*, ed. Detmer, 531–32).

76. I.e., the appointment of the curate was in the gift of the cathedral chapter.

and everyone went home. All of this was run by the priest (Stutenberent) together with Knipperdolling and his fellows and the other rebaptizers who were in the city.

Everyone forced to accept rebaptism and non-Anabaptists driven from the city

Now came the Friday after that Monday.[77] After they'd chosen the new council, at seven in the morning on that Friday they ran through the city, up and down the streets, shouting, "Get out, you godless people! God's just about to wake up and punish you!" They ran like this through the city with their weapons (guns, pikes, and halberds). They threw doors open [11v] and then by force chased out of the city everyone who was unwilling to have himself baptized. These people had to abandon everything they had, house and home, wife and child, and in this piteous way they had to depart from their possessions and abandon them. So men and women, maidens and children, and all the clergy withdrew from the city in the morning on a Friday (the second one in Lent). On that Friday, there was savage weather, with rain, snow, and strong winds.[78] A dog should not have been chased from the city on that Friday, so savage was the weather on that Friday. The other burghers and the clergy had left before that Friday. If they had waited until that day, they would still have had to leave along with the others. Once these people moved out of the city, there was a great crying in the city of Münster from the women and children. Those who remained in the city—men, women, and maidens— were forced to the baptizing, as you'll [12r] presently hear. So the burghers and women who'd remained in the city on that Friday had to go to the marketplace and have themselves baptized. This baptizing lasted about three days. Those who had themselves baptized on the Friday went to the houses of the burgher masters Kibbenbrock and Knipperdolling (both were burgher masters of the rebaptizers), and they each had their name

77. For a more detailed account of the origin of the plan to expel the non-Anabaptists, see Kerssenbrock, *Anabaptistici furoris*, ed. Detmer, 532–33. On Wednesday, February 25, 1534, Mathias urged in a sermon that all the godless in the city should be killed. The next day, Knipperdolling argued that such killing would call down the wrath of neighboring states upon the city, and he proposed instead that those who refused immediate baptism were to be expelled the following day (Friday, February 27). For Kerssenbrock's version of the expulsion itself, see ibid., 534–40.

78. Kerssenbrock too emphasizes the bitterness of the winter weather (*Anabaptistici furoris*, ed. Detmer, 538).

written down. It would certainly be fair for those among the men and women who had themselves baptized on the Friday to be granted mercy. I can't say much about those who were baptized before the Friday. Those who had themselves baptized on the Friday went before the preachers and had themselves baptized. Three or four preachers stood up there at the marketplace and baptized the people. The preachers said to the people they were baptizing that they should give up evil and do good. They had a pail of water placed there in front of them. The people went and fell to their knees before the preachers. Then the preacher baptized them with three handfuls of water in the name of the Father, Son, and Holy Spirit, amen. These were the words that they baptized them with, but their intent was not so good. It had an entirely different meaning to it, as they eventually learned, as you will presently hear. The preachers baptized in their own houses some old men and women who could not go to the marketplace and also some who wouldn't go. [12v] They also baptized some of the old and sick people in this way with good words.

Nobody imagines things would turn out as they did

When the rebaptizers took control of the city of Münster on Friday and forced these people to be baptized or else they had to leave the city and abandon everything that they possessed as the others had done, those who were baptized on Friday stayed in the city with the same poverty that they had,[79] and did not imagine that things would go so far. The other burghers, women, and clergy, who left the city or were driven from it by force before the Friday or on it, also didn't imagine that things would go so far, imagining that they would return in three or four days. O Lord God, how they betrayed the folk one way or the other[80] and did in the well-being of all of them and the life and possessions of some! If those who had themselves baptized on Friday had known in advance what the preachers had in mind with the baptizing, not one child would have stayed in the city that day, and they all would have left together.

79. The point is that it was predominantly the well-to-do who fled, whereas the mass of Anabaptists were of lesser social standing. For the plundering of the houses left by those who had been driven out, see Kerssenbrock, *Anabaptistici furoris*, ed. Detmer, 542–43.
80. I.e., whether they stayed or left. For the same expression used under similar circumstances, see 41r.

Anabaptists tighten their control

Once they'd chased the people away like this on Friday, they were lords in the city of Münster. Knipperdolling and Kibbenbrock were the burgher masters, and they had control of the city by themselves. Knipperdolling went through the whole city that Friday afternoon, shouting, "Father, Father, grant, grant!" as loud as he could shout. He looked up into the air [13r] and had a savage look about him, no different than if he were a madman, and he was pale in the face. Knipperdolling didn't shout like this alone. There were ten or twenty others who were also shouting in all the streets and lanes, so that on that Friday there was such a wondrous rule and regime that it is impossible to write or tell about this regime, and no one can conceive of or express it. On the third day they had it announced throughout the whole city in all the streets and lanes that the council ordered that all those who hadn't had themselves baptized who were still in the city should remove themselves by sunrise or else they would be killed.[81] This sounded so shocking that the folk in the city were seized with horror. The announcement was made by a city servant (master of heralds) named Teba. Those who hadn't been baptized left the city straightaway.

Anabaptists control the city watch and have a vision

The two burgher masters (Knipperdolling and Kibbenbrock) and all the council that the rebaptizers had chosen appointed the city servants, appointing six masters of force[82] and as many other servants as they needed.[83] The masters of force had to keep a watch every night in the beginning, and every night they kept an army pan with a fire up at the marketplace.[84] At night, the burgher masters Knipperdolling and Kibbenbrock, some other members of the council [13v] and the watch commanders, and John of Leiden would go around the city and inspect the watch.[85] Once, they went

81. Apparently, Sunday, March 1. Kerssenbrock makes no mention of this supplementary decree.
82. *Gewaltmeister* in High German. The duty of this office was to supervise the night watch and (in connection with this) to detect and suppress any activities, seditious or otherwise, that threatened public order (see Kerssenbrock, *Anabaptistici furoris*, ed. Detmer, 108, 884).
83. Kerssenbrock mentions the watch briefly in his discussion of the establishment of a military force in the city (*Anabaptistici furoris*, ed. Detmer, 553).
84. The phrase "army pan" ("heer panne") apparently signifies a brazier kept in the field at night during military operations for the purpose of providing illumination. In this instance, the purpose is presumably to prevent any conspiratorial activity against the new regime at night.
85. The presence of council members on watch duty is also mentioned by Kerssenbrock

around the city one night and saw a great fire outside the city. By the fire they saw two swords just like battle swords. The fire lay in between and blazed up the height of a man into the air. The fire was seen by John of Leiden, both burgher masters, and two of the masters of force, as well as two or three members of the council and the highest secular judge, who all saw the fire. John of Leiden and the two burgher masters said that the fire was a sign out of heaven from God that God would keep watch outside the city. They fell to their knees and gave thanks to God. My Gracious Lord of Münster,[86] however, had begun to besiege the city and keep watch around it at night, and it's my view that the landsknechts that the bishop of Münster had stationed outside the city had made that fire while they were keeping watch at night.[87] Knipperdolling also said that at night they saw a face in the moon and people standing by the moon, and that the look in their faces was just like a Moor.[88] Knipperdolling would see many things of this nature in the air at night. For the others who were standing by him he would point [14r] with his fingers into the air towards the moon, but they couldn't see it the way he did. He would see many things of this nature day and night. Those who couldn't see this the way Knipperdolling and the other rebaptizers did they didn't consider to be so holy, and they didn't have faith in the way that Knipperdolling and the other rebaptizers did. They would see many of these things and informed the common people in the city of Münster of them. They said that at night they saw three cities in the air. The cities stood above Münster, and one was Münster, the second Strasburg,[89] and the third Deventer.[90] God had selected these cities (as named by me)

(*Anabaptistici furoris*, ed. Detmer, 553).

86. The Cologne manuscript originally read "the bishop of Münster" here, but the first part of the phrase was scratched out and replaced with the printed text. Presumably, Gresbeck decided when revising the clean text that it was better to use a more polite way of referring to the bishop, which perhaps reinforces the idea that the prince-bishop was the intended recipient of the account.

87. Gresbeck here alludes rather incidentally to the fact that on February 28, the prince-bishop's forces took position outside the city, thereby putting the city under a rather laxly enforced siege (see Kerssenbrock, *Anabaptistici furoris*, ed. Detmer, 545–48, for details of the military dispositions).

88. One wonders what anybody in Münster knew about the appearance of Moors (the Moslem population of the North African coast and Spain).

89. The religious reformers of Strasburg made the city renowned among those favoring anti-traditional thought. Melchior Hofman accorded it a prominent role in his millenarian vision of the impending end of the world, which was to come in 1533, but the city's leaders did not appreciate the compliment and imprisoned him in that year for his troublemaking in the city (he would eventually die in prison a number of years later). Clearly, the lukewarm reception he received in Strasburg had yet to impress itself upon the minds of his followers, who continued to view the city as leading the way to the new regime on earth.

90. Deventer, a city in Holland, was at this time embroiled in a great deal of Anabaptist activism,

and wished to keep a holy folk in them. There God's word was to emerge anew. For His word had been obscured for so long. It would then spread over the entire world, but it would go forth from these three cities first. They preached about that fire for more than half a year, saying that they'd seen it outside the city in the way that I've mentioned.[91]

John Mathias and John of Leiden intimidate a gathering of menfolk

John Mathias and John of Leiden were both prophets and were, along with the burgher masters and the council, the leading men in the city of Münster. The leading prophet in the beginning was John Mathias, [14v] and John of Leiden wasn't the leading prophet then. But it was John Mathias who said that it was revealed to him that John of Leiden was to be raised high up in the world and become a great prophet. These prophets, preachers, and real rebaptizers from all lands who had come to the city in this way were all of one mind as to what they intended with the baptizing. The two prophets, John Mathias and John of Leiden, had all the menfolk that were in the city gather together in the cathedral square with their weapons and armor, and they formed ranks seven deep. The prophets then started shouting in the square that the door to mercy was shut, there was no more mercy. Rather, God was angered. They shouted that those who'd been baptized on the Friday were to go stand by themselves on one side, and these people went and stood by themselves on one side. Then some members of the council and preachers came and said to those who were standing by themselves that each one should lay down his weapon and take off his armor.[92] So they laid down their weapons. The members of the council and the preachers also bound the weapons from their bodies and removed their armor by force.[93]

---

much of it depending upon the influence of men who brought news of the events in Münster (see Mellink, *Wederdopers in de Noordelijke Nederlanden*, for a collection of evidence). Note that Deventer was the town where Henry Graes was to muster the Anabaptists who were to raise the siege of Münster (see 75r).

91. Since the incident with the fire seems to have taken place soon after the Anabaptists took control of the city council in late February, Gresbeck would seem to think that talk of this wonder must have ceased sometime not long after late October. Could it have been given up around the time of the abortive plan to send missionaries to the surrounding communities in mid-October (see also note 405)?

92. Apparently, Gresbeck refers here to those who had not been baptized and were left standing when those who had been baptized moved to the other side.

93. The context seems to demand "unbound," but even if we read something like this (which is a simple change paleographically), the sentence still seems odd in that it was just said that the men had already laid down their weapons. Also, even with "unbound," in what way can a weapon be said to be

74

Then the men had to lie on their faces and pray to God that they might stay in the city and receive mercy. [15r] The prophets and preachers said that God didn't want to have anything impure in the city of Münster, and that God wanted a holy folk who would praise His name. They lay on their faces for an hour crying and praying, and every moment they expected that the prophets and preachers along with the other rebaptizers would fall upon them and kill them all. What they intended to do was to kill them together. Some also said that they wanted to drive them naked and bare from the city. In that case, the landsknechts of the bishop would certainly have killed them. This is how they forced the others who hadn't been baptized on Friday to be baptized. These men numbered about three hundred. Once they were lying down in great fear up at the cathedral square, they eventually had to get up and leave their weapons on the ground, and they led them to St. Lambert's Church. They entered the church together, and there they stayed on their hands and knees for three hours, having to pray to God that they might stay with the holy folk. They shouted out in a loud voice, "O Father, O Father, O God, have pity on us and admit us to mercy." Men and women held each other by the arm, and embraced themselves in a crosswise manner, and danced like this, and they had to worship the Father in this way. There were also some small [15v] boys and womenfolk in the church with them who shouted so loudly that there was a terrible noise in the church. There were also some rebaptizers in the church who'd been baptized before the Friday, and they went up and down the church saying, "Pray, pray, pray to the Father truthfully," going by one person first and then by the next, until the end.

A false vision

There was one man there who lay still for a long time and didn't shout. Eventually, he raised himself up and shouted in a loud voice, "O Father, grant!" Then he lay down again for a while. Soon he raised himself up again and stuck his hands up into the air and shouted in a loud voice, "O Father, grant mercy!" Then he lay down again and remained still for a while. Then

---

"bound" to the body? The sentence seems garbled. Perhaps the mention of "weapons" here is a mental slip, and the intended sense was that their *armor* was to be unbound and removed from their bodies by force? Certainly, there is no easy solution, and the flow of the sentence suggests that the fault was one of composition rather than transcription.

he raised himself up a third time and shouted out again. Another man stood by him. He held him by the arms and said to him, "Hold fast, hold fast! Pray truthfully!" The man prayed so long that he fell back down again, and he stuck his hand up into the air just as if he were seeing a sign or an angel coming out of heaven. When the man standing beside him shouted, [16r] "Where? Where is he, where is he?" he pointed with his hand to the vault of the church. The only thought of the folk in the church was that God had revealed himself or that an angel had come from heaven. But in that church there was a painting of God on the underside of the vault, and the man sat directly in front of it while he was shouting like that and pointing with his fingers, and when the other man asked him, "Where is he?" he showed the way to this God.[94] John of Leiden and some preachers were all of one mind about this buffoonery of shouting in the church. John of Leiden and Schlachtschap were standing outside the church listening, and after the shouting and the pointing with fingers had taken place, they threw the church door open and went into the church. John of Leiden then went to stand on an altar and said, "Dear brothers, I shall inform you for God's sake that you have mercy from God and are to remain with us and be a holy folk."

Another false vision

One time they also prayed to a weathercock on the top of a house that was made of brass. The sun was shining upon this weathercock so that this weathercock, being made of bronze, gave off a shining just like the gleaming of the sun. They prayed to this weathercock, imagining that the Father [16v] was sitting upon the house. They took the weathercock down from the house so that they shouldn't pray to it anymore. This praying to the weathercock took place before the siege of Münster began.[95]

John of Leiden's special horse

After the shouting and the pointing with fingers in the way that I have mentioned before was finished, with John of Leiden and Schlachtschap coming

94. This is the cynical explanation of the ecstatic experience by someone who lends it no credence.
95. This incident appears in Kerssenbrock (*Anabaptistici furoris*, ed. Detmer, 501–2), where it appears right after the victory celebrations of the Anabaptists that followed the successful outcome of the uproar that started on February 9. Here the anecdote is a digression called to Gresbeck's mind by the similarity of the delusions by which divine signs were imagined to be present when Gresbeck (and others) held the signs to be nothing but natural phenomena.

into the church and announcing to the people that they were to remain in the city and be a holy people, John of Leiden and Schlachtschap announced how a horse had run to the city and they had taken it inside. They said that God had sent it into the city, and that it had come running to the city from God Himself. This horse belonged to a nobleman from whom it had run away. John of Leiden would ride it when he became king. Eventually, when they had nothing more to eat, John of Leiden said that God had revealed to him that they should eat horse and that the king would be the first to eat his horse. John of Leiden then had this horse that God had sent him killed and ate it in his court. When the hunger [17r] eventually became so great, John of Leiden received this revelation about eating his horse. Then they ate the other horses. Accordingly, John of Leiden (the king) had to be the first to eat the horse that God had sent him and that had come running into the city from Him. So they brought things to an end in the church. John of Leiden and Schlachtschap went up to the chancel[96] and stood facing each other, and they had all the folk go up between them. They blessed them, placing their hands on their heads. Then they went back to the cathedral square, and everyone retrieved his weapon and went home.

A gathering of women intimidated as the men had been

The next day, the women and maidens went to the cathedral square, and they had them assemble there just as they had done with the men. Some preachers (Schlachtschap, Klopriss, and Gerard Krechting[97]) were present there, too, and they applied duress to them just as they had on the men. The womenfolk cried and lay on the square in the same way. The preachers pressed the womenfolk to believe in the baptizing so urgently that some of them fainted. With this [17v] fainting on the part of the women, the preachers baptized them, with (some of) them not even knowing that they

96. I.e, the latticework screen that separated the choir (where the priest officiated) from the congregation.

97. Presumably, Bernard Krechting is meant. There were two brothers named Krechting who held important places in the Anabaptist regime. Bernard had been pastor in Gildehaus, and after moving to Münster he became a councilor of King John of Leiden and later his lieutenant (he was eventually executed with the king and shared a place with him hanging in a cage from St. Lambert's church; see 145r), while his brother Henry, who had been bailiff in Schöppingen, became the chancellor of the twelve elders (24r) and held the same position under John of Leiden. Since the correct form of Bernard's name is given on 145r, the name here is presumably a mental slip.

were being baptized. Eventually, the womenfolk left the square and went into the cathedral. There they lay down and shouted as the men had done before in St. Lambert's Church. Eventually, God revealed to them that they were to stay in the city, that God had admitted them to His mercy, and that they should be a holy folk. The preachers revealed this to the womenfolk just as they had to the men in St. Lambert's Church. These womenfolk were also all forced to the baptism on the Friday. These womenfolk that they had forced to be baptized (otherwise, they would have killed them or driven them from the city) numbered about two thousand.[98]

Special token for the Anabaptists

They had tokens minted, as big as a heller.[99] These were inscribed with the four letters for "The word becomes flesh."[100] In St. Lambert's Church they gave this token to all the men and women, everyone who was in the city, and they listed everyone under his name. They sewed the token up on a little chain and hung it around their necks. Four weeks later, they gave out another token, also inscribed with the four letters [18r] for "The word becomes flesh." These tokens were the size of a corn cockle white halfpenny.[101] John of Leiden distributed them in Knipperdolling's house. These too they hung around their necks.

A man arrested for speaking against the Anabaptist leadership

There was a burgher in the city named Hubert Smit who was supposed to serve on the watch one night.[102] He said during the watch, "The prophets

98. For Gresbeck's discussion of the city's population under the Anabaptist regime, see 69r.

99. A heller is a halfpenny coin (i.e., not a large one). For an illustration of such a token (plus discussion by Berndt Thier), see Albrecht et al., *Das Königreich der Täufer*, 36.

100. I.e., the initials of the phrase (Low German "dat wort wirt fless" equals High German *Das Wort wird Fleisch*). The reference is to John 1:14, and the sense is that the reformed Anabaptist regime is literally the manifestation in human form of the kingdom of God.

101. A "white penny" was a standard silver coin (also called an "aldus penny" or a "groschen"), with "white" signifying the color of the metal. A common issue of this denomination was minted in Mainz and had as a device on it the city's symbol, the corn cockle (this was a weed that used to be common in wheat fields, "wheat" being designated with "corn" after the English usage).

102. The same basic story appears with some variation of detail in Kerssenbrock, *Anabaptistici furoris*, ed. Detmer, 559–61. Kerssenbrock gives the man's name as "Hubert Ruesscher the blacksmith." The form here presumably reflects the not yet fixed nature of last names in the early modern period, the man's profession being used as a last name ("Smit" equaling smith). In any event, according to Kerssenbrock (*Anabaptistici furoris*, ed. Detmer, 518), Ruesscher had participated in the travesty of

and preachers, they'll prophesy until they do us in, and they must have a devil in their body." It was reported to the prophets and preachers that he'd made such a statement during the watch. The prophets and preachers set to it and had him arrested and thrown into the tower.[103] The next day after this, they had all the menfolk gather together in the cathedral square with their weapons. The men formed ranks five deep, and they formed a circle and held a common assembly. Eventually, they had the burgher come into the circle and stand before the common man. The prophets and preachers set to it and accused the burgher of having said against God and His prophets, apostles and preachers (the apostles were the preachers) that they would prophesy "until they do us in and that they must have a devil in their body." At this point, the common man asked whether this was true and had happened. He said yes, because he couldn't [18v] deny it since he was convicted by men who'd heard it from him. At this point, the preachers said he was worthy of death, he had to die, he'd angered God, and this was God's will. God didn't want anything impure in the city, and everything that was in sin had to be eradicated. God wanted a holy folk. Then they led the burgher to the cathedral. Then John of Leiden took a halberd and slashed the burgher twice in the body but couldn't run him through. How this happened I can't write. They took him back to the prison in the tower.

Botched execution of the man

They all then remained up at the square, and again they formed ranks five deep. There the prophets and John of Leiden and John Mathias shouted that the door to mercy was shut, that there would never ever be mercy anymore, and that they would all be damned together. Eventually, John of Leiden tore the shirt from his body and shouted in a loud voice that the door to mercy was shut, God was so very angered, had a glowing sword in His hand, and would inflict punishment. They would all burn up in hellfire. All the menfolk lay facedown on the ground, and cried and shouted. Some womenfolk also were standing up at the cathedral [19r] square and looking on. They too stood there shouting and crying, so that it was

---

Catholic ritual that Gresbeck relates above (4v) without naming the participants. See also Kirchhoff, *Die Täufer in Münster*, 594.

103. It was common procedure in German cities during the early modern period to use one of the towers in the city walls as a prison.

wondrous behavior what the people up there carried on. It would be impossible to write or tell of this. Eventually, they had the burgher hauled from the tower to the square. He cried piteously and asked for mercy. The door to mercy was still closed. John Mathias, who made himself out to be a prophet, wanted to place the burgher against the wall and shoot him with a gun. The burgher wouldn't stand against the wall and threw himself face down upon the ground in the form of a cross, crying piteously and asking everyone for mercy. So John Mathias took another pistol and wanted to shoot the burgher through the body. But the pistol wouldn't prime, so he primed it again, put the barrel to the man's back as he lay before him on the ground, and shot him through the body and then threw the pistol away. At this point, the burgher heaved himself about, crying piteously, and didn't die right away. Then they dragged him to his house. John of Leiden came to him and said, "He's getting better, he's getting better," since he wasn't dead right away, [19v] so they brought him home. Then two or three days later, the prophets and preachers came to him in his house and said to him for God's sake that he would keep his life and not die. But within eight days the burgher died.

Two ex-burgher masters arrested and pardoned

The prophets and preachers remained even longer up at the cathedral square and looked for more people who were still supposed to be in sin. The prophets took out of the group the one burgher master, Kibbenbrock, and Henry Redeker and Mollenhecke, who had been councilmen (aldermen[104]) before the baptizing in the city of Münster, and two of them, Henry Redeker[105] and Mollenhecke, were also councilmen during the baptizing.[106] The

104. Here and in 48v, Gresbeck seems to treat "alderman" as an alternative term for "councilman" (for the correct distinction between the terms, see introduction, section 3.1).
105. As an alderman in the regularly elected councils of 1532 (Kerssenbrock, *Anabaptistici furoris*, ed. Detmer, 213) and 1533 (ibid., 392), and as a councilor in the supplementary council elected in October 1532 (ibid., 271), Redeker showed himself to be a radical (ibid., 215, 279, 470, 480), and he urged at the time of the council elections in February 1534 that the voting should be in accordance with the spirit and not the flesh, a sure sign of Anabaptist inclinations (ibid., 519). He stood up to the Anabaptists in the name of regular legal procedure early during the Anabaptist regime (see also note 106), but would later play an instrumental role in putting down the July 1534 uprising against polygamy (see Kerssenbrock, *Anabaptistici furoris*, ed. Detmer, n256). He would then be appointed as one of John of Leiden's four royal councilors (ibid., 647, 663). See also Kirchhoff, *Die Täufer in Münster*, 548.
106. The Anabaptists were right to harbor suspicions about Mollenhecke, who would later lead an uprising against the establishment of polygamy (see 48v–49r). For more on him, see Kerssenbrock, *Anabaptistici furoris*, ed. Detmer, n254. As for Redeker, in Kerssenbrock's account (ibid., 560), he and

preachers had them too taken to the tower (the cellar[107]), and all the people were still lying on the ground up at the square. Knipperdolling lay on the earth and shouted how he was possessed. He lay facedown on the ground and rooted in the earth with his face like a pig, burrowing out a great hole in the ground with his hands, feet and face.[108] Eventually, they had the men brought back to the cathedral square from the prison. The preachers placed them facedown on the ground, so that they too should ask for mercy. The other folk didn't imagine anything other than that these three would also die. [20r] John of Leiden went up to the cathedral square. He looked into the air and prophesied. He said to himself, "It's turning white, it's turning black, it's turning white, it's turning black." Someone went up to him who alone (and no one else) heard him going on like this and prophesying, "It's turning white, it's turning black," so that no one but this man heard this. The man who heard this was still alive when the city was captured, and he was pardoned by the lord.[109] After John of Leiden had prophesied long enough, he went to the burgher master and the other two. He raised them up and informed them that they had mercy from God and should improve themselves. In this case, the door to mercy opened up, while they did the other burgher in. At the same time, Tilbeck, who had been a burgher master before the baptizing and eventually became the king's master of the court in the city, was standing there. He cried, being afraid that he would go to prison, but he wasn't taken to the tower.[110] He'd helped the bishop of Münster in getting his cavalrymen and peasants into the city, but in the end he defected from the bishop and adhered to the rebaptizers. On account of the cavalrymen and peasants having gotten into the city, Tilbeck was afraid [20v] that the prophets would shoot him too. This is how the prophets and

Tilbeck had intervened to halt the initial proceedings against Hubert on the grounds they violated normal legal procedure (i.e., they were objecting to the disregard of traditional governmental practice by the Anabaptist leadership). Though Gresbeck says nothing of it, Redeker would later join Tilbeck in temporarily taking over the leadership of the Anabaptists when the remaining leaders were arrested during the rebellion led by Mollenhecke (see ibid., n256).

107. I.e., the cells for prisoners were below ground level.

108. Kerssenbrock says nothing about Knipperdolling in his version of this event. Since there seems to be no motivation for his appearance here and nothing comes of it, perhaps Gresbeck has erroneously intruded into this incident some other occasion when Knipperdolling abased himself similarly (perhaps in connection with some other legal proceedings, which may have led Gresbeck to associate that event with the present affair).

109. I.e., by the prince-bishop.

110. Kerssenbrock (*Anabaptistici furoris*, ed. Detmer, 561) claims that it was Redeker and Tilbeck who were arrested, making no mention of Mollenhecke. Gresbeck's detailed account is to be preferred.

preachers ruled in the city of Münster at the time when the city was first put under siege. This was also the first time that they shot someone like this or inflicted punishment like this.

Landsknecht arrested and executed for speaking against a preacher

There was a foreign landsknecht in the city. He'd said that he would shoot Schlachtschap with his gun and load it with grapeshot. This knecht[111] held a grudge against Schlachtschap, having quarreled with him so that they were enemies of each other. It was reported to the prophets and preachers that he would load his gun with grapeshot and shoot the preacher. The prophets and preachers had the knecht arrested and put him in the prison. Straightaway the next day, they summoned a common assembly up at the cathedral square and had the landsknecht brought before it. The prophets and preachers set to it and accused the landsknecht of having spoken against the preacher Schlachtschap and of wishing to load his gun with grapeshot and shoot him. Having spoken against God's apostles and being worthy of death, he should die. So they bound the landsknecht to a tree and shot him with a gun.

Communal ownership of precious metals instituted

[21r] So the prophets and preachers, along with the whole council, took counsel and wished to have all property in common. They first issued a proclamation that all those who had copper money should bring it up to the council hall. A different kind of money would be given to them in return. That is what happened. Next, they came to an agreement and decreed that all property should be common, that everyone should bring up his money, silver and gold, just as each had done the last time.[112] After the

---

111. "Knecht" is merely the second element in the word "landsknecht" (it is cognate with the English "knight," though the two words have diverged in status; both basically mean "military retainer," but the English word has come to signify a much higher social status). Perhaps it could be translated as "soldier," but given the obvious association with the full form, it seemed best to retain the original form in the translation (it turns up fairly frequently).

112. Kerssenbrock also places the confiscation of gold and silver right after the death of Hubert the smith, asserting that fear of his fate deterred any opposition to the order (Kerssenbrock, *Anabaptistici furoris*, ed. Detmer, 561–62). Kerssenbrock ignores the early decree about copper money and erroneously associates the monetary decree with the later confiscation of excess clothing. The chronology of these decrees is rather vaguely attested, but it seems clear that John Mathias was a driving force and that

prophets and preachers reached this agreement with the council, they had it announced in the preaching that all property should be common and that one person should have as much as the next. Whether they'd been rich or poor, they should all be equally rich, the one having as much as the next. So they said in the preaching, "Dear brothers and sisters, now that we're a single folk, brothers and sisters, it's absolutely God's will that we should bring together our money, silver and gold. The one person is to have as much as the next. So everyone should bring his money up to the registry next to the council hall. The council will sit there and receive the money." The preacher Stutenberent continued, "It's not appropriate for a Christian to have any money. Be it silver or gold, it's unclean for a Christian. Everything that the Christian brothers and sisters have belongs to one person as much as to the next. You shall lack nothing, be it food or clothing, house and hearth. What you need [21v] you shall get, God will not let you lack anything. One thing should be just as common as the next, it belongs to us all. It's mine as much as yours, and yours as much as mine." This is how they convinced the people, so that they (some of them) brought their money, silver and gold, and all that they had. But in the city of Münster, the idea that the one person was to have as much as the next turned out unfairly.[113]

Not everybody turns in his wealth

There were some people in the city who brought up all their money, silver and gold, and retained nothing at all. Some people brought up a part and also retained something. Some brought up nothing at all. Those who brought up their money, silver and gold, and retained nothing were good Christians and held God's word dear.[114] The others who brought up something and also retained something were still two-faced and still had a little doubt. Yet, those who become good Christians were still to receive mercy,

---

the initial institution of communal property must have taken place in March (after the driving out of the non-Anabaptists on February 27 and before Mathias's death around Easter on April 5).

113. Gresbeck's resentment about how unfair the institution of communal ownership of property turned out to be in practice will be one of the recurrent themes of the narrative.

114. From this sentence to the end of the paragraph, Gresbeck appears to be giving the Anabaptists' interpretation of events. In particular, the last three sentences are actually in the present tense, and although he does occasionally use the present tense in past narrative, this usage is not very common, and perhaps he is lapsing into the present as he is reproducing the sentiments of the Anabaptists at the time. Or conceivably (though less plausibly) this phraseology reflects Gresbeck's basic acceptance of the Anabaptist tenet of economic equality in the Christian community, his dissatisfaction arising merely from disillusionment with the Anabaptists' hypocritical (as he saw it) application of the principle.

though they had to pray truthfully to God.[115] The others, who retained their money, silver and gold, and brought up nothing at all, were forced to be baptized on the Friday. They are Christians by force, and are still godless. These people still have to all be stamped out by us.[116]

John of Leiden preaches the necessity of communal ownership

[22r] So they had the folk come up to the marketplace together, and they gave a sermon there. John of Leiden said that it was God's will that everyone should bring up his money, silver, and gold. "This money, silver, and gold, is for our best benefit in case we need it." They preached so fearsomely and imposed such a dire penalty for it that no one dared to retain anything. When they were informed of someone who'd retained his money, silver, and gold, they drove him from the community and imposed such a punishment on him (beheading some) that when another person thought of it, no one dared to retain anything.

Deacons seize foodstuffs

The bringing up of money lasted about two months, since their preaching and punishments were so fearsome that no one dared to retain anything.[117] They also had it said in the preaching that anyone who still retained anything should bring it up freely, boldly, and openly. He would still receive mercy. After this time there is no more mercy, and the door to mercy will close.[118] Whoever still had something brought it all up, allowing themselves to be convinced.

---

115. Seemingly, this sentence was recomposed during the writing of the manuscript. At first, the text read "had to" (past tense: "moesten") with an infinitive no longer recoverable. This version was scratched out and replaced with the present tense ("moten") and the infinitive given here.

116. The end of this sentence doesn't appear in Cornelius's text, and the text isn't fully visible in the Cologne manuscript. After the clearly legible phrase "still have to be stamped out," the text continues with "and all still X by/from us," the X representing a word that disappears in the inner margin of the page. This may be an infinitive (something like "leave"), but conceivably the fact that Cornelius's text omits the final phrase means that it was composed defectively (certainly, there's only room for three or so letters, which seems to rule out a suitable infinitive). Since the visible part of the phrase largely repeats the phraseology of the earlier section of the sentence, it may simply be that it's a garbled repetition with the additional information that the "stamping out" is to be done "by us" (rather than "from us"; the preposition "van" can take both meanings).

117. This would seem to extend no later than May.

118. Again, this sentence is in the present tense, which presumably means that it is to be taken as an indirect quotation of the Anabaptists' own thoughts.

Registration of communal property

After the property became common in this way, [22v] they appointed three deacons in each parish who were to guard the property consisting of produce, grain, and meat, and any sort of foodstuffs that there were in the city.[119] These deacons entered all the houses and examined what in the way of food, grain, and meat each person had in his house, and they wrote a list of everything that each person had in his house. These deacons went through the city. Each group of deacons went around their parish and were to examine what sort of poor people there were in the city and not let them lack anything. At first, they did this two or three times, but this practice was eventually forgotten because they still had provisions enough in the city. It was with a good appearance that they carried out this procedure in Münster. After they drew up the list for each house, no one had control over his possessions. But if they'd hidden on the side something that wasn't listed, they were able to retain it.

Communal meals

They had a house by each city gate. This was a "community house." Everyone who was keeping watch outside the gate and working on the walls or in the canal went there to eat. There was a captain in charge of each gate, and a preacher as well as squad masters. The captain also had a lieutenant who kept the people under duress. They would also preach in this community house in front of the gate every day in the morning, before noon.[120] [23r] The deacons had to make arrangements for the food in the community

119. For Kerssenbrock's discussion of the deacons, see *Anabaptistici furoris*, ed. Detmer, 557–58, 737. Kerssenbrock gives the names of seven, and another source specifies their number as eight. As the city had six parishes (St. Martin's, St. Lambert's, St. Ludger's, St. Giles's, St. Mary's, and the Jew Fields), Gresbeck's statement here would seem to indicate that there should have been more. For their later activities in connection with the control and distribution of "communal" goods, see 22v–23r, 27v, 45r, 62r–v, 68r, 88v, 91r, 95v–96r, 97r, 125v–126r.

120. The preposition translated here as "in front of" is "vo(e)r." Somewhat counterintuitively from an English point of view, when used of the city gates, the preposition can signify either side of them. Most of the time, it means "before" the outer side, in which case I've translated it with "outside." However, the movement of the king described on 96v makes it clear that the same preposition can be used to describe something taking place in front of the inner side of the gate (see also the usage with street names on 108r). Usually, the context makes it clear which side is meant, and I've used "outside" for activity in front of the outer side, and "in front of" for the inner side. In a few instances, like the present one, the sense is not self-evident. Whereas one might think the watch should be held outside the gate, presumably eating a meal would be safer on the inner side, under the protection of the walls against sniping from the besiegers.

house, each deacon in front of his gate. In each parish they appointed an innkeeper for the community house who had to see to the cooking and look after the house. When it was past noon so that the people sat down and ate, a young man stood there and read from the Old Testament (the Prophets). Once they'd eaten, they sang a German hymn. With this, they got up and went to their watch post. Then the captains and the assistants sat down to eat.

Inept management of the food supply

The deacons took the meat, bacon, and grain from the monasteries and from the houses from which they had driven out the burghers, and they also took what was up at the cathedral square and in the vicarages. They provided food with this in front of every gate for as long as it lasted. When it was used up, they began to rummage around in the houses for what they'd listed, and then they began to make people poor. In this way, they ate ten or twelve hundred cows and other cattle in one summer, as well as other meat, butter and cheese, and also stockfish and herring,[121] so that in this way they at first feasted and were openhanded. They would carry entire barrels full of herring up to the walls in front of the gates where they were keeping watch. [23v] They wouldn't eat the herring, and threw it away. With time, the food began to give out. Then they certainly would have eaten the herring that they at first didn't like. Then everyone who had anything at home had to go there to eat. But they didn't have much at home. They had taken everyone's property from him, and they could not get it back when the hunger began to arrive.

City council replaced with twelve elders

The prophets reconsidered and didn't wish to have any government at all in the city of Münster. The prophets and the preachers, the Hollanders and Frisians (the criminals), the real rebaptizers—these men wished to be lords by themselves, so they appointed as twelve elders those in the city who were supposed to be the wisest men and good Christians.[122] These elders were

121. "Stock fish" refers to fish preserved, without salt, through drying in the sun, whereas herring were usually "soused" (preserved through immersion for a period of time in a lightly salted pickling solution).
122. For Kerssenbrock's discussion of the appointment of the twelve elders, see *Anabaptistici*

to rule the people and lead the way for them and to hold sway in the city.
So they deposed the burgher masters and the council that they'd appointed
as well as all the guilds and aldermen, so that there would no longer be
any government apart from the twelve elders and the council (it was the
same thing). But it was awful that the foreigner wanted to have the city by
himself, as they in fact did. The foreigner had control of the city. So the
prophets chose the twelve elders just as the children of Israel had done.[123]
They would do the same. For they said that Münster was the New Israel
and they were Israelites. The preachers selected from here and there in Holy
Scripture [24r] what supported them. The twelve elders didn't rule wisely,
however much they had the Holy Scripture lying open before them when
they took counsel.

Deliberations of the twelve elders

So the prophets and preachers chose the twelve elders in Münster. The
twelve elders would go to take counsel every day in the council chamber,
where the council used to sit before. When the twelve elders went to take
counsel, they sat around a table and had the Bible (Old Testament) lying
open in front of them on the table, as they wanted to pass judgment according to it. John of Leiden would stand there and would give counsel for
every evil as well. The chancellor would also sit there and write down their
business (what they had to take care of). This chancellor was also good at
every evil, and he's named Henry Krechting. He kept his life but he was
a real rebaptizer.[124] Whoever had something to take care of in the city of

---

furoris, ed. Detmer, 575–76. There is some dispute about the time of the replacement of the regular city
council with the twelve elders. The elders issued an important edict containing legal provisions, which
bears the date April 8, 1534 (ibid., 582–88). Unfortunately, this document is not preserved in the
original, and otherwise there is no proof of their existence before May. Detmer (ibid., 574n2) doubts
that the elders were created before the death of Mathias on about April 5 (as the issuance of such a long
document so soon after his death seems to imply) and suggests that perhaps in the date of the document
the month "May" has somehow been replaced with "April" (he has no explanation for this). It must be
noted, however, that Gresbeck's chronology here clearly places the establishment of the new magistrates
before Mathias's death (related below, 62r).

123. See 134r for another instance of the Anabaptists modeling themselves after the ancient
Israelites.

124. Krechting had been the *Gaugraf* (bailiff) of Schöppingen (a small town in the bishopric to
the northwest of Münster), and after converting to Anabaptism, he moved to Münster in February
1534 with his family and a number of his subjects (see Kerssenbrock, *Anabaptistici furoris*, ed. Detmer,
509–10). On the way, he was captured and imprisoned, but his son fled to Münster and informed
the Anabaptists, who sallied forth and rescued Krechting. Detmer (ibid., 509n1) cites this text in
support of the idea that Krechting would later escape from the capture of the city and go on to found

Münster went before the twelve elders up in the council chamber, where they sat and heard everyone's need. They wished to pass judgment according to the Scripture and be holy in this way.

Group of landsknechts arrested for bad behavior, and two executed

One time, it happened in the city that there were ten or twenty landsknechts.[125] They were staying in a house in the city, and they had a drinking party [24v] and were of good cheer. They were boisterous, as landsknechts generally are. Their host and the hostess didn't wish to tap the keg for them anymore. So the landsknechts said, "Hostess, if you won't tap the keg, then we will," and they insulted her. The host in the house was not at home.[126] This host is named Everett Remensnyder.[127] The host and the hostess set to it and accused the landsknechts before the twelve elders and the prophets and preachers of having used violence in their house and insulted the hostess. The twelve elders went and had the landsknechts arrested and thrown into the tower.[128] Straightaway on the next day, they had a common assembly held up at the cathedral square and had the landsknechts come there.[129] The landsknechts were accused there of what they had done, with Chancellor Henry Krechting (the criminal) standing there and reading out what the landsknechts were supposed to have done. They were tied in pairs, and they fell upon their knees and asked for mercy. They said that if they could

---

a family named Krefting. (Detmer based himself on Cornelius's text with the pluperfect ["hadde dat leven beholden"], which is inexplicable, but now we know that Gresbeck used the perfect ["haeyt . . . beholden"].) The point of "but" is presumably that the "real" (i.e., committed: 14v, 23v, 24r, 35r, 87r, 99r, 117r, 122r) rebaptizers should have been killed, but Krechting escaped the fate he deserved. Henry's brother Bernard thought uncertainly that his brother escaped, it being stated in his confession of July 25, 1535, that Bernard reported that his "brother Henry . . . escaped, as he imagines" ("broder Henrich . . . is ontkomen, als hy meint"; Cornelius, *Berichte der augenzeugen*, 381). There are also reports to the effect that Henry was killed in violation of the agreement by which some rebaptizers were allowed to depart on the day of the city's capture (see Kerssenbrock, *Anabaptistici furoris*, ed. Detmer, 848n2), but these reports apparently confuse him with his brother Bernard.

    125. For Kerssenbrock's account of this incident, see *Anabaptistici furoris*, ed. Detmer, 612–13. He dates the party to June 28.

    126. For some reason, this sentence was struck out of the Cologne manuscript. Certainly, it contradicts the previous statement that both the host and the hostess were unwilling to keep the beer flowing.

    127. For Remensnyder's later activities, see Kerssenbrock, *Anabaptistici furoris*, ed. Detmer, n658.

    128. For the use of the tower as prison, see Kerssenbrock, *Anabaptistici furoris*, ed. Detmer, n105.

    129. According to Kerssenbrock (*Anabaptistici furoris*, ed. Detmer, 613), the trial took place two days after the party, on June 30. He presents the trial as taking place on a single day, whereas Gresbeck makes it clear that it was spread over two days, presumably June 29 and 30.

get mercy, they would work every day in the canal where conditions were worst of all. There was no mercy for them, and then they begged for mercy. Eventually, the door to mercy opened up a little, so that some got mercy, and some had to die. There was one who said, "Well, then, if I'm going to get no mercy, where am I to die, here in the circle?" The twelve elders said no. They took him to a linden tree on the square,[130] tied him to it, [25r] and shot him with a demi-arquebus and a handgun.[131] He's named Gerard Schmoester, and had been brought as a prisoner to the city, having held the rank of captain in the besieging army outside the city.[132] After he was dead, they tied another to the tree and then shot him that way, too. They shot the two that day and took the rest back to the prison. Everyone then went back home.

Four more executed

The next day they came back up to the cathedral square, and once more held a common assembly. Then they had the landsknechts brought again from the prison. They (these landsknechts) begged for mercy anew and fell upon their knees. The door to mercy was again closed. Eventually, the door to mercy opened up a little again, so that some knechts kept their lives. They tied four knechts to the tree and shot them with guns. They shot these knechts on account of an insult or a drink of beer.

Anabaptists rule through intimidation

These prophets and preachers and all the Frisians and Hollanders and all the rebaptizers that had rushed to the city from other cities were all afraid of

130. The linden tree was associated in medieval Germany with justice. Judicial assemblies were regularly convened in locations protected by trees, and lindens were frequently planted for this purpose (such trees being known as *Gerichtsbäume* or *Gerichtslinden*). The linden was suited for this purpose through both its abundant foliage and its long life. Thus, the linden was a very suitable tree for an execution. See *HRG*, s.v. "Gerichtsstätten," col. 174.

131. Kerssenbrock emphasizes the unprecedented nature of the executions, which cowed the populace into acquiescing in the Anabaptist regime.

132. According to Kerssenbrock, it was this man who insulted the innkeeper's wife. Gresbeck seems not to have realized the full importance of the man. His full name was Gerard Münster the Smoker (i.e., someone who cures meat; the exact significance of the nickname, which Gresbeck presents in a garbled form as his last name, is unknown to me). He was one of the two generals in command of all the infantry forces besieging Münster (Kerssenbrock, *Anabaptistici furoris*, ed. Detmer, 524) and was taken into the city by the Anabaptists after a raid of theirs on the besiegers. Kerssenbrock flatly states that he went over to them voluntarily, but a letter written on May 18, 1534, to the duke of Cleves-Jülich by his military councilors who were present at the siege says in connection with the loss of this man that it was unclear whether he had defected or been captured (Cornelius, *Berichte der augenzeugen*, 234).

an uprising in the city so that they would have had to give up the city. For this reason they used such great duress [25v] in the city. Whoever had done anything had to die straightaway, provided they could get there halfway respectably.[133] They did this because they knew in advance that if the city was taken, they could receive no mercy from the lord.[134] The foreigner in the city had fled from his own possessions—wife and children and everything they had. So they knew full well that they couldn't return to their possessions and that they'd forfeited their lives and property. For this reason, they used great duress in the city and would hold the city to the last man. So the foreigner had possession of the city of Münster and ruled in the city this way until the city was taken.

Mathias prophesies his own death

There was this prophet John Mathias. One time, he was invited with his wife as a guest to the house of some countrymen of his for a wedding. (This wife later became queen right after John Mathias's death, marrying John of Leiden too.) After John Mathias arrived at the house with his other fellows, they sat at the table and were joyful. (When rebaptizers were gathered together like this, they would always be joyful with the Lord and wouldn't[135] say it was all supposed to be about God. They always keep Paul in front of them or the Prophets, and they sat like that and would teach each other. They would always behave in a holy way like this, but it was all conducted with the fool.) As they were sitting around the table and were joyful with the groom and bride, when the roast was supposed [26r] to be dragged up, the spirit of the baptist came upon John Mathias. He sat for an hour long, clapping his hands together, nodding his head up and down and sighing heavily, just as if he was about to die. The others who were with him kept quiet and looked at his business. Eventually, he started to wake up again and said with a sigh, "O dear Father, not as I will but as you will."[136] He stood up, gave everyone his hand, and kissed them on the mouth. He said, "God's peace be with you all," and went on his way with his wife. (At that

133. The last clause is rather enigmatically expressed. Presumably, Gresbeck means that the Anabaptists would carry out an execution so long as they had a halfway plausible justification.
134. I.e., from the prince-bishop.
135. Logic seems to indicate that the text should read "would" instead of "wouldn't."
136. Clearly a reference to the words of Jesus in Gethsemane, when he accepts, with resignation, the fate that awaited him (Matthew 26:39; cf. Mark 14:36, Luke 22:42).

time the rebaptizers didn't have so many wives yet.) The others returned to their seats and were joyful. Eventually, they got up and each went home. They said good night with peace and departed from each other.[137]

Mathias dies during a raid and is replaced as leader by John of Leiden

The next day John Mathias went from the city for an exchange of gun-fire, taking with him ten or twenty men who went with him.[138] When he reached the enemy with his companions, they exchanged fire, and hit one another in large numbers. John Mathias was hit along with his companions (not many got away). John Mathias was stabbed through with a pike. The landsknechts cut off his head, chopped the body into a hundred pieces, and hit each other with them. They stuck the head up in the air on a pole. The landsknechts then shouted to the rebaptizers in the city that they should bring back their burgher master. The landsknechts didn't know that he [26v] was the chief prophet in the city. This John Mathias was a big, tall man with a big black beard, and he was a Hollander. Now that he was dead, all the Hollanders and Frisians and all the real rebaptizers were very downcast at having lost their prophet. All the rebaptizers in the city said that God had revealed this to him at the place where he'd been invited as a

---

137. For the sense of "with peace," see Gresbeck's elaborate description of an Anabaptist farewell (29r).

138. For Kerssenbrock's account of the death of Mathias, see *Anabaptistici furoris*, ed. Detmer, 568–70. Most sources are vague about the exact date (they also place it around Easter). In his confession of July 25, 1535, John of Leiden specified the date as Easter itself ("to paeschen"; Cornelius, *Berichte der augenzeugen*, 371), but in another undated confession he dates it more vaguely to "around Easter" ("umbtrent paschen"; Niesert, *Münsterische Urkundensammlung*, 178). In both instances, he clearly dates the death to eight days after a revelation that he had received, so he must have had a fairly clear idea about the temporal relationship of the death and the revelation, and he could hardly have forgotten that it took place precisely on Easter if it had. Hence, it makes more sense to take the reference to its being "on" Easter as an inaccuracy. It has been argued that Mathias was attempting to fulfill a prophecy that the siege would be lifted on Easter (in particular, see the groundlessly emotive presentation of the events in Kirchhoff, "Die Endzeiterwartung der Täufergemeinde zu Münster," 39, from which later views are mostly derived). Although it is true that Kerssenbrock speaks of Mathias's foolhardy attack as if it was intentionally suicidal, the failure of Gresbeck to specify any particular date strongly suggests that the death did not take place on Easter itself. Surely, such a coincidence would have been remarked upon at the time, and Gresbeck could certainly have made some sort of ironic notice of this in his account to deflate the pretensions of the prophet if the death had taken place then. It is also to be noted that Gresbeck finds nothing remarkable to say about the date of the wedding party at which Mathias has his revelation of his impending death, but if the death took place on Easter, then the party was on the preceding day, the Easter vigil. This was certainly an inappropriate time for a feast by the standards of traditional practice, and although the Anabaptists would have had no compunctions about violating Lenten taboos, it would be expected that Gresbeck would remark upon such an impropriety.

guest the previous evening, while he had been sitting at the table. The Hollanders and Frisians, the preachers and the rebaptizers held more about this John Mathias than they held about God.[139] John of Leiden then became the chief prophet. He was the only one, and he began to preach, saying in the churchyard at the Grey Monks,[140] "Dear brothers and sisters, you shouldn't be despondent because our prophet John Mathias is dead. For God will raise up another one who will be even greater and higher than John Mathias was. For it's God's will that he should die in this way. His time had come. It was not without reason that God had brought it about that he died this way. The purpose was that you shouldn't believe in him too much, that you shouldn't hold him above God. God is mightier than John Mathias was. What John Mathias did and prophesied, he did through God. He didn't do it by himself. So God can certainly raise for us another prophet through whom He will reveal His will."[141] With such words John of Leiden calmed the folk in the city. The prophets and preachers had informed the folk that God was to strike their enemies in the heart, so that they would [27r] flee before them and not have the power to harm them. So the rebaptizers had marched with John Mathias out of the city against the enemy, believing that the enemy couldn't kill them.

John of Leiden consoles the Anabaptists amidst manic behavior

John of Leiden was now the leader along with Knipperdolling and his fellows and Stutenberent and all the preachers. So he ruled from then on, and he preached at the Grey Monks that God felt satisfaction in the folk and they should be a holy folk. "Everything that is unrighteousness and is still in sin must be stamped out, since the example is ready. You have entered into the Apostolic Church[142] and you're holy. Holy is the Lord

---

139. Surely, if Gresbeck believed that Mathias had died on Easter Day, he could not have failed to make some ironic comment at this point about the Anabaptists' being depressed about the death of their prophet rather than happy at the resurrection of Jesus.

140. "Grey Monks" signifies the monastery of Franciscans, which was now occupied by Anabaptist refugees from elsewhere (see 118r and also note 602).

141. See *Anabaptistici furoris*, ed. Detmer, 570, for Kerssenbrock's rather different version of this speech (based on earlier printed accounts).

142. "Apostolic Church" means that ecclesiastical setup that was supposed to have existed among the apostles in the aftermath of the crucifixion of Jesus as recorded in the book of Acts. It was a common aim of the reformers to return the present church to their conception of what things had been like in that distant period. Certainly, this meant a rejection of the traditional practices that had arisen in the

and you're His folk. Now that the example is ready, it shall spread over the entire world, just as it began here in this holy city." Some men shouted, "O Father, O Father, give love, give love!" and danced. The menfolk (some of them) ran with drawn swords through the city in all the lanes and streets, shouting that the Father had given them the sword so that they would punish unrighteousness, and that God couldn't wait for anyone who wouldn't convert. After this sermon was done, some women and maidens remained up at the churchyard, dancing and shouting in a loud voice, "O Father, O Father, O Father, give, give, give!" They jumped up, and stretched their hands into the air and clapped them together, with their hair hanging loose at the nape of their necks or down their backs. They looked towards the sun like this and their only thought was that He was sitting by it. They imagined only that God would [27v] reveal Himself in the sun. Eventually, they divided themselves into pairs, taking each other by the hand, and then they danced around the churchyard and then through the city, across the marketplace, first up one street and then another. Eventually, they danced back to the churchyard that they'd danced out of before. There they danced and looked at the sun some more until they could dance and shout no more. Eventually, they went back home. The women and maidens who danced like this were as pale and white in the face as if they were dead. They were distorted in their expression, just like corpses.

A communal meal prepared

The prophets and preachers arranged to hold a supper, each captain and preacher by his gate. The deacons took care of what they needed for the supper, and they held it with a spread like a wedding feast. The preachers had it said to the common folk in the preaching that they would arrange a supper and that everyone who wished to go to the table of the Lord should cleanse himself of sins and put aside all unrighteousness and idolatry, that if there was anyone who still had money, silver and gold, he should bring it up, and that whoever had some litigation with another, they should come to an agreement and pray for forgiveness.

---

intervening centuries, but a major element of this effort in the present context is the communal possession of property attested in Acts 4:32–5:10 (see Kerssenbrock, *Anabaptistici furoris*, ed. Detmer, 631, for a citation of apostolic procedure in this connection). The severe persecution faced by the apostles (e.g., 5:17–8:4) no doubt confirmed in the Anabaptists' minds their own righteousness in the face of the persecution that they faced themselves.

Treatment of the guests

[28r] So they arranged a supper in front of each gate. They had boiled and broiled meat for the meal and beer at the table. The preachers went along the tables and preached to the folk after their fashion. They asked each person, young and old, whether they really believed that this supper was a real supper just like the one that Christ had instituted. So they said yes. Would they also be willing to suffer for the sake of God everything that would befall them, be it fire or water or the sword?[143] They all said yes, they would gladly suffer what they could for the sake of God. Where could the poor common folk turn?[144] One person was compelled to this and the other not. They beheaded or shot whoever was unwilling to act like the prophets and preachers and like the others. An old woman was sitting at the table and wished to take part in the supper. The preachers asked the woman what her faith was and what she believed in. The woman answered by saying, "I believe in God." They next asked her what she held about Mary and about the saints. She answered that Mary was a pure maiden and the mother of God, and that the saints had suffered much for the sake of God. They next asked her whether she also kept saints (wooden images) in her house. She said yes. Then the preachers abused the poor woman and chased her from the table. She had to go back home. The preachers then said, "Listen, dear brothers and sisters. This devil still has saints [28v] and idols in her house. She is not worthy of coming to the Lord's table and holding this supper with us." The preachers didn't merely rebuke the women because of the saints that she had in her house. They also meant that she held about Mary that she was a pure virgin and that she was the mother of God. For the rebaptizers didn't hold this about Mary, as you will hear later.[145] So this woman went back home and wasn't allowed to take part in the supper.

143. "Fire, water, and sword" refers to various modes of execution. Burning at the stake was the normal method of executing heretics, but the Catholic authorities frequently disposed of unrepentant Anabaptists by throwing them into a river with a rock chained to their neck as a sort of mockery of their attitude towards baptism (this jocular touch no doubt added a welcome note of levity to the otherwise dreary solemnity of eradicating religious deviants). Beheading was probably the least unpleasant mode of death that a condemned heretic could expect.

144. This rhetorical question is Gresbeck the narrator speaking retrospectively. He means, what other choice did they have?

145. See 77r–77v for a discussion of the Anabaptists' views on Mary.

Rosendale convent used a prison

There was a cloister (sister house[146]) in the city, where there'd been ten to twenty nuns in residence. Some of them had left the city, and some had stayed in the convent. The house is called "the Rosendale."[147] The prophets, preachers, and twelve elders would have everyone brought to it who was still an unbeliever about the rebaptizers and wouldn't adhere to the baptizing. They also had those who'd stayed in the city without having themselves baptized and all those who'd still retained money, silver and gold, and had kept aside something in the way of food or grain brought to the Rosendale. There they sat as prisoners. The preachers would go to the people in the Rosendale (the cloister) and would instruct and teach them. Whoever didn't choose the right path like the preachers had to die. There were many people in the city who never had themselves baptized. Many people who'd let themselves be baptized and wouldn't stick to the baptizing also moved out of the city. As for what those who hadn't let themselves be baptized got in the city, [29r] it took a lot before they could get mercy. Some had to die because of this.[148]

Meaning of the supper explained

They then held the supper, and the preachers preached what it meant.[149] They wished to hold the supper just as Christ had done with his disciples. Eventually, they had a little round flatbread as big around as a hand's breadth. The preachers laid the flatbread on the table and said, "Look, dear brothers and sisters. You will all do for us afterwards what we do for you first." So, the preachers each broke a flatbread apart, and they ate a piece of it. Then all the folk broke the other flatbreads, and each ate a part of

---

146. A German expression for a "convent of nuns" ("sister" being Gresbeck's regular term for "nun").

147. Low German "tho den rosendale."

148. I.e., for not getting baptized.

149. The Anabaptist leadership would frequently go out of their way to explain to the congregation how their new procedures were an improvement over the traditional Catholic rites that they replaced (for Rothman's long discussion of the sham mass, see 106r–v; for another occasion on which the flatbread and wine are explained, see 71v). In this instance, a purely symbolic feast replaces the traditional celebration mass, with the bread (Gresbeck uses the diminutive of the word *koke*, meaning "bread," "roll"; seemingly the latter signifies unleavened bread) and wine being in no way converted to the flesh and blood of Christ (whether the substance was changed via transubstantiation, as Catholics held, or the body was sacramentally united with the bread, as the Lutherans taught). A rejection of the formality of the traditional mass was characteristic of most forms of the radical reformation.

one, and they each had a drink of wine with it. Then they sang a song of praise, and they stood up and each went home. The preachers stood before the doors, and said good night to everyone, giving them their hands and kissing them on the mouth. They said, "Dear brothers and sisters, go in the name of the Lord, and God's peace be with you." Then they went away. They numbered about four hundred, the first ones to hold this supper. Then the others who had been keeping watch came to the same city gate and [29v] also held the supper just as the first group had done, and the first group then kept watch again for the same length of time. John of Leiden rode from one gate to the next around the city, from one supper to the next. He also preached, and informed the people as well. This supper took place by one gate, and they held it by all the gates in the city of Münster.[150]

Failed plot to kill the prince-bishop through a woman's wiles

The criminals—the Hollanders and Frisians and the proper rebaptizers and Knipperdolling along with some other burghers in the city of Münster—didn't know how to get the bishop of Münster away from the city. They took counsel in secret without the common man's knowledge.[151] This council was held by the prophets and the preachers and all the leaders of the rebaptizers in the city. They prepared a woman who was to request permission from the prophets and the preachers so that she was to say that God had revealed to her that she was to march from the city to the camp and convert My Gracious Lord of Münster and the landsknechts.[152] It was also

---

150. The procedure is not so clear here, but elsewhere (132r–v) when a similar event takes place separately at all the gates, Gresbeck describes at length the specific event at his own gate (the Cross Gate), and then succinctly adds that the same thing took place at the other gates.

151. Presumably, Gresbeck wants to make it clear from the start that he had no prior knowledge of this attempt on the prince-bishop's life! Gresbeck belabors this point in his account.

152. The woman's name was Hille Feicken (for Kerssenbrock's account of her attempt at assassinating the prince-bishop, see *Anabaptistici furoris*, ed. Detmer, 605–10). For a treatment of her, see Huebert Hecht, "Hille Feicken of Sneek." According to Kerssenbrock, she left the city on June 16. Here Gresbeck indicates that the Anabaptist leadership put the woman up to it, but all other documentary evidence contradicts this view. In their confessions, both John of Leiden (Cornelius, *Berichte der augenzeugen*, 402) and the preacher John Klopriss (Niesert, *Münsterische Urkundensammlung*, 132) state that the woman came up with the plan on her own, and in his confession (Cornelius, *Berichte der augenzeugen*, 404), Knipperdolling claims that she had told John Mathias that the Father had instructed her. The preacher Dionysius Vinne implicitly agrees with this when he states in his confession (ibid., 275) that she asked for permission to leave the city in order to kill the prince-bishop. Feicken herself basically confirms this in her own confession (Niesert, *Münsterische Urkundensammlung*, 44) when she states that she informed the preachers and Knipperdolling (and someone whose name she couldn't remember!) of

supposed to have been revealed to her that she was to go from the city to the camp in daylight. This woman moved out from the city for the camp and took along as much money as she wanted. In this way, she came to the camp and came to the bishop. The plan that the prophets, preachers, and other leaders undertook with the woman wouldn't come to pass. Instead, My Gracious Lord of Münster was informed of the villainy.[153] [30r] The prophets and the preachers had prepared this woman to poison My Gracious Lord of Münster and to fornicate with him or to do him in, in whatever way she could bring this about.[154] If the woman had been able to bring this about, she was to have returned to the city. So the woman was away for a long time and was with My Gracious Lord of Münster. Once My Gracious Lord of Münster found this out about the woman, His Grace had her arrested and put in prison. She confessed that if she'd been able to bring it about, she would have done it and poisoned (done in) My Gracious Lord's Grace. My Gracious Lord then set to it and had her pay the penalty. He had her head cut off, and she was placed on a wheel.[155] She imagined that the hangman wouldn't have the power to execute her. For she imagined at the time that she was too holy. But the hangman cut off her head. This woman was a Hollander's wife,[156] and she was still a beautiful young woman, so that the Hollanders and Frisians (the criminals) imagined that My Gracious Lord of Münster would be done in in this way. These criminals imagined that if they'd done in the bishop, they would have gotten their way from then on. The prophets in the city said how they could get (cap-

---

her already conceived plan.

153. According to Kerssenbrock (*Anabaptistici furoris*, ed. Detmer, 608–9), Herman Ramers was an anti-Anabaptist who had remained in the city to protect his family and property, and upon learning of the plot, he defected to warn the prince-bishop, leaving the city on June 18.

154. Feicken was to conduct herself upon model of the Old Testament figure Judith, whose story forms the main narrative of the apocryphal book of Judith. To make a long story short, when the Israelite city of Bethulia was under siege, the beautiful and pious widow Judith went to the enemy camp, where she used her feminine wiles to get the enemy general drunk and then beheaded him. She managed to escape, and when the besieging army learned that their general had been killed by a woman, they fled in terror. It is surprising that Gresbeck makes no mention of this background to the plot (it would readily lend itself to his wry sense of humor). His reference below to the possibility of using fornication as part of her attempt indicates that he knew of the overall conception.

155. "Placing the body on a wheel" means tying the body to a wheel, which was then attached at the hub to a pole and raised up in the air to expose the body as warning to potential malefactors. This was a common method of dealing with the bodies of executed criminals.

156. She was from the town of Sneek, which she herself accurately describes in her confession as being in West Frisia (Niesert, *Münsterische Urkundensammlung*, 40). Kerssenbrock, however, says (*Anabaptistici furoris*, ed. Detmer, 627) that it's in Holland, despite the fact that his account was based on her confession.

ture) the bishop—he would not have escaped with his life. The prophets in the city said that the woman had sent a letter [30v] to the city saying how it had been revealed to her that she would convert many folk, how God had revealed to her in the city that this would soon happen, and how she'd converted the folk in the camp. The prophets and preachers informed the people, so that the poor people in the city imagined that it was all true. Some in the city wouldn't believe it. But the common man was not informed that My Gracious Lord of Münster had had the woman executed, and that she'd moved out from the city in order to do in My Gracious Lord of Münster. All those who rushed to the city after she'd been executed were forbidden on pain of death so that they wouldn't dare to say anything of this in the city, so that the common man wouldn't be informed of it.

Burning of documents

They had it ordered in the preaching that anyone who had books or charters in his house should bring them up to the cathedral square.[157] Some people brought their books and charters, as well as all the books from the churches and the cloisters. They piled these books and charters into five or six heaps and burned them up. They also took from the council chamber all the charters and all the privileges[158] that the city of Münster had, and they piled them up in a heap in front of the council hall and burned all these up too. These books and charters burned for about eight days before they were burned up. Some people retained their charters and books.

Start of destroying churches

[31r] They now began to tear down the churches and monasteries, as you'll eventually hear.[159]

---

157. Kerssenbrock (*Anabaptistici furoris*, ed. Detmer, 558) includes the destruction of private documents in a vague notice of the creation of the deacons and the confiscation of gold and silver. He had earlier mentioned the destruction of ecclesiastical documents at the time of the violation of churches in the aftermath of the expulsion of the non-Anabaptists on February 28 (ibid., 553–54).

158. I.e., documents granting the city various "liberties" (rights).

159. For Kerssenbrock's account of the devastation of the churches, see *Anabaptistici furoris*, ed. Detmer, 571–73. This activity began after Knipperdolling claimed on April 9, 1534, to have received a divine inspiration that they had to be torn down. Presumably, this early activity is what led Gresbeck to give the vague notice here. The process of destroying the churches went on for some time, and Gresbeck summarizes it later (see 111r–114v; also 118r–v, 136r).

Gunpowder production

They made gunpowder in the city day and night. They had two oil mills on which they made explosive (gunpowder), and in the old cathedral they made a pestle mill on which they also made gunpowder, so that they had enough gunpowder throughout the siege.[160] For the only thought of the Hollanders and Frisians was that they had a winning hand.

Houses to be left unlocked

They also wanted all things to be free, one thing as much as another, house and home, with no exception. So they would never lock the door. Be it day or night, at all times houses were supposed to be open, so that one person could go into his neighbor's house if he wished to. In front of the house doors there was supposed to be nothing more than a grill so that the pigs wouldn't run inside. In the end, they had no problem with the pigs running in.[161] Cats and dogs, they too stayed out of the houses in the end.[162] They were certainly able to leave the doors open day and night, because they had no problem with any domestic beasts.

Anabaptist schooling

They opened up five or six schools in the city, where they taught the children.[163] The young boys and girls had to learn to read and write the German hymns. Everything they taught was all [31v] about baptizing, after their fashion. They would teach the young children this way in their youth, and they were supposed to grow up with the baptizing. Every week, the children from all the schools would go in pairs to the cathedral along the streets. They would preach to the children in the cathedral, wishing to instruct them for a time. When the sermon was over, the children sang a German hymn and then went home in pairs. When the children went to

160. Kerssenbrock (*Anabaptistici furoris*, ed. Detmer, 543) also mentions the provisions for making gunpowder (including the erection of a mill in the old cathedral).
161. This is an ironic way of saying that there were no pigs left during the starvation that afflicted the city towards the end of the siege.
162. These animals were also consumed (see 138r), so there were no cats or dogs to get into the houses.
163. Kerssenbrock speaks of the Lutheran school instituted in 1533 to compete with the older traditional schools (*Anabaptistici furoris*, ed. Detmer, 386, 401–2), but makes no mention of Anabaptist schools.

school, they would sing a German hymn in school before they began to learn. When they later left the school, they also sang a German hymn, and then went back home.

Anabaptist coinage

They also had money coined in the city just like Joachimsthalers and they also had guilders of eight or nine guilders coined.[164] They often had talks with the landsknechts in the trenches. When they did so, they prepared someone and he went outside the gates and held talks with the landsknechts in the camp. The man who held these talks had guilders with him and gave this money (Joachimsthalers) to the landsknechts in each camp. They meant to get the landsknechts into the city in this way, and they did in fact get some. When the prophets and preachers and the leading men in the city had that money coined, this is why they did it. All other money, be it silver or gold, was not to be valid any longer in the world. The money that they'd coined and would later have coined was to be valid over the whole wide world. They'd already coined some of this money before John of Leiden became king. When they had it coined, it was to be valid in the whole world, as the rebaptizers said, and according to their plan [32r] they wouldn't have had any need of money. They said that they were Christians and a Christian should have no money. It was all unclean for Christians, and one Christian shouldn't strike a deal with another. They should make exchanges with each other, and one city should make exchanges with the other.[165] This was supposed to happen throughout the whole world. But it was so awful that they took the money from the people in the city. It was all villainy what they were engaged in.

164. A "guilder" ("gulden") was properly a gold coin. In practice, actual gold coins seldom circulated, and the term was used as a unit of account (known as a "current guilder") to signify a fixed amount of actually circulating coins (silver or copper). Presumably, Gresbeck means that the minted guilders were worth eight or nine current guilders. In fact, the Anabaptists minted two denominations, one full-sized and the other half as large (see Kerssenbrock, *Anabaptistici furoris*, ed. Detmer, 666–67). For an illustration of a half thaler struck under the twelve elders and another of a thaler minted under John (with discussions by Berndt Thier), see Albrecht et al., *Das Königreich der Täufer*, 56, 71.

165. The last provisions were meant to establish a barter economy in which goods were exchanged for each other without the medium of money. Those who have no theoretical understanding of the economic function of money could easily blame it for the social inequalities that are manifested in the possession and use of money. The attempt to stamp out money was apparently meant in earnest, as Gresbeck later records instances of people being executed solely on the grounds that they still had money in their possession (78r–78v, 178v; in the second instance, it's explicitly noted that the money was used to purchase something).

Anabaptists play a dirty joke on the besieging troops

They undertook an act of villainy and wished to cover the landsknechts' trenches in shit.[166] The prophets and the preachers and leaders placed a wine barrel in a wagon and filled it from a privy, wishing to take it to the trenches. This happened when the bishop of Münster first had the trenches dug outside the city.[167] With this, the prophets and preachers made derisive fun of the digging of trenches and of My Lord of Münster's having hired landsknechts, brought such heavy artillery outside the city, and put himself on the defensive in this way. That was what they made their derision with. For the prophets and preachers imagined that God was walking with them on earth. They imagined that no one could oppose them, imagining that they already had a winning hand. So the prophets and preachers and the leaders in the city gathered with a company of the rebaptizers, and by St. Maurice's Gate they rode out of the city with the wine barrel in the direction of the trenches. When they reached the trenches with the wagon, they chopped the barrel apart, and the filth ran all along the trenches. Having befouled the landsknechts' trench in this way, they returned to the city.

Another joke

[32v] They went even further in making derisive fun of My Gracious Lord of Münster and all those who were stationed outside the city. They didn't know what sort of villainy they would commit. They made a bishop out of some hose and a shirt, and they filled it with straw and made a head on top.[168] They hung an amice around the mannequin and put a mitre on its head, and then tied the mannequin to a horse.[169] They decked the horse

---

166. For Kerssenbrock's account of this unhygienic story, see *Anabaptistici furoris*, ed. Detmer, 588.

167. The placement of the story in Kerssenbrock suggests that the event took place in April, but Gresbeck indicates early March here.

168. Kerssenbrock (*Anabaptistici furoris*, ed. Detmer, 558) relates this prank, explicitly dating it before the escapade with the barrel of filth.

169. An "amice" is a white cloth draped over a priest's neck and shoulders while he celebrated the mass, and a "mitre" is the distinctive headgear of a bishop. Presumably, these two items were chosen for dressing the mannequin in order to make fun of the fact that Bishop Francis was not in fact an ordained priest (he would not be ordained until 1543).

out with charters,[170] and brought it to the city gate.[171] They then released it into the trenches, driving it away from themselves with a slap. The horse with the made-up bishop ran towards the camp along the trenches. The landsknechts ran out of the camp and ran after the horse along the trenches, wanting to catch it and the man riding on it because they imagined that a live man was seated on it. When they came up to the horse, the man on it turned out to be a mannequin made of hose and a shirt stuffed with straw. The landsknechts got angry and chopped the horse and the mannequin into pieces. The prophets and preachers along with some of the rebaptizers stood outside the gate looking at the horse, and they laughed at having duped the landsknechts in this way with the horse and the mannequin riding it.[172]

Anabaptists raid the besieging troops

[33r] The rebaptizers would often fall upon the landsknechts from the city and exchange fire with them.[173] They were very clever at this exchanging of fire as if they'd engaged in warfare for twenty years, and everything they did they did with cleverness, deftness, and good sense. For the prophets, preachers, and leaders in the city had strictly forbidden anyone in the city to be so bold as to get really drunk, so that they would all stay in their senses. The result was that no one dared get drunk and they were always sober, and when they marched out, they did so with wisdom and deftness. So they had many exchanges of fire with the landsknechts, and they often suffered losses on both sides. The rebaptizers often left the city at night on an adventure, so that they often fell on the fully armored watch and brought them into the city. Whenever the rebaptizers would march out at night, they would pull a shirt over their armor. This was their identifying token. They did this often and a lot at night. One night they went out on an adventure,

---

170. According to Kerssenbrock, these documents were indulgences and papal bulls. The game of pinning documents to a mare and sending it out to the camp as a form of derision had been played before on Good Friday (April 3, 1534), when the Anabaptists drove out a horse with the text of the treaty that the prince-bishop had made with the city the previous February (Kerssenbrock, *Anabaptistici furoris*, ed. Detmer, 568).

171. St. Maurice's, according to Kerssenbrock.

172. According to Kerssenbrock, the Anabaptists fired into the gathered landsknechts, killing most of them. Gresbeck's account obviously suggests otherwise.

173. For details about raids (which sometimes took the Anabaptists far from the city), see Kerssenbrock, *Anabaptistici furoris*, ed. Detmer, 554, 591.

and they got some prisoners and were so close to the Gelders[174] blockhouse that they heard them singing the song "So, we'll crash the danger signals, then. Look, friends!" and talking, and they sat on the blockhouse. Then the rebaptizers came back to the city, and they too sang, "So, we'll crash the danger signals, then. Look, friends!" At that time, they imagined that they didn't keep a good watch, and said that they [33v] could certainly have taken a blockhouse from them, imagining that they didn't keep a good watch. They would even march out a bit during the day because they would have gladly had prisoners in the city in order to get fresh news about how things stood in the camp and what talk was going around in the camp. So they forbade so strictly anyone from getting drunk. They also did this because they were always afraid that everyone would discover their villainy, imagining that someone who was drunk would likely dare to say something that a man in his senses should leave out, while a man in his senses often makes himself convincing with fair words. This is what the criminals (the prophets and preachers) also did. With their cleverness and deftness, they tricked the folk in the city of Münster, and they also tricked the other burghers from other cities and in the bishopric of Münster, who followed the false prophets and preachers, leaving behind wife and children, house and home, and everything they had, to follow criminals.[175] If they'd known at home what they learned at Münster, they would certainly have stayed at home.

Anabaptists spike besiegers' artillery

The landsknechts too would often run out for an exchange of fire. They often ran right up to the city, and often suffered heavy losses. This suffering of heavy losses happened to them when they were drunk and didn't know how to defend themselves. For this reason they often got shot. One time, the rebaptizers fell upon their artillery from the city, wanting to spike it.[176] They spiked some pieces, burned up some of their powder, [34r] and took some cannonballs for demi-culverins and falconets.[177] But they didn't carry out this spiking of the artillery without losses. In this they suffered many

174. Outside the Jew Fields Gate; Kerssenbrock, *Anabaptistici furoris*, ed. Detmer, 547.
175. This category of foreigners duped by Anabaptist preaching is discussed at greater length below (45v–46r).
176. This raid is described at greater length below (34v–35v).
177. For a discussion of the various sorts of artillery mentioned by Gresbeck, see introduction, section 3.2.

dead on the retreat, when they wanted to march back to the city. They also got some prisoners by the artillery, whom they brought back with them into the city. This included a gun master that they wished to bring back, but he refused, so they shot him dead when they withdrew.[178] If this gun master had been willing to go along, he would have kept his life.

Anabaptists collect shells fired during bombardment of city

When My Gracious Lord of Münster had the city bombarded, they collected all the shells from the siege artillery that were shot into the city in a pile up at the marketplace. They also fired tumblers into the city, and these shots they also piled up by the others.[179] There were no more than sixteen of these tumbler shots, but there was no counting the others. Some that they didn't get were fired too high and landed in the canal.

Failed storming of the city

The captains in the camp outside the city made a plan. They fell upon the city, unleashing their assault on Whitsun Monday at eight o'clock in the evening.[180] [34v] This storm (assault) wouldn't succeed for the landsknechts, and they had to retreat. They suffered losses, and the rebaptizers in the city also suffered losses, including many dead. In this storm the rebaptizers suffered greater losses than they did during the final assault.[181] When the landsknechts retreated, the rebaptizers brought all the assault ladders into the city and piled them up by the council house and in front of it, so that

178. This position ("bussenschutter" or "bussenmester," High German *Büchsenmeister*) was a professional in charge of managing a piece of artillery, which he may even have cast himself. The Anabaptists would have sorely needed such men to help man their own cannons.

179. "Tumbler" (Low German "tumelers") is an old-fashioned term that dates back to the time before the invention of cannons, when catapults were used to hurl large stones that tumbled through the air. "Tumbler" continued to be used after the introduction of artillery for stone shot (and the term was sometimes understood to refer to the propensity of such projectiles to tumble along after hitting the ground).

180. May 25, 1534. For Kerssenbrock's account, see *Anabaptistici furoris*, ed. Detmer, 592–94. A preliminary bombardment commenced on Thursday, May 19, and the storming of the city was to have taken place on Tuesday, May 26. On Monday, however, the troops at the Gelders camp got drunk and decided to launch their attack that evening in order to get more plunder for themselves. As the other camps learned of this premature assault, they launched their own attacks, but the lack of coordination allowed the defenders to defeat the separate attacks in a piecemeal fashion.

181. As Gresbeck would claim credit for the plan that led to the capture of the city, he is here subtly indicating the superiority of his plan (see 151v for his claim that if his plan had been carried out to the letter, losses among the attackers would have been minimal).

there was a great pile of them. So the rebaptizers were strong in the city in the first summer, and also had a very strong city, so that it could not have been readily taken by force. There was never a day that landsknechts didn't come into the city, and there was also seldom a day or night that Hollanders and Frisians didn't all come rushing into the city. They (the rebaptizers) came from all lands, so that in this way they were strong enough in the beginning. If the bishop's troops had attacked immediately when they chased away the burghers and all the folk on that Friday,[182] they would have taken the city from them, since it would have been the case that landsknechts could have been gotten in as quickly at that time as happened in the end, My Gracious Lord of Münster.[183]

Stutenberent fires up the Anabaptists for the spiking raid

When the prophets and preachers made the plan to spike the artillery, as I described before,[184] they set to it and had it said in the preaching that whoever was eager to march out should be up at the cathedral square at one o'clock in the afternoon. For it was God's will, and the prophets had [35r] received a revelation about it. Those among the landsknechts and the real rebaptizers who were eager then moved out. Since this had been revealed to the prophets, they didn't care whether they died or not. Those who wished to take part in the march out came up to the cathedral square. So many of them came that half had to stay in the city, and one man wanted to march out in place of the other. The priest Stutenberent stood up in the middle of the folk up at the square and preached to those who were going to march out, informing them that God had revealed to the prophets that they should march out. This man Stutenberent, he could speak so well that there wasn't his equal in yammering deftly. He fetches it here and there from everywhere—it's impossible to write or speak of his orating. (The king's chancellor Henry Krechting, the criminal, could also

---

182. I.e., February 27 (for Gresbeck's account of the expulsion, see 11r–12r).

183. The final phrase seems to be an address to the prince-bishop. If so, this is the only indication within the text of the intended reader. Cornelius, *Berichte der augenzeugen*, takes the phrase to be an error and excises it from his printed text. It's interesting that the only time when Gresbeck feels the need to address the prince-bishop directly is one instance when he's pointing out how the siege could have been ended much earlier if the plan that he later proposed for the city's capture had been followed earlier.

184. See 33v–34r.

speak just like Stutenberent.) This Stutenberent said, "Dear brothers, it's God's will that we should march forth. Whoever is willing to march forth for the sake of God and risk his life for the sake of God, stick up a finger." At this point, they all stuck up a finger, wishing to march forth all at once and happy to risk their lives for the sake of God, since it had been revealed to the prophets that they should march forth.[185] Stutenberent said, "Dear brothers, this marching out shall not be so distressing for the following reason. You mustn't have such great fear, since it's God's will. Now, dear brothers, I realize that the flesh has fears. [35v] Your spirit urges you on and is willing!" He preached a lot. Eventually, they attacked from the city, and they spiked some artillery pieces, and some men died. This is how they fulfilled the revelation.

Anabaptists reluctantly adopt traditional military practices

When the city of Münster was first put under siege, the rebaptizers would have no pipes and drums, and also wouldn't have banners. In the beginning, they didn't want captains.[186] Whenever they came up to the cathedral square, they did so without drums and without pipes and banners. The prophets said that it wasn't appropriate for Christians to have pipes and drums. This was something in accordance with the flesh and the world, and they mustn't have such wild living as the godless had. The rebaptizers wouldn't do otherwise,[187] but then they had a revelation from the prophets, or rather the prophets had a revelation from God. Eventually, the prophets and preachers got a revelation from God that the children of Israel had had units[188] and all sorts of instruments. This they found in the Bible. (When

185. For a similar ploy on Rothman's part of making men volunteer in public for dangerous duty, see 135v–136r.

186. Drumming, piping, and banners are basic elements in early modern military maneuvers (see 91r and esp. 152r; for a modern discussion, see Arnold, *Renaissance at War*, 67–68), whereas fiddles are just for entertainment (see 91v, where they do appear with drums and pipes). Note the illustration on Arnold, *Renaissance at War*, 62, a contemporary print showing a drummer, a piper, a sergeant with halberd, and a standard-bearer with flag. These figures represent the major elements in the by no means easy task of maintaining order in the dense battle formation in which the landsknechts fought. The point of the passage is how "puritanical" sensibilities had to give way before military practicality.

187. I.e., they wouldn't deviate from their refusal to use traditional military discipline.

188. The connection of banners and units isn't self-evident, but banners played an integral role in maintaining the cohesion of regiments of landsknechts in battle (see also note 457). Hence, the lack of banners was very detrimental to regular military discipline. Thus, in "discovering" that the ancient Israelites had military units, it was implicitly indicated that the use of banners met with divine approval.

the prophets and preachers found something in the Bible that was helpful to them, they would say that God had revealed it to them. One person in the city realized that they'd taken it from Scripture in this way and another didn't. A part of the rebaptizers didn't imagine anything but that whatever the prophets said and did they had from God, and that He had revealed it to them.) When they got the revelation that they were allowed to have pipes and drums, and that they should also have banners, they prepared pipes and drums and banners and appointed captains [36r] and officers, and every morning and evening they went to the watch and from the watch with pipes and drums. Whenever they went to the cathedral square and held a common assembly, they also all went with pipes, drums, and banners and began to become soldiers, just as the landsknechts held their assemblies.[189] One time, they launched an attack with banners out of St. Maurice's Gate against the trench by the mill mound.[190] They exchanged fire with the landsknechts and drove them out of the trench, so that they got possession of the mound. That night, the landsknechts took back possession of the mound and kept it for as long as the camp lay before the city, until they made the blockhouses.[191] After the rebaptizers had this exchange of fire, they marched around the city along the wall with pipes, drums, and banners. When they reached the wall opposite the Gelders camp, he[192] shot at the banner from the camp with a siege cannon. He shot the piper dead and shot five or six men under it who were wounded. The banner marched on, and the other men remained lying there. At this point, they got tired of marching around the city with the banner.

Sappers fill the moat

They undertook to dig outside two of the city's gates, St. Maurice Gate and the Jew Fields Gate. They dug so close outside one gate that they threw the dirt into the canal. Many landsknechts had rushed into the city, which had

189. As hired mercenaries, the landsknechts were not completely subordinate to their officers in the way that a modern soldier serving a nation-state is expected to be, and (whatever oath they may have made to the prince or other authority that they were serving) they held meetings among themselves to discuss common interests (see 52v for an assembly about strategy and 154v for the numerous meetings held by the landsknechts when they were unhappy with the distribution of booty after the fall of the city).
190. I.e., the mound upon which a windmill was located.
191. Gresbeck is referring to the later tightening of the siege, when the siegeworks were made into a continuous circuit with blockhouses constructed as major stations for the besieging troops (158r–v).
192. For "he" Cornelius has "someone," which makes more sense.

certainly often been the case previously in a siege where they had also dug just as they did outside Münster. [36v] So some landsknechts set to it and dug through the wall there so that they could reach the canal, which they wanted to fill up.[193] What they then threw into the canal during the day, they took back out at night. These landsknechts who were carrying out this digging in the city in order to counter-dig in this way had previously been miners, so that they knew how to engage in digging. The rebaptizers would work this way in the earth at night and stood in a row, so that one man took from the next the earth and the tall shrubbery and other wood that the others had thrown into the canal. They did this in the city for three or four nights. Eventually, they threw in so much that they could no longer remove it and gave up taking it out at night. This digging took place outside the Jew Fields Gate.

Besiegers and besieged fire on each other

Next, they also dug outside the city along the canal, digging so close that the peasants had to have osier mats over their heads. They shot stones from the city, and the landsknechts shot stones back into the city. Eventually, they gave up the digging. So the rebaptizers made slings in the city. These slings were made on a pole, and with them they could throw a boulder at the landsknechts or the peasants, who were continuing to dig in the trenches. When a landsknecht or a peasant exposed himself, so that he would be a hand's breadth above the trench, they shot at him right away from the city, and when the rebaptizers exposed themselves on the wall, [37r] the landsknechts shot back at them. They shot many men dead on both sides, the rebaptizers shooting into the trenches and the landsknechts at those up on the wall, one man lying in ambush for the other.

Anabaptists make catapults

The rebaptizers made large slings with which they would throw things as heavy as a vat of butter. This sling was made with a long pole (lever). One

---

193. I.e., the renegade landsknechts in the city are attempting to thwart the efforts of their erstwhile comrades outside the city. The subsequent use of "they" becomes a bit confusing at times, but the shifting between the two groups is clear enough if one bears in mind that the outsiders are trying to fill the canal in with various detritus during the day and the insiders are seeking to remove this same material at night.

end had a weight, and the sling hung between two strong uprights. They brought the sling up onto the wall by the Jew Fields Gate. When they wished to make a shot with the sling, the sling wouldn't have the follow-through to fire. They loaded this sling two or three times with a great stone and released the weights of the sling. The stones went up into the air and fell down onto the ground right in front of the sling. They couldn't throw the stones over the wall. The landsknechts in the trench stood up, and when they saw this shooting with the sling, they laughed and shouted. They threw stones at the sling, so that they had to flee from the sling and abandon it.[194] They had two of these slings built in the city, a small one and a large one. They couldn't shoot with either of them. They took back the small one (the one with which they'd first shot), and gave up the other one as a bad idea.

Another contraption

[37v] They undertook to make another machine. This was to be shaped like a gallows, and in the gallows a clapper from a bell was to hang. This clapper was to hang on a swinging beam, with a peg tied to the beam, so that they would ring this clapper like a bell. They wanted to set up this gallows on the wall. Then they would ring the clapper whenever the landsknechts were about to launch an assault. The clapper was to go in the gallows just like a bell that one would ring. Whenever the landsknechts attacked, the clapper was to smack them in the head.[195] They also had panels made that were as long as a man and half-a-man broad, and in these panels they made loopholes.[196] They also wanted to have these panels if an assault was in the works. Then they would lie behind them and shoot through them. They would set up these panels on the palisade when necessary, and when they

194. The first "they" is the besiegers and the second the rebaptizers.

195. The whole description of this gadget sounds confused. In the first place, how could one make a sound with a clapper, whose purpose is to make a bell sound? In any event, the final sentence seems to contradict what precedes it. Now it appears that the contraption was meant to act as a device to whack the heads of any attacker who made it to the top of the wall (presumably up a ladder). Perhaps the latter was the actual intention, and Gresbeck became confused because the instrument was made out of parts for a bell (see also 112v–113v, where Gresbeck discusses a contrivance for a nighttime alarm system, which may have influenced his account here). Since the device was given up before being used, Gresbeck may have had to rely on his own imagination to figure out what its designers were up to.

196. A loophole is a narrow opening in a wall to allow the defenders to shoot outwards without much opportunity for attackers to shoot through it at the defenders. The contraptions described here are basically "mantelets" (temporary cover for gunsmen).

wished, they would take the panels back down. When My Gracious Lord of Münster had the city bombarded for the assault, all these plans that the Hollanders and Frisians had undertaken proved to be idiot's work. They did carry out the setting-up of the panels on the palisade and the bringing of the gallows up onto the wall, but the sounding of the clapper they didn't. The Hollanders planned this and spoke of it, but it was all Hollanders' and Frisians' work, all foolishness, what they undertook.[197]

A landsknecht executed in the city

[38r] There was a knecht in the city who was denounced before the prophets and preachers and all the leaders of the rebaptizers. The common man in the city was not informed of what this knecht had done. They would say in the city that he'd lived in marriage breaking (adultery[198]). (At that time, the men didn't have more than one wife.) What this knecht had done, I can't say. The knecht was also not brought before the common man up at the cathedral square the way they did with the others that they wished to kill. So they brought the knecht to the Jew Fields Gate, where they bound him to a column and then raised the column with knecht up onto the wall. The knecht stood there attached to the column for half an hour, so that the landsknechts should see the knecht from the trench. Eventually, the rebaptizers shot the knecht with guns, then they let the knecht stand for half an hour more. Eventually, they took the knecht down from the wall, and they untied him from the column and buried him.

Losses on both sides

While the camp was outside Münster, the rebaptizers suffered great losses outside two gates, St. Maurice's Gate and the Jew Fields Gate. The most trenches were dug there, and they were shot the most there by the landsknechts, [38v] from the camp or from the trench. Outside these two

---

197. This is the first instance of an ongoing joke on Gresbeck's part. He has converted the phrase "fool's work" into "Hollander's work" (see 69r where both are used in conjunction: "doren werk . . . Hollanders werk"). He usually just uses "Hollander's" in this phrase, but here extends it to the Frisians too. Although he frequently pairs these two groups in referring to the "real baptizers," he had a worse attitude about the Hollanders, not otherwise saying anything derogatory about the Frisians specifically (see 93r for his view of Hollanders' limited intelligence, and also note 484 for a word for "clown" or "fool" that refers specifically to Hollanders).

198. Gresbeck uses two synonyms in German.

gates, the rebaptizers lay buried in large numbers in the walls and in the farms outside the two gates. The landsknechts also suffered great losses outside the two gates.

On matrimony[199]

Now, John of Leiden took matrimony in hand with the preachers and the twelve elders, so that one man was supposed to have more than one wife.[200] The prophets, the preachers, and the twelve elders took matrimony in hand, secretly for as long as they were of one mind. The prophets and preachers found in the Bible the phrase "grow and increase yourselves."[201] There were also some Old Fathers, such as Abraham, David, and Helkmaen and others of them, and they had more than one wife.[202] They wished to go on according to this practice and accepted matrimony.[203] So the prophets and preachers proclaimed matrimony in their preaching, how it was God's will that they should accept a kind of matrimony in which God would have a good pleasure,[204] so that man should increase the world—for God wanted to establish a new world—and that it was God's will that each brother should have more than one wife and increase the world.

199. This is the only time that Gresbeck provides a heading of his own.

200. For Kerssenbrock's account of the introduction, see *Anabaptistici furoris*, ed. Detmer, 619–21n555). For the inaccuracy of his explanation of the motivation for this innovation, see note 554.

201. The quotation is a common German rendering (but not Luther's version) of Genesis 1:28, God's injunction to the newly created first man and woman to procreate.

202. "Old father" reflects the German phrase for "patriarch." Strictly speaking, only the biblical figures Abraham, Isaac, and Jacob were patriarchs, but the term can also be used more broadly of the characters attested in Genesis between the creation of mankind with Adam and the proper patriarchs. Here, however, the inclusion of David in the list shows that the term simply signifies a prominent figure in the stories of the Old Testament. In the treatment of polygamy in his book *Restitution*, Rothman cites "the holy oldfathers . . . Lamech, Abraham, David, Helkana [=Elkanah], etc." (Stupperich, *Die Schriften B. Rothmanns*, 264), and Gresbeck's list here is obviously a shortened version of Rothman's list, which Gresbeck presumably became familiar with from his preaching (there's no indication that he read the book). Lamech, Noah's father, is said to have had two wives (Genesis 4:17). Abraham's barren wife Sarai (later called Sarah) gave him her servant Hagar as a second wife from whom he could have children (Genesis 16:4). Sarah herself later became pregnant in old age, giving birth to Isaac (Genesis 21:1–3). King David had eight wives (the first is mentioned in 1 Samuel 18:27, and the rest appear in the list of his children in 1 Chronicles 3:1–9). Elkanah (who should precede David chronologically) had two wives, Peninnah and Hannah. Peninnah had many children by him, but Hannah was barren and was derided for this by Peninnah (1Samuel 1:2–6). Eventually, Hannah's prayers were answered, and she had the prophet Samuel by Elkanah (1 Samuel 1:19–20). Gresbeck has somewhat garbled the name of this comparatively obscure figure in rendering it as "Helkmaen."

203. In this passage, Gresbeck frequently uses the neutral term for the state of marriage ("eystand") as if it signified polygamy specifically.

204. "Good pleasure" is the standard English rendering of the Latin *beneplacitum*, a term of medieval theology signifying God's sovereign will (and apparently underlying the Low German "wohlbehagh").

Polygamy proclaimed

John of Leiden with his bishop,[205] preachers, and the twelve elders proclaimed the matrimony, [39r] saying that it was God's will that they should increase the world, that everyone should have three or four wives, as many of them as he wanted, but they were to live with the wives in a godly way, as you'll eventually hear. This pleased the one and not the other. There were men and women opposed to this, so that they wouldn't uphold the matrimony, and for this reason many a person would eventually have to die.

Polygamy enforced

John of Leiden was actually the first to take another wife in addition to the first wife that he'd taken in Münster.[206] (They would say that John of Leiden had another wife at Leiden in Holland.) John of Leiden took more wives every day, so that he eventually had fifteen wives.[207] So the

---

205. The bishop chosen by the Anabaptists was Julius of Franken from Frisia (for the appointment, see Kerssenbrock, *Anabaptistici furoris*, ed. Detmer, 542). Kerssenbrock says that the purpose of the appointment was for him alone to perform baptisms, though what the title has to do with that function is not clear. The appointment was made in the aftermath of the expulsion of non-Anabaptists on February 27, and presumably he was meant to exercise the functions of the prince-bishop within the traditional constitution of the city. (In this case, the position would be comparable to the *archon basileus* or "king magistrate" in the ancient Athenian democracy and the *rex sacrorum* or "king of [sacrificial] rites" in the Roman Republic, both being "kings" who carried out the indispensable sacral functions of the king after the abolition of the monarchy, though in this instance it would be the political and not the sacral functions that would be exercised. A political parallel might be the role of the king or queen in modern constitutional monarchies that have democratic governments.) If this is so, the position would have been rendered superfluous with the abolition of the old form of government and its replacement with the twelve elders a month or so later, and perhaps it's at this point that the position was used for the performance of baptism. The man had little chance to do much under John of Leiden's reign, as in October 1534 he was sent as an apostle (73v) to Coesfeld and executed (ibid., 705; see 72r, 73v–74v for Gresbeck's discussion of these events).

206. John of Leiden's first wife in Münster was Knipperdolling's stepdaughter Anna (see also note 554 for the term used to describe her relationship to Knipperdolling and the false interpretation given to it by Kerssenbrock). In his confessions, John clearly states that he married Mathias's widow on July 25 (St. James's Day) and that he had previously married Knipperdolling's "maid" (Niesert, *Münsterische Urkundensammlung*, 178; Cornelius, *Berichte der augenzeugen*, 371). This second marriage was the culmination of the three-day campaign of preaching in favor of polygamy that started on July 23 (Kerssenbrock, *Anabaptistici furoris*, ed. Detmer, 620). Kerssenbrock says that *after* the suppression of Mollenhecke's uprising against polygamy, John straightaway became the husband of three wives, including Mathias's widow (ibid., 626). This dating is clearly wrong, as the rebellion took place at the very end of the month in response to the introduction of polygamy (ibid., 621), and as for the three wives, these were presumably John's first wife back in Holland, Knipperdolling's stepdaughter, and finally Mathias's widow. It should be noted, however, that Gresbeck later speaks as if he thinks that John's first wife was Mathias's widow (see 54r and also note 290).

207. Fifteen is the number that Gresbeck gives for John's wives (88v, 91r, 110r, 139r), while Kerssenbrock's list (*Anabaptistici furoris*, ed. Detmer, 657–59) gives sixteen. For the various figures given in

Hollanders, Frisians, and all the real rebaptizers also took more wives in addition to their first wife. They compelled their first wife to go and fetch them another wife. At this, the devil had a laugh. Those got their wish who then had old wives and could now take young wives. This was also supposed to be taken up by the menfolk in the world who were not rebaptizers, who had old wives and could have a young one in addition, since it was godly. These rebaptizers in the city of Münster considered it proper according to their understanding.[208] The leaders like John of Leiden and the preachers and the twelve elders—they'd taken away all the money (the silver and gold), and had driven everyone away from their property, and were residing in their [39v] houses (their goods), and wished to have ten or twelve wives each to boot! I say that this was certainly the proper baptism for them.[209] They hadn't touched the proper water with which they baptized.[210] Let everyone be on his guard against using such water for baptism! If the rebaptizers had gotten their way, imagining as they did that they would have taken possession of the whole world and driven out all the lords and princes and every government in the world, they would have corrupted the world, just as they did to Münster, and done in many a person, just as they did outside and inside Münster. God didn't wish for them to get their way.

Rationale for polygamy

The prophets and preachers and the twelve elders had a plan: each man who had a young or old wife who wasn't fruitful, it was God's will that this man should take another who was. If she became fruitful, he should have nothing to do with her until she delivered.[211] If the man can't abstain from a women during the period when the wife is with child, he may take another.[212] If

contemporary sources, see ibid., 657n1.

208. The play on words here is a little hard to convey in English. "Proper" is the Low German "recht" (related to English "right"), which also means "real." Gresbeck uses the same word below, where the better translation is "real," but I've used "proper" throughout the passage to try and preserve Gresbeck's image. Basically, his point is that the Anabaptists abused the "real" sense of baptism, since their interpretation of it wasn't "proper" (both notions being conveyed by the single Low German word).

209. I.e., the (re)baptism was in Gresbeck's mind just an excuse for greed and lechery.

210. I.e., the Anabapists failed to grasp the spiritual sense of baptism.

211. "Fruitful" now means "pregnant."

212. On the strict prohibition against having sex with pregnant wives, see Kerssenbrock, *Anabaptistici furoris*, ed. Detmer, 630. This policy is defended at length by Rothman in his book *Restitution*, and confirmed in their confessions by John of Leiden (Cornelius *Berichte der augenzeugen*, 375) and Knipperdolling (Niesert, *Münsterische Urkundensammlung*, 190; Cornelius *Berichte der augenzeugen*, 379).

the man then takes another wife who also becomes fruitful, then he should leave her alone too. If afterwards the man can't abstain from womenfolk, he may take yet another, as many women as he wants to have, so that they will increase the world. So the man had to have nothing to do with the women who had conceived, and they always took another one. [40r] In this way, they wished to increase the world with the matrimony that they'd established. The matrimony that God had established they didn't wish to uphold.

Polygamy takes on a life of its own

This is what the rebaptizers wanted at first to have with the taking of wives. They'd made an ordinance along with it, and in this way they wished to live with their wives in a godly way, according to their faith. But in the end they took wives wherever they could get them. Whether they became fruitful or not, they would have just that many wives. In the end, they took little girls who were not yet old enough for childbearing, as you'll eventually hear.[213] So they slept first with one wife and then with the other. They did all this with a holy pretense, so that they would increase the world.

Women urged to accept polygamy

The prophets, preachers, and the twelve elders had it stated in the preaching, "All womenfolk, virgins, maidens, and widows, all those who are marriageable,[214] whether they be noble or non-noble, spiritual or secular, they should all take husbands, and the wives who have husbands outside the city who've fled from us should also take other husbands, since their husbands are godless and have fled from the Word of God and aren't our brothers. Dear brothers and sisters, for so long did you live in heathendom in your marriage, and it was not a real marriage." In this way, [40v] the preachers had the common folk informed in their preaching that they should take husbands in this way. There were some women willing to do this, and others not, and of the maidens and other servant girls,[215] some were willing

---

213. 47r–v.

214. The Low German word "manber" literally means "man-able," so "marriageable" here signifies "sexually mature." Gresbeck later complains that the Anabaptists would marry pre-pubescent girls (47r–v).

215. Gresbeck frequently uses a construction in which "other" is used in the sense of "as well." Properly speaking, "other" should imply that the item it modifies is another member of the group indicated by the preceding noun, but in this usage there is no such implication (that is, the "other"

and others not. There were some women who remained in the city and had let their husbands take part in the departure before or on the Friday, imagining that they would come back to the city in four days or so. If the burghers of Münster had stayed in the city and guarded it and had taken a look at whom they'd let in, that would certainly have been better. It was even better that they departed from the city rather than letting themselves all be baptized, even though they saw that it couldn't go on.[216]

Women had been left behind when their menfolk opposing Anabaptism left the city

Some women let their husbands take part in the departure so that they wouldn't have anything to do with the business, and these women stayed in the city with their property, their house and home, and their children to protect them, not expecting that their husbands would stay away for so long, and that such a business would arise from this. If these women had known before and on the Friday what they would eventually learn, they would have abandoned everything that they had and left the city with their husbands. Since they'd stayed in the city, they had to do just as the other women did and just as the prophets [41r] and preachers wished. If the common man in the city, consisting of men and women and the maidens, young and old, who'd let themselves be baptized on the Friday—if they'd known in advance what they would come to know after the Friday, not one child would have remained in the city, as I stated before.[217] Then it was too late, and they were piteously betrayed one way or the other.[218] Many is the person who eventually ran secretly from the city, by day and also by night.

Men seek more wives

So the order went out in the city that they should all take husbands. Then the Hollanders and Frisians and all the rebaptizers who'd rushed into the

---

noun is simply a further item in the list without being a new manifestation of the previous category). Presumably, that's the usage here (that is, "servant" girls are simply added to the "maidens" without necessarily being "maidens" themselves. On the other hand, as young girls "servant girls" may have been conceived of as being mostly maidens.

216. Presumably, what "couldn't go on" was the Anabaptist regime.

217. Presumably 12v is meant (where the reference is to no child having stayed). For similar ideas, see 33v, 40v, and 93v.

218. For the meaning of the phrase "one way or the other," see note 80.

city and some of the burghers in the city of Münster, they ran into every house throughout the whole city in which they knew a woman or virgin or young maiden. Five or six of them would run after her, first one man and then the other, because the one wanted to have more wives than the other. The more wives they had, the better Christians they were. This running about in the city in search of wives took place so swiftly that the prophets and preachers and the twelve elders together with their bishop had a prohibition given out in the preaching that they should not run after the womenfolk. "Dear brothers, you should send word to the sister or go alone to her in her house, and you should ask for her hand in marriage. If it's the case that her spirit doesn't attest to her willingness to have a husband, or if she's betrothed to someone else, then he should leave her alone and go to someone else. For as long as God puts this in her mind [41v] and her spirit then attests to it, then it's God's will that she should then get someone that God assigns to her." The preachers continued, "Dear brothers and sisters, when the brother works to get a Christian sister, so that they both wish to become a married couple, they should pray to God for three days that it should be His will that he take her and that he may live with her, that this may be God's good pleasure, that it should be for His praise and for His glory, and that He may increase the world with her and with all the women that you get."

Women forced to enter into polygamous marriages

This attesting of the spirit by these women and virgins and maidens before they would take a man fell out of use. If the Christian sister's spirit wouldn't attest, then the Christian brother's spirit attested that he would have her, so that the Christian sister no longer dared to refuse.[219] Whether the brother who wanted to have her had a wife or not, she had to take him all the same. If she was still unwilling, she had to come before the preachers, and they forced some womenfolk in the city to take the men, whether they were willing or not. Otherwise, they said they deserved death.

---

219. Kerssenbrock refers several times (*Anabaptistici furoris*, ed. Detmer, 589, 614, 628) to this male attesting of desire, which he quotes in the form, "Father, my spirit desires your flesh" or the like ("Father" presumably being an invocation of the Anabaptist deity and not the person whose flesh was desired).

Woman dies under suspicious circumstances

Once the matrimony had taken this course of a man having to have as many wives as each wished, this pleased one man and not the other, and many would be killed because of this, [42r] as you'll eventually hear. Many a person in the city was upset on account of the matrimony, to the point of death. As soon as they adopted this matrimony, the one was all opposed to the other right until the end. One time, they found a woman lying in the water, and she was drowned. She was floating on the surface and still had her clothes on. This woman was drowned in the city. The common people didn't know how she was drowned, whether the prophets and preachers had had her drowned or the woman had drowned herself. So the common folk couldn't learn how the woman was drowned. Some people would say that prophets had had her drowned. Some people would say that she'd drowned herself on account of the matrimony. This woman was lying on the water unbound, so the people in the city thought that she'd drowned herself because she was so upset about the matrimony.[220] I can't write anything more about what the situation was with the woman. This woman wasn't a resident of the city of Münster, and they didn't know where she was from. For she was known in Münster and they'd missed her in the city. They took the woman out of the water and buried her.

Strife among polygamous wives

From now on, they couldn't get along on account of the matrimony, and there was now great ill will in the city among the women. Whenever two [42v] or three women were together in one house and had one husband together, there was always criticizing and quarreling among the wives. For the first wife always wanted to be next to the husband, and the other wives that the husband had taken in addition to the first wife also wished to be by the husband and to keep themselves with him just as the first wife did. So they couldn't get along together, so that they never had peace among themselves, and every day some accusation came before the prophets and preachers and the twelve elders. Hence, they eventually set to it and took some of the women who were the first wife of their husband and cut off their heads,

---

220. I.e., if she had been drowned against her will, her hands would have had to be tied. Since they were not, this was taken by some as evidence that she had committed suicide.

so that the other wives would think of this and be at peace with the other wives (concubines). In this way, they compelled their first wives, whom they'd had for ten or twenty years, and they had children together. Then they lived in ill will like this. With this, the first wives had to keep quiet and dared not speak against it. Otherwise, they were all taken and beheaded.[221]

Recalcitrant women arrested

The prophets and preachers would at first place them for a while in the Rosendale, as I mentioned before.[222] They couldn't compel the women with the Rosendale. Then the preachers, especially Stutenberent, said, "I say to you verily, the Rosendale won't work any longer. We recognize that you can't be compelled by it anymore. Punishment must be by the sword." In this way, they kept the women quiet for a while, [43r] but this didn't last long. Hatred was now widespread among them because the devil ruled the matrimony and the wives, so that there was no solution for it. The prophets and preachers carried out severe punishment with the sword, executing many. Eventually, they couldn't compel the wives. Eventually, the preachers said, "It won't succeed until you go to the cathedral square in your pelt.[223] Then you'll certainly sing a different tune." But it was too late. There was no solution to it. They had to solve the problem with all the women in some other way if they were to get along, so that three or four women should be at peace with one husband.

Anabaptist leadership backpedals on polygamy

The prophets and preachers and the twelve elders went to take counsel about how they could succeed with the women, so that they should be at peace together. So they had it said in the preaching by the preachers that all the womenfolk who'd been compelled to marry and had husbands, who would gladly leave those husbands, should come up to the council hall and have themselves listed. They would be divorced, since the preachers

---

221. Another example of Gresbeck's tendency to generalize from specific examples.

222. See 28v. For the use of the Rosendale convent as a prison, see also Kerssenbrock, *Anabaptistici furoris*, ed. Detmer, 629.

223. At the bottom of 44r it becomes clear that the women took the requirement to wear the pelt as a sign that they would be executed (presumably, because the pelt could be worn with the neck exposed).

had made a mistake with the matrimony.[224] How clever it was of John of Leiden, Stutenberent, and the twelve elders, and of some other preachers, to say that the preachers had made a mistake with the matrimony! With this they meant the preachers that they'd [43v] sent out to Soest, to Warendorf, to Coesfeld, and to Osnabrück, wishing to absolve themselves on the grounds that they hadn't consented (agreed) to the matrimony and to shift the blame to the other preachers.[225] They knew full well that those preachers were dead, having been executed in the cities. They imagined that they would pay the price for them for this situation with the matrimony. So it happened that they divorced the people at the end of the first summer, when the city was under siege and they'd sent out the preachers.[226] "Since the preachers have made a mistake with the matrimony, you should come up to the council hall and have yourselves listed. You will be divorced. No one will be compelled to it; marriage should be voluntary. Whoever it pleases may do it. Whoever it doesn't please may leave it be." But when they had this proclaimed, it was too late. They'd had all the men marry the womenfolk in the city,[227] and some of the women had already been executed on account of the matrimony. "A man can certainly live in a godly way with one wife, and a man can also certainly live in a godly way without wives, and a woman too can certainly live in a godly way without a husband." How they overturned it, being tired of the many women, and certainly seeing that the situation with the matrimony was not godly! But they'd gone so far into it that they couldn't get back out.[228] They set a period (eight days) for the women to have themselves listed. [44r] About one hundred married women, young and old, had themselves listed. The little girls also had themselves listed, having also been forced into it, as you'll eventually

224. "Divorce" has a rather modern, legalistic sound to it, and "separate" would be a better translation, but the modern associations of the word would suggest a temporary separation rather than the permanent one intended.

225. For the dispatch of preachers to these towns and their eventual execution, see 71v–74v. As for the variant "agreed" given as an alternative to "consent," the German verb "consentieren" clearly has the sound of a borrowing from Latin, and Gresbeck has given a normal German synonym (*bewilligen*).

226. Gresbeck's memory of the chronology seems to have failed him here, since the missionaries were sent out in mid-October and executed soon thereafter (73v–74r).

227. This clause is defective in the Cologne manuscript. All it says is "they had all the men the womenfolk in the city [*sic*]." The verbal form(s) that should (apparently) go with "had" is omitted, and the translation here is conjectural.

228. Here, as elsewhere, Gresbeck believes that the Anabaptist leaders "knew better" (e.g., 60r, 74r, 77v, 95r), that is, they actually accepted traditional beliefs but cynically subverted them for their own immoral purposes. There is, however, no reason to doubt the sincerity of the Anabaptists, even if one takes their ideas to be at times rather misguided.

hear. To these women who had themselves listed they gave a date when they were to come back. When the women came back, they asked each woman, young and old, if they had really been forced to their lord. (The womenfolk would call their husbands "lord.") Anybody that was forced into marriage who could prove it they divorced. Many womenfolk in the city who'd been forced into it didn't have themselves listed because they were afraid that the prophets and preachers had something else in mind, being afraid that they were to go up to the cathedral square in their pelt because they would be beheaded. If they'd known that they would divorce them, hundreds more would probably have had themselves listed. When it happened that the wives were divorced from their husbands, the preachers gave a sermon on the topic (these womenfolk) and pronounced the curse that they belonged to the devil body and soul (they had to have this reputation afterwards), and then the benediction.

Old women obliged to take a guardian

Those women in the city who were too old to take husbands had to choose a guardian.[229] The old women held these guardians just as the young women held their lord. So the old women went through the city [44v] and chose guardians. The old women could chose whomever they wished, and the guardian had to keep the old woman as if she were his legitimate wife, and keep an eye on her. So the young and the old women would go up the streets and ask each other, "Have you by chance seen my lord?" and they (some of the women) played the fool with this looking for their lord. They would ask each other what their spirit attested to, and they made a lot of loud yammering with this looking for their lord and attesting of their spirit. Some women attested to the spirit that it was not right for one man to have five or six wives, for they got it into their heads that one man had enough with one wife, and he could certainly content himself with that. In the city, they attested to this same spirit that the men should not have more than one wife. For the saying goes that many pigs make the slops thin.[230]

229. Once again, the main problems were the women left behind when their male relations had fled the city back in February. Normally, these men (fathers or husbands) would have had legal charge of these women, and in the absence of such males (and without the possibility of a new marriage for these older women) a male guardian had to be found.

230. Clearly a proverb, meaning that if too many animals eat from a given quantity of food, none of them get enough.

So these women had so much talking in the city since the women in the city were of two sorts, just as the men were. Some women said that My Lord of Münster should capture the city and that it was all buffoonery what the prophets and preachers were engaged in. Some said that it was God's work what they were engaged in. So they lived in such doubt and were so confused, not knowing what views they should hold and what they should believe. Eventually, the prophets and preachers forbade the women to go along the streets yammering, "Have you by any chance seen my lord?" and attesting to their spirit. They were not to call their husbands "lord" anymore, [45r] and they were to call them as they would in the past, so that the expression of calling them "lord" fell out of use, and they were to conduct themselves just as was appropriate for legitimate couples and leave behind this tomfoolery.

Guardians to provide for their aged wards, but eventually starvation sets in

So these guardians had to keep an eye on the old women and make sure that they remained in the faith, and they had to instruct them. If the old women wouldn't be obedient to the guardians, then he had to accuse her before the prophets and preachers, and then they were punished. Before the womenfolk were punished, the guardians first had to teach and instruct them. If they didn't allow themselves to be taught, they were accused before the prophets and preachers, and if they didn't let themselves be instructed by them (the prophets and preachers), then they had to die, the men as well as the women, young and old, the one as much as the other.[231] The guardians had to provide the old women with food and clothing, just as the deacons had previously done, so that they would lack nothing. Instead, the sick, old women and the poor people would have as much as the other rebaptizers or the rich people.[232] But he who was poor remained poor, and he who had something at the end had to grab onto it, even though property was supposed to be held in common. The hunger befell the poor people first, and

231. The generality at the end of this sentence seems inappropriate for the context (recalcitrant old women). Presumably, Gresbeck is speaking of the common practice in the city of executing those who refused to adhere to official policy.

232. Here, Gresbeck's mention of care for the destitute leads to a long digression on the care of the poor in general and their eventual starvation. It was this sort of "associative" composition that infuriated the early modern editor of the text.

they suffered great distress. When the time arrived that the hunger became great in the city, the prophets and preachers and the deacons didn't consider that they'd taken each man's property from him and that the common poor people would have been happy to eat, and in the end they let them starve to death in this piteous way. [45v] But in the beginning the poor common people would get enough in the way of food and clothing, so that they had no want. When they got something at that time, they didn't stop until they'd used it up, but some of the poor people didn't do that. When some women got something, they didn't stop and they sang and jumped and were of good cheer. They thanked the kind Father for having consoled them so richly, and they ate and drank as long as they had something. But when the food began to give out, when the Father could no longer console them so richly, they kept quiet about the Father, and they no longer sang about the gracious Father or jumped with the gracious Father. With time, they began to take a staff in their hand and could no longer walk because of the great hunger, so that some died in the end.

Foreigners duped by the preachers' eloquence

These foreign burghers, who'd rushed to the city and followed the preachers from other cities from all lands and who'd let themselves be led astray in this way by the false prophets and preachers, also had to take wives, just as much as those who had no wife did, as many as they wished to have.[233] At home, they had wives and children, house and home, and some were rich men, and they'd abandoned what they had, following the preachers and letting themselves be convinced in this way.[234] Now, there are some people in the world who think and even say that they shouldn't have been convinced by the preachers to follow them. These prophets and preachers would certainly have led the devil astray from this world with their orating and preaching. It's impossible to say just [46r] how they could orate. For this reason, there was still many a person in the city who was in doubt. This

233. This category of noncommitted Anabaptists who were won over by the enthusiastic preaching of the "real rebaptizers" was discussed above (33v).
234. Note the emphasis on the wealth of those who were convinced by the Anabaptist preaching. Although modern scholars sometimes emphasize that Anabaptism appealed to members of the lower classes of society, Gresbeck makes it clear that rich people also found the new ideology of the sacrifice and communal sharing appealing (among the local converts one can think of Knipperdolling and Kibbenbrock, who belonged to the highest levels of society).

was the result of the length of time that they preached and of their having adopted so many regimes.[235] These burghers who'd rushed to the city certainly would have preferred to be out of the city, back with their property, their wives and children, and their house and home. But then it was too late. Some of the burghers, who'd left behind and given up great property, succumbed to a chagrin and died, being so piteously betrayed. Some of the burghers did this and some did not. For the prophets and preachers had instructed them to give up everything that they had and follow the Word of God—they would get a twofold repayment. This is how they convinced the people.

Traditional marriages considered invalid

All the menfolk who'd previously had legitimate wives, whether they'd been burghers in the city of Münster or foreign burghers who'd moved to the city with their wives—all the men who'd had legitimate wives before the baptizing and kept their wives had to get married to their wives again if they wished to remain with each other. The matrimony in which they'd been for so long hadn't been a real matrimony, and for all that time they'd been in fornication and lived like heathens. So the women and men had to get married once more, though they'd been together for ten, twenty, or thirty years. They had to do this because they'd been baptized anew and become Christians. [46v] For the prophets and preachers said that in the time since they were born they'd not known of the Christian faith or the Word of God, and they also hadn't really been baptized and had lived for that time like heathens. So God would now finally wake up and establish a new world.

Unmarried women seek husbands

Now that they were in the midst of the matrimony and saw that no womenfolk could escape having to take a husband and that they'd put the women under such great duress to get married that they had to do this, every

---

235. Seemingly, Gresbeck means that that large number of changes in the structure of society advocated by the Anabaptist leadership (first as implemented by the Anabaptist-controlled city council, then by the regime of the twelve elders, and finally by the kingship of John of Leiden) left many people confused. He may mean that people (including himself?) became disillusioned with the increasing radicalism of the later reforms, some of which, such as polygamy, obviously came as a disagreeable shock to at least portions of the population.

female looked for a man. There were some womenfolk who didn't want a husband who had a wife and they took a man who was still without a wife. So the womenfolk looked around when what they had to do was get a husband each. Those who were glad to be together came together. There were also men in the city who didn't want to have more than one wife and didn't want to live just like cats and dogs. There remained among the men and women in the city many pious people who were good Christians and wished to have nothing to do with the business, and they were forced to it. May God be compassionate to those who died for this reason and had no guilt in it! God must forgive the truly guilty person for his sins.[236] John [47r] of Leiden and Knipperdolling beheaded and executed so many, personally bringing so many pious men and women to their deaths with their own hands, and they starved so many to death, and they took their property from everyone so piteously and drove them from their property, and made so many people poor, that God may well have pity.[237] Everything that they did was necessarily right, it was all God's will. Knipperdolling beheaded more people than John of Leiden did, since Knipperdolling was entrusted with the sword in the beginning.[238]

Even small girls married

Now that all the womenfolk in the city of Münster had to take men, eventually it was the small girls and they too had to take men. These girls were eleven, twelve, thirteen years old (I dare not write how young they were).[239] They were still children and hadn't yet come of age, so that they were not yet marriageable. So these girls had to take husbands, even though they were too small, being children still. So the Hollanders and Frisians (the criminals) and some burghers in the city of Münster took these girls in addition to the first wives that they'd taken before. Those men who had old wives also took some of the girls, and in this way they divided up the

---

236. By "must" Gresbeck means that it's up to God alone to determine whether to forgive the guilty, not that God has to do so. Presumably, the implication is that no human is in a position to do so.
237. For more talk of the guilt of the leadership (especially the "limping prophet," John Dusentschuer), see 63r.
238. For Knipperdolling being assigned the position of "sword bearer" in the beginning, see Kerssenbrock, *Anabaptistici furoris*, ed. Detmer, 573.
239. Kerssenbrock (*Anabaptistici furoris*, ed. Detmer, 627) specifies exactly the same ages. In saying that he dares not write their ages, Gresbeck is indicating his reluctance rather than suggesting that the ages were in fact lower.

girls, one taking them here and another there, because they had to take men in this way. When the preachers, the Hollanders and Frisians, and all those who had taken the girls did so, they were nonetheless too small for the criminals. The Hollanders and Frisians [47v] kept the girls for so long with their evil will that they wrecked all the girls, breaking their bodies down, because they were not in fact capable of servicing the men. There was a woman in the city who was a female doctor, and she healed these girls, so that they became healthy, though some girls died because they were wrecked.[240] This woman had fifteen of these girls that she made healthy again. These girls also had themselves listed at the council hall so that they would be divorced from their husbands,[241] because the Hollanders and Frisians in the city wouldn't relent.

Discontent with polygamy results in an uprising

An uprising arose in the city of Münster on account of the matrimony, because some burghers and pious people and landsknechts from other cities wanted to revoke the matrimony, and everyone was to have his own goods back and the burgher masters and council were to be restored, so that things would all be as they had been before, and they wanted to surrender the city.[242] So these burghers and landsknechts had taken John of Leiden, Knipperdolling, and some other preachers prisoner, and had put them in the prison in the city cellar at the council hall. They'd also taken a preacher named Schlachtschap prisoner.[243] They hauled him from bed in between two women, and two women lay below him on a trundle bed. So they had placed him along with someone else in the stocks. Some women came before the stocks, and they threw muck

---

240. Kerssenbrock (*Anabaptistici furoris*, ed. Detmer, 627) says that this woman, who was the wife of a man named Knupper, practiced surgery. In the late medieval and early modern period, performing actual operations was considered a menial task beneath the dignity of properly trained doctors, and the "surgeons" who worked on living bodies were generally of lowly status (often barbers, because such men were used to dealing with sharp instruments). Although this occupation is somewhat surprising for a woman, there is no doubt from the terminology that she wasn't merely a midwife (the term used by Gresbeck is "arstinne" [=High German *Ärtzin*], which is just the regular word for "doctor" with a feminine ending added to it, not a common word at all).

241. I.e., in the procedure discussed earlier (79v–80r).

242. See *Anabaptistici furoris*, ed. Detmer, 621–25, for Kerssenbrock's narrative of these events. He dates the start of the uprising to July 30, but a contemporary document indicates that the nocturnal activities that began the uprising took place the evening of the preceding day (ibid., 621n2).

243. Kerssenbrock adds the names of the preachers Rothman, Klopriss, and Vinne (*Anabaptistici furoris*, ed. Detmer, 621). Perhaps Gresbeck specifies Schlachtschap alone merely because the lascivious detail related in the next sentence stuck in his mind.

and stones at him and reviled him, asking if he wanted to have even more wives, and if he wasn't satisfied with one wife. Many folk gathered up there at the marketplace in front of the council hall, [48r] and they had a look at how the uprising would turn out. They went up to the marketplace for a long time, and had possession of it for half a day. Eventually, the Hollanders and Frisians and Tilbeck[244] and also some other burghers gathered together. They took possession of all the gates around the city, so that they couldn't get possession of any gate.[245] Those who'd started the uprising up at the market wanted to send someone from the market on horseback to have a look.[246] There was one man who was willing to ride to the gates. They wouldn't trust him, so he had to go back.[247] So they sent out someone else on horseback. He rode there, wishing to have a look, and some men accompanied him on foot. When the man on horseback reached the gate, they took him prisoner and of those who were on foot, some were also taken prisoner and some escaped from them.[248] Then news reached the market that the man on horseback was captured along with some of the others who were on foot. So they sent out someone else once more to see if this was so.[249] In this way, they found out that it was true that they were captured.

Tilbeck leads the Anabaptists and Mollenhecke their opponents

Tilbeck and some of the twelve elders came back to the market, and they wanted to reach an agreement among them that they would put an end to the uprising, so that everyone should go back home.[250] The burghers and the landsknechts wouldn't leave off—they wanted everything to be as it had been. Tilbeck saw that they wanted everything to be that way again. Tilbeck then went around the city [48v] and fetched the Hollanders and

244. For his earlier career, see also note 62.
245. The second "they" refers to the rebels.
246. According to Kerssenbrock (*Anabaptistici furoris*, ed. Detmer, 622–23), twenty men were sent out to examine the attitude of the Anabaptists only after the people whom the rebels summoned indiscriminately to the marketplace as reinforcements decided to go over to the Anabaptists once they concluded that the Anabaptist forces were stronger.
247. Presumably, the man had stepped forward to volunteer, and was now obliged to "go back" to his original place.
248. According to Kerssenbrock, twelve of the twenty men dispatched were captured.
249. Kerssenbrock makes no mention of a second mission.
250. This is the same ploy that Tilbeck had used to deflect the earlier uprising back in February (9r).

Frisians and all those who adhered to rebaptism from the watches, and they now occupied the city all around. So these men (the Hollanders and Frisians) gathered together and marched in battle order against the others in the marketplace, being five or six hundred strong. Those whom they'd taken prisoner (the man on horseback and the others on foot) they'd allowed to go back. This took place on Tilbeck's advice, because the Hollanders and Frisians were afraid that they would keep the upper hand.[251] The leader among the burghers and landsknechts was a burgher named Mollenhecke. He'd been an alderman in earlier days, so he was in opposition and wanted things to be as they had been.[252] One time, Knipperdolling and this man Mollenhecke came together and had a face-to-face meeting. Knipperdolling would hold that the baptizing was right, and so was everything that they undertook, and Mollenhecke the alderman was opposed to it, because everything that they undertook with matrimony and the common ownership of property and everything that they undertook—it was all wrong. Knipperdolling and Mollenhecke's having this disagreement took place on the street in the city. This man Mollenhecke started shouting into the air to God in heaven, as hard as he could, "O God in heaven, look down here and punish the great wrong that's taking place in this city, and whoever is wrong, may You punish him!" After Mollenhecke had shouted like this to God in heaven, he said to Knipperdolling, "How does it please you, this shouting to God in heaven?" Then Knipperdolling said, "Well, then, things will soon change." Shortly after this time, Mollenhecke [49r] gathered the burghers and landsknechts in his house at night, when they took John of Leiden, Knipperdolling, and the other preachers prisoner, so that the uprising came into being in this way.[253]

251. "They" refers to the rebels.

252. Henry Mollenhecke's profession is variously described by Kerssenbrock as a locksmith (*Anabaptistici furoris*, ed. Detmer, 392) and blacksmith (ibid., 621). He had been chosen as one of the electors for the city election of 1533 (ibid., 392), and was trusted by Anabaptists in the beginning, because he was one of the two men appointed by the twelve elders to look after the artillery (ibid., 584). For Mollenhecke's earlier run-in with the Anabaptists, see 19v–20v. Here, Gresbeck is presumably once more using "alderman" to mean "councilman" (see also note 104), and in any event, this isn't true, because Mollenhecke was simply an elector. See also Kirchhoff, "Die Belagerung und Eroberung Münsters," 465.

253. This final sentence shows that the dispute between Mollenhecke and Knipperdolling took place before the uprising, and in some way caused the uprising to break out. Gresbeck's interest in the event is centered solely on the acrimonious outcome of the meeting, but one has to wonder why Mollenhecke bothered to tell Knipperdolling of his desire for a restoration of the old ways in the first place. Could it be that Mollenhecke was trying to win Knipperdolling over to the effort to overthrow the (foreign) Anabaptist control of the city (cf. 140r, where Gresbeck indicates that even at the end

Rebels hemmed in at the city hall

Now that the burghers and landsknechts learned that the Hollanders and Frisians had gathered with Tilbeck[254] and would march on the marketplace and do battle with them, before they would let things become the way they'd been again or give up the city, these burghers drew themselves up in battle order, had the drums sound the alarm, and prepared themselves for defense.[255] The Hollanders and Frisians (the criminals) came with their retinue to the marketplace in battle order and defeated the burghers and landsknechts, so they took flight to the council hall. One of the burghers was shot in the doorway of the council hall and died right away.[256] When the Hollanders and Frisians saw that they were taking flight to the council hall, they kept up the pressure and chased them upstairs in the council hall, as high as they could reach. In this way, the Hollanders and Frisians with their retinue took possession of the council hall, and they wanted to storm it then and kill everyone who was up in the hall. So they shot upwards from below at the burghers and landsknechts through the ceiling with demi-arquebuses, and they brought a demi-culverin[257] up to the front of the council hall and shot up into the council hall through the window. [49v] The burghers and landsknechts who were up in the council hall returned fire and threw down stones from there, just as if they were making an assault by storm together or as if a storm assault

---

of the siege, Knipperdolling still retained enough influence with the natives of Münster that if he'd been willing to overthrow John of Leiden, they would have followed him)? If so, the meeting ended in discord, with Mollenhecke showing his hostility to Anabaptism and Knipperdolling adhering to it, and the realization that there was no help to be expected from Knipperdolling presumably impelled the opponents of Anabaptism to seize the leading Anabaptists and then undertake a rather ill-conceived attempt to seize control of the city.

254. According to Kerssenbrock (*Anabaptistici furoris*, ed. Detmer, 622), the leader of the Anabaptists after the preachers were arrested was Henry Redeker, the man who had previously gotten into trouble with the Anabaptist leadership after he cooperated with Tilbeck in trying to curb John Mathias's encroachment on traditional legal procedure (19v and note 106). For whatever reason, Gresbeck paid no attention to Redeker's actions in the present events, and only Tilbeck's involvement stuck in his mind.

255. According to Kerssenbrock (*Anabaptistici furoris*, ed. Detmer, 622), in the morning after they seized the preachers, Mollenhecke and the other anti-Anabaptist leaders summoned the populace to the marketplace to increase their numbers. This was a move of dubious utility as the loyalties of these new forces turned out to be unreliable, and they went over to the Anabaptists. Kerssenbrock claims that this was simply a rational decision based on the perceived military superiority of the Anabaptists, but one has to wonder whether they didn't go over to the side they really favored once they determined the actual situation.

256. This man was named Herman Kramp (Kerssenbrock, *Anabaptistici furoris*, ed. Detmer, 623).

257. For a discussion of the various sorts of artillery mentioned by Gresbeck, see introduction, section 3.2.

were being launched against the other side. It was assault enough for the burghers and landsknechts. Some still had to die because of it.

Rebels surrender

Eventually, the burghers and landsknechts saw that they'd lost and had to surrender, so they stuck their hats out the window and asked to be taken prisoner. The Hollanders and Frisians wanted to kill them all at once, but eventually they took them prisoner, capturing a hundred and twenty.[258] The rest of them had escaped when they saw that the Hollanders and Frisians had assembled. But if the burghers had then gained the upper hand along with the landsknechts, they certainly would have remained with them. They placed these one hundred and twenty men in a prison up at the council hall in the cellar. That they were taken prisoner and defeated was caused by Tilbeck. Otherwise, they would have surrendered the city. If, on the same night when they started the uprising and took John of Leiden and Knipperdolling prisoner, the burghers and landsknechts had taken possession of a gate, they would have kept the upper hand. That's just what took place when the city of Münster was captured. At that time, the landsknechts looked for plunder rather than seeing that the gates were kept in possession, so that they were almost defeated.[259] The burghers did the same thing after taking Knipperdolling, [50r] John of Leiden, and some preachers prisoner. At that time, they too looked for money rather than seeing to it that they got possession of a gate, and they stuffed their sleeves full of gold and sat the whole night in their cups, drinking wine so that they got drunk.[260] For this reason, they were defeated, so that the Frisians and Hollanders got the upper hand.

258. Kerssenbrock (*Anabaptistici furoris*, ed. Detmer, 623) indicates that the prisoners were roughly handled at first.

259. See 151v.

260. Kerssenbrock mentions that after the surrender, one man (a *miles* or landsknecht) was found to have concealed in his clothing the surprisingly large sum of four thousand florins (guilders) that he had stolen from the city registry, but he makes no reference to drunkenness. If there had been drinking, it would have had to take place in the evening before the showdown at the marketplace, and it's hard to see how this could have changed the course of events as Gresbeck relates them. Since Gresbeck clearly has in mind the parallel between the present situation and the later events when the city would have been taken without any losses (in his reckoning) if his plan had been followed, but instead the attacking troops were more interested in looking for plunder (151v), perhaps he has confused the present events with the failure of the first attempt to storm the city because of the drunkenness of the troops, a circumstance that he himself, surprisingly, does not mention (see also note 180). In any event, Kerssenbrock claims that once the man's theft was discovered, he was compelled to admit that he had planned to use the money to escape and bring the prince-bishop's troops in through St. Ludger's Gate, and that this revelation led to the general demand for the execution of the prisoners.

Some rebels pardoned, others executed

Of these hundred and twenty prisoners, John of Leiden, Knipperdolling, the preachers, and the twelve elders had forty-seven killed.[261] The others were pardoned. Those who were pardoned had to produce witnesses before the twelve elders, John of Leiden, and the preachers that they hadn't been present there at night, that they arrived there in the morning, and that they'd not been there in the beginning.[262] Whoever could produce witnesses that he'd arrived there in the morning kept his life. The others had to die. Those whom they'd killed they shot with demi-arquebuses and they hacked them up with short daggers.[263] They set (some of) them against the walls, and they shot them that way. They beheaded some of them. Whoever desired to kill someone was allowed to take him and kill him.[264] How he did him in was just awful. This killing lasted three or four days. Up at the cathedral square, they made two great pits in which they placed the dead. Every day they did in ten or twelve until they were all dead. Then they held the people under great duress, so that they got their way with the matrimony. After this time, no one dared [50v] say in opposition to it that the matrimony was wrong, since everything they did was necessarily right. There was one among the prisoners, and he too was supposed to die with them and go with them to the cathedral square. He was a burgher in the city of Münster, and he kept asking to go home and speak to his wife and to his children before he was to die. They wouldn't grant him this request. When they were going to take this burgher from the council hall to the cathedral square, the others were bound in pairs and the burgher was bound alone. All of a sudden, he made a run from the others, wanting to run home and speak to his wife and to his children. So they ran after him

261. Kerssenbrock (*Anabaptistici furoris*, ed. Detmer, 624–25), states that the following morning, ninety-one men were executed at the discretion of the leading Anabaptists. Other contemporary evidence (ibid., 625n2) agrees with Gresbeck in putting the number in the upper forties. Mollenhecke was among the executed.

262. I.e., they had to demonstrate that they had simply answered the alarm set off by the rebels to summon reinforcements and were not guilty of taking part in the earlier stages of the rebellion during the preceding night, merely becoming involved in events whose significance they didn't really comprehend.

263. Kerssenbrock (*Anabaptistici furoris*, ed. Detmer, 624–25) claims that twenty-five were shot, and that in order to save gunpowder and prevent the enemy finding out about the discord within the city, another sixty-six were beheaded (mostly by Knipperdolling, but also by John of Leiden when anger impelled him).

264. See 98v for a later reference to someone who had been an active participant in the executions.

and some came opposite him, and they caught him between them. They hacked him into pieces with short daggers, and then they took him by the feet and lugged him back to the others in the cathedral square. The pieces that they'd hacked off of his body and head they put on his body when they carted him to the cathedral square. Then they killed the others straightaway and threw them into the pits.

Pardoned rebels make public apologies

The other prisoners, who received mercy, they had them assemble in St. George's Monastery, in the lords' refectory. There Schlachtschap sat in a high chair and gave a sermon about how God had revealed to him that he should give a sermon to those who'd been present at the uprising. So this preacher spoke seated in the chair [51r] and gave a sermon about how they'd acted against the will of God, and how they should thank and praise God for having granted them mercy. He said that each one should pray in the common assembly in front of his own gate, when a sermon was given before the brothers and sisters.[265] Whether they'd acted against the will of God and the matrimony and whether there was some brother or sister against whom they'd said or done something that was against God's will, they would, he said, forgive them for this. This is what happened, and they prayed for forgiveness in the common assembly. Then they were granted mercy. This preacher wrote down each man under his name,[266] and they were then at peace again, and became their brothers again.

Anabaptist weddings and divorces

From then on, they got their way with the matrimony, so that all women, virgins, and girls had to take husbands. When a pair wished to get married, they didn't get married as they had at first, by the preachers. The one that went in to the other brought along one or two people (his friends), and they held a staff together and gave each other their hand. With that they were a legitimate couple. If they could get along when they were together, then they remained with each other. If they couldn't get along, they left each other. When a pair came together who wanted to become a legitimate

265. I.e., pray for forgiveness.
266. Presumably, this means that Schlachtschap attended each common assembly and drew up a list of those who asked for and received forgiveness.

couple according to their marriage even though the man was not marriage-able and had a young wife, then they divorced them.[267] [51v] It happened often and a lot in the city that they were divorced in this way in the common assembly. Then the woman took another husband.[268]

Anabaptist marriage officiants

After they held the city by themselves, having driven the burghers and women from their property on the Friday, they had a house in each parish in which they would preach in the morning.[269] Of these preachers, some were renegade priests and monks, and some were other burghers, Hollanders and Frisians, all of them being preachers.[270] Whoever could read anything became a preacher. At that time, they still upheld matrimony as it's upheld in the world. Some who performed marriages had been parish priests and some who performed marriages were not parish priests, these others being burghers. When they got married, they did so in the common assembly before all the folk, each in his own parish. But this didn't last long. When all property came to be held in common, matrimony too came to be held in common along with the wives. Provided they weren't brothers and sisters from the same mother and father, they married each other and became legitimate spouses. They wouldn't pay any attention to the other sorts of kinship. They wouldn't make a big deal about paternity or kinship.

Second unsuccessful storming of the city

So My Gracious Lord of Münster had another storm assault launched on the city at six gates, [52r] after midsummer on a Monday (on Grever Market[271]), in the morning as it was becoming light.[272] They'd carried out an assault bombardment and knocked down six gates and some towers as well,

267. Apparently, Gresbeck means that the man was considered underage.
268. I.e., the divorced wife of the young man remarried.
269. For Anabaptist preaching houses, see 2r.
270. Another overgeneralization. Clearly not all of the Hollanders and Frisians could have been preachers, though apparently it seemed that way to Gresbeck.
271. Grever market ("grever markt") was a Westphalian market. Gresbeck here uses the medieval practice of referring to dates not by their numbering in the month but by their relation to fixed festivals and holidays in the month.
272. For Kerssenbrock's account of the assault, see *Anabaptistici furoris*, ed. Detmer, 673–79. According to him (ibid., 676), the assault began at dawn (five o'clock in the morning) on August 31, which was in fact a Monday.

and they'd had assault trenches dug around the city.[273] Once they realized in the city that the landsknechts were about to storm the city, the rebaptizers took up position up on the walls with all the women that were in the city, young and old. Not one person remained in the city, apart from the sick and the old. So they manned the walls in strength, and took up defensive positions in expectation of the coming attack of the landsknechts. The rebaptizers longed for the assault and were in great fear. They would shout from the city, "When will you come, then? We've been baking and brewing for three or four days,[274] and the porridge has been ready for a long time. Would you like to come some other time?" In the city, they had made preparations for the assault by boiling water with lime and making tar wreaths[275] and equipping themselves with artillery, and with everything just as if they considered it a matter of life or death. Once the landsknechts were about to launch the assault in the morning, they carried out a bombardment from the camp into the city throughout the night.[276] In the morning, the landsknechts fell upon the city at the six gates and stormed it. The rebaptizers put up a great defense from the city of Münster, shooting and throwing stones and pouring hot water and throwing the burning wreaths, so that the landsknechts had to retreat.[277] The landsknechts launched two assaults outside each gate. [52v] At some gates they launched three. When the landsknechts retreated, they shouted from the city, "Come back! Will you retreat already? The storming had to last at least a whole day!" The rebaptizers had a good shout, since they had a stout city. But if the landsknechts had launched the attack an hour and a half earlier, they would have captured the city. For they waited too long for the day, so that it was too light. When the landsknechts were about to launch the assault in the morning, they held a common assembly outside the city, because they were unwilling to attack since they couldn't agree about the assault. The rebaptizers in the city heard

273. According to Kerssenbrock (*Anabaptistici furoris*, ed. Detmer, 673), the preliminary bombardment began on August 28. He reports that it was so large that it could be heard as far away as sixteen Westphalian miles (about seventy English miles or nearly 120 kilometers).
274. I.e., since the start of the preliminary bombardment.
275. I.e., wreaths covered in pitch that could be set alight and dropped down on the troops attempting to reach the tops of the walls by ladder.
276. Perhaps Gresbeck means that there was a more intensive bombardment directly before the assault. At any rate, this bombardment seems different from the one mentioned above that damaged the gates and towers.
277. See Kerssenbrock, *Anabaptistici furoris*, ed. Detmer, 677–78, for the horrific effects of the boiling water and the wreaths.

this holding of an assembly, and learned that the landsknechts were in disagreement like this. Once the landsknechts retreated, they moved back to their camp. Then the rebaptizers rose up and sang, "If God were not with us at this time, we would have had to fail." They all fell down on their knees and sang. John of Leiden then went around the city with the preachers, and they sang and jumped and were joyous, saying, "Dear brothers, don't we have a strong God? *He* helped us. It's not through our might that this has happened. Let us now be joyous and let us now thank the Father." The Hollanders and Frisians (the criminals) imagined, when they defeated the assault, that they had a winning hand, that they had gotten possession of the whole world. But if the rebaptizers had gone and sat down, leaving the strong God (their Father) to halt the landsknechts' assault, truly [53r] the landsknechts would have won the city from the strong God (the Father).

Aftermath of the victory

Once the assault had taken place, the rebaptizers rebuilt the gates and everything that had been bombarded, and outside every gate they placed a great earthwork, making the city just as strong as it had been before. Then the preachers proclaimed that their relief would come soon. They imagined that the Hollanders and Frisians and all those who were on the side of the baptizing would come and relieve them. This was the relief they counted on. For the preachers informed the common folk that God would descend from heaven and relieve them. If it was the case that God didn't relieve them, then, they would say, there was no God in heaven. They said that Christ would descend from heaven, and walk with them on earth for a thousand years, and rule with His folk, and establish a new world. After the thousand years were over, then the day of the Lord would come and Christ would then turn over His folk to His heavenly Father.[278] They also said, "There are among us here some brothers who will not taste death and are so holy that they'll ascend to heaven." Here they were tempting God too much.[279] If Christ had descended from heaven just as they said, they would have acted [53v] just as the Jews did and stoned Him, when He wouldn't give a sign.[280]

278. This is a fairly clear exposition of the Last Days as laid out in the Book of Revelation. Melchior Hofman expected that these events were to begin to take place in the year 1533.

279. Seemingly, Gresbeck conceives of the Anabaptists as generally tempting God, but here they have gone too far in his estimation.

280. This conception is a peculiar conflation of several biblical passages. In a story in Mark and

John of Leiden has a revelation of his own exaltation

Now, a great revelation came to John of Leiden, that he would be a king over New Israel and the whole world, and would be next to God.[281] In the whole world, there would be no king or lord but John of Leiden, and in the whole world there would be no government but John of Leiden and

---

Matthew, Jesus is asked for a sign by the Pharisees as a means of testing him, and he refuses on the grounds that this request is made in bad faith (Matthew 12:38; Mark 8:11–12). In Mark, he simply leaves after the rebuke, whereas in Matthew this story is connected with a further statement to the effect that the present faithless generation will be given no further sign but the miracle of Jonah (this statement is derived from the so-called Q source; see Luke 11:29–32 and Matthew 12:39–45). Whatever the compositional history of this story, there is no stoning. In John, the Jews, who are portrayed as being collectively hostile to Jesus because of his claims to divinity, threaten to stone him three times. In the first instance, Jesus slips away when the Jews picked up stones after he implies that he's God (8:59). In the second, after Jesus confronts the Jews again, he explicitly validates his claims on the very grounds that he *has* performed miracles (9:32), and soon thereafter people across the Jordan refer to John the Baptist as not having performed "a miraculous sign," in contrast to Jesus, who presumably has. In any case, the Jews reply that they will stone him not because of his miracles but because of his blasphemy (9:33). This time, Jesus doesn't simply slip away but eludes the Jews' attempts to seize him (9:39). Finally, in John 10:31–33, the Jews yet again menace Jesus with stoning, this time not for miracles but for blasphemy. Though the Jews actually do say that they "are stoning" Jesus, seemingly no stones are actually cast, as Jesus then continues to argue with them (10:34–38), and in the end he escapes once more after they try to seize him (10:39). In the present passage, it would seem that these stories are being conflated, so that the Jews' wish to stone him for blasphemy despite his miracles is transferred to the Pharisees' attempt to entrap him by asking him to perform a miracle and his refusal to do so. It should also be noted that the Jews never are actually represented as stoning him, even in John. This version in Gresbeck is simply a reflection of the visceral hostility towards the Jews that was prevalent in late medieval/early modern Germany, where people believed the worst of the Jews and garbled the (already unfavorable) stories in the New Testament to cast the Jews in the most anti-Christian light possible.

281. For Kerssenbrock's account of John of Leiden's installation as king, see *Anabaptistici furoris*, ed. Detmer, 633–39. Kerssenbrock casts the prophet John Dusentschuer (introduced below in a different context; see 62r–63v) as the driving force behind this move (and this is corroborated by a wide range of confessions, including those of John of Leiden and Knipperdolling; see ibid., 634n1). Gresbeck, however, doesn't introduce "the limping prophet" (he apparently cannot even remember the man's name) until after his description of the newly installed king's royal estate (see 55r–60v). Gresbeck indicates that the prophecy that led to the proclamation of John as king came to John himself, but other sources attribute the revelation to Dusentschuer (John of Leiden claims in his confessions that he first received a revelation that God would raise up a new David in the "last days," and that he would fulfill this role, but John prayed to God that he should have someone else make this revelation public, as people would otherwise not believe it. The person who did so was John Dusentschuer. See Niesert, *Münsterische Urkundensammlung*, 178–79; and Cornelius, *Berichte der augenzeugen*, 372). Even if Gresbeck has the details about the revelation wrong, however, he is correct in placing the installation after the defeat of the second storming of the city. Kerssenbrock is somewhat unclear about the exact date, but he states that Dusentschuer's machinations began "after St. James's Day" (ibid., 633), that is, after July 25, the time of the introduction of polygamy (see also note 206 above), and describes both the installation and the establishment of the royal household and government (Kerssenbrock, *Anabaptistici furoris*, ed. Detmer, 646–67) before his description of the second assault. Other literary sources place the installation even earlier, but any dating before the second assault is disproved by various contemporary sources that indicate that the installation took place in the first week or so of September, in the aftermath of the defeat of the second assault (see ibid., 633n3). Gresbeck doesn't give an exact date for the installation, but he clearly agrees with the later sources in placing the installation directly after the defeat of the assault.

whoever of the rebaptizers he appointed. So John of Leiden proclaimed the revelation to the common folk, saying that God had revealed to him in this way that he would be a king of the righteous and punish the unrighteousness in the world and be next to God. The common folk in the city kept quiet. As for the revelation, one person believed it and the other not. The leaders in the city of the rebaptizers—the preachers along with Knipperdolling and Bernard Krechting and Henry Krechting and Tilbeck and even more of them—agreed about this. It was them, the leaders of the rebaptizers, who made John of Leiden a king. The common man in the city didn't make John of Leiden a king. John of Leiden continued, "Now God has chosen me as a king over the whole world. But I say to you, dear brothers and sisters, I would much rather be a swineherd and much rather hold the plough or dig ditches than be such a king. What I do, I must do, [54r] for God has chosen me for this. Dear brothers and sisters, let us thank God for this." Then they got up and sang a German hymn, "To God on high alone be glory"[282] and each then went back home.

The new king sets up his court

Then the king decked himself out in accordance with his royal estate, and then appointed councilors[283] and all the commanders, as befits a territorial lord.[284] First, he abolished the twelve elders, as I stated earlier.[285] After that, he appointed Knipperdolling as a viceroy,[286] and Tilbeck became master of the court,[287] and he manned his court with burghers and Frisians and

282. This is the vernacular version of the Gregorian chant "Gloria in excelsis deo."

283. There were four regular councilors (Gerard tom Kloster, Bernard Krechting, Henry Redeker, and Gerard Reyning) with Christian Kerckering acting as a sort of chairman to settle disagreements (Kerssenbrock, *Anabaptistici furoris*, ed. Detmer, 647).

284. "Territorial lord" ("landesher") signifies the ruler of a land in the Holy Roman Empire who has no sovereign above him apart from the theoretical (and ineffectual) powers of the emperor himself. In practice, such rulers held full governmental power. For Kerssenbrock's account of the king's court, see *Anabaptistici furoris*, ed. Detmer, 646–50.

285. The mention of the abolition of the twelve elders actually follows (54v). Either the reference here is a mistake or perhaps Gresbeck thinks that the abolition is implicit in John of Leiden's indication that the revelation appointing him as king also dictated that only those appointed by him would hold office (53v).

286. See *Anabaptistici furoris*, ed. Detmer, 646, for Kerssenbrock's discussion of the appointments. In the regular practice of the bishopric, upon the death or resignation of the bishop, his administrative duties were carried out by a board until the chosen successor was duly confirmed. The term for the members of this board was *vicarius* in Latin and *stadtholder* in the vernacular (ibid., 194). This title was adapted to designate the king's "deputy" (the German term literally means "placeholder"), and so is translated as "viceroy" here.

287. I.e., *Hofmeister*. See Kerssenbrock, *Anabaptistici furoris*, ed. Detmer, 647, for this appointment.

Hollanders, so that the king had a great retinue. The king also appointed attendants, cooks, butlers, all offices, just as befits a lord. In this way, the king filled all the offices, apart from that of executioner. This office was performed by the king and by Knipperdolling themselves.[288] Whoever in the city of Münster wished to could carry out the office.[289] Then John of Leiden, the new king, made his first housewife a queen.[290] The king didn't make his other wives queens. These were the queen's underwives, being the king's concubines (play wives).[291] The queen also appointed her own councilors and servants and attendants, just as the king did.[292] So the king held a court by himself with his servants, and the queen held a court by herself with her fellow wives and her servants.

The new king establishes a cavalry force

[54v] The king had all the horses that were serviceable for riding brought together up to the cathedral square. The king took all the horses and kept them in his court, and to each of his chief officers he gave a horse. He read out the names of all those who could ride and were strong enough to bear a lance. These men had to go on horseback, and he grouped them all together. He also grouped together those who were to ride as marksmen. In this way, he made a company of cavalrymen. The king rode up and down up at the cathedral square and examined the horses. The cavalrymen divided into two companies. Those with the lances rode by themselves over on one side, and the marksmen rode by themselves over on the other. Eventually, the two companies ran against each other, the riders with lances against the marksmen, just as if they were going

288. Knipperdolling had been appointed to this post back at the time of the creation of the twelve elders (Kerssenbrock, *Anabaptistici furoris*, ed. Detmer, 573).

289. Presumably a reference to the procedure by which anyone who wished could participate in the execution of those who had joined Mollenhecke's rebellion (50r).

290. On 147r, Gresbeck makes it clear that Mathias's widow was his queen, and so it seems that in the present passage, she is the one being described as the "first housewife." If this is meant to be a chronological reference, it's wrong, as Knipperdolling's stepdaughter was his first wife in Münster (see also note 206). Perhaps, however, Gresbeck is using the term "first" to signify precedence (it's clear that the connection with Mathias's widow the queen had dynastic overtones, although nothing much is made of Knipperdolling's generally unnamed stepdaughter; see 147r). Could Gresbeck have confused precedence in status with temporal priority?

291. "Play wife" is a way of rendering of "spilfrouw," a comparatively uncommon Germanic term (=High German *Spielfrau*) for the Latinate word "concubine" and literally means a "woman for play" (as opposed to the proper wife). For a list of John's wives, see Kerssenbrock, *Anabaptistici furoris*, ed. Detmer, 657–59.

292. For Kerssenbrock's account of the queen's court, see *Anabaptistici furoris*, ed. Detmer, 661–62.

to fight a battle together, so that they would learn how to marshall themselves, whether they were to come to the enemy right away or on the morrow.

The king replaces the military commanders

So the king renovated everything in the city. He removed the twelve elders, who'd held power in the city, and he removed all the commanders—captains and other officers—who'd previously held command. Everything had to be renovated. The king also appointed new captains and a new chief captain.[293] This man was to be the field captain over all the captains in the city.[294] There were as many captains as there were gates in the city, [55r] and the chief captain was above them all.[295] Whenever the captains now had something to take care of, all the captains had to come every Friday to the chief captain in his house. Whatever need there was among the captains they reported to the chief captain. Or if the captains had someone who was unwilling to follow orders, he would be accused there before all the captains. The chief captain would have any man who was accused fetched (have him come before him). If he couldn't explain himself, he had to go sit in chains. Depending on how his faith had been and what help he'd given to the rebaptism or whether he'd been opposed to the baptizing, he received mercy and they winked at it.[296]

The king announces the appointments of his new officials

The king had a great chair covered on all sides with pieces of silk cloth placed up at the marketplace.[297] The king arrived very magnificently with

293. "Hoeptman" signified the commander of a regiment of landsknechts, and the word gives rise to the modern German term for "captain." The phrase "oberster hoeptman" ("chief captain") signifies the regimental commander who held overall command when there were several regiments operating together, and the term gives rise to the High German term for "colonel" (*Oberste*).

294. The "field" captain would hold overall command during an expedition in the field, outranking the captains of individual regiments. In effect, this is a functional term for the "chief captain."

295. See *Anabaptistici furoris*, ed. Detmer, 650, for Kerssenbrock's list of the new officers. This list is based on the positions for a field army (see also note 383 below), and so does not correspond to Gresbeck's conception here. Kerssenbrock's list refers to the later establishment of the field army, which, as Gresbeck makes clear (69v), was not established until October as part of the planned departure for the Promised Land. Only then were the field officers appointed. There is no way to know which if any of these eight positions was held at this time by the men later appointed as officers in the field army.

296. Logic dictates that Gresbeck should have added "or was punished," but he seems to have lost track of the start of the sentence and ends as if he had begun with "anyone who was a real rebaptizer."

297. For a similar description of the court of justice and the royal procession, see Kerssenbrock,

his councilors and master of the court and his attendants and his vice-roy Knipperdolling and all the preachers, and the king sat on his horse, which was covered with a cloth. The king went and sat on his throne. He was magnificently decked out with velvet and silk garments and gold chains and gold rings on his fingers,[298] and they carried the sword before the king. Once the king was sitting on his throne, the councilors sat around him, and the preachers and the attendants stood around him. [55v] Stutenberent then went and stood up on a bench and read out a list in which were written all those who would be the king's servants. He called up each in the common assembly by name, reading each out, "Knipperdolling, a viceroy. Tilbeck, the king's master of the court. . . ." In this way, he named each one in a row, indicating what office each would have. When this reading was done, the king had them invited to his house, where he held court. Eventually, the king said, "Dear brothers and sisters, as for my having chosen my councilors and all the servants that I need for my royal estate, the only reason why I do this is so that each one should learn and know how to marshal themselves if I have to go forth right away or on the morrow. Otherwise, I have no further need of servants and also don't want a viceroy within Münster, except right away or on the morrow when I'm going to go forth into the world for the sake of God." In this way, the king came into his estate and he remained in this estate right until the end.

Regalia of the new officials

On the next day, the councilors and all those who were to be the king's servants came to him in his court. The king then addressed them, instructing each one as to how he should conduct himself. The king straightaway liveried all his servants,[299] the hoses clearly distinguished crosswise red and grey, the one red and the other grey,[300] and on their coats dress sleeves onto which was stitched the world with a cross above

---

Anabaptistici furoris, ed. Detmer, 662–68.

298. "Gold chains" signifies a golden necklace that served as a sign of office. For two examples of surviving gold chains that could conceivably date to the Anabaptist rule in Münster and for a copy of an excessively large gold coin that was probably struck to serve as decoration (with discussions by Berndt Thier), see Albrecht et al., *Das Königreich der Täufer*, 68–70, 76.

299. See Kerssenbrock, *Anabaptistici furoris*, ed. Detmer, 655–56, for a much shorter description of the servants' clothing.

300. Presumably, what Gresbeck means is that the red stocking had a grey cross and vice versa.

and two swords stuck through it.[301] He also liveried his attendants, with magnificent silkwork, velvet doublets, and hose of the best cloth all made à la landsknecht, [56r] and they wore clothing that was all slit up.[302] (In the beginning, when they started the baptizing, they didn't have any slit clothes. At that time they wanted to be so holy that they wouldn't wear such clothes. These clothes were in the manner of the world and the flesh. A life like this, the way the godless lived, they couldn't have.) At first, the king's cavalrymen had a distinctive sort of clothing made out of vestments. Out of the absolutely smoothest silkwork they had the cavalrymen's overcoats made for half the body, so that the one arm[303] was without sleeve and the breast was half without coat, so that it was impressive[304] on horseback. That's how the king liveried his cavalrymen, too. The king then liveried all his household staff in red coats covered over with grey trim, the sleeve also having the world stitched on it, just as the other livery was made. All his other servants, be it garment cutters or shoemakers, bakers or brewers—whatever the office, they all wore the king's livery. The king had a gatekeeper in front of each gate, and they too had a distinctive livery, also red covered with grey trim, with a key stitched on one sleeve, so that they would remember to unlock and lock the gates. Each of his servants had a gold ring on his finger, some a ring of five guilders, some one of eight guilders, some one of twelve guilders, and some one of twenty guilders. Depending on what the man was like and what his command was, he got a corresponding ring.

301. For a fuller discussion of John of Leiden's coat of arms, see 56v.

302. The point of the reference to landsknechts is that they were reputed for flamboyance, and a particular element of this was to have their outergarments slit, so that their colorful undershirt could be pulled through the slits and thus become conspicuous. For an extended discussion with illustrations, see Richards, *Landsknecht Soldiers*, 30–42.

303. The word translated as "arm" is "ermel" in the original. Etymologically, this is a diminutive of the word "arm," and in High German is the regular word for "sleeve" ("ermel"). The regular word in Low German for sleeve is "moüüe" (used quite frequently by Gresbeck), and clearly it's meaningless to say that the "sleeve was sleeveless." Since the normal "sleeve" was a fairly bulky item that was attached to the garment (it could be removed) and was used for storing things (for such a use, see 50r, 141r), perhaps "ermel" is used here to indicate a tight-fitting covering of the upper arm (otherwise, the arm would be bare).

304. The original reading ("ruchtych") means "well-known, with a (good or bad) reputation," but the corrector changed this to a reading ("ruterich") meaning "like a knight, cavalryman." This certainly seems to make more sense with the subject "it" and the adverbial phrase "on horseback," though perhaps the original expression was a somewhat clumsy way of saying "so that wearing this attire on horseback made an impression that was much talked about."

The king's own regalia

Once the king had chosen all his servants, great and small, noble and non-noble, he had them in his court.[305] [56v] But they didn't wish to keep the one better than the other, and the one was supposed to have as much as the other. But with this they took a false step.[306] The king had also decked himself out. He'd done so a little at the time when he'd received the revelation that he was to be a king. But with this they were playing the fool (buffoonery). Now he decked himself out magnificently along with his servants, and he had himself made a velvet coat, and magnificent hose and doublet of magnificent silkwork, and a magnificent golden cap, and a velvet bonnet with a crown, and a sword with a golden sheath, and an armor dagger[307] with a golden sheath, and many golden chains, which he wore around his neck.[308] The king had a golden chain, and on this chain he had the world hung, just like his coat of arms, with a golden round orb.[309] This was a blue speckled (colorful) orb, and the stone on top was grey and blue. I can't write any more about whether the stone was a gemstone. This stone was mounted all around just as the world is painted, being hung around with gold,[310] and on top of the orb there was a golden cross, and there were two swords stuck through it. The king would wear this chain around his neck. He also wore silk cords around his neck, and on these were bent the most beautiful gold that there

305. This sentence is somewhat defectively composed, and this is a conjectural restoration of sense.
306. That is, Gresbeck is objecting to the evident contradiction between the ideal of egalitarianism underlying the communal ownership of property on the one hand and the elitism inherent in the court hierarchy and its material manifestation in varying attire and decorations on the other. Once again, Gresbeck's words seem to suggest that he accepts the Anabaptists' principles (though if he'd been challenged on the point, he could have said that he was simply pointing out their hypocrisy).
307. An "armor dagger" ("panser degen") was a short dagger with a straight blade used for stabbing.
308. For the king's attire, see Kerssenbrock, *Anabaptistici furoris*, ed. Detmer, 650–55.
309. The coat of arms is described at length in Kerssenbrock, *Anabaptistici furoris*, ed. Detmer, 652–53. Note that it contained the motto "Ein koninck der gerechticheit über all" ("A king of righteousness over everything/everywhere"), which signified his pretensions to universal rule (cf. 59v for similar phraseology about the king's claims).
310. Perhaps Gresbeck is referring here to the sorts of roundels that appear around the edge of early maps of the world. The gold setting of the stone could be conceived of as surrounding it in a similar way.

was in the city, consisting of ducats,[311] rose nobles,[312] angelots,[313] crowns, and gold guilders,[314] so that the king decked himself out very magnificently. What the king had on his horse—the equipment and trappings—was also all covered with gold. For I hold that there was silver on the trappings, [57r] and it was gilded. The king also had two gilded spurs. I also hold that these too were made of silver and gilded over. It may well have been pure gold. On the saddle the trappings were also gilded. In this way, the king decked himself out magnificently along with his servants. It was all the Father's will that he should deck himself out in this way. For the king said that he was dead to the flesh and had no arrogance in this, but was doing it for the glory of God. For this reason he was certainly allowed to wear it, and all those who were dead to the world and the flesh were free to wear anything. They would still sit on silver seats and still eat from a silver table setting. No more attention should be paid to silver and gold than to muck and other stones, so worthless should gold and silver be. Yet, the common man couldn't get any of his money or his silver and gold back. But the king and the councilors who wore this and had it in their hands[315]—this king and the preachers would say to the folk that they shouldn't live in accordance with the flesh and the world, and that there should be nothing but the spirit in a person. So completely was he supposed to be dead to the world! And every one of the preachers, Hollanders and Frisians, and the real rebaptizers still wanted to have just as many wives as they wished. Whenever the flesh would be dead like this in a person, he wouldn't covet so many wives, and he should actually live without a wife. In the end, [57v] they were dead to the flesh, and being nothing but skin and bones,[316] they were so starving that they let all their wives go.[317]

311. The ducat was a variety of gold coin first minted in Sicily in the twelfth century. The denomination proved very popular, and local issues were minted all over Europe, the most famous of which is that of Venice. The name is derived from the fact that the legend of the coin includes the Latin word *ducatus* ("duchy").

312. A current variety of English gold piece worth eighty pence (one-third of a pound).

313. This is the French term for a variety of English gold piece from the fifteenth century worth ten shillings. The name comes from the fact that the coins had an angel on the obverse.

314. The terms "crown" and "guilder" are rather too vague to specify which coins in particular Gresbeck has in mind.

315. Again, Gresbeck is noting the hypocrisy of the royal magnificence, and at the same time he seems to be making something of a joke. The expression "to have in one's hands" is used elsewhere by Gresbeck to mean "to engage" in an activity, but here this metaphorical phrase is quite literal (given that the king and his retinue are wearing other people's gold as rings!).

316. More of Gresbeck's wry sense of humor. He refers to the starvation that would soon strike the city.

317. For the Anabaptists' dismissal of all but their first wives because of their inability to feed them, see 139r.

Chains of office and rings for the new officials

So the king decked out himself, and his councilors and his building masters and viceroy and chief captain and his chancellor. For each of them he had a great silver chain around the body made, and this chain went around under the arms and over the head across the shoulders. The chain had great, wide links and was finely made. They also had landsknechts' daggers made, the scabbard covered with silver and the cover on the dagger studded with silver. They also had some short armor daggers, which also had silver sheaths. They also had great gold rings on their fingers, and they were magnificently clothed with magnificent coats. They got these coats in the city, from the rich people that they'd driven out of the city. They would wear this livery on the street when they accompanied the king. The other captains and officers didn't have this. They got no more silver than a chape[318] on the dagger and a gold ring and the livery (as I've described).

Regalia of the queen, her officials, and the viceroy

Now that the king had decked himself out along with his councilors, he decked out his queen along with all the wives. The king [58r] decked out the queen along with her servants very magnificently, just as magnificently, indeed, as he'd done for himself. But all his wives were not as magnificently decked out as the queen was. The queen had also liveried her servants just as the king had liveried them, in red, not two colors. Similarly, the viceroy had also liveried his servants, red coats with a sword stitched on the sleeve and blue clouds stitched under the sword. The king had commanded the viceroy to take the sword, so that he should execute with it. So the viceroy would carry out the executions himself, or his servants would. In the end, the king would also carry out executions. When the viceroy would go through the streets or sermons would be given, he had two great battle swords carried behind him. One time, someone fled from the camp to the city, and he was a landsknecht.[319] They brought him to the heathen house.[320] They wanted

318. A *chape* is a metal tip for a leather scabbard to prevent the tip from poking through the leather.

319. This anecdote seems to have no connection with what precedes except as an illustration of an execution carried out by the sort of battle sword used by the viceroy's servants.

320. Actually, there were two "heathen houses," that is, houses in which the non-Anabaptists (considered heathens, 40r, 46r) would be instructed in the new faith. According to Kerssenbrock (*Anabaptistici furoris*, ed. Detmer, 632), these were set up in the aftermath of the suppression of Mollen-

to have him taught the faith, and then he was to have himself baptized. Once the knecht was in the city, he'd certainly wished to get away again, so he asked the king for permission to go off. The king said yes, he would have permission to be gone. So they brought the knecht to the gate in the evening and were going to set him on his way. [58v] They said to the landsknecht, "Now go off on your way," so the knecht went off on his way. Presently, someone came up behind him with a battle sword and cut off his head. They said, "Now go on to wherever you wish." Many a landsknecht rushed to the city in the beginning, thinking that they would receive their monthly pay, and some landsknechts fled to the city from the camp who were still in the service of My Gracious Lord and had received their pay. They acted as criminals. That man[321] killed them for the most part in the city, shooting the one, beheading the other.

Magnificence of the court

Once the king along with his queen and all the king's and the queen's servants had decked themselves out, they had it proclaimed to the common folk in the preaching that no one should get angry with the king or the queen or the councilors or the other servants, and that no one should take offense at them, because God had selected them for this and set them in their estate, and everyone should stick to the estate that was their calling.[322] One time, the king together with his queen rode in this magnificent way to the market, and they were going to give a sermon. The king had his throne covered magnificently with silkwork, and the throne stood so high that he sat above everyone,[323] and below the throne many benches stood in a circle in front of it. The queen had a house on the marketplace, directly opposite the throne. [59r] There, the queen fitted this house with a half-door hung with drapes and two silk cushions of red velour (velvet).[324] So one morning

---

hecke's rebellion at the instigation of John of Leiden as prophet.

321. I.e., the king?

322. The conception here is somewhat untranslatable. The medieval notion was that everyone had a status (estate) to which he was called (his "vocation," to use the Latinate term), and it was a violation of the natural order for a person to step out of the place to which he had been called (by God).

323. According to Kerssenbrock (*Anabaptistici furoris*, ed. Detmer, 663), it was on a dais that was three steps above ground level.

324. A "half-door" signifies a door split in two horizontally, the two halves being capable of opening or closing separately. Such doors were normally used as a counter from which sales could be made, but the point here is to allow the queen to observe the activity in the marketplace while remaining in the house. Oddly enough, such doors are called "Dutch doors" in North America. Perhaps their origin

the queen rode to the marketplace and had a riding horse on which she sat, and it was decked over with a cover. The king had his councilors walk in front of him, and all his servants walked in front of and behind him, as did his master of the court with a white staff, and his lackey[325] ran beside the horse, and his attendants ran on all sides of him.[326] In this way he rode to the market when a sermon was about to be given. The queen had similarly decked herself out, and also had a courser decked out with a sidesaddle and a cover hung around. In this way, the queen too rode to the marketplace. When the king reached the marketplace, all the folk, male and female, young and old, were already there, having come to see the king, and they did reverence to him. The king went and sat on his throne, and his councilors, attendants, and preachers, and all his servants went and sat below on the benches. The viceroy[327] went and sat at the king's feet. The viceroy went and sat next to him, and then the councilors did so and preachers. Once the king was sitting on his throne, two small youths stood on either side of the king. The young man on the right-hand side had a book in his hand, which was the Old Testament, and the other young man on the left-hand side had a drawn sword in his hand.[328] The young man who stood on the right-hand side and had the Old Testament in his hand signified that the king would set himself in God's place and seat himself on the throne of David (in David's place), [59v] and was to proclaim anew the Word of God, which had been cast in shadow for a long time. The young man on the left-hand side with the sword signified that he was a king of the righteous and a king over the entire world, and was to punish all unrighteousness. Now that the king entered into the Holy Place,[329]

---

is not from the Netherlands proper but from the whole lowland territory of northwestern Europe, including Westphalia.

325. Caspar Wynschenck (Kerssenbrock, *Anabaptistici furoris*, ed. Detmer, 648).

326. See Kerssenbrock, *Anabaptistici furoris*, ed. Detmer, 663–64, for the royal procession. The master of the court was Tilbeck, and the attendants numbered twenty-eight (ibid., 649, with names).

327. Knipperdolling.

328. One of the young men was Christopher of Waldeck, the natural son of the prince-bishop. One day during the siege, he inadvertently strayed too close to city and was captured by the Anabaptists, who brought him into the city. The king was pleased with the young man's appearance, and used him as a prop in his court. For the two young attendants and the identification of one as Waldeck, see Kerssenbrock, *Anabaptistici furoris*, ed. Detmer, 664, and ibid., 664n3.

329. The phrase translated as "Holy Place" ("das hillige") is seemingly derived from Hebrews 9–10. There, Paul (or whoever wrote the book) makes a comparison of the sacrifices of the Jews at the Temple with the sacrifice of Jesus at the crucifixion. The "Holy Place" refers to the inner sanctum or holy of holies, the innermost room of the Temple, which was entered only once a year, by the high priest alone, to give sacrifice in atonement for the sins of the nation. Jesus is said to have entered the Holy Place as a metaphorical high priest (9:10–11). Paul then indicates that because of Jesus's sacrifice of himself, the Christians may also enter this metaphorical "Holy Place" (10:19). The present passage

and the Apostolic Church was ready,³³⁰ and the king had converted all the folk in the city of Münster (New Israel), because he'd reproclaimed the Word of God anew and had punished all unrighteousness within the city of Münster (but only in the city), Münster was an example to the entire world. The king as well as the preachers imagined that they would take possession of the entire world, just as they had Münster. So the king switched the two small youths who stood beside him. He placed on the left hand the young man who had stood on the right-hand side, and he placed on the right hand the young man who had stood on the left-hand side. This switching of places signified this much, that he had once more brought forth the Word of God. When the king placed on the left hand the young man with the Old Testament who had stood on the right hand, this signified this much, that he had reproclaimed the Word of God anew and was going to prevail. That the young man with the sword on the left hand had to go to the right hand signified that he was to go on punishing all unrighteousness and had punished it. The king and the preachers imagined that in this way they would take possession of the whole world and would have the upper hand just as they did in Münster (and the king together with the Hollanders and Frisians and all the rebaptizers along with their retinue did have it). So [60r] they carried out this foolishness with the young men with the book and the sword before the common folk, and made the poor people (some of them) so blind. Some who helped carry out this rule did know better, but as for some of the simple people, they didn't know any better and imagined that things were to be so. Those who already knew better had to keep quiet,³³¹ and they dared not reply that they'd undertaken such buffoonery, or the king would have had them all beheaded. So the king went and sat on his throne between the two young men. These two young men always stood beside the king until the end.³³² Whenever they gave sermons

---

would seem to imply that John of Leiden resembled Christ in entering the Holy Place by himself. Later, the image seems to refer to the entry of all the Anabaptists (83r), as in the later section in Paul, and in another passage (94r–v), the phrase "enter the Holy Place" clearly means to become an acceptable member of the Anabaptist community. Note also that Hebrews 9:23–24 refers to "examples" of things, and the German word for this ("vorbild") is also the word that appears at the end of this sentence.

330. For the "Apostolic Church," see also note 142.

331. Note the adverb "already." Seemingly, Gresbeck counts himself among those with reservations. Could the adverb imply that he was already beginning to have doubts at this stage? If so, was this actually the case or is he retroactively importing into earlier events his later disillusionment?

332. Actually, Christopher of Waldeck fled the city on June 2, 1535 (see Kerssenbrock, *Anabaptistici furoris*, ed. Detmer, 648n8), but this took place after Gresbeck's flight from the city and presumably he was unaware of it.

up at the marketplace, the king would always arrive magnificently like this up at the marketplace. When there was going to be a sermon, a preacher would always stand up on a bench in front of the king, and he would have a pulpit standing in front of him on which his book lay open. When there was something of importance to the king to be said, Stutenberent would normally give the Word. He was the king's orator (his pleader).[333] Once the preaching was going on, the queen followed on horseback with her servants and attendants, with a lackey beside the horse. When she arrived up at the market, she had to ride through the folk to the house in which she would take her place. Some of the people had to stand up and let her ride through with her servants and fellow wives. These fellow wives followed her in a row two by two. So the queen went and took her place at her window and also listened to the sermon. Once the sermon was over, the king got up from his throne [60v] and went back and sat on his horse, and he rode back home with his servants just as he'd ridden out. The queen too rode back home just as she'd come. The other folk then sang a German hymn, and they too went home. This was the first time that the king with his queen rode so magnificently to the market for a sermon.

The king's progress on horseback

Now that the king was decked out like this, he one time rode magnificently through the city to all the gates, and then went out the gate and inspected the camp. But he didn't ride out far from the city, from one gate to the next outside the city. The king had on a velvet overcoat, and what he had on him was all gold—gold chains and sheaths. The inlay on the trappings that the horse had on was all gilded. His spurs were all gilded, as I've described before.[334] All the cavalrymen and servants on horseback and on foot rode with the king, and the attendants ran on all sides of him. The king rode in the middle of the cavalrymen, and the marksmen rode in front of the king together with his master of the court and the councilors (some of them).

---

333. Kerssenbrock calls Rothman the "royal orator" (*Anabaptistici furoris*, ed. Detmer, 647). The term "orator" signifies someone who pleads the case for a prince or state in diplomatic transactions. In his original text, Gresbeck gave two alternative German expressions for this position: *vorrderner* ("representative speaker") and *worthelder* ("pleader"). The better-educated editor of the text replaced the first with *advocatus*, the corresponding Latin term.

334. See 57r.

The master of cavalry[335] along with the other cavalrymen rode behind the king, and beside the king his lackey also ran beside the horse. This is how the king rode through the city. When the king rode in this way through the city, the folk ran up the streets to see him. [61r] Wherever he rode before the folk, they did reverence to him. They curtsied and bowed to him.[336] The old women stood in the streets and said, "Welcome in the name of the Lord! Praised be the Father!" Some men and women would certainly have been glad if he'd been before a thousand devils.[337] The old women imagined only that the king was God Himself, so blind had he made these old women. They were led astray (grace is better than right).[338]

Henricus becomes a preacher

Now that John of Leiden was king, they had no prophet who could produce any lies, so there arose a prophet who produced great lies.[339] His name was Henricus, and he was a schoolmaster in the city. He knew that the baptizing was in Münster.[340] To this prophet something was once revealed. He expounded this before the common folk in a sermon—how a voice had

335. John of Kursener (Kerssenbrock, *Anabaptistici furoris*, ed. Detmer, 650).

336. It's clear from the description on 102v that "nigen" (Higher German *neigen*) signifies the physical act of honor known in English as a "curtsy" (i.e., lowering the body by extending one leg forward at the knee and bending the other backwards, while at the same time lowering the head). Although in English, curtsying is restricted to females, in Münster men would use this practice as well. As for the "bowing" here, the German here literally says "bent themselves," which presumably signifies bending the upper body forward at the waist.

337. The expression "be before a thousand devils" is apparently a popular expression meaning to "be consigned to the worst section of hell." Here, "devils" means the lesser demons subordinate to the devil (Satan).

338. The parenthetical phrase is a legal proverb. It normally means that it's better to be merciful than to enforce the law strictly (cf. the English "a king's face should give grace"). In the present context, this presumably means that it's preferable to adopt the view that the old women had been fooled by the Anabaptist regime into acting as they did (thereby shifting the blame to the Anabaptist leadership) rather than to assume that they knew full well what they were doing (also recall how elsewhere Gresbeck contrasts those who acted out of ignorance with those who knew better; see also note 228). It should be noted that the use of this proverb seems to imply that Gresbeck's view was that the women were in fact culpable.

339. Gresbeck doesn't really mean that John of Leiden was the only liar among the Anabaptist preachers, and the statement here is merely an indication of his distaste for the new preacher, who yields pride of place as chief liar only to John of Leiden (and in the next paragraph is displaced by a new liar!). Cf. the statement at the end of 63r that "they were all together" responsible.

340. This is Henricus (Henry) Graes of Borken. Nothing is known about how he became a schoolmaster or the background to his emergence as a prophet (apart from what Gresbeck says here). He becomes prominent only later once he's captured during his mission as an apostle to Osnabrück and betrays the Anabaptists (see 74v–75v). Like many men of higher education in late medieval and early modern Germany, he adopted a Latinate form of his name by which he was known even by speakers of the vernacular (like Gresbeck).

come to him at night and three times said, "Prepare, prepare, prepare!" He had been terrified at this and was in great fear, not knowing what this voice meant. The voice came back the next night at midnight, and again it said three times, "Prepare!" He was terrified again, not knowing what the voice meant and what he was supposed to prepare. The third night, the prophet didn't go to bed but sat up all night on his knees in his bedroom, praying to God to reveal to him what he was supposed to prepare. Then the voice [61v] came back to him, and three times more it said, "Prepare!" So he sat on his knees and said, "Dear Father, what am I supposed to prepare?" The voice answered to him, "You're to proclaim great joy to My people." Then the voice went away again. The prophet then stood up and thanked the Father. He then informed the king and the prophets of this revelation. On the next day, the king had a sermon given. The prophet stood up on a bench in front of the king and proclaimed his revelation to the people, how three nights in a row a voice had in this way said to him, "Prepare!" and how on the third night he'd gotten on his knees in his bedroom and prayed to God to reveal what he was supposed to prepare. The voice said to him that he was to proclaim great joy to His folk. When the prophet had uttered this, the king stood up and said to the common folk, "Dear brothers and sisters, let us thank the Father for this," and he went onto his knees. The folk then went on their knees, and they sang a German hymn and praised the Father for his good deed. Then everyone went home. Henricus then remained a prophet. This revelation was lying and buffoonery, as it all was.

The limping preacher sets a limit on clothing

[62r] So there stood up another prophet after this prophet. He too could produce great lies.[341] He would say that there would never ever be any more mercy, and they were all going to sink down into hellfire and burn up. Because he could shout and terrify the folk this way, they made him into a prophet. This prophet had much rule in the city, and would curse all the folk who they imagined were still unfaithful and wouldn't be obedient. The king and the councilors and the preachers informed the common

---

341. This man was John Dusentschuer. He had previously played the major role in the installation of John of Leiden as king (see also note 281), but Gresbeck seems entirely to have forgotten about this and only introduces him here, after his discussion of the new royal court. Apparently, Gresbeck recalled only his involvement in the clothing decree and the subsequent dispatch of the apostles to various towns. It's remarkable that Gresbeck has apparently even forgotten the man's name.

folk that God had made him into a prophet. But it was the king and the councilors and the preachers who'd made him a prophet. Whenever the prophet produced a lie, he would say, "God has said to me" what had supposedly been revealed to him. One time, it was revealed to him how much clothing a Christian brother and a Christian sister were supposed to have.[342] A Christian brother was not supposed to have more than one coat, two pairs of hose, two doublets, and three shirts.[343] As for hoods and bonnets and for shoes, no decision was made about how many of these each individual should have. A Christian sister was not supposed to have more than one chemise, one dress, one pelt, two collars, two pairs of sleeves, two pairs of hose, and four shirts. Whatever further clothing each of the men and women had, they had to turn over. They also left each bed according to how many people were in the house,[344] four pairs of sheets for each bed. Throughout the city, the deacons then went around with a wagon in each parish, stopping at each house. The deacons went [62v] into the houses and said, "God's peace be with you, dear brothers and sisters. I've come at God's behest, as our prophet has proclaimed for God's sake, and I'm to examine what you have in your house. If you have more than you need,

342. John of Leiden twice says in confessions that Dusentschuer became known as a prophet because of his preaching that in light of the siege everyone had to turn over property, in one instance specifying "their money and property, clothing and jewelry" (Cornelius, *Berichte der augenzeugen*, 372) and in the other speaking more generally of making "all property common" (Niesert, *Münsterische Urkundensammlung*, 178). Here, John is confusing Dusentschuer's specific preaching about excess clothing with the much earlier confiscation of gold, silver, and money (21r–22r and also note 114). In any event, John dates the decision about clothing to the period after the suppression of Mollenhecke's rebellion and before his own installation as king (that is, August 1534). Given this confusion on John's part and Gresbeck's own confusion in forgetting about Dusentschuer's role in John's installation as king in early September, it's somewhat hard to choose between their varying dates for the clothing decision (John's in August and Gresbeck's apparent date in September after John's installation), but it seems difficult to imagine that John could have forgotten whether Dusentschuer became prominent through his own installation as king or was already prominent at the time of the installation. Since Gresbeck has apparently forgotten Dusentschuer's involvement in the installation and cannot even recall the man's name, it's perhaps easiest to conclude that John is basically right about the chronology and that Gresbeck was confused about whether the prophesying about clothing took place before or after the second assault on the city. Kerssenbrock gives a short reference to the clothing decree among a list of measures that he attributes to John of Leiden as prophet in the aftermath of the suppression of Mollenhecke's rebellion. In this case, he states (*Anabaptistici furoris*, ed. Detmer, 630) that John of Leiden was following the lead of a sermon given by Schlachtschap.
343. For Kerssenbrock's version of the maximum amounts of clothing allowed, see *Anabaptistici furoris*, ed. Detmer, 638–39.
344. As it stands, the text seems to make little sense (each bed could hardly be left according to the number of inhabitants). Since the number of people who would occupy a bed could vary by status (for instance, younger siblings would presumably share a bed, not to mention the complications of polygamous sleeping arrangements), presumably what Gresbeck means is that the number of beds allowed would have to be determined on an ad hoc basis (rather than by a fixed formula, as with the clothing).

we'll take that from you for God's sake and give it to those who need it. If you need or lack something, we are to give it to you in your necessity for the sake of God." So the deacons examined what each person had in his house. Whatever each person had in the way of clothing beyond what the prophet had proclaimed they took from the people and threw it up into the wagon. But for those who needed something it was difficult enough to get anything back. Some got so little back that they died because of this.[345] The deacons took as much in the way of men's and women's clothing as they could carry away, so that they got a house full of clothes. They gave this clothing to the foreigners who came rushing to the city. (These people had no clothes.[346]) Whether landsknechts or Hollanders and Frisians, these people were clothed with some of the clothing. The deacons kept back the best clothing in expectation of the coming relief. They were expecting a great company of folk who would come to Münster. They were going to clothe them with this, and in expectation of these people, they also slaughtered some cattle, intending to clothe and feed them. The folk who were in the city were supposed to march out, and the foreign folk were supposed to have lived in the city, so that the foreign men would have jointly had the city. They said to the folks that when the foreign brothers and sisters came, whoever [63r] had a big house should receive them as guests until the time when God then revealed who should join the march to the Promised Land,[347] and that so many people were going to come to Münster that six or eight couples would live in one house, and so many brothers and sisters were going to come to Münster (New Israel) that they would be located around Münster for the distance of a half mile.[348] "Our brothers will be placed where the enemy and godless are now placed.[349] Those people are building the houses for our benefit.[350] That's how it will

345. Gresbeck is referring here to the later situation when starvation struck the city, and he's confusing the confiscation of excess clothing relevant to the present passage with the communal possession of food (95v–96r).

346. Obviously, these people were not actually naked. What Gresbeck means is that they didn't have the full (though comparatively limited) wardrobe that a regular person would own.

347. For the impending (and, as it turned out, abortive) "march to the Promised Land," see 66v–70r, and also note 375.

348. It has to be borne in mind that a German mile was substantially larger than an English one, so the distance indicated here is something like two-and-a-half English miles (four kilometers).

349. There's no overt indication in the text that these words are a quotation, but the shift to the present tense and the use of the first person plural forms suggests that Gresbeck is portraying the words that would be said (presumably in sermons) in the city.

350. What is meant is that the construction being carried out by the besiegers would be seized by

IOHAN MATHYS VAN HAERLEEM EEN PROPHEET DER GEESTDRYVERS.

Plate 1: Christoffel von Sichem (1546–1624), *John Matthias*, copper engraving, ca. 1605/6, © Stadtmuseum Münster.

There is no contemporary portrait of Matthias, the charismatic and domineering first leader of the Anabaptists in Münster until his death in battle around Easter 1534. After Matthias's death left a power vacuum in Münster, John of Leiden took advantage of his connection to Matthias via his marriage to Matthias's widow, Diewer, to seize the leadership of the Anabaptists.

A

Plate 2: Heinrich Aldegrever (ca. 1502–55/61), *John of Leiden*, copper
engraving, 1536, © Stadtmuseum Münster.

This is one of the most famous portraits of John of Leiden. The text at the top reads, "John
of Leiden, a king of the Anabaptists at Münster: a true portrait." The text below reads, "Haec
facies, hic cultus erat cum septra tene(rem) / Rex ἀναβαπτιστῶν, set breve tempus ego,"
an elegiac couplet ("This was the face and this the attire when I held the scepter as king of
the Anabaptists, though the time was brief"). Then, after a line indicating that Heinrich
Aldegrever of Soest made the portrait in 1536, the king's motto appears: "Gottes macht ist
myn cracht" ("God's might is my power"). The king's coat of arms appears to the upper left,
which he also wears around his neck, along with rings of office hanging from his shoulders
and his scepter in the crook of his arm.

C

WAERHAFTICH·GEKONTERFET·BERNT·KNIPPERDOLLICK
DER·XII·HERTOGEN············EYN·THO·MONSTER·

IGNOTVS·NVLLIS·KNIPPERDOLLINGIVS·ORIS·
TALIS·ERĀ·SOSPES·CVM·MIHI·VITA·FORET·
HINRICVS·ALDEGREVER·SVXATIĒ·FACI
1536

Plate 3: Heinrich Aldegrever ca. 1502–55/61), *Bernd Knipperdolling*,
copper engraving, 1536, © Stadtmuseum Münster.

The text above reads, "Bernd Knipperdolling, one of the twelve dukes at Münster, truly painted." Below is the elegiac couplet, "Ignotus nullis Knipperdollingius oris / Talis eram sospes, cum mihi vita foret" ("I, the Knipperdolling who was nowhere unknown, looked like this while I was alive"). The final line indicates that Heinrich Aldegrever of Soest made the portrait in 1536. To the upper left is the "sword of righteousness" with which Knipperdolling carried out executions at the behest of John of Leiden. Knipperdolling was a member of the traditional patrician ruling class of Münster, but threw his lot in with John of Leiden. Gresbeck describes the rather fraught relationship between the two men, with Knipperdolling sometimes supporting John as his chief executioner, but sometimes challenging him for the leadership of the Anabaptists. Gresbeck is bitterly hostile to Knipperdolling for supporting the foreign Anabaptists to the detriment of the native population of Münster.

D

Plate 4: Anon., after a portrait by Heinrich Aldegrever (ca. 1502–55/61), *John of Leiden*, woodcut printed in Nuremberg, © Landschaftsverband Westfalen-Lippe.

The heading reads, "John of Leiden, king of the Anabaptists at Münster, absolutely truthfully painted by A.G [=Aldegrever?]." To the left, the box reads, "at the age of twenty-six." The one to the right reads, "Gottes macht ist myn krafft" ("God's might is my power") and above it is John's coat of arms as king.

Plate 5: Anon., after a portrait by Heinrich Aldegrever (ca. 1502–55/61),
Diewer of Haarlem, woodcut, © Landschaftsverband Westfalen-Lippe.

The heading reads, "Gertrude of Utrecht, queen of the Anabaptists at Münster, absolutely truthfully painted by A.G [=Aldegrever?]." To the left, the box reads, "at the age of twenty-four." This portrait is obviously meant to form a pair with the preceding one, the elements in them being mirror images of each other and the two spouses intended to face one another. As for the inaccurate name (John of Leiden is nowhere attested as having a wife with this name), presumably Aldegrever did not know the queen's name and made one up. In any event, the clear intention is to portray John's main wife, Diewer of Haarlem. The (apparently fictitious) coat of arms in the upper left is a split one, with John of Leiden's arms on the right and an odd image of three locusts with the head of kings on the left. It has been hypothesized that the latter is a made-up device meant to signify Diewer's previous marriage to John Matthias (the imagery being suggested by Revelation 9:3–10). Diewer played a crucial role in John of Leiden's royal regime by serving as his main wife and giving John of Leiden legitimacy among the Münster Anabaptists through her connection with John Matthias as his widow and the mother of his child. This is the only contemporary portrait of her, though it is presumably a fantasy drawing of the artist's imagination.

Plate 6: Daniel Hopfer (ca. 1470–1536), *A landsknecht with his wife*, etch-
ing, © Stadtmuseum Münster.
The landsknecht's clothing clearly shows the slit clothing that was imitated in the livery of
John of Leiden's retainers.

Plate 7: Hans Burkmair the elder (1473–1531), *Group of landsknechts*,
    woodcut, © Stadtmuseum Münster.

The flamboyant clothing of this group shows how the landsknechts wished to distinguish
themselves with their individualized garments. Note also the large battle swords that they
brandish.

H

Plate 8: Erhard Schön (after 1491–1542), *Siege of Münster*, woodcut, ca. late 1530s, © Stadtmuseum Münster.

Though the scene is incorrect in its overall topography, the exactitude of certain details suggests that the Nuremberg artist Erhard Schön made this image on the basis of images drawn by an eyewitness. The details perhaps are meant to show the schematic overview of the situation in the fall of 1534: the double moat with earthworks in front, the use of the tower of St. Lambert's as a watchtower, the absence of spires on the cathedral's two towers, the execution place in the main square, the burning windmills, and above all the bombarding artillery in the lower right and the troops approaching the city with storm equipment.

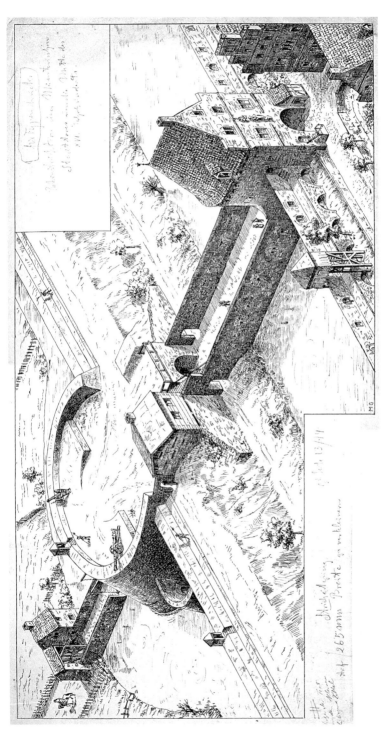

Plate 9: Max Geisberg (1875–1943), *The Cross Gate in 1535*, drawing, ca. 1900, © Stadtmuseum Münster.
The reconstruction of the Cross Gate as it would have appeared in 1535 was drawn by Max Geisberg around 1900 on the basis of his own study of plans and views of the city. This was the gate by which the troops led by Little Hans of Longstreet made their entry into the city using the plan formed by Little Hans and Gresbeck.

Plate 10: One-thaler coin, 1534 (obverse), author's collection.

The surfaces of both sides of this one-thaler coin issued by the Anabaptist regime in Münster are entirely covered by texts that serve as propaganda, laying out the religious and secular claims of the new government. The words that go clockwise around the outside of the observe and continue on the reverse are based on John 3:5: "Whoever is not born of the water and spirit may not / enter into the kingdom of God" ("We nicht gebore(n) is vth de wat[er] vn[d] geist mac nich[t] / in gaen int rike gades"). The outer legend on the reverse then continues: "One king raised over everything [or 'everywhere']" ("Ein koninch upreg over al"). In the center of the obverse is the crucial Anabaptist text (John 1: 14): "The word became flesh and dwells in us" ("The wort is fleisch ge worden vn[d] wanet in vns"). The inner circle on the reverse reads, "One god, one faith, one baptism" ("Ein god, ein gelove, ein doepe"), signifying the Anabaptists' claim to have the one true faith, which is reflected in their believers' baptism. Finally, the innermost text on the reverse gives the date and origin of the coin: "1534 in Münster" ("1534 Tho Munster").

Plate 11: One-thaler coin, 1534 (reverse), author's collection.

L

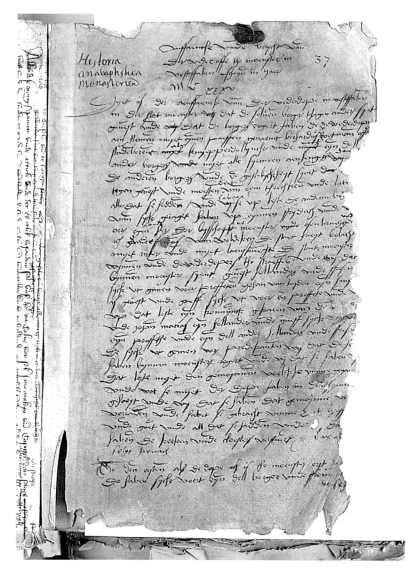

Plate 12: Opening page of the Gresbeck manuscript, © Stadtarchiv Köln.
This the first page of the manuscript of Gresbeck's work that was preserved in the City
Archive (Stadtarchiv) of Cologne. The manuscript was subject to the damage caused by the
collapse of the building housing the City Archive in 2009, and its fate remains unknown
(it was likely freeze-dried along with the other material that suffered water damage, and
may well be recovered at some date in the future). One can see paper loss on the right, but
such loss is mostly restricted to the beginning and end of the manuscript, with the majority
of the paper preserved intact. The somewhat clumsy writing of the main scribe is obvious
to the eye. The Latin heading in the upper left ("historia anabaptistica monasteriensis" or
"Münster anabaptist history") was added by a subsequent reader of the text.

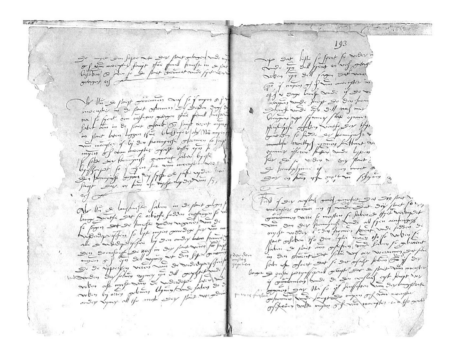

Plate 13: Pages from the end of the Gresbeck manuscript,
 © Stadtarchiv Köln.

These pages (the second and third from the end) illustrate some features of the Cologne manuscript. One can clearly see the headingless "paragraphs" into which the text is divided. In the last paragraph, the dark marginal insertion was made by the original scribe, while the two in lighter-colored ink (and sloppier handwriting) were made by a later reader, who also made changes in the first, second, and ninth line of the paragraph. The later editor also begins at the bottom of the last page here, a long strike-out of text that continues into the text of the next page (the last of the manuscript). All these later changes were incorporated into the derivative manuscript on which Cornelius's 1853 publication of Gresbeck's text was based. One can also see how the last letters of the page on the left begin to disappear into the tight binding of the text into the codex in which the manuscript is preserved. The letters lost to view are few here, but on some pages a few from the of each line become invisible in this way, and the (temporary?) loss of the original manuscript has made it impossible to check the original to ascertain these letters.

N

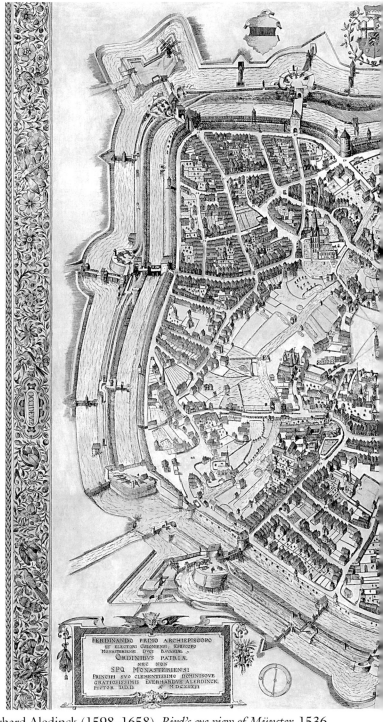

Plate 14: Everhard Aledinck (1598–1658), *Bird's eye view of Münster,* 1536,
    © Stadtarchiv Münster.
This famous overhead map of Münster was created in 1636 by the prominent local painter

O

Everhard Aledinck. Even after the passage of a century, it provides a very clear and accurate
sense of the layout of the city at the time of the Anabaptist regime.

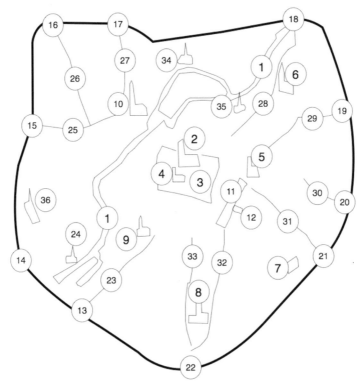

Legend to outline of Alerdinck map of Münster

1. River Aa
2. Cathedral
3. Cathedral Square
4. St. James's Church
5. St. Lambert's Church
6. St. Martin's Church
7. St. Servatius's Church, Nichting's Monastery
8. St. Ludger's Church
9. St. Aegidius' (Tilgen's) Church, St. Tilgen's Monastery
10. Church of Our Dear Lady, Convent-Across-the-Water
11. Main Marketplace
12. Council Hall
13. St. Tilgen's Gate
14. Bisping's Gate or the New Work
15. Our Dear Lady's Gate
16. Jew Fields Gate
17. Cross Gate

18. New Bridge Gate
19. Horst Gate
20. St. Maurice's Gate
21. St. Servatius's Gate
22. St. Ludger's Gate
23. St. Tilgen's Street
24. Bispinghof, St. George's Monastery
25. Our Dear Lady's Street
26. Jew Fields Street
27. Cross Street
28. New Bridge Street
29. Horst Street
30. St. Maurice's Street
31. Salt Street
32. St. Ludger's Street
33. Traditional King's Street
34. St. John's Monastery
35. Grey Monks
36. Brothers' House

look around Münster in terms of houses. The burghers in Münster, who will then leave house and home, will get in other cities in the Promised Land three times as much as they left."

Origins of the limping preacher

The king's councilors, the preachers, the Frisians, and Hollanders intended that all the people in the city should move house, so that they would make an exchange of houses. They all wanted to do this so that the foreign man would have the best houses that there were in the city. This was all undertaken by the preacher that I named before. The common people (the burghers in the city) were unwilling to do this. But some of the burghers were willing, and they moved out of their own houses and moved into other houses that were better. In this way, everyone who wished to remained in his own house.[351] This prophet had been born in the bishopric of Münster, in a city named Warendorf, which lies about three miles from Münster.[352] He had been a goldsmith and was a great swindler. He was responsible for every single thing, just as they all were together.[353] This goldsmith came to Münster at the same time as the [63v] rebaptizing. At first, he made himself out in Münster to be a gunner. For they held this goldsmith to be a half idiot, and he walked with a limp in one leg, since one of his legs was shorter than the other. He was a venturesome person, and he wanted to know about everything. Some people were astonished that this goldsmith had become a prophet, so that the common man was doubtful that he should be a prophet. This prophet would question the menfolk in the street that he knew didn't have more than one wife. He would ask them, "Do you have no more than one wife? You must take even more wives," because he wanted every man to take four or five wives, as many as they wished.

---

the triumphant Anabaptists and turned to the use of the besieged populace of Münster.

351. Seemingly, Gresbeck's words mean that no one moved unless he expected to acquire a better home. Since those who held the better homes would presumably not be willing to move, this scheme makes sense only if there were unoccupied (better) homes for those who moved to occupy, and these were presumably the houses abandoned by the burghers who left the city after the forcible rebaptism. See Kerssenbrock, *Anabaptistici furoris*, ed. Detmer, 611, for an earlier decree of the twelve elders prohibiting the transfer of possession of a house without their permission, supposedly to make sure that no house fell into the hands of people deemed unsuitable.

352. I.e., about fourteen English miles (twenty-two kilometers). The town is actually about twenty-eight kilometers to the east of Münster, which is closer to four German miles.

353. Another reflection (in rather exaggerated form) of Gresbeck's conception that outsiders were responsible for the city's transgressions.

Two possessed girls, and the possession
of the leading Anabaptists[354]

One time, there were two small girls in the city. These girls took it upon themselves to be mute, and the people would also say that they were supposed to be mute. They actually were, having an evil spirit on them. They went up the street during the day and looked for all the menfolk who had elegant garters tied around their legs.[355] When they came upon menfolk who had elegant garters, they stood in front of them and pointed with their fingers, giving out a noise just like a person who was mute. If the man was unwilling to have the garters taken off, the girls would get angry and shriek. If the man willingly let the garters be taken off, the girls were quite satisfied, and they jumped up into the air and clapped their hands together and looked into the air with their faces and acted just as a mute person would. These girls also went through the city and looked for womenfolk who had on elegant neck scarves that were [64r] stitched or untrimmed.[356] If the womenfolk had silkwork around their bodices or sleeves, the girls would leap at it and want to have it too. The women were supposed to take it off, and they jumped at the women's neck and pulled it from whoever

354. There is no section break at this point in the Cologne manuscript, but there clearly is a break in sense. Somebody drew a cross in the margin of the manuscript opposite the first line of this section, presumably as an indication that the sense break was noted.

355. As is often the case, Gresbeck focuses in on one particular detail and isn't very clear about the general context. Here, he seems to tell the story of the two mute girls because their being possessed by a demon allows him to speculate about the possibility of John of Leiden being similarly possessed. The overall story can be sorted out as follows. The preachers apparently issued a prohibition in their sermons against the wearing of ostentatiously luxurious clothing on the grounds that this was a sign of un-Christian pride (Kerssenbrock doesn't record the incident, but Article 16 of the ordinance of the twelve elders does prohibit the production of "new and unusual clothing"; *Anabaptistici furoris*, ed. Detmer, 584). The prohibition at first led to some women abandoning their efforts to make themselves pretty (note the breaking of mirrors), but some (both men and women) continued to wear fancy clothing in public. The two mute girls then took it upon themselves to accost such people and to demand that they surrender their offensive garments. This harassment led women to give up wearing such items. Apparently, the girls did so in Anabaptist ecstasy and even "infected" other women who came to their aid. After eight days or so, the Anabaptist leadership halted the disturbance being caused by the harassment by keeping the girls at home. Nonetheless, the prohibition remained in force, and after about three weeks, some young women suddenly began to "push back" by dressing in men's caps and walking like soldiers. As a result, the preachers partially backed down with the prohibition, allowing some of the older clothing to be worn again. The story seems to have no particular setting in the narrative (it begins vaguely with "one time" and the subsequent section on John of Leiden's possession is likewise apparently not fixed in the narrative), but presumably the prohibition took place during the time of John Dusentschuer's prominence in the late summer and early fall of 1534.

356. "Untrimmed" ("getagen"=High German *gezogen*) refers to cloth whose nap is left uncut; see Grimm, *Deutsches Wörterbuch*, s.v. "gezogen," col. 7191.

didn't hand it over willingly. There was a period of time in the city when the womenfolk wouldn't wear untrimmed neck scarves or silkwork on their bodice and sleeves. They also wouldn't wear little Eifel scarves.[357] They also used to wear under their wimpel some padding to attach their scarves to. They took these off and wouldn't wear them any longer. Some threw them into the fire along with the padding, and they broke their mirrors apart and burned them up. They didn't wish to be proud, wanting to be humble and pure and not to live in sin. But it didn't last long. It lasted for three weeks, actually, that they went about in wimpels like this. They didn't want to go around any longer in such a bare way with a wimpel, and they put on men's small bonnets, little black caps. The young women then came with a marching up just like landsknechts. For in Münster you couldn't find many maidens apart from those who were too small.[358] The wearing of nightcaps took place very quickly. They had the red nightcaps, which were red, made black. The women's flesh wouldn't become dead for them.[359] They all kept a stinger on them in showing such pride with the caps that the preachers again tolerated their wearing their shawls once more just as they had done before. But as for wearing these little Eifel scarves and the bib and the padding, [64v] the preachers at first forbade these items to the womenfolk for a good while, so that they had to lay these aside. The girls who were mute burned up such garters as they got from men and whatever they got from women in the way of neck scarves and silkwork from their collars and sleeves. They went around in the city like this for eight days, carrying out their rule like this. The girls sometimes had an astonishing appearance about them, and they lay on their backs and threw themselves about and tugged themselves by the hair and acted so horrifyingly with their faces that a person was terrified at it, his whole body trembling from it. Some men in the city once saw the girls so conducting their business and the spirit so handling them that the men couldn't get over it in a single day. Whenever these girls were vexed with the spirit that they had on them, and all those who were with them were likewise vexed by the spirit, so that it

357. The Eifel is a mountainous region in western Germany between Aachen and Trier.
358. I.e., too young for marriage. Gresbeck's thought here is a bit elliptical. Does he mean that because the number of mature young women was small, their value as potential spouses gave them leverage to flout the preachers' disapprobation of their flamboyant clothing?
359. An ironic allusion to John of Leiden's and the preachers' talk about the flesh being dead for the Anabaptists (57r).

seemed to them that their heart would jump out of their throat, and they had to fall down on their backs until they were released from this, some women stood by the girls when they behaved this way. One woman took them by the foot, another by the other foot, and the others took them by the arms, and they stretched the girls. When they were vexed, the women were also vexed, so that they also stood and shouted, "O Father, O Father, give mercy! Christ was put on the cross, and we must be shaped the same the same as Him!" [65r] This shouting and marching of the girls lasted for two or three hours every day while the girls had the spirit with them. It's impossible for me to write or say the wonder that the girls created. What the girls did took place so quickly that much talk of it spread through the city and the people were half bewildered. Eventually, the king set to it with the preachers and the preacher bishop,[360] and they had the girls come before them, wishing to examine the girls and ask what sort of spirit they had with them. When they looked around, they had an evil spirit with them.[361] They then had the girls taken back home, specifying that they mustn't come among the people and that no one could come to them until they were released from the spirit. The preachers didn't have much to say about this, and they were secretive about their having an evil spirit with them. They would say in the city that the girls had a flying spirit with them.[362] These girls became healthy again, and were eight or ten years old, no more. One time, there was a period of five or six days when the king was mute and didn't speak. I can't write whether he had an evil spirit with him or what the situation was, but he was mute for a while. For the common folk also said [65v] of the king that he was mute. Some people said that the spirit of God was ruling him, so that he should receive a revelation from God, and some people said that he had an evil spirit with him, and some people said that he did this out of buffoonery, imagining that they would certainly make him speak if this was the situation. Eventually, the king started speaking again, having received a revelation that God had been angry at him for not

360. For the Anabaptist bishop see also note 205.
361. The term "evil spirit" (*böser Geist*) was the standard German term for a demon that possessed or otherwise harassed a human; Grimm, *Deutsches Wörterbuch*, s.v. "Geist," cols. 2636–38.
362. In the first version of the Faust story, when Mephistopheles appears to Faust in the start of chapter 4 and offers his services, he is first described as "the flying spirit" ("der fliegende Geist"). There, as often, "spirit" signifies a demonic being, and the demons were generally conceived of as having the ability to fly through the air (and at times conduct humans with them). It's not clear why such a conception is relevant here.

having done right by His affairs and not having carried out punishment as he should have. God had now granted him mercy, and he was to improve himself. As for spirit that the king had with him (the mute spirit), one could certainly have driven it out of him with a short cudgel or a handled spear.[363] It was a fool's spirit. But as for the two little girls, they had an evil spirit with them. This is what they said in the city as the truth. The men and women would go up the street during the day, and were possessed in this way by the spirit.[364] They would go up and down the city, and some danced and looked in their expressions like nothing but a possessed person. They would go around and laugh, just as someone would laugh in buffoonery, beaming. Everything they said was about the Father and "pray to the Father." Whenever the rebaptizers had the spirit with them like this, they weren't in their right mind, and they felt as if their hearts would burst out of their bodies, so great was the dread that they had within. So it's certainly to be believed that the rebaptizers had their own peculiar spirit [66r] that would vex them, and so one can certainly think that it must not have been a good spirit. God preserve us from such a spirit! Knipperdolling too stayed in his house for a while and was crazy, so he wouldn't go out and the people in the city spoke much of this. Eventually, Knipperdolling did go out again. I can't write about what the situation was with him, but he would often have the illness that the spirit would vex him. One time, a revelation came over Knipperdolling, and he went around the city to all the gates where the common people were working on the earthworks. At each gate, he had the people gather together, and he said, "Dear brothers and sisters, God has revealed to me that I am to proclaim great joy to you for the sake of God. If it's the case that I'm lying, may the devil take me away body and soul!" He straightaway turned around, and he laughed to himself a little. The other folk then thanked God and sang a German hymn, and Knipperdolling went on his way.

The king possessed at a meal

Now the king was magnificently established in his court with his councilors and servants. He would invite the councilors and all his captains and

---

363. More of Gresbeck's wry sense of humor.
364. Gresbeck now refers in general to the ecstatic experiences of the general population of the Anabaptists.

leading servants and preachers as guests along with some wives. The king's messenger would run around in the city (he had a silver box[365] in front with the king's coat of arms). When they were then [66v] sitting and eating at the table, the spirit of the baptizer came upon the king, and he often sat like that for an hour and had his business. Eventually, the king came back to his senses. So they ate and drank and were of good cheer. The king had his wine tasted[366] and had himself served at the table, just like a territorial lord. He had his organist and a portable organ in his house, and the organist played while they ate.[367] Sometimes, a young man read a chapter from the prophets (the Old Testament). Sometimes, the spirit would vex the king in the way I mentioned before. After they'd eaten, pipes, drums, and lutes started up, and they began to dance and court the pretty ladies. This holding of court would certainly last all night.[368] This was all the will of God.[369]

Special meal to be held before a general attack by the Anabaptists

After this, they had another supper[370] prepared that they would hold up on Mt. Zion.[371] (That is, up at the marketplace. They had given the marketplace this name, so that it was called Mt. Zion.[372]) This supper was not sup-

---

365. The word "busse" could conceivably also mean "gun," but it's hard to see how the gun would bear the king's arms (or why a herald would carry one).

366. Gerard Kibbenbrock performed this duty (Kerssenbrock, *Anabaptistici furoris*, ed. Detmer, 648). Wine tasting was necessary only for princes who feared poisoning.

367. For details about the royal organist (Lubbert Oestermann), see Kerssenbrock, *Anabaptistici furoris*, ed. Detmer, 648.

368. For the royal festivities, see Kerssenbrock, *Anabaptistici furoris*, ed. Detmer, 666.

369. Another instance of Gresbeck's sarcasm.

370. The German word ("aventmail," or *Abendmahl* in the High German form) translated here as "supper" is both a term for a normal evening meal and the technical term for the Christian Eucharist (on 71r the regular meal that preceded the "supper" is distinguished with the term "maltit"=High German *Mahlzeit*). Since the Anabaptists rejected the view of Catholics and of Lutherans (and other magisterial reformers) that there was some sort of presence of the body and blood of Christ in the bread and wine used in this sacrament, and instead held that the meal was merely a commemoration of the Last Supper, it seems that the rather formal sounding term "Eucharist" is inappropriate for the present context, even if that is the most obvious translation. For Rothman's treatment of the Eucharist supper in his book *Restitution*, see Stupperich, *Die Schriften B. Rothmanns*, 256–58.

371. For Kerssenbrock's account of this meal, see *Anabaptistici furoris*, ed. Detmer, 697–704. According to him (ibid., 696–97), the meal was held on October 13 and had been announced the preceding day by John Dusentschuer as a way of cheering up the fraught situation after a disturbance caused by the attempt of a disgruntled Knipperdolling to usurp royal authority. The connection with Knipperdolling's activities, which are described below by Gresbeck (97v–103v), is incorrect (see also note 374), but there is no reason to doubt the date given for the meal (confirmed by the departure of the apostles that takes place at the end of the meal; see 71v–74r) or the involvement of Dusentschuer.

372. This new name was part of the attempt to equate the reestablishment of the kingdom of God

posed to take place until God revealed it to the prophets, so it was revealed to the limping prophet that the trumpet[373] of the Lord would go off three times and be blown.[374] When it went off for the third time, everyone was to be up and march to the Promised Land.[375] They were to gather up on Mt. Zion, and then would march out of the city. They would leave behind everything that they had, house and home, and were not to bring along more than just what they had on. Not a single person would be left in the city. The city would be deserted and would be altogether destroyed, and there would be wild beasts in the city [67r] and a wilderness in the city.[376] The people in the city (some of them) were afraid in expectation of the time when the trumpet of the Lord would go off, and they would march off towards the world and then march through camp in the midst of the enemy. For they (some of them) were afraid that the enemy would kill them, as in fact would have happened if they had moved out of the city. The king and the prophets and preachers informed the common folk that God would

---

373. The word for "trumpet" is also used in Low German for the trumpets that appear in Revelation 8–9.

374. As becomes clear from Gresbeck's subsequent narrative, the preparation for the departure was a protracted affair. It was first proclaimed that the trumpet would have to go off three times, and two weeks are specified between the first and the second blast, but the interval between the second and third is not stated (67v–68v). Given that the third blast resulted in the meal, which can be dated to October 13, the preparatory preaching must have started towards the end of September (further evidence that Kerssenbrock's association of the meal with an attempt to clear the air after Knipperdolling's antics is false; see also note 371).

375. Since the planned departure failed to materialize, it's a bit hard to understand what exactly the plan was. Clearly, the intention was in some way modeled on the story in Exodus in which the Israelites were rescued from their captivity under the oppressive pharaoh and led to the Promised Land by God (the initial promise is given to various patriarchs in Genesis [12:1, 7; 15:18–21; 28:13], but its final fulfillment comes when the Israelites return in force to the land of Canaan after their sojourn in Egypt [Deuteronomy 1:8]). Note that in his description of measures taken by John of Leiden in the aftermath of the suppression of Mollenhecke's rebellion, Kerssenbrock indicates that the Anabaptists thought that God was walking in their midst, just as he did when he miraculously saved the Israelites and destroyed their persecutors during the crossing of the Red Sea (*Anabaptistici furoris*, ed. Detmer, 632). Clearly, there was a sense that God would deliver the new Israelites from persecution, just as he had in the past. In this regard, it's perhaps significant that the phrase "Promised Land" is not used in the story told in Exodus but comes from a passage in Hebrews (11:9) that directly follows a section that provides a source of imagery mentioned elsewhere by Gresbeck as part of the Anabaptist discourse (see also note 329 for the "Holy Place"). But where was the destination of the coming departure from the city? Since Gresbeck gives no hint of this, presumably there was none. Perhaps the failure of any of the leaders to come up with a goal (or to get one by "revelation") had something to do with the eventual abandonment of the plan. Gresbeck indicates later (69v–70r) that it was dropped as a result of popular opposition, but this could have been a convenient pretext for the leaders to give up an untenable plan (see also note 384 at the end).

376. Peculiarly, the imagery of the desolation of the city seems to be reminiscent of the description of Babylon's destruction in Jeremiah 51 (see verse 39 in particular for the wild beasts that will live in the empty city). Strange words to use of the New Jerusalem!

strike the enemy in the heart so that they would flee before them just as if they had been struck by force. Five would kill a hundred of them, and ten would kill a thousand.[377] The poor people didn't imagine anything but that they were to march out, and they had fitted themselves out with clothing for this, and so they were on the watch for the time when the trumpet of the Lord would blow. Some people didn't imagine anything but that an angel would descend from heaven among the clouds and blow the trumpet. Eventually, the limping prophet went through the city in all the streets and alleys holding a horn in his hand, and he blew it in every street in every corner of the city, just the way one blows as a cavalryman on horseback. After the prophet blew this way, some of the people came to have a look. One person looked at the other, and they dared not say anything against it but kept quiet. For they'd imagined that God had let the blowing happen in the way I mentioned. The preachers and the Hollanders and the Frisians and the real rebaptizers went up the streets and wished each other peace, saying "dear brother" to one another. [67v] "Dear brothers, the Lord will perform wonders, the trumpet of the Lord has been blown one time, we'll soon be up, the Lord will march with His folk to the Promised Land." The prophet now kept quiet with his blowing for fourteen days. The preachers preached every day that everyone should prepare himself in expectation of the time when God would blow the trumpet a second time. They didn't know when God would be up, they watched for this every hour. So the trumpet blew the second time. The same prophet again hobbled through the city and blew just as he had the first time. Then the Hollanders and Frisians (the criminals) again went around in the city: the trumpet of the Lord had gone off a second time, so the Lord would soon be on guard with His people, and they would march to the Promised Land. The one person was joyful and the other distressed that they would march out in this way and leave everything they had, not knowing where they would go. Some of the men and women didn't believe that they would march out and the city would become empty, or that the enemy would run away from them as if they'd

377. In his description of measures implemented by John of Leiden as prophet in the period between the defeat of Mollenhecke's uprising and John's installation as king, Kerssenbrock notes in connection with the confidence of the Anabaptists their belief that five of them would suffice to defeat the prince-bishop's forces (*Anabaptistici furoris*, ed. Detmer, 632). A confession made in February 1535 by an Anabaptist who had been in the city states that in the period when the king had to console the people because of the failure of relief to materialize (see 86r–87r), he said that five of the Anabaptists would be able to withstand the godless (Niesert, *Münsterische Urkundensammlung*, 139).

been driven off by force. There were some people in the city who had faith and didn't imagine anything but that God would perform such great signs, and they were watching for this every hour and fitted themselves out for it. So the king and prophets and preachers had it proclaimed that the supper would soon take place, the Lord would soon let the third trumpet blow. Everyone, whether a brother or a [68r] sister, who wanted to give something as a contribution to the fare, whatever each one had, they were to bring this to the deacons. They made a slip of the tongue with this food that they were supposed to contribute.[378] For they said that all the people who were in the city were to march to the Promised Land, and the city would be empty. They hadn't had any need for everyone to have given something as a contribution. They may as well eat everything up first rather than leave anything in the city. Everyone gave something as a contribution for the festivities. One person gave a ham, another a side of bacon, so that in this way they got a great festivity from each other. The preachers had it proclaimed that whoever had benches, sawhorses, or tables should bring these up to Mt. Zion (the cathedral square). They set the benches and tables up in order, so that the one side of the cathedral square was filled with tables and benches. (The cathedral square in Münster is a large square[379] of level ground.)

The special meal is held

So the king and the prophets and preachers had it proclaimed that when the trumpet of the Lord went off for the last time, each brother should then come up to Mt. Zion with his wives and his household. Each brother was to come with his armor and weapon that he would live or die with, and the march from the city to the Promised Land would then take place. The womenfolk were to take along for necessity the clothes in which they wished to walk. [68v] They were not to weigh themselves down with clothes—they would get clothes where they came to. "When you're on your way marching to the Promised Land," they informed each other, they wouldn't grow tired from walking or have hunger or thirst. They wouldn't need anything. The preachers said, "Now we'll certainly see who is an unbeliever and who dares

378. Apparently, this was the explanation given by the Anabaptist leadership when the plan for a mass expedition was abandoned and the food that had been contributed for this purpose was now used instead for a feast.
379. "Square" in the sense of a public place.

to abandon himself to God, and who dares to go to the end for Him and who will hide himself in the nooks and crannies. If someone is discovered over there, they must all be stamped out. For the unbelievers should report themselves and stamp themselves out." Then the trumpet of the Lord went off for the third time. The limping prophet went through the city one morning between five and six o'clock,[380] blowing with the horn just as he'd done twice before. All the folk were in the cathedral square right away as if they would march out right away. All the men and women, young and old, came up to the cathedral square, and each had prepared and fitted himself out as if they would march out, the men with their armor and their weapons, and the women (some of them) having packed in sacks and baskets everything that they wanted to take along. So up to the cathedral square came all those who could walk, the women carrying the little children that they would take along in their arms, having slung the children in kerchiefs. There also came up to the cathedral square womenfolk who'd only just taken to the childbed and had hung the babies from their necks, the babies being no more than two or three days old. Such a rule did the king and the prophets and the preachers [69r] have at that time in the city, chasing all the folk together—it was all Hollander's work, all fool's work! There went up to the cathedral square many a distressed person among the old and the sick, who walked with canes and could never walk. They were still supposed to march out. The preachers said that the lame people who couldn't walk were going to start walking. Knipperdolling said, "Look, there stands a blind man." And there stood a blind man. "He will start to see again! Such signs will God do among us!"[381] But the lame and the blind remained just as they were. Such signs wouldn't happen up at the cathedral square. Now that they were up at the cathedral square, the men went and stood in their ranks seven deep, old people and young, everyone who could bear arms. The women all went over and stood by themselves on one side in a company. With old and young, the men were two thousand strong. They (the arms-bearing rebaptizers) were never stronger than fifteen hundred in the city. Of the women in the city, young and old, there were eight or nine thousand, more or less (I don't know about this exactly).

380. Nine a.m. according to Kerssenbrock, *Anabaptistici furoris*, ed. Detmer, 697.
381. This attempt to make the blind see (based on the action of Jesus in Mark 8:23) is attested in the confessions of the captured apostles; see Kerssenbrock, *Anabaptistici furoris*, ed. Detmer, 692n3.

Of small children who either could or couldn't walk, there were also probably ten or twelve hundred.[382] So these men stood in their ranks up at the
cathedral square, and the women in their company, awaiting the king and
the queen. Eventually, the king and the queen arrived very magnificently,
the king with his councilors and all his cavalrymen, and [69v] they all sat in
their full armor, the cavalrymen with their lances, and the marksmen with
their firearms. The king rode in the middle of the group in his full armor,
with a young man behind him with a lance who carried the king's helmet
for him. The king had a golden crown on his head. (This crown was two
hands' breadth high. He'd laid the crown on a hat, so that the king was very
magnificent. All that he had in the way of adornment and the trappings on
the horse, this was all gold.) The attendants ran on all sides of him, and his
lackey was beside the horse. In this way, he rode around the cathedral
square and inspected the folk. The queen halted with her carriage in front
of her court with her fellow wives. The king appointed new captains and
officers and ensigns,[383] and they made a main company and a lost company
and some skirmishers.[384] Eventually, they had a battle against each other,

382. Kerssenbrock (*Anabaptistici furoris*, ed. Detmer, 700) gives the figures of sixteen hundred
arms-bearing men (minus those on watch duty), five hundred old men and boys, and five thousand
women (see ibid., 618n314, for other contemporary evidence).

383. These new officers were necessary for the field army, which is about to be created. Here
Gresbeck speaks of new officers, but presumably the old ones were for the most part given new titles
(see 54v–55r for the old arrangement by which the commanders were appointed with reference to the
defensive layout of the city). In connection with the appointment of the officials at the time of the
establishment of the kingdom, Kerssenbrock gives a list of commanders according to their positions
in a field army (the dating is wrong; see also note 295). He lists two commanders-in-chief, one cavalry
commander, one commander of all the infantry, one commander of the main body, one commander of
the vanguard, three ensigns, one commander of skirmishers, two arms masters, two sergeants (i.e., the
men who kept the pikemen in proper order), and one drummer (see also Kerssenbrock, *Anabaptistici
furoris*, ed. Detmer, 650n11, for a long list of minor military positions omitted by Kerssenbrock).

384. Gresbeck's account here makes it clear that the troops in the city hadn't previously been
arranged for open maneuver in the field. Methods of warfare had been undergoing rapid developments
since the 1490s, and the new tactics required a strict military order and great discipline on the part of
the troops. In deploying the landsknechts for battle, a distinction was made between the main company,
which was marshaled in a tight battle formation of ranked pikemen, and a special force, which fought
in front of the main company as a vanguard. The main force is called "der geüeldyge hoeypt" (High
German *der gewältige Haufen*, literally the "forceful group"). *Haufen* is often translated as "regiment"
in English, but the other uses of the word here in the German suggest the use of "company" as being
appropriate for both uses, which at times overlap). The vanguard is called "der verlaren hoeypt" (High
German *der verlorene Haufen*). The exposed position of the vanguard force made it a particularly dangerous unit to serve in. It bore the initial brunt of battle in both defense and offense, and the losses to
be expected led to its odd designation ("the lost company"; the phrase is sometimes mistranslated as
"lost hope" as if the second element were the Higher German *Hoffe*, or "hope"). The troops in it fought
individually without the strict regimentation by ranks characteristic of the main body. For this reason
one might refer to them as "skirmishers," but this term is more appropriate for lightly armed troopers
who fought at a distance as opportunity presented itself, and quickly withdrew when pressed (here

the main company against the lost company, just as if they were upon the enemy (were to have a battle in the field). The cavalrymen charged up and down the square, and they had their blood up. The drums sounded the alarm. Their only thought was that they would move out of the city right away and smash open the camp, and then would march into the Promised Land. After they'd played the fool long enough up at the cathedral square, the king's chief captain said, "Dear brothers, my lord, the king of the righteous, orders the following to be announced. Now that you're marshaled in the main company and the lost company, and so are all you captains and officers and ensigns, right away or on the morrow you know how to marshal yourselves again, just as you are now marshaled, in case we are to march out [70r] right away or on the morrow." They wouldn't go out the gate. The Promised Land was too far from Münster. The trumpet of the Lord hadn't been blown properly. They played the greatest foolishness, so that nobody should have believed it. The captain continued, "Dear brothers, we will not march out and leave the city empty and let the godless come back into the city. This is not the will of God. This is nothing more than a temptation[385] of you as to what you would do by the Father, whether you would be obedient. Now, dear brothers, let each one take his wives and set himself down at the table of the Lord. Set your arms beside you and be joyful with the Lord!" Everyone then sat down with his wives. The king then rode back to

---

called "loepers" [High German *Läufer*], literally, "runners"). The vanguard was manned with volunteers who received extra pay. For what it's worth, Kerssenbrock seems to have been somewhat unclear about this terminology in the Latin terms he uses in his list of the royal military establishment in *Anabaptistici furoris*, ed. Detmer, 650. He reasonably enough translates the "main group" as the "principal army" ["praecipuus exercitus"] and the "skirmishers" as "runners" ["cursores"], but he calls the "lost company" merely the "regular soldiers" ["gregarii"], a term that seems to betray a misunderstanding of what the purpose of the formation was. The Humanist Willibald Pirckheimer of Nuremberg made a rather different choice for translating the "lost group" in his Latin history of the Swiss war that he had served in as a doctor, calling it, in a circumlocution worthy of Classical Latin idiom, the "squad that they call lost" ["turma quam amissam vocant"; see *Opera politica, historica, philologica*, 84]. In any event, the lack of adequate training among the troops may have contributed to the decision to abandon the plan to depart for the Promised Land. The forces in the city had certainly gone out on raids against the enemy in the preceding months, but that's by no means the same thing as the massed maneuvering necessary for open battle in the field; see 79v, 82v–83r for the later drills that the troops would engage in once a week to hone the necessary skills for open battle. As it turned out, the army never took to the field for open combat with the besiegers, and the field army seems to have fallen into abeyance until the preparations for the Easter salvation (see also note 457).

385. The Latin verb from which "temptation" is borrowed literally means to "test." As used in modern English, "temptation" signifies testing a Christian's morality by offering him a "tempting" pleasure to lead him astray from adherence to Christianity's often strict moral dictates. In the speech of the Anabaptists, the corresponding German word ("versokynge"=High German *Versuchung*) refers to God's putting his people "to the test" through inflicting on them difficulties that will try their faith (as with Job). "Temptation" and "tempt" are regularly used in the translation in this sense.

his court with all the cavalrymen, and all the cavalrymen then rode back home, took off their armor again, and went back to the king. The king had adorned himself magnificently with a velvet overcoat and golden chains, with the golden crown sitting on his head. The queen was also magnificently decked out with a velvet dress. She also had a golden crown on her head. Then the king along with the queen went up to the cathedral square, very magnificently, with his councilors and servants, and he had it announced that everyone should sit down with his wives, and he had all those called up who held command from the king. They were to stand up with their wives and serve at the table, and the king himself would serve at the table with the queen. "And when you've held the supper, some of you will stay here and serve us in turn at the table." So these men stood up and served at the table. The king together with his queen [70v] went along the table and addressed his guests and held them back so that they should be joyous with the Lord. The preachers did the same, saying that they should make themselves joyous with the Lord. They certainly had to chat together, and they had to sing and praise the Lord. They stood up and sang the German hymns. Every man sat beside his wife. The preachers asked, "Brother, how many wives do you have?" The brother answered, "two" or "three" or "four," depending on how many each had. One man sat there who said, "These four women are my wives." He[386] then replied, "Praised be the Lord for that! You surpass me, because I have no more than three!" In this way, the preachers went along the table and addressed the brothers and sisters. The brother who had no more than one wife sat shamefaced. Such a man was still an unbeliever, and he wasn't yet a real Christian. Then the preachers said, "Here on Mt. Zion there are still some people, and before the clock strikes twelve, they'll be alive and dead." The common folk didn't know how they meant that, and they were supposed to take it to mean that they (some of them) would die and become alive again. They imagined that such signs would not take place. They sat eating and drinking, and were of good cheer. Up at the cathedral square, it didn't look as if anyone was going to die. Each brother sat beside his wives, and in the evening he could go to bed with the one that he hankered after. They could think of that, they didn't think about [71r] dying. It didn't seem

---

386. Presumably, Dusentschuer (though conceivably just any old preacher who asked the question).

deadly there. Knipperdolling kept asking one time that the king should cut off his head—in three days he would rise again from the dead.[387] The king wouldn't do it. But if it had been some fellow, the king would have cut off his head. The king couldn't do without Knipperdolling, however. He was a good hand in the cards for him, since Knipperdolling held rule and was the king's viceroy. He was the first and the last.[388]

The general attack is cancelled, and missions are sent to four neighboring towns

Eventually, after the meal had taken place, they held the supper in the end, just as if they were going to the sacrament.[389] The king and queen, Knipperdolling, and the king's councilors went and stood in the middle of the cathedral square, and they had small round flatbreads and broke them apart. All the folk, men and women, young and old, walked up in between the king, the queen, and Knipperdolling, and then each ate a piece of the flatbread and then had a leisurely drink of wine along with it.[390] This is how they held the supper. Once they had held the meal, the prophet had all the folk form a company. All the preachers were together, and so were the leaders of the rebaptizers. They fetched a high stool and placed it right in the middle of [71v] the folk. The preachers stood up on it, one after the other, and preached what the supper signified. Eventually, the king himself stood up on the chair and said that God had deposed him, and he was no longer king. He'd angered God by not ruling as he should. He said, "Dear brothers and sisters, the intention was not that we should march out of the city like this, and this is not the will of God. For it was nothing more than a temptation of you." When John of Leiden (the king) said this, he started laughing to himself. His thoughts were unknown to me.[391] If the king and prophets and the preachers together with the leading rebaptizers had marched out of the city, all the common folk, men and women, would all

387. The phrase "one time" indicates that this anecdote is from a different date and is related here simply to illustrate the belief among certain Anabaptists that they could return from death. For another story showing Knipperdolling's strange passive-aggressive relationship with the king, see 102v–103v.

388. The phrase "the first and the last" comes from the concluding words of Christ in Revelation 22:13, when he announces his impending return (see also Isaiah 41:4). Presumably, the phrase here simply signifies "all important" and doesn't bear any further connection with its original context.

389. I.e., they held their own version of the Eucharist (see 29r–29v for a similar rite).

390. For the significance of the flatbread and wine, see 29r and also note 149.

391. Note that Gresbeck was apparently present at this feast.

have marched out of the city, so that not one person would have remained in it. Eventually, the limping prophet stood up on the chair and said that he had a revelation from God that the preachers were to march out and march to four cities: Soest, Osnabrück, Warendorf, and Coesfeld.[392] The prophet had a list in his hand and tore this list into four pieces. He first read one list ("Item.[393] The preachers are to march to Warendorf") and called up the preachers by their names, and they came up before the prophet. The prophet said to the preachers, "You dear brothers, I say to you as a Word of the Lord that you're to march into Warendorf in broad daylight, and to walk into the city and proclaim the peace to them. If it's the case that they won't accept the peace, [72r] then the city will sink down on the spot and burn up in hellfire." The prophet took the list and threw it at the prophets' feet, saying, "I throw the register to you as proof." Then the preachers picked up the list and said that they'd carry it out in this way for the sake of God.[394] The prophet then read out the second list in the same way: these men were to go to Soest.[395] He also said to the preachers that if they wouldn't accept the peace, then that city too would sink down. The prophet then read out the third list and also called up these preachers. They were to go to Coesfeld.[396] If they too wouldn't accept the peace, then they too would sink down on the spot. The prophet then read out the fourth list and called up those who were to march to Osnabrück.[397] If they too wouldn't accept the peace, then they too would sink down on the spot. The prophet then got the preachers together and said to them, "I say to you as a Word of the Lord that you're to march into the cities and proclaim the peace to them. If the four cities won't accept the peace, then all four are to sink down on

392. Towns in the general vicinity of Münster, chosen to represent the cardinal points of the compass (see Kerssenbrock, *Anabaptistici furoris*, ed. Detmer, 704–6), respectively south, north, east, and west. Note that Dusentschuer already has the list of missionaries to the various towns written out. Presumably, the decision to abandon the general expedition and replace it with the dispatch of select missionaries had already been taken before the special supper at which the cancellation of the expedition was announced.

393. "Item" literally means "likewise" in Latin, and it was used in late medieval/early modern Latin to indicate additional "items" in lists. The word was adopted with this sense in the vernacular (both in German and English; hence the modern English meaning of the word with an extension in application). The word was presumably used to mark the start of each list of names after some introduction indicating the purpose of the four separate lists of names.

394. For the list of men sent to Warendorf, see Kerssenbrock, *Anabaptistici furoris*, ed. Detmer, 706.

395. For the list of men sent to Soest, see ibid., 704–5.

396. For the list of men sent to Coesfeld, see ibid., 705–6.

397. For the list of men sent to Osnabrück, see ibid., 705.

the spot!" This prophet moved out with them and journeyed along to Soest with his companions. At that time, the prophets said, "Do you now see that we must stand up for this? We won't shrink from any fire or water or the sword![398] For a long time, some of you've said, 'We don't dare to come up on the walls'[399] or 'against the enemy.' But we must now be the first, and we will march out in the name of the Lord!"

Missionaries are dispatched and the meal continues, with the king executing a man

[72v] The prophet said to the king, "Brother John of Leiden, God orders you to keep on ruling and to remain a king as you were before, and to punish unrighteousness." With this, the prophet made John of Leiden into a king again. God was supposed to have revealed this to him. The preachers moved out of the city the same evening, and they brought them through the camp.[400] Each one went to his city, one group to Warendorf, the second to Coesfeld, the third to Soest, and the fourth to Osnabrück. They divided themselves up this way and got past the camp. Once each group of preachers arrived at the cities, they bid them peace, but the cities wouldn't accept the peace.[401] The cities didn't sink down on the spot as the limping preacher had said and prophesied. Instead, all four cities put the preachers in prison, and they were all executed, apart from one named Henricus, who'd given himself out as a prophet, as I related before.[402] Now that this had taken place up on Mt. Zion, the king said to all the folk that everyone should go home, and some should stay there and serve at the table. The king and the queen and the councilors and all those who hadn't yet held the supper were also to go and sit at [73r] the table of the Lord, and they too would hold the supper. So the king and his queen with all his wives, and the councilors with all their wives, and all the king's servants with all their wives went and

---

398. A reference to the modes of execution used by the secular authorities against the Anabaptists (see also note 143).

399. I.e., during the two attempts on the part of the besiegers to take the city by storm.

400. This seems to mean that the Anabaptists got the missionary preachers past the blockhouses (for a similar expression with "come by the blockhouses" used below of Henricus Graes's planned return to Münster through the fortifications, see 75r).

401. For more detail, see below, 73v–74v.

402. For the recognition of Henricus (Graes) as a prophet, see 61v–61v. Because the events surrounding Graes's capture and the way in which he alone kept his life took place beyond Gresbeck's ken, Gresbeck has nothing to say on these topics. For details, see also note 407.

sat at the table and were joyous, and they held the supper just as the first group had done. They served the king very magnificently at the table. For every course that they set before the king, someone stood there with a coronet and blew a fanfare. Once the king had almost completed the supper, the spirit of the baptizer came to him, and he sat for a while without speaking. Eventually, he woke up again and became lively once more. He'd received the revelation from his God (the devil[403]) as to what he should do. He said to his servants that they should fetch him a prisoner from the prison. The servant asked the king, "Will my lord the king have them all at once?" Then the king said, "No, bring me the one, the landsknecht, and bring me the executioner's sword.[404] It's the will of God, the man must die." So they fetched the knecht and the executioner's sword. The king then said to the knecht [73v] he had to die when he got down on his knees. The knecht was unwilling to get down on his knees, so that he would die so hastily. The king said that he'd better sit down, or he'd hack him apart in the middle. The knecht asked for mercy, but he had to die. So the knecht got down on his knees, and the king cut off his head. With this, the king fulfilled the revelation. They left the knecht lying on the cathedral square that night until the morning, when they buried him. In this way, then, was the supper fulfilled. Then the preachers moved out of the city for the four cities, as I described before.

Failure of the missions

The limping prophet was gone with the preachers and their bishop, and they journeyed to the cities. The king, the Hollanders and Frisians, and the real rebaptizers wondered how things might be going for the preachers. Eventually, the king got news that the preachers had probably gotten across, that each group of the preachers was where they were supposed to be, and that they had control of the four cities and were going around preaching, and also how the folk were having themselves baptized in the cities. Eventually, the king and all the rebaptizers got the real news, how all the preachers [74r] were prisoners, and how My Lord of Münster had

403. Obviously Gresbeck's retrospective (re?)-evaluation of the nature of John of Leiden's "spirit."
404. Apparently, there was only a single landsknecht being kept prisoner among a number of others. Gresbeck gives no indication of the general background or of the reason why John of Leiden had it in for this man in particular.

control of Warendorf. For the king's only thought was that they'd taken hold of Warendorf and Soest. Eventually, the news came that they were all executed.[405] Then there was a distressed company in Münster. Eventually, after the king with his company saw that they could never get the cities for themselves and that everything that they undertook was lost, he comforted the folk, saying, "This had to happen, it was God's will that they had to die this way, because after the preachers there are still other preachers to come who will expound and preach the Word of God much more clearly." In this way, the king comforted the folk and kept them quiet. Those who by now knew better had to keep quiet and grant that he was right in all things. The plan wouldn't succeed for him. If this had succeeded for him and they had taken possession of one or two of the cities, they imagined that they would take possession of the whole world. For the four cities did not sink down on the spot as the prophet had said, the prophet having said to the preachers when they were about to march out that no one would be able to hurt or harm them, that the godless would not have the power to take the least hair from their bodies. As it was, [74v] the four cities wouldn't accept the peace, and remained in their faith, being unwilling to believe the false prophets. Had these four cities accepted the rebaptizers and believed the preachers, things would have gone for them just as they did for Münster.

The prophet Henricus returns as a spy

This prophet Henricus, who'd made himself out to be a prophet, as I mentioned before,[406] came back. He said that God had revealed to him in prison that he should go once more to Münster in New Israel and visit the city once more. The folk welcomed him back, giving him their hand and kissing him on the mouth with the kiss of peace. The prophet told them how he got out of prison, how he dropped out of a window, and how he walked at night until he came to the holy city.[407] The prophet told how he

---

405. For Kerssenbrock's account of the various embassies and the executions of the apostles, see *Anabaptistici furoris*, ed. Detmer, 708–24. Though his account isn't entirely clear, it would seem that he dates the feast at which the missionaries were chosen to October 13 (ibid., 697), and he has Klopriss arrive at Warendorf on October 14 (ibid., 708). Certainly, the missions all came to a bad end within a week.

406. 61r–61v.

407. This story told by Graes is all lies. He was captured along with the other apostles dispatched to Osnabrück. As a schoolmaster, Graes had been educated in Latin, and when he and other captives were in the presence of the prince-bishop, he asked in Latin, "Doesn't the king have the power to release someone in chains?" As a result, he won the favor of the prince-bishop, who spared his life and had

was to march out of the city again, and in daylight would walk up to the blockhouses. The godless wouldn't have the power to hinder or harass him. This Henricus took counsel with the king and his [75r] councilors and was informed of all their plans. The king with his councilors agreed with Henricus that he should march to Deventer in Holland,[408] and after assembling their brothers together, march back by force to Münster.[409] They also gave Henricus two hundred guilders, in case the rebaptizers in Holland needed money.[410] The king also gave Henricus a banner. Henricus was to have let it fly in Deventer at the marketplace (at the edge), and the rebaptizers were to have turned out under it.[411] This banner was a banner of the righteous, a Christian banner. Once Henricus let the banner fly and had all the rebaptizers together, he was to have moved back to Münster by force. Once he reached the blockhouses, he was to have let the banner fly. This was to have been their symbol. Then the king would have sallied forth with the biggest company that he had, and would then have fetched them into the city. As for this white banner, the one that Henricus was supposed to have had with him when he moved out of the city the last time and to have let fly in Deventer, this is what the common rebaptizers in the city of Münster said. I can't write exactly whether that happened. Anyway, Henricus did move out of the city and also got the two hundred guilders, and he was supposed to assemble the rebaptizers, but he got no further from the city of Münster than [75v] the blockhouses, and went to My Gracious Lord of Münster.[412]

---

him sent back to Münster as a spy (Kerssenbrock, *Anabaptistici furoris*, ed. Detmer, 724–25). (Clear proof of the value of a classical education!) Graes then revealed to him everything he knew about the Anabaptists in Münster and promised to tell how the city could be captured if the prince-bishop would grant him his life. The prince-bishop agreed, provided that Graes went back to the city to find out the king's secrets. In effect, Graes was to act as a double agent.

408. Kerssenbrock (*Anabaptistici furoris*, ed. Detmer, 728) mentions Wesel, Deventer, and Amsterdam as the destinations (confirmed by the confession of Bernard Krechting; Cornelius, *Berichte der augenzeugen*, 380). On the significance of Deventer, see note 90.

409. Gresbeck makes it sound as if the decision for Graes to set out in order to drum up support was reached after calm deliberation, but according to Kerssenbrock, once he learned as much as he could, Graes decided to leave before word of his secret mission could be revealed by any turncoats, so he feigned a crazed revelation from God ordering him to leave as he did. Presumably, Gresbeck wasn't privy to the details of the deliberations.

410. The figure is confirmed by the confessions of John of Leiden (Cornelius, *Berichte der augenzeugen*, 383), Bernard Krechting (Niesert, *Münsterische Urkundensammlung*, 189), and Knipperdolling (Cornelius *Berichte der augenzeugen*, 378, 380). Kerssenbrock puts the sum at three hundred (*Anabaptistici furoris*, ed. Detmer, 729). In any event, the deceitful Graes was clever enough to get the Anabaptists to give him a nice parting gift for himself!

411. For the military significance of the banner, see note 457.

412. The letter of good faith that John of Leiden gave Graes for his journey (see note 416) is dated January 2, 1535, and he's recorded as being at Iburg (a stronghold of the prince-bishop's) by January 4,

Henricus moved out of the city at night and took a knecht with him, and in this way they sent Henricus on his way between the blockhouses. Henricus with the knecht went to within some distance from the blockhouses, and he brought the knecht to a house and said that he should wait for him.[413] The knecht did this, and Henricus went to the blockhouse (to My Gracious Lord of Münster). The knecht kept watch, but Henricus didn't come back. Then the knecht headed back for Münster and returned to the city. He then told the king how Henricus the prophet had gone from him and he was supposed to wait for him, and that Henricus didn't come back to the knecht. At this, the king and his councilors along all his retinue were distressed that Henricus the prophet had done such a thing. They would never have believed it! When word got out, so that the common man learned that Henricus was such a false prophet and that he was with My Lord of Münster, there was much talk in the city. Some people said that it was all buffoonery what they were engaged in, with the prophet having defected from them like this, and that it should all be considered buffoonery what he'd prophesied, as I mentioned before: what had been revealed to him in his bedroom, and what [76r] he'd announced to the common folk up at the market.

The Anabaptists justify their treatment of Henricus plus how they dealt with a letter from him (and also a later letter from the landgrave of Hesse)

Eventually, the king and Stutenberent had a sermon given up at the market. Stutenberent said in the sermon, "Dear brothers and sisters, some of you are going around grousing and grumbling that Henricus the prophet has defected from us. Dear brothers and sisters, don't let yourselves be surprised at this! Such false prophets are supposed to arise among us, and Henricus is one of these.[414] We couldn't care less that Henricus has been informed of our plans and now the bishop is also being informed of them."[415] The king would certainly have preferred that Stutenberent had not made the statement, "We couldn't care less that they're being informed of our plans."

1535 (Kerssenbrock, *Anabaptistici furoris*, ed. Detmer, 729).

413. Presumably, this is just some random house outside the city.

414. The reference to false prophets comes from Matthew 24:11 and Mark 13:22.

415. For the sorts of things that Graes revealed to the prince-bishop, see Kerssenbrock, *Anabaptistici furoris*, ed. Detmer, 729–30.

This statement was heard by the whole community in Münster at that time. This statement was silently retained in memory by some people, and some whispered among themselves, "What sort of plans do they have among themselves that they would care about if word of their buffoonery would finally get out?" Stutenberent continued, "Dear brothers and sisters, we gave Henricus two hundred guilders for the journey. This was to have been for the benefit of the brothers he was supposed to fetch. Dear brothers, two hundred guilders is a small matter, and that's also all the money that we've sent out of the city. [76v] But to the preachers and those whom we've sent out with letters[416] we've given travel funds before and after. So we haven't sent a penny out of the city."[417] Some people would say that the king was supposed to have sent six or eight thousand guilders out of the city. I can't write any more about what the truth of this is, but I could well believe that he sent a sum of money out of the city. They preached a lot about this Henricus and the two hundred guilders, so that everyone had to keep quiet. The king and the preachers would be right. So they distanced themselves from Henricus, and he was supposed to be a false prophet, as in fact he was, and so were all the prophets and preachers who were in the city as well as the king. At that time, Henricus could have harmed the king along with all the rebaptizers by getting the king to sally forth with all the arms-bearing men.[418] But what the situation is with this is unknown to me. This prophet Henricus wrote to the city a letter[419] about how he was with My Gracious Lord of Münster, addressing the king and the whole community. The things that the preachers and the rebaptizers were undertaking with the king and his councilors were, he said, all buffoonery. It was nothing [77r] but them deceiving the poor people, and they would do in their lives and property and everything they had. He said that they should convert—they would still receive mercy from My Gracious Lord of Münster. He wrote, "All your prophets and preachers and your king are prophets and preachers and a king just as I am a prophet and preacher and am a king. They're all

416. Kerssenbrock (*Anabaptistici furoris*, ed. Detmer, 728–29) reproduces a letter that John of Leiden gave to Graes for him to show to people as proof of the legitimacy of his mission.
417. Seemingly, the argument is that expenses for a journey are not a form of sending money out of the city, and the only exception was the large sum given to Henricus, which was not meant for the costs of the journey.
418. I.e., if he had raised the standard as a sign of his return with relief, the king's forces could have been ambushed when they sallied forth to meet the supposed relief.
419. For the text, see appendix, document 1.

false preachers and prophets along with the king in the city of Münster, just as I was a prophet."[420] The chancellor[421] stood and read the letter up at the market in the common assembly. I do hold that the chancellor did not read the whole letter (what was written in the letter). The king would do this whenever they got letters in the city and didn't want to inform the common folk of what the letters contained. One time, the landgrave[422] wrote to the city, and this text was copied from the text that they'd sent from the city about the baptism.[423] The rebaptizers of Münster wouldn't hold anything about Mary. It was written in the text that the landgrave had written to the city how Christ had suckled at Mary's breast, and that Mary was the mother of Christ and had conceived Christ from the Holy Spirit. Stutenberent stood and expounded that. He read out that Christ had suckled at Mary's breast and that Christ was supposed to have received flesh and blood from Mary.[424] At this point, Stutenberent presented a determination[425] before the whole community, saying, "If Christ is supposed to have received flesh and blood from Mary in this way by suckling at her breast, then we humans would belong to the race of cows and beasts. For we consume the milk of cows, and small children consume the milk and are reared with it. In that case, we would all have to belong to the race of cows

420. In the original: "The previous prophets were all prophets just like me, so that you poor stupid people couldn't recognize that it's lies and seduction by which you are being done in."
421. Henry Krechting (Kerssenbrock, *Anabaptistici furoris*, ed. Detmer, 24v).
422. I.e., Philip I, Landgrave of Hesse (1504–67). Philip was one of the chief proponents of religious reform among German princes, and as his territory was nearby, it was natural for the Anabaptists in Münster to solicit his support. For his part, Philip attempted to get the radicals in Münster to moderate their views, to no avail.
423. The word translated here as "baptism" is missing in the manuscripts, which merely read, "van der" (presumably, "dope"). For the extended correspondence between the regime in Münster and Philip I, Landgrave of Hesse, see Kerssenbrock, *Anabaptistici furoris*, ed. Detmer, 754–61; for the Anabaptists' long disquisition to Philip, see Stupperich, *Die Schriften B. Rothmanns*, 414–22. Presumably, the statement about text being copied from the text sent to the landgrave by the Anabaptists means that the landgrave was responding to their text and quoted it. The letter from the landgrave is mentioned here out of chronological order because it came to Gresbeck's mind only as another example of the procedure by which the leadership in the city supposedly read out only excerpts of hostile correspondence. Rothman wrote the book *Restitution* in October 1534, and the letter mentioned is presumably the refutation of Rothman's book that the landgrave wrote in March 1535 (see Kerssenbrock, *Anabaptistici furoris*, ed. Detmer, 758n3).
424. There is an untranslatable similarity in words in the German, in that the same verb (High German *empfangen*) is used of both Mary's "conception" of the child Christ from the Holy Spirit and the child's reception ("conception") of his bodily substance from her.
425. I.e., an official statement of doctrinal interpretation ("boscheyt" [=High German *Bescheid*] corresponds to *determinatio*, a term from the Scholastic exegesis of theology signifying the authoritative decision of the issue under discussion). For Rothman's treatment of the incarnation of Christ in his work *Restitution*, see Stupperich, *Die Schriften B. Rothmanns*, 226–30.

and beasts!" The rebaptizers imagined that Christ was supposed to have received flesh and blood from Mary's milk, and the rebaptizers also imagined that when they [77v] consumed the milk of cows, they were supposed to receive flesh and blood from them. Stutenberent knew better about this, except that he said it out of derision and mockery, not knowing what he would say to the people about the text.[426] For they would say that Christ had brothers and sisters as well.[427] It was to be understood as far as Mary's milk goes that Mary wasn't supposed to have conceived Christ in purity through the Holy Spirit.[428] I can't write any more about what instead they

426. Here Gresbeck seems to believe that Rothman knew better, that is, that he accepted traditional doctrine, but made his derisive counterargument because mockery was the only way he knew to refute the truth. This is just a reflection of Gresbeck's retrospective hostility to Anabaptism. There's no reason to doubt the sincerity of Rothman's views.

427. Presumably, the sense is that Rothman would have agreed that Mary did suckle, since she must have done so with Jesus's siblings, but used mockery as a way of refuting the landgrave's argument, since he couldn't do so directly. For more on disputes about whether Jesus had siblings, see also note 592.

428. This topic pertains to arguments of Christology (the nature of Christ). The relationship between Christ as the son of God on the one hand and God himself on the other was the subject of much dispute in antiquity. The matter was generally uncontroversial during the Middle Ages, but became a matter of great dispute at the time of the Reformation. The notion that had been accepted as orthodox since antiquity held that the three "persons" of God (Father, Son, and Holy Spirit) were seen as manifestations of a single God, and this threefold conception of God is called the Trinity. A different line of thought in antiquity known as Monophysitism held that the divine nature of Christ supplanted the humanity of the fetus of Jesus that was conceived in Mary, and Melchior Hofman adhered to a similar idea that arose in the 1520s (he famously compared the arrival of Jesus in the world through Mary to the passage of water through a pipe). In his final days after his capture, John of Leiden showed himself willing to recant a number of his views, but he balked at the notion that God was born of a human (Kerssenbrock, *Anabaptistici furoris*, ed. Detmer, 872). Here, Gresbeck shows a garbled understanding of the Anabaptist doctrine on this topic, confusing his discussion of the Anabaptist view on Jesus's incarnation and birth by introducing the related but irrelevant topic of their view on the question of whether Jesus had siblings. It is true that the Anabaptists held (against the traditional view), that Jesus did have siblings, and the connection in Gresbeck's mind must have been that if the Anabaptists thought that Joseph and Mary procreated in the natural human manner in the case of the siblings, then they must have done so in the case of Jesus as well. At any rate, that seems to be the logic here of jumping from a statement about the belief in the existence of the siblings to the conclusion that they denied the doctrine of the virgin birth of Jesus. But the question of the existence of the siblings pertained to the issue of whether Joseph and Mary had sexual relations *after* the birth of Jesus (see 117r and also note 592). The virgin birth, on the other hand, is the idea that Mary conceived and gave birth to Jesus as a virgin, that is, through the operation of the Holy Ghost without having had sexual intercourse with her husband-to-be Joseph (Gresbeck is clearly describing this doctrine in speaking of the virgin giving birth "in purity through the Holy Spirit"). And Gresbeck is flatly wrong in claiming that the Anabaptists rejected the virgin birth. In his treatment of the topic in his treatist *Restitution* (chapter 4, see Stupperich, *Die Schriften B. Rothmanns*, 226–30), Rothman makes it abundantly clear that the Anabaptists did not reject this doctrine. Rather, they rejected the traditional interpretation of its significance. During antiquity, the question of the human versus the divine nature of Jesus was hotly disputed, and the view that eventually prevailed and became the orthodox view of the medieval church held that Mary conceived Jesus through the intervention of the Holy Spirit (or Ghost), and that as a result, Jesus was both divine and human in nature. The Anabaptist view as outlined by Rothman is based fundamentally on the centrality of the statement in John 1:14 that the Word of God was made

believed on this point. He read more things from the text that he imagined they would repudiate in this way with foolishness. Eventually, Stutenberent gave this text to the chief captain and said, "Dear brothers and sisters, this text is too long to read, so I've given it to the chief captain. He's to give it to the captains. One captain will take it from the other, first one, then the next. So you're to read it out yourselves, each captain to his folk in front of his gate." So Stutenberent handed over the text before the community. But this text went no further than the chief captain. The common man couldn't learn what the text contained. In this way, the prophet Henricus wrote to the city. He abandoned the baptism and converted, receiving mercy from the lord[429] and remaining alive.

Stutenberent writes a book to drum up foreign support, and the relief expected at Easter fails to materialize

Now Stutenberent with the king and the [78r] preachers undertook a second plan. Stutenberent wrote a book, and this book is called *Restitution*.[430] They had the book published, and they sent it to Holland and Frisia and threw copies of it into the camp in front of the blockhouse, sticking them

---

into flesh (note that this phrase was emblazoned on the tokens minted in Münster by the Anabaptists, see 17v–18r, as well as on the coins minted by them, though Gresbeck doesn't mention this; see Kerssenbrock, *Anabaptistici furoris*, ed. Detmer, 666–67). He equated the "Word of God" with God himself, and therefore asserted that Jesus was entirely divine. Such a view was entirely in keeping with the Monophysite teaching of Melchior Hofman. Rothman's overt "confession" (formal summary of belief) is that Jesus was "conceived by the Holy Spirit and born out of the Virgin Mary" ("entfangen van dem hilligen geiste, gebaren vth Marien der Junckfrouwen"); Stupperich, *Die Schriften B. Rothmanns*, 230, see also 199–200. The exact same phrase is used by the captured Anabaptist preacher Dionysius Vinne in his confession of October 1534; Cornelius, *Berichte der augenzeugen*, 273. Rothman is at pains to demonstrate that the talk in the Bible of Jesus being of the family of David is purely metaphorical and that Jesus did not take on ("annemen") any flesh from Mary, being the literal incarnation of God himself (in the form of the "Word of God"). Accordingly, Gresbeck is wrong to claim on the basis of the Anabaptist view on the existence of the siblings of Jesus that they denied the doctrine of the virgin birth. Note that in the following sentence, Gresbeck admits to being unable to explain what they positively did believe regarding this issue, which shows that the introduction of the topic of the siblings simply reflects Gresbeck's own attempt to make sense of something he didn't really understand.

429. I.e., the prince-bishop.

430. The book *Restitution* (full title: *Eyne restitution edder eine wedderstellinge rechter vnde gedunder christliker leer, gelouens vnde leuens vth gades genaden durch de gemeinte Christi tho Munster an den dach gegeuen* [A restoration or reestablishement of correct and sound Christian doctrine, belief and life, given to the light of day from the grace of God through the community of Christ at Münster]) was published in October 1534 (for the original text, see Stupperich, *Die Schriften B. Rothmanns*, 210–83). This date accords well with dispatching the book as part of a new plan for relief after the failure of the dispatch of missionaries in October. The association of the dispatch of this book with the notion that the city would be relieved on Easter is false (Rothman wrote two more books in the interim, see also note 453).

onto sticks and putting them in front of the blockhouse at night, so that the landsknechts would get them, intending to get landsknechts into the city from the blockhouse. But these books wouldn't help. The people that they'd sent out to Holland and Frisia with the books came back, and they got letters from Holland and Frisia saying that they'd assembled there and would come to Münster and save them, and would bring along provisions. When the letters arrived, the king got a great revelation from God that the relief was to take place at Easter.[431] The king proclaimed this in the preaching up at the marketplace in the common assembly, and he had a landsknecht that he'd had fetched from the prison stand before him, wishing to cut his head off. This knecht was the king's barber.[432] He wanted to leave the king and march home, and kept requesting permission from the king, asking that he give him travel money for the journey.[433] The king said to the knecht, "You still have travel money." The knecht said, "I have no money." The king said in response, "Why are you lying?" The knecht said, "If it's the case that I'm lying, cut off my head." [78v] So the king searched the knecht to see if he did have money on him. The king found two Joachimsthalers[434] and also some small change on him. For this, the knecht had to die. For he'd been betrayed to the king as still having money.[435] [79r] Now that the king said that the relief was to happen on Easter, he said, "If it's the case that the relief does not take place on Easter, then do to me as I will do to this criminal who stands here before me, and cut off my head too."[436] The knecht was no

431. Gresbeck apparently makes a major chronological blunder as a result of his associative method of narration. He connects the dispatch of *Restitution* in the fall of 1534 with the expected relief the following Easter (March 28, 1535, something like six months later) because of the fact that, in connection with the first event, John of Leiden cuts off someone's head and says that the people should do the same to him if the city isn't relieved by Easter. Gresbeck then goes on to describe how John weaseled his way out of this problem of his own making. The decision to discuss the preparations for the abortive Easter relief at this point in the narrative (78r–81r) leads to all sorts of chronological complications, because a number of events related later in the narrative clearly preceded Easter, but Gresbeck treats them as they followed the failure of the relief to show up at Easter.
432. See Kerssenbrock, *Anabaptistici furoris*, ed. Detmer, 649, for the appointment of a barber named Winold (the last name isn't preserved).
433. The way Gresbeck tells this story in the perfect tense seems to imply that the following conversation about the money took place after the knecht was hauled before the king, but presumably all this story about the discovery of the two coins took place previously, and at the time of the main narrative the knecht was simply brought forward for execution after having been previously condemned.
434. On this coin, see also note 743.
435. See note 165 for the significance of still having money in violation of the earlier decree confiscating money.
436. For Kerssenbrock's mention of this statement, see *Anabaptistici furoris*, ed. Detmer, 772. In a confession, John of Leiden is said to have indicated, in connection with a letter that he sent out proclaiming the relief to come on Easter, "how the king prophesied this long before and had consented to

criminal, he would have been glad to get away from the criminal, the king. The poor people all imagined that the relief would come on Easter. Some people didn't believe that the relief would come on Easter. This knecht fell to his knees before the king, and asked for mercy, bidding all the people in the community to plead for him. The door to mercy remained closed. Many of them then fell to their knees before the king, but they couldn't attain mercy, because the door to mercy was always closed. In the end, the door to mercy was closed in the case of the king.[437] The king had the knecht brought to the city gate, and had his head cut off, for the sake of the two Joachimsthalers, and for having said, "If it's the case that I am lying, cut my head off."

Expectations of relief on Easter, and the Anabaptists' fighting spirit

[79v] Now that the king had proclaimed that the relief would take place on Easter, the people looked forward to Easter. The menfolk equipped themselves with weaponry and armor and clothed themselves in hose and doublets, made à la landsknecht.[438] The king had all the men come up to the cathedral square once every week with their weaponry in their main company and lost company. There, they went into battle order and had a battle against each other just as if they were upon the enemy, so that they would learn how they should conduct themselves whether they would fight a battle with the enemy right away or on the morrow. All the folk who were capable of arms equipped themselves like this, fitting themselves out just like a company of landsknechts. For they dared to exchange fire with the landsknechts every day, just as if they'd pursued warfare all their days, so brave and stout were they.[439] If they killed a person, they made no more of it than they would of killing a dog. If the rebaptizers were killed, they (some of them) didn't even have any regard for this. If one of the rebaptizers died,

---

have his own head cut off provided that such did not take place" (Cornelius, *Berichte der augenzeugen*, 373).

437. I.e., after the city's capture.

438. For the significance of dressing like landsknechts, see also note 302.

439. Note that this statement makes it clear that even though a few landsknechts may have joined their ranks, the Anabaptists were basically composed of people who hadn't served as soldiers before.

they said that they'd striven[440] in piety [80r] and earned the crown.[441] He was with the Father. In this way God would soon save His folk. When they died like this, it was all the will of God.

A wagon fort is prepared for the relief, which fails to arrive

So the king had a wagon fort made in expectation of the arrival of the relief.[442] They were going to march out into the field with it when the brothers arrived from Holland and Frisia.[443] This was the relief on which the king relied, and they informed the common folk in the city that God would relieve them. If God had relieved them, they wouldn't have needed any wagon fort. If God had been with them, no one would have been able to act against them. It was all buffoonery what they engaged in. So they fitted out the wagon fort and had artillery placed in it consisting of demi-culverins and falconets and demi-falconets and serpentines (they also had a full field culverin cast).[444] They also installed guns on carts, just like organ pipes standing side by side, consisting of full[445] arquebuses. These were installed side by side on the carts, so that six or eight of the arquebuses lay side by side. Whenever they fired them, they would go off at the same time. They made the wagon fort of no more [80v] than fifteen or sixteen wagons because they didn't have the wood to make a bigger one. They also placed

440. The Low German word used here can mean both "stride" and "fight." Presumably, both senses are meant, and the translation is an attempt to convey this ambiguity.

441. The "crown" refers to the crown of martyrdom.

442. Although the use of wagons as an ad hoc defensive device dates back to antiquity, the early modern use of them begins with the Hussite revolt of the early fifteenth century, where the Hussites scored a number of successes by forming wagons into a square behind which they could place guns to defend themselves. The novelty was that the wagon train equipped with guns could move across the comparative open territory in the Czech lands and be formed into the wagon fort (*Wagenburg* in modern German, and "wagen borch" in Gresbeck's Low German) when needed. The practice spread to the south among the Hungarians and Ottomans, but it attained only a short-lived usage in Germany, where the forests and rolling landscape made it less suitable. As recently as the Peasants' Revolt of 1524–25, it was used (to no avail) by the rebels. For a general discussion, see Arnold, *Renaissance at War*, 82–83 (he uses the term "war wagon").

443. Gresbeck clearly associates the construction of the wagon fort with the expectation of relief on Easter (80v), but he later associates the abandonment of the project (86v) with the relief expected from the Anabaptist rising that was suppressed in January 1535 (86r and also note 463). It seems more likely that such a large project would have been undertaking at the earlier (December?) rather than in the final stages of the siege, when the Anabaptists' powers and spirits would have been flagging.

444. For a discussion of the various sorts of artillery mentioned by Gresbeck, see introduction, section 3.2.

445. The point of "full" is to show that these were full-sized arquebuses rather than the smaller demi-arquebuses.

a palisade around the wagon fort.[446] This palisade was arranged so that it could be carried in sections. Each section could be raised into position, and they could be spread apart. These palisades had sharp iron shafts in front, and the bottom side had an iron peg, with the palisade standing up and leaning against an iron pole. If they'd hauled the wagon fort into the field, they would have fixed the palisade around the wagon fort. This palisade was for the cavalrymen, who couldn't ride onto the wagons on account of the horses, because otherwise they would have run the palisade into the horses' bodies.[447] In this way, the king made preparations in expectation of the arrival of the relief, and he would have moved out of the city in force, imagining that he would take possession of the world. So Easter arrived,[448] and the relief stayed away. The common folk then said that it was all a lie what they were engaged in, saying, "Let that one cut off the king's head, just as he said."[449] The king was [81r] informed that the people in the city were going around saying that the relief stayed away and didn't come on Easter, as the king had said, and that if it was the case that the relief didn't come on Easter, they should do to him just as he would do to the knecht whose head he'd cut off. So the king had a warning (sermon) given. He said in this sermon, "Some of you go around saying that the relief hasn't come as I announced to you, on Easter, and that if it was the case that the relief didn't arrive on schedule, you should do to me just as I would do to the knecht who stood before me. No, dear brothers and sisters, have you retained that so reliably in your memory? Will you set a schedule for God? No, God will not have a schedule set. You must first be free of sin, of all sin. In that case, God will certainly relieve us."[450] In this way, the king quieted the folk, so that they had to keep quiet. For the king would not have been able to quiet everyone, if he hadn't had his retinue—Knipperdolling and the other burghers who adhered to him, and the Hollanders and Frisians (the criminals)

446. A palisade consisted of stakes (usually with an iron tip) that were erected in front of a fortification to make it difficult for attackers to approach.

447. It's hard to imagine anyone in his right mind riding his horse up onto such a wagon. Presumably, the palisade was intended to ward off attacking infantrymen.

448. March 28, 1535.

449. For the original statement, see 79r. Presumably, "that one" refers to the man who had executed the barber for the king.

450. In the previously quoted confession of John of Leiden, directly after his offer to be beheaded if the relief did not arrive on time at Easter is mentioned (see also note 436), the text continues: "But Easter came, and the relief failed to appear. He said how he had meant not the external relief but the internal one, in the spirit." For Kerssenbrock's version of the king's excuse, see *Anabaptistici furoris*, ed. Detmer, 792–93.

and all those [81v] who adhered to the king. Whatever *he* said and did was all said to him by the councilors and preachers.[451] What one didn't know, the other did. On top of that, there were a great number from all lands.[452]

Stutenberent writes a second book to drum up foreign relief

So the king along with his retinue did not know what course of action he was going to take. The relief didn't come. So Stutenberent came up with one more plan, and he wrote one more pamphlet. This pamphlet was supposed to be *On Vengeance*.[453] They had it printed and also sent it to Holland and Frisia, where they knew rebaptizers. It was written there that everyone should get up, take the sword in his hands, and march to New Israel. The vengeance of the Lord would start any minute, and they should put themselves on the defensive and come by force. The king and Stutenberent imagined that they would gain use of the folk in the world, so that they would rescue the city. This was the relief that they spoke of, that they kept speaking of. When the king got news (got letters) from Holland and Frisia, [82r] he informed the common folk that he had a revelation from God, it having been written to him by letter.[454] Now that the book was sent off, the relief was supposed to happen in three weeks,[455] and he had

451. Note Gresbeck's conception here that John of Leiden was not really in charge of events and was simply implementing policies determined by the councilors and preachers, and that among these "powers behind the throne" only Knipperdolling deserved to be named.

452. Presumably, Gresbeck means places other than Münster itself and Holland and Frisia.

453. *Vengeance* (full title: *Eyn gantz troestlick bericht van der Wrake vnde straffe des babilonischen gruwels, an alle waren israeliten vnd bundtgenoten Christi, hir vnde dar vorstroyet, durch die gemeinte Christi tho Munster* [A completely consolatory report on vengeance against and punishment of the Babylonian abomination, to all true Israelites and allies of Christ, scattered hither and yon, through the community of Christ at Münster]) came out in December 1534 (for the original text, see Stupperich, *Die Schriften B. Rothmanns*, 285–97). According to the surviving fragment of the confession of an unknown Anabaptist, one thousand copies were sent to neighboring towns and villages (Niesert, *Münsterische Urkundensammlung*, 147). Gresbeck's explanation that the text was written in response to the failure of the relief to arrive on Easter is clearly false. Rothman wrote one more text during the period of the siege, but it goes unmentioned by Gresbeck; *Concealment* (full title: *Van Verborgenheit der Schrifft des rykes Christi vnde van dem daghe des heren durch de gemeinte Christi tho Munster* [On the concealment of scripture and on the day of the Lord through the community of Christ at Münster]), which came out in February 1535 (for the original text, see Stupperich, *Die Schriften B. Rothmanns*, 299–72). Conceivably, Gresbeck has confused these two works of Rothman, and the second was written in response to the suppression of the gathering Anabaptist relief in Holland in January (see note 461).

454. I.e., he claimed that the news he alone (and presumably his advisors) received in the letters had been made known to him in a revelation.

455. Given the dating of this attempt to the period after the failure of the Easter relief to arrive on March 28, some date in late April is implied. However, since the relief discussed here failed because of

it proclaimed in the preaching that all those who wished to join the march out should come up to the cathedral square, and those who wished to remain in the city should go to their watch where there had been assigned so far. "No one will be forced to join. Whoever will not happily join the march out of the city, let him be free to remain in the city, because we also need people in the city, since the city must be defended. It's much better for that person to remain in the city who is afraid that he would be struck (shot) to death than for him to join the march out, because these people don't have the real faith. They're praying to God to get the real faith. For those who wish to join us in the march out must fundamentally have the faith in God to believe that God is with us. If God is with us, who can oppose us? The godless won't have the power to take the least hair from our bodies." That's what they had proclaimed in the preaching.[456] "If there are womenfolk or sisters who would be happy to join the march out, they should also come up to the cathedral square. [82v] For we'll need the sisters when we travel in case some people become ill or they get shot." They were also fearful about how faithful they were.

Preparations for the new relief

All the men (all those who wished to join the march out) then assembled and came up to the cathedral square together and were then listed. Each one had his weapon and armor with which he would take part in the march. The king appointed captains and officers anew. They then made five banners, and they made a lost company and a main company.[457] They then did battle against each other as if they'd come upon the enemy, the way they'd been accustomed to do in the past.[458] They would come up to the cathedral square one day every week, on Thursday. The king had made

---

Schenck's crushing of the Anabaptist uprising in late January (86r and also note 461) and the book that started it was written in October, it would appear that the start of this three-week period would have been somewhere around New Year's (to allow time for the Anabaptists in the Low Countries to gather their forces and move on Münster, though there's no way to know how practical the plan actually was).

456. Gresbeck feels compelled to interrupt the quotation to express his (retrospective?) incredulity at the absurdity of the preceding assertion.

457. A "banner" signifies not just a flag, but by metonymy it's a term in military language for the unit of men who stood underneath the flag (a regiment notionally numbering about five hundred landsknechts, but clearly there were fewer in this instance). Apparently, the organization of the field army set up back in October (69v) had not been maintained in the interim, so the organization had to be reestablished and the relevant officers appointed anew.

458. For similar exercises, see 55v, 69v, 70v.

them have a game day every week. They would assemble together up at the cathedral square, and they formed their ranks and had a battle among themselves. But they never went out the gates and fought a battle with the enemy apart from exchanging fire with them. When they now had nothing to do up at the cathedral square, they came there all the same [83r] when it was their game day and played every sort of game. One played cards, another threw the ball or played with the bow, or they ran against each other or played at rhyming around just like children (for the king and the leaders had taken away the money), and the others played at rhyming around.[459] This game day went on with half of the city's men playing and the other half remaining on watch duty. But in the end the game day was abolished. The king got it into his head that they would again become too wild, too foolish. For they'd reached the Holy Place, or they would have fallen again into sin.[460] The king realized that it would do him no good. For this reason, the game day had to go, and they abolished it.

Determination of who would march out to meet the relief

On the next day, the men who wished to remain in the city came up to the cathedral square. They numbered about three hundred, young and old. The king came up to the cathedral square with Stutenberent, and they inspected these men who wished to remain in the city. Some [83v] of the others who wished to take part in the march out also came up to the square and inspected those who wished to remain in the city, and they were contemptuous and derisive of their wishing to remain in the city. The king went into the cathedral with Stutenberent and all the men, and Stutenberent went and stood on a bench. He said, "Dear brothers, here we have another large company, and with it we'll man the city walls all around. If it's the case that we need more men in the city, we'll take them from the other company and place them with you, so that you'll be strong enough." Stutenberent continued,

459. Presumably, what he means is that adult competitions involving rhyming normally included a wager of money, but because of the confiscation of money in the city, the contestants had to play the way children did—without betting. The form of the compound verb ("vmme-remen") seems to imply some sort of "round" competition, but I can find no parallel for this compound in either High or Low German, so its exact significance is unclear to me.

460. For the "Holy Place," see also note 329. The sense must be that now that the Anabaptists had implemented the will of God in their community, they couldn't slide back into the pagan ways of the rest of humanity.

"Dear brothers, the intention is not that in this way we'll march away from you. Rather, when we're gone, we'll be more concerned about you than about ourselves. For we'll mostly leave our wives and children here. We won't march away very far, and we'll soon be back with you." So they were divided up, and the king spoke: "Now, dear brothers, each of those who wish to remain in the city is to go up to his watch post, and the others who wish to take part in the march out should come up to the [84r] cathedral square." In this way, it happened that one group went up to the watch, and the other went up to the cathedral square. The king went around the city with his councilors and inspected every watch to see how many there were in each. Where there were too many of them, he took some away. He assigned these men where there were too few. The king placed an officer over each watch to rule the folk when the king had moved out of the city with the other brothers. This officer assigned to the men in his watch, each separately, where he was to stand guard when the king with the others were out of the city in their company. In this way, they arranged the men for the defense. The king took away some more of those who wished to join the march out and put them too on the watch (those who were to stay in the city), so that they would always be strong enough to hold the city.

Women chosen for the march out

[84v] The next day, the womenfolk who wished to join the march out came up to the cathedral square. These numbered about three hundred. The king wouldn't take along all the womenfolk, and he reviewed them. He took those who served his purpose out of the company, and the rest went home. Those womenfolk who wished to take part in the march out also came up to the cathedral square with their weaponry, one with a halberd, another with a handled spear, and in this way they formed ranks. The womenfolk who wished to take part in the march out whom the king wished to take along numbered about fifty actually, and they were listed under their names.

Determination of which women would march out

They had all the womenfolk who wished to stay in the city, consisting of the youngest womenfolk, come up to the cathedral square the next day. They too came with their weaponry and went around the square [85r] in their ranks, just like a company of landsknechts. The king and the captains ordered the womenfolk around the city along with the men who wished to remain in the city. They divided the womenfolk into as many companies as there were gates around the city. Each company of womenfolk went by itself and stood in ranks, three deep. Each company left the cathedral square in ranks, and they got up and sang a German hymn, "A Mighty Fortress Is Our Lord God." Each company went to the gate to which they'd been assigned. The captains then went around the city and ordered the womenfolk up to the earthworks and along the walls. Whenever all the men who would march out came up to the cathedral square, the other men who would remain in the city had to keep the watch on the earthworks and the walls during that time. Whenever there was an alarm so that they struck the assault bell, each person would run to his assigned post, so that everyone knew where he was to take his stand. [85v] The womenfolk did likewise and also ran to the posts where they were assigned with their weaponry.

The relief fails to materialize

Up at the cathedral square, they would walk around quickly, but it wouldn't happen that they marched out the gate in a company. The relief wouldn't come. They firmly expected that the Hollanders and Frisians would come and rescue them. There were supposed to be a hundred thousand of them who would come to Münster and rescue them. That was the rescue they were watching for. For they informed the common folk that God would relieve them. If they'd come in such numbers, they would first have taken control of the bishopric of Münster, then the bishopric of Osnabrück, then the bishopric of Cologne and the territory of Cleves, and then they would have gone on to take control of the whole world.

Excuses for the failure of the relief

When the relief didn't come, it was all the fault of their sins, because they weren't righteous the way they were supposed to be. The king found out that there were rebaptizers on the way [86r] who would move to Münster. These rebaptizers took possession of a monastery, and Jorgen Schenk besieged them in it and stormed the monastery three times.[461] The third time, Jorgen Schenk's assault was victorious, and he killed them all, hanging the

---

461. For Schenk's campaign against the gathering Anabaptists, see Kerssenbrock, *Anabaptistici furoris*, ed. Detmer, 776–77. The date of these events is January 1535.

leaders from the walls. The king had found this out, that Jorgen Schenk had defeated them. Then they realized that they couldn't make it through the territories, so that they realized that everything in their situation was lost. The Hollanders and Frisians also said how the rebaptizers in Holland had possession of three cities, so that the rebaptizing would then spread over all of Holland. The king then had a great sermon preached up at the market. There, Stutenberent stood up on a bench and said, "Dear brothers and sisters, as it seems to us, we're relying on our foreign brothers who are supposed to come to us. This is not what we should rely on.[462] God will certainly relieve us when it's our time. But if they come, we'll take them as reinforcement. We'll certainly take even the devil from hell as reinforcement if we can fulfill the will of God." (The criminals meant their own will.) "But you shouldn't rely on the brothers. But if they come, that will happen through the will of God." That's how they pulled the wool over the common people's eyes, [86v] as long as they could, right to the very end. Mightily though they preached, the relief never came. They'd prepared everything in terms of artillery and their wagon fort—none of it would happen in the way that they would have been happy to see.

The Anabaptists refuse to give up, and starvation strikes

When the king, his councilors, and all the leaders of the rebaptizers noted that the other rebaptizers in Holland or Frisia or wherever they were gathered together couldn't make it through the territories, they knew full well that they were holding a losing hand. Still, they wouldn't give up. If they'd still surrendered the city, many people could still have received mercy from the lord.[463] It was revealed to the king that they shouldn't use the wagon fort but should abandon it, for it wasn't God's will for us to defeat our enemies with our might.[464] "It's not by our might that it's done. God will strike

462. As it stands in the narrative, this sermon follows the failure of the abortive relief mission that was the new plan after the failure of the relief expected on Easter. Given the chronological confusion by which the Easter relief (78r–81r) was related before the present relief effort, which in reality seems to have taken place in January but is narrated as if it took place after the Easter effort, it seems that the present sermon with its talk about not relying on outside assistance should be dated to a period after Easter. That is, because of his chronological confusion, Gresbeck is placing it in the correct historical date but the wrong one in terms of his own narrative.

463. I.e., from the prince-bishop, not God.

464. Gresbeck slips into the first person in his indirect speech before quoting the king's words directly.

them in the heart, so that they'll run away, as if they were struck by force. Dear brothers and sisters, we've angered God by having counted on our intelligence and cleverness. We must await the time when [87r] God will relieve us." So the wagon fort was given up and they abandoned it. They re- alized that it wouldn't happen, that the relief stayed away. The relief came a bit earlier than they would have preferred.[465] For the hunger and woe came to hand. Whoever couldn't fast had to rush from the city and get himself killed. That was a harsh relief for them. Relief is what they wanted, for the real rebaptizers said that before they surrendered the city and gave up the baptizing, they'd starve to death for it. If they then died of hunger, they did this for the sake of God, and for this they would later have heaven.[466] So the hunger stood up among them, and it became the one prophet for them, saying the real truth to them and telling them no lies about the relief. So they set everything aside and waited for their Father, but the Father stayed away for too long.

Entertainment held as a distraction

So they now had other foolishness in hand, setting everything aside and defending the city as long as they could. [87v] It was revealed to the king that wonder after wonder was to take place, so great was the joy they would see.[467] The king had one third of the city meet up at the market, men and women. This lasted for three days. For the city was divided into thirds, so that watch duty took place in the city every third night.[468] So the third part come up to the cathedral square. Once this third was gathered together, and they'd looked at and watched what sort of great wonder would take place there, the king with his queen came up to the cathedral square with his councilors and all his servants, and he walked up to his house and went

465. More of Gresbeck's irony, since this "relief" will come in the form of death.
466. I.e., attain entry into heaven for their death in the service of God. For a more explicit expres- sion of this sentiment, see 140v–141r.
467. The following long narrative of three-day festivities (87v–94v) has no explicit indication of date. However, the fact that the deacons are reduced to serving only beer and bread (88v, 91r) and the failure to ask for contributions (unlike the procedure for the feast held in October, 68r), which indicates that people no longer had any food to spare, suggest that the date of the festivities took place during the famine in the spring. This impression is confirmed by the decision to ease the social restrictions and allow the young people there to engage in dancing despite the objection of the more steadfast Anabap- tists (92r, 94v), which likewise suggests a late date when the regime's increasing desperation forced the king to give in to the desire of people to go back (in part at least) to the old ways.
468. Presumably, what Gresbeck means is that those assigned to watch duty (all the adult males) were divided into three groups, and each group was on duty only once every three nights.

and took his place by a window. The king had his place at the window, having decked himself out magnificently with gold chains and silk pieces. The queen had decked herself out similarly along with all the councilors and attendants. The king had a book lying in front of himself in the window, and this was a book of the kings. He read out a chapter from it, and the chapter that he read was supportive of the king. [88r] He read how King David had striven,[469] how he'd slain his enemies, how the angel came out of heaven with a glowing sword and struck King David's enemies away before him.[470] "Dear brothers and sisters, this can very well happen among us too. The same God still lives!" After the king read a little like this, the preachers stood below the window where the king had his place, up at the cathedral square. The preachers and schoolmasters had some young boys with them, and they sang the German hymn in discant, just as the students sing out the cantilena.[471] The preachers and the schoolmasters sang the one verse in discant with the small boys. The common folk who were standing around them sang the second verse in German. Once they'd sung one verse, the king read on again. Then the preachers started singing again. Eventually, Stutenberent

469. For the sense of "striven," see note 440.

470. Gresbeck is apparently recalling the content of the reading by memory alone and didn't consult any biblical text (note the vagueness of the citation "a book of kings"; presumably, he had one of the Books of Kings in mind). At any rate, in no passage does an angel descend from heaven with a glowing sword to smite David's enemies. In 1 Chronicles 21, an angel with a drawn sword is seen by David, but it is threatening Jerusalem with destruction in vengeance for the enumeration of the people by David, which had annoyed God (God eventually relents and instructs the angel to put the sword away once David offers to build an altar to God). The chapter that seems the most likely candidate as a text that could have led to this garbled recollection on Gresbeck's part is chapter 22 in 2 Samuel (known as 2 Kings if the books of Samuel and Kings are counted together as Kings 1–4), where David thanks God for "delivering him out of the hands of his enemies." In his recounting of the events for which he is thankful, David notes that God "bowed the heavens also, and came down . . . he rode upon a cherub, and did fly" (2 Samuel 22:10–11). This passage may have led to Gresbeck's memory of the angel. God is said to have "sent out arrows, and scattered them; lightning, and discomfited them" (22:15), which may have something to do with the glowing sword (perhaps this is also connected with some dim recollection of the events of the Apocalypse). David says that God "delivered me from my strong enemy, from them that hated me; for they were too mighty for me" (22:18). This seems consonant with Gresbeck's recollection, and would be a very appropriate text for John of Leiden to have cited as evidence that divine relief was at hand (see the further statements to this effect in verses 38–49). Note also that earlier Gresbeck has John of Leiden refer to God's having a "glowing sword" as a sign of his righteous anger (54v).

471. "Discant" signifies traditional polyphonic ecclesiastical singing, in which the text is chanted alternately by various groups of singers. Describing the singing as "discant" is somewhat surprising in that the elaborate discant style of the late medieval period, which generally obscured the actual text by drawing out the words in a way that rendered them unintelligible, was rejected by the reformers. Perhaps Gresbeck is merely alluding to the responsive element of discant without meaning that the singing here actually followed the traditional practice. "Cantilena" signifies a form of singing that is less complicated than discant, with a main voice on top of the music with contrapuntal voices below.

too went and took his place in the window and preached. Eventually, he said, "Dear brothers and sisters, [88v] all those who are assigned here should remain up here at the cathedral square. The others should go back home or go to the watch post to which they're assigned."[472] Those who remained up at the square sat down, each one beside his wives. The king then came with his queen and all his wives (fifteen[473]) and with his councilors, attendants, and preachers along with their wives, and they too sat down. The king had had a place prepared for him, where he sat with his royal household. They sat there, just as if they would lay out a supper. The deacons had bread and beer set out on the tables, and nothing else. They sat and ate, and they were joyful. But the king had enough to eat and drink on his table. The preachers went by the tables saying, "Dear brothers and sisters, this is how you must endure, with God's help, on bread and beer, until God makes things better, until our relief comes. For you're going to come to even greater temptation [89r] before you're relieved. God wants to assay and test you, wishing to see whether you too will fall away from His Word, whether you'll actually hold to Him because you promised Him. For He wants to keep for you the promise that He made to you. Then He will hold to you." In this way they convinced the people, so that they were joyful. They would gladly suffer for God's sake what they could suffer. When this meal was over, everyone would certainly have eaten some more. Those who still had something to eat at home could go home and eat. As for the great wonder and joy that took place there, they couldn't get their fill from it.[474] Eventually, Stutenberent said, "Dear brothers and sisters, if anyone wishes to go home, he may do so and come back. Here even greater joy is going to take place." So everyone went away home, and the king went home with his queen and councilors. The king equipped himself on horseback along with all his cavalrymen and marksmen in their full armor. The king was in his full gear from head to foot, [89v] with his golden crown up on his head, and he came riding up to the cathedral square, with his councilors riding in front of him and in back. In this way, he rode around the cathedral square. All the folk came back to the cathedral square, and they saw the king in his estate. The queen also came with her fellow wives, and they watched what

472. Seemingly, in addition to the one section of the watch that had been summoned to the square, other people were also present (including women).

473. See also note 207 for the number of his wives.

474. More of Gresbeck's irony. He means that their hunger wasn't satisfied by the mental diversion (see also 93v, 121r).

sort of wonder was going to take place there. Eventually, they then set up two poles, and on the poles they hung a wreath of rosemary, which was as large as a hand's breadth around. The one pole was for the king and the cavalrymen who carried lances, and the other pole was for the marksmen who carried short firearms. Eventually, the king took the lance and the helmet from his page. He laid the lance on his gear and ran at the wreath with full force, so that he would win the wreath with the lance. Once the king was running like this at the wreath, the trumpeter started blowing and the drums sounded the alarm. The king had a run at it first, and the other riders with the lances followed him and also ran at the wreath. The king missed several times, and then he did win it, and the other cavalrymen [90r] also won it. The marksmen ran at the other wreath, one after the other. This running went on the whole day long. The trumpet and drums would go off again, whenever the king would start up running again. When the king won the wreath, one saw great joy. Then the king had the prize, and there was laughter at this. At this point, the queen stood up with her fellow queens, and they saw the great joy and laughed. They had a good laugh. The king still had enough to eat. The others were beginning to become sick from hunger, so that they began to walk with canes. The king imagined that he would entertain them with holding court in place of their eating. This wouldn't happen. No holding court takes the place of eating. So they carried on this joy up at the cathedral square with the target practice of running at the wreath. There were some people up at the square watching, and some also played and threw a ball. After the tournament took place like this, the day came to an end. Then they had all those folk gather in a company. [90v] The king's chancellor, Henry Krechting, then said, "Dear brothers and sisters, what took place here today up on Mt. Zion is not foolishness or jesting. I tell you truly, this is all God's will. God wants to have it so. It took place for His praise and glory. For this let us thank the Father." Then they stood up and sang a German hymn, "To God alone on high be all glory."[475] When the song was over, everyone went home.

Second day of entertainment

The next day, the second part of the people came up to the cathedral square. The king again took his place in the window, and he again read out of the

475. For the identification of the hymn, see note 282.

book, just as he'd done the first day. The queen and his councilors were all beside him, and the preachers also stood below the window with the small boys. They sang the German hymn in discant, and the other folk sang in German, just as they'd done the day before. Stutenberent again took his place in the window and preached. Eventually, he said, "Dear brothers and sisters, those who are now [91r] assigned here should go up to the council hall and sit down there, each with his wives." They did this, and the others went back home. The king also came with his queen, his wives (fifteen), and with his councilors and all his servants, and he walked very magnificently up to the council hall. The king sat up in the council chamber with his councilors and his wives, and the common folk sat up in the council hall.[476] The deacons had salt and bread and beer laid out on the tables, and up in the council hall they piped and drummed and they sang. They also preached to these people that they had to endure with God's help, and that they would be tempted in this way, speaking before them just as they'd done the first day. Eventually, after the meal was over, the king stood up with his queen and went from the council hall onto the marketplace in front of the hall with all his wives, to the accompaniment of piping and drumming. The king took the queen by the hand, and performed the opening dance. [91v] His councilors followed him with the other wives. After this took place and the dance was over, the king went back with his queen and his councilors to the council chamber in the council hall, where they'd sat before. Up in the chamber they had piping and drumming and lute playing and fiddling, and then went on dancing with their wives. This was all God's will, in honor of the Father. The other common folk up at the council hall also danced, and they also had piping and drumming. Those who desired to dance were allowed to dance. Then the young fellows and the young womenfolk danced, and some said, "Things will now become good again. If there's going to be dancing again, then things will become good again, in the old way." There the young folk danced and ran riot the whole day up at the council hall, just as if they'd been released after having been in prison. When they were allowed to start up dancing again because they had permission from the king and the preachers, with their foolishness they sustained

476. The council chamber is the room for the city council's deliberations in the council hall. It was here that the Treaty of Westphalia that ended the Thirty Years' War was signed in 1648, and for this reason the room is known as the Peace Hall (*Friedenssaal*).

the folk in this way right until the end. Eventually, Stutenberent came [92r] from the council chamber. He went and stood on a bench, and he gave a sermon. Eventually, he said, "Dear brothers and sisters, this joy that has taken place here is God's will. For I've recognized that some of you are going around with a sour look on your face, and are scornful that dancing has started up again. There's no warrant for this. They may look as they please, for we Christians are free in everything that one may enjoy in the world, be it dancing, be it singing, jumping, or playing. Every sort of joy that we can enjoy we may certainly enjoy—provided we have no harm by it—to the praise and glory of God. All the joys that the godless have and enjoy we too may have and enjoy. These are freely available to us. We praise God with them, and the godless praise the devil with them." He said that whoever still desired to dance was to dance some more, as long as they wished, and make themselves joyful with God's help. So they all kept on dancing until the evening. Eventually, the king came from the council chamber with his councilors and his captains and [92v] officers. These men walked in front of and behind the king, with silver chains hanging from their necks and wearing very costly coats that they had on. These coats belonged to the burghers and squires that they'd driven out of the city. The king walked in their midst, with his scepter in his hand and a golden crown up on his head, and his master of the court[477] in front of him with a white staff. In this way, he went home. The queen also went home with her servants and her fellow wives. Then the common folk also went home. In this way, they carried on such great joy for the day in the city.

Third day of entertainment

So, on the next day, the third section of the folk in city came up to the cathedral square. The king again took his place in the window with his queen and his councilors and all his officers, and he again read from the book, just as he'd done twice before. The preachers and the schoolmasters and small boys again sang just as they'd done twice before. After the king finished his reading, Stutenberent came to the window and preached, [93r] just as he'd done before. Eventually, he said, "Dear brothers and sisters, all those who are now assigned here should go up to the council house and

---

477. Tilbeck.

sit down there." There they went and sat down together, and the king with his queen again came very magnificently in his estate, going and sitting in the council chamber. They again had piping and drumming, and ate salt and bread, and danced and sang. And there they also carried on great joy. In the end, it was all finished with the fool. It was all Hollander's work.[478] When a Hollander is seven years old, he's the most intelligent that he'll ever become. They started so much foolishness that there's no speaking of it. They're generally half idiots. It's impossible to write or to say it, and you can't even retain it all in memory. The common people in the city could realize that their situation wasn't right, that it was all buffoonery what they were engaged in. For they were overpowered, because the foreign man had possession of the city. So they had to keep quiet, and they hoped that things would all get better, that they would give up the city. If some people had [93v] learned before what they later learned, not one person would have stayed in the city on the Friday apart from the rebaptizers, John of Leiden, Knipperdolling, and Stutenberent along with their fellowship.[479] Now eventually, once they'd danced enough up at the council hall and eaten salt and bread, and carried on great joy, the king went with his councilors to the cathedral square, along with the queen and all the folk. There, the king made great joy. The king had a race with his councilors and servants. The king beat all the others at running, so quick was he at running. The others also raced and played other games, whatever they wanted. The queen with her fellow wives and some other women stood and watched the running, the great joy that took place there. Eventually, the king grew tired of running, and some of the people went home. They would have been much happier to eat something if they'd had anything. There's poor holding of court where there's no bread![480] For they didn't become full from the joy that they saw there.[481] [94r] So the king adjourned the racing, and they went on dancing again with the women. Eventually, the king had his attendants gather together. They had to tie their daggers to their sides, and they bound the sheaths of the daggers to the cross guard, so that the daggers

478. For the notion, see also note 197.
479. For similar expression, see 12v, 41r, 33v, 40v, and 93v.
480. The same phrase is used on 139r. It sounds like a proverb but is presumably Gresbeck's own coinage.
481. For the same idea during the previous day's festivities, see 89r.

would not come out, so that they didn't cut themselves on the daggers.[482] Then the musicians had to strike up a dance. The attendants then danced with the daggers, the way they would dance through swords, as if it were Shrovetide.[483] This was all a real idiot's piece (Hollander's work).[484] So, they danced for a while, the king and the queen with her fellow wives, and the other wives watched this dancing, the great joy that the attendants carried on with the dancing. These attendants were partly landsknechts and partly renegade priests, who'd rushed to the city or were prisoners in the city.[485] Whenever these prisoners came back out of the heathen house,[486] learned the faith, and were baptized, the king would take them into his court, and they then became his attendants. They too had entered the Holy Place.[487] Little Hans of Longstreet [94v] had also entered the Holy Place and was also an attendant of the king.[488] So the last are supposed to have had as much as

482. The text actually reads "so that the sheaths would not come out," but this is an obvious slip of the pen. In the first place, sheaths can hardly fall out, and it's equally obvious that the danger of getting cut comes from the daggers themselves falling out of their sheaths.

483. "Dancing through swords" ("doer de swerde danssen") is a German expression to describe the formal sort of dancing known as the linked-sword dance. This practice consisted of a long line of males (generally around twenty, but sometimes many more) who each had a sword (or something similar like a staff) in one hand and grasped the end of the sword of the next man with the other. Sometimes the elaborate dancing involved movement through or over swords held out by certain of the dancers (hence the phrase used here). The origins of this European form of dancing are disputed, but it became popular in the wealthy cities of the Low Countries in the fourteenth century, and from there spread to Germany, where it was particularly widespread in the sixteenth century. At first, the dancing was performed by traveling entertainers, but it soon became associated with guilds, which put on shows as an expression of civic and corporate pride. In Germany, these events were particularly associated with Shrovetide at the end of Carnival. The practice died out in Germany in the late sixteenth and early seventeenth centuries. There appear to have been two causes of this. First, the more dour attitudes brought about by the Protestant Reformation and then the Catholic Counter-Reformation led to attempts to stamp out the frivolous entertainments associated with Carnival. Second, the protracted period of warfare during the Dutch struggle for independence from Spain and the Thirty Years' War was not favorable to these sorts of festivities, which were expressive of municipal pride. (For a general treatment of this form of dancing, see Corrsin, *Sword Dancing in Europe*, esp. 42–51, for our period in Germany.) As for the dancing with daggers here, this seems to have been similar to sword dancing in that the dancers were linked to each other by holding someone else's weapon, but presumably because the attendants hadn't practiced, they held on to the sheaths of the daggers rather than open blades.

484. The phrase "clownish Hollander" ("mael Hollander") was a proverbial expression of German contempt for Hollanders (it also appears in 111r); the Hollanders apparently returned the feeling (see Schiller and Lübben, *Mittelniederdeutsches Wörterbuch*, s.v. "mal").

485. I.e., the landsknechts were prisoners or renegades, but the priests were all renegades.

486. For the heathen house, see also note 320.

487. For the sense of "Holy Place," see also note 329.

488. This sentence was struck out in the Cologne manuscript and is omitted in Cornelius's text. Seemingly, the point of this extended description of the dancing by ex-Catholics is for Gresbeck to get a dig in at Hans of Longstreet by indicating that he was in fact an active member of the king's court (this is stated explicitly on 147r). The implication of this sentence was presumably not lost on the editor of the Cologne manuscript to judge by its excision. Kerssenbrock (*Anabaptistici furoris*, ed. Detmer, 649) also lists a John Longstreet among the king's attendants.

the first.[489] Eventually, after the dancing was over, Stutenberent had the folk gather together, and he said, "Dear brothers and sisters, what took place here is all God's will, so that nobody should view this in irritation or see it as foolishness. If anyone doesn't like it and is scornful of it, we can let that happen. For it's God's will like this. Let us now go home, and let us thank the Father for His good deed." So they got up and sang a German hymn, and then everyone went home.

It was just a deception

In this way, they fulfilled a prophecy—this joy—and they played the fool three days long. This was supposed to be the will of God, and one was supposed to be praising God with it. So it was all God's will. Whether it was good or evil, it all had to be right. For there was nothing else for them to do. When the relief didn't come, they had to use up their time. God might well pity the regime that they carried on in the city—[95r] such a devil's rule as they had in hand, with them deceiving all the folk, and putting them in such a piteous condition with it, and making so many people poor. Many a simpler poor person knew no better—just as one does find many naive people in the world—who couldn't grasp this and could get no understanding out of it. But many did know better and helped exercise rule with the king, and there was no sympathy for them. Now they've gotten their reward, and now they've been punished. God forgive them their sins. Let everyone protect himself against false prophets and preachers like these, and not let himself be led astray. Let him take an example from the city of Münster and the other cities in the world, be they in the High or Low Countries,[490]

489. The reference is to Matthew 19:30 ("But many shall be last that are first, and first that are last"). With the preceding sentence about Hans of Longstreet left out, the point of the quote becomes obscure. As it is, Gresbeck is presumably alluding to the perceived unfairness of the collaborator being rewarded for the capture of the city, whereas Gresbeck, who claims to have come up with the plan first, received nothing for his efforts (156v). Thus, the man who was first (Gresbeck in coming up with the plan) is last (in rewards), whereas the man who was last (Hans) is now first.

490. In Low German, the term Upper Country (*overland*) normally signifies the comparatively mountainous regions of southern Germany in contradistinction to the plains of the Lower Country (*nederland*) along the coast of the north. The latter term eventually came to be associated with the Burgundian territories along the North Sea (the modern-day Netherlands and Belgium), while the overland had a more restricted sense, signifying specifically the Rhineland to the southwest. Given Münster's proximity to the Netherlands, it's conceivable that Gresbeck has the narrower geographic sense in mind, but since he seems to be speaking rather broadly, it appears preferable to imagine he has the more general understanding in mind. See Lübben, *Niederdeutsche Grammatik nebst Chrestomathie*, 92, for a Low German grammarian of the mid-fifteenth century who used the term "Upper Country people" ("averlender") to specify speakers of High German (as opposed to Low German).

and not allow the rebaptizers to burst in as deeply as they did in Münster. Whenever they get the upper hand, they'll do just as they did in Münster. Let everyone protect himself against this! Behave as holy as they wish, they are not to be believed. Let other cities be wary about this.

Starvation worsens

[95v] The hunger became great in the city—so much so that women and children began to cry for bread.[491] The deacons had no more to give to the folk than a piece of bread that everyone still got occasionally. But so long as they still got a piece of bread, they could quiet all the folk, and for as long as they still had grain, the king had it forbidden that anyone should be so bold as to do his own baking or brewing in his house. The king and the councilors imagined that in case they[492] had something secretly hidden that the deacons hadn't gotten, they would still get it and had an order given in the preaching that if someone still had meal or grain, they should bring it up and give it to the deacons.[493] "For the deacons are to go around the city once more and examine the houses and look in all the nooks and crannies. If the deacons find something that you've hidden away, they'll take it from you, and you will be punished for it. Whatever more the deacons get will then be divided among the community." So the deacons went around the city in each parish, and they entered all the houses and examined all the corners. The deacons found much more that the people had secretly [96r] hidden away. One had hidden it in the bedding (in the straw), the other had hidden it stuck in the attic (in the rafters)—in many secret crannies where someone had hidden something. The deacons examined all the crannies

491. After his (chronologically confused) account of the various attempts to rescue the city from the siege through the intervention of outside forces, Gresbeck turns to the regime's measures to deal with the starvation that developed during the last stages of the siege in the spring of 1535.
492. I.e., the general populace.
493. The position in the narrative of this discussion of the confiscation of foodstuffs seems to imply that this took place after Easter 1535, but evidence from confessions made in December 1534 shows that the procedure whereby grain and meal were confiscated by the deacons and then distributed by them was already in force at that time (see Kerssenbrock, *Anabaptistici furoris*, ed. Detmer, 737n2). As it turns out, Gresbeck is rather vague about the earlier confiscation of food by the deacons. He notes at the time of their initial appointment that they inventoried the food people had in their houses (22v), and when they conduct another examination of people's houses to see about confiscating excess clothing, he also refers to their later refusal to give back the food that they had confiscated (62v). Whatever the exact date, the search described here clearly took place late in the siege, when supplies were giving out and the Anabaptist leadership were desperate to rout out any additional foodstuffs that they could lay their hands on.

that they could think of, and everything they could find they took away from the people and went off with it. Those who still had something hidden that the deacons couldn't find kept it and were able to eat from it as long as they could. For they couldn't get anything back from the deacons. Those who still kept something secretly, whether meal or malt, would bake or brew at night. The king was informed of this and had an order issued to the millers that they shouldn't mill for anyone, whether for baking or brewing, except for the king's bakers and brewers.[494] Now, the miller colluded and secretly milled for the people all the same. So the people would go at night to the mill and have the milling done. The miller was willing, provided that he got a share and made his fee from this. If the king and the councilors had been informed of this, they would have had all the millers who were in the city hung. Now that the king [96v] had noted that the provisions were beginning to give out, he had his cares and took care of himself with wine and beer.[495] He had the best wine and the best beer that there was in the city brought to his court, and he also had enough grain and meat brought to his court, so that the king with his royal household would certainly have held out for another half year,[496] since the king had taken good care of himself with provisions. If the king and councilors had been able to hold out for so long, and many others besides them, then the other common folk that were in the city would have starved to death. The king with his councilors and his court and many others besides would not have been able to hold the city by themselves. The king would say that he would hold the city with the help of four others.[497] He could just as well have said that he would hold it by himself. One time, the king ran around the city at night along the walls, wearing his shirt and with his head uncovered and his feet bare, shouting, "Israel, rejoice! The relief is almost at hand!" At this, the landsknechts shouted from the camp that he should [97r] go back to bed, they would keep on holding the watch. The poor folk rejoice at this, imagining that the relief would soon arrive. But it stayed away for too long, and the hunger came on forcefully.

494. The prohibition on personal baking and brewing was also already in effect in December 1534.

495. The verbal play on the word "care" ("do haeyt der konnynch in *sorgen* geüeft vnde haeyt syck do *besorget* . . .") is more of Gresbeck's wry humor (here alluding to the king's hypocrisy in that his "care" applied only to himself).

496. The same figure is given in 153r.

497. Kerssenbrock vaguely refers to this notion as a sentiment held by the Anabaptists in the city; *Anabaptistici furoris*, ed. Detmer, 632.

Abortive preparations for relief

The king still imagined that the Hollanders and Frisians would come, so that they all imagined that the relief would come.[498] Everyone who was going to take part in the march out was still supposed to equip himself, and the others who were going to remain in the city were also supposed to equip themselves so that they could protect the city when the others were away. The king had an order issued that all those who had sacks should bring them to the deacons, and all those who had more firearms than they needed should bring these up to the council hall. Whether on horseback or on foot,[499] they were to bring these together. That is what happened. The people brought the sacks to the deacons, so that they had a great pile of them gathered together. They were going to take these bags along when they moved from the city to the Promised Land. They would then send them back to Münster full of grain and reprovision the city. But the sacks remained unused. They never came. It would never happen. [97v] It was all in vain what they started. When it wouldn't happen, it was all the fault of their sins. It was often the fault of their sins when they noticed and got news that displeased them. The landsknechts would shout from the camp to ask where they were staying with the sacks, and whether they wouldn't bring the sacks—they would fill them full of grain for them.[500] So the relief once more stayed away. They gave it up, and they all went on keeping watch.

Knipperdolling acts up

A rumor arose in the city that a great wonder would take place that was supposed to have been revealed to the king, and this was going to take place

498. This sentiment is in direct contradiction to the one expressed after the failure of the last relief effort (86v), where the Anabaptists abandoned any hope of relief. Presumably, Gresbeck has lost track of the general progression of his confused narrative. Perhaps the talk here of preparing supplies for a sortie that would result in bringing back foodstuffs to the city was some short-lived plan bruited about to assuage the starving populace in the aftermath of the failure of the Easter relief to materialize. At any rate, the plan seems to dissipate into futility without much ado.

499. Presumably, this clause means whether the weapons were for infantrymen or cavalrymen.

500. This sentence is representative of the problems that Germanic languages can at times get into because of the fact that there is only one regular third-person plural pronoun, so that a sentence involving two or more groups can at times get confusing (Latin would solve the problem through the use of separate demonstrative pronouns, and modern English would normally use nouns or names in place of the pronouns to avoid confusion). If one converts this sentence into a direct quotation of the landsknechts' taunt, then the first and second person pronouns make it perfectly clear who is who.

up at the marketplace. So the king had a sermon given up at the market. All the people that were in the city gathered there, apart from those who were on watch duty. There, the king sat magnificently upon his throne with all his servants, and the preachers preached one after the other, just as if they were holding a disputation together.[501] The folk sat and listened. The preachers had the habit that when they stood preaching, they would pause in the sermon two or three times, and then they went on preaching. One time when the preacher went on preaching, Knipperdolling suddenly jumped up [98r] and began to shout and rave, shouting, "Holy, holy, holy is the Lord! Holy is the Father! And we're a holy people!" He began to dance and behaved so inhumanly that all the folk began to look up and the preachers halted their preaching.[502] Knipperdolling danced before the king and said, "Lord King, this came to me overnight. I will be your fool." He said, "Lord King, good day! How are you sitting here, Lord King?" He did reverence and curtsied to him,[503] and he placed his hands on his sides, and he jumped up and down in front of the king, and he went and sat at the king's feet, and he threw his head back and looked up at the king as if he

501. Gresbeck is referring to the sort of public debating that was a common element in the Scholastic methodology of the late medieval universities.

502. Here begins a long account (down to 103v), spread over several days, of confrontation between Knipperdolling and John of Leiden. Gresbeck's account at first gives the impression that Knipperdolling was just engaging in some sort of stunt or shenanigans, and it's only later that it becomes clear that Knipperdolling's behavior was meant to undermine the king's authority before Knipperdolling challenged him directly. In his account (*Anabaptistici furoris*, ed. Detmer, 690–94), Kerssenbrock makes it clear that Knipperdolling was actually posing a serious challenge to the king with his claim to a new inspiration from God (101v–102v). Presumably, this sort of "dueling spirits" meant nothing to Gresbeck (or at least he chose in his retrospective account to show no hint of having understood what was actually at issue). The only source to give a specific date for these events is Kerssenbrock, who dates them to October 12, 1534, and sees them as the cause for Dusentschuer's summoning of the meal at the end of which the apostles were dispatched to Soest, Osnabrück, Warendorf, and Coesfeld (ibid., 696–97). This association of the meal with Knipperdolling's behavior is clearly wrong (see note 371). Detmer (ibid., 691n1) asserts that Kerssenbrock is nonetheless generally correct and is simply using the time when Dusentschuer summoned the meal to date the goings-on that gave rise to the meal and that Gresbeck is inexact in setting these events so late (seemingly well after Easter 1535). His grounds for this interpretation are that Knipperdolling's activities already appear in the confessions of the captured apostles (i.e., were already known in October 1534), citing no particular event described in these confessions as proof of his assertion. In any event, although Kerssenbrock's account is pretty clearly a compilation based on a number of sources and events, it remains the case that the early fall of 1534—the period soon after the installation of John of Leiden as king, when the new regime had not yet become firmly established—would seem the most "reasonable" time for Knipperdolling to have attempted to challenge the king's authority through a counterclaim of divine validation. As for Gresbeck's implied chronology, it's hard to see why he placed his version of these events at this point, but subsequent passages also seem to relate to earlier events. In any event, a statement at the end of the section ending on 102v makes it clear that Gresbeck himself has no clear sense of when exactly this confrontation took place.

503. For "curtsying," see note 336.

were a real fool. Eventually, Knipperdolling jumped up from the king and grabbed a halberd[504] from one of the attendants, and he laid the halberd on his shoulder and marched like that before the king, saying, "Have a good look, Lord King! We'll go like this when we march out in our ranks, and we'll punish the godless!" Eventually, Knipperdolling called the attendant up, saying to him, "Come here and follow me!" He walked off in front of all the folk and the attendant followed him. He said to the attendant, "This is how we'll step when we march off." Knipperdolling [98v] gave the attendant the halberd and laid it on his shoulder, saying to him, "Go off now and show how you're to go right away or on the morrow when you come to the enemy, the godless." Eventually, Knipperdolling said, "Go and sit down now." Another attendant was sitting there, and he called him up: "Come here now! You know how to behead the godless. Follow me! This is how we will go through the world and punish the godless. God commands you to behead, just as you did to the others, all the godless who won't convert." This attendant had killed many of the burghers and landsknechts who'd one time taken the king and Knipperdolling prisoner when they wanted to revoke the matrimony.[505] This attendant was a leader in the killing, and that's why Knipperdolling called him up. So the attendant went and sat down again, and Knipperdolling went on dancing. In his expression he looked like a dead man. He seemed as if he was possessed, and the truth wasn't much better. All the rebaptizers had a distorted color in their face, being pale and yellow under the eyes and having an inhuman expression. You could tell from their [99r] expressions which one was a real rebaptizer. Eventually, Knipperdolling went and stood on his head, and he jumped in among the women over the benches, first over one, then over the other, and he tumbled round about like this, just like a tumbler or a juggler, acting no differently than if he were out of his mind. Eventually, Knipperdolling straightened himself up again and walked on his feet, and he blessed men and women—some of the men and some of the women. He didn't sanctify them all.[506] To those that he did bless he gave his hand, and kissed them

504. The halberd was the instrument used by a sergeant to maintain order in the ranks of the pikemen when they were drawn up in battle order.

505. By "matrimony," Gresbeck means "polygamy" (see note 203); for the executions carried out after Mollenhecke's uprising and the permission granted to anyone who wished to take part in the killing, see 50r.

506. Here there's something of a play on words in the German that is hard to represent in English, all revolving around the word "hillig" (=High German *heilig*) or "holy." The verb is "hilligen" or "hal-

on the mouth. He said, "You're holy, God has sanctified you," sanctifying a number of men and women in this way. For Knipperdolling got it into his head that they weren't all equally holy, that some of them were still unfaithful. For this reason, he wouldn't sanctify them all. He came to a peddler, and this peddler was sitting on his wares. Knipperdolling said to him, "You are becoming holy, but you won't abandon these wares. You sit on them like a brooding hen in case you can get chicks from it. The wares are your God. You must abandon them if you wish to be holy." Knipperdolling wouldn't sanctify him. But in the end he did. [99v] Knipperdolling walked on and sanctified more people. He came across an old woman that he should also have sanctified. He wouldn't sanctify the old lady. Knipperdolling said, "There comes an old woman running towards me. Am I supposed to sanctify *her* before I'm ready? I had it in mind that I would rather have punched her in the snout. Should I sanctify her before I'm ready?" He wouldn't sanctify the woman. Knipperdolling went on and sanctified more people, saying "Holy you are, God has sanctified you," and kissing them on the mouth. The king sat on his throne, and along with all his councilors and servants and preachers and all the common folk, he watched what Knipperdolling made go on like this. Some people that he wouldn't sanctify stood and cried. Some of them—the simple people—didn't know better. Some people realized that the devil was ruling him.[507] Each one had to keep quiet. Knipperdolling sanctified not one of the king's councilors, preachers or attendants, and he sanctified the other common folk (some).[508]

The king is despondent

Now that the king was sitting like this up on his throne and watching, the spirit of the baptizer came to him.[509] He fell from his throne, and his scepter [100r] fell from his hand. He folded his hands together, and sat like that

---

low," which basically means to "make or call holy." "Hallow" isn't really appropriate for the context; "bless" would be the normal English translation, but that word sounds as if it refers to a statement indicating the fortunate nature of the person's situation rather than his sanctity (it's also to some extent related to the sense of the Latinate term "benediction"). Since the Latinate "sanctify" corresponds in etymological sense to the German, I've chosen to use it as the not entirely satisfactory translation.

507. For a similar contrast between the simpleminded people who didn't realize what was going on and the more intelligent ones who did but couldn't say anything, see 95r.

508. Though Gresbeck makes no such connection, Knipperdolling's surprising failure to sanctify those who were leading figures in the king's government may have had something to do with his later attempt to challenge the king's authority to rule. For the sense of "other," see note 215.

509. For an earlier example of the king being seized by the "spirit of the baptizer," see 65r–66r.

for a long time, as if he were unconscious. He sat there with his whole body as if he was quivering as if he was very terrified, and said nothing, until the end. At this, the women also started shrieking and shouting, and they were dismayed. The spirit began to vex some of them too, so that a person who saw the fuss could have taken fright. It's impossible to say or write, and no one can believe, the way it happened. Now that Knipperdolling saw that the king had fallen from his throne and that the spirit was ruling him—the poor people didn't imagine anything other than that he was endowed with the spirit of God, that God was ruling him—Knipperdolling ran up to the king and suspended the sanctifying. He grabbed the king around and sat him back on his throne, and then he blew the spirit into him. Then the king revived and said in a quivering voice, "Dear brothers and sisters, what great joy I see! The city is going around in a circle, and you all look like angels. The one is more beautiful than the other and brighter than the other, so holy are you all!" Then [100v] they began a shrieking among the women, and a shouting of "Father" up at the marketplace, because the king had received such a revelation. The spirit befell the king once more, but this didn't last long, and he sat down again. In the end, he revived again and said, "Look, dear brothers and sisters! The house is coming forward, the city is still going around in a circle. This means this much—and it's a sign from God—that we're still going to march around the world, and that I'm still going to be a king over the world and to lord over it." His spirit (the devil) then left him, and he came back to his senses. The king called out of the company someone who was standing in the middle of the folk. The king said to him, "Brother, come here, you with the grey cap." This man went to the king. The common folk imagined that the king was going to cut his head off, just as he used to do, and just as he would also do later, when it was convenient for him. So the fellow with the grey cap went up to the king, and the king said to him, "Climb up here by me on my throne." The fellow climbed up onto the throne. Then the king took the fellow and grabbed him in his [101r] arms. He swung the fellow to either side, from one side to the other. Eventually, he also blew the spirit into the fellow, just as Knipperdolling had done to him. The king then pulled a ring with a gemstone off his finger and placed it on the fellow's finger. The king did this as proof that he'd received the prophecy from God for the whole community, that they were all a holy folk, that the one was more beautiful than the other, and they looked like angels, and that he was going to be a king over the world and to lord over it. So the king told the fellow to climb down now, and the fellow climbed down. The fellow was supposed to thank the Father for having become so holy. Knipperdolling said to the fellow, "I had told you that you would become so holy and so great." Once the fellow came away from the king and walked once more upon the ground, he rose up right away and shouted, "Pray to the Father and praise the Father and thank the Father for His good deed!" He jumped up and danced, behaving just like the king and Knipperdolling. [101v] This is what happened with the king and the fellow. Knipperdolling went back among the people, and went on sanctifying as he'd done before. The fellow danced until he couldn't dance anymore, and Knipperdolling also got tired of sanctifying the people.

Knipperdolling tries unsuccessfully to inspire certain men as apostles

Knipperdolling had those men fetched who'd been prisoners with him in the tower of the Church of Our Dear Lady when the peasants and the cavalrymen that My Gracious Lord of Münster had sent into the city before the siege had possession of the city.[510] These men came up to the marketplace. They were also burghers in the city, just like Knipperdolling. These men that Knipperdolling had fetched up to the marketplace he sat up on a bench and blew the spirit into them too. But he couldn't blow the spirit into them. These were poor people and sick people, and they didn't know how to assist the buffoonery the way the king or Knipperdolling or the preachers did.[511] They stood on a bench and looked into the air and folded their hands together and stood and danced. They remained standing like that in one spot and hopped up and down, but [102r] Knipperdolling couldn't blow the real spirit into them. Knipperdolling stood by them and whispered into their ears, saying to them, "He'll emerge, He'll come. If you want to see Him too, pray truthfully."[512] But it wouldn't happen, the spirit wouldn't come out. Knipperdolling couldn't blow the spirit into them. There were four or five of

510. For Knipperdolling's arrest, see 47v.

511. Gresbeck must mean that he considered the spiritual possession exhibited by the king and Knipperdolling to be an intentional fraud, one that the others here weren't privy to, so that they failed to "play their part."

512. Since the German word for "spirit" is masculine (*Geist*), it's conceivable that the third-person pronouns in this quote should be translated with "it," but presumably, something like the Holy Spirit is meant, in which case the pronoun would be masculine in English too.

them that he wanted to blow the spirit into. Nothing would come of it. He then named each of them just as the Apostles were named.[513] One was to be called Paul, another Peter or James or Simon, and so on.[514] These apostles couldn't receive the spirit from Knipperdolling, and they remained just as they'd been when they came up to the marketplace. Knipperdolling carried on his rule with these apostles so long that the king said he would go home and that everyone else should go home. Knipperdolling said he wouldn't go home yet, and they should stay there some more. He imagined that he'd blow the spirit into the apostles. It wouldn't happen with the apostles. Eventually, the king said, "Dear sisters and brothers, we'll praise and thank God, and go home." For the king [102v] was afraid that Knipperdolling would let the fool peek out too far,[515] so that word of their buffoonery would get out, in just the way that Knipperdolling made things go on up at the marketplace.[516] When the king named the sisters first and the brothers last, Knipperdolling said, "Lord king, you're saying that wrong. That's not how I taught you. You should name the brothers first and the sisters next. That's how it ought to be. And you brothers, when you wish to curtsy to the king and do reverence to him, you should curtsy to him over the right leg.[517] And you sisters, you should curtsy to our lord the king and to your husbands over the left leg. This is how you should be obedient to your husbands. Learn this and do it as I've said to you." Eventually, Knipperdolling said to the apostles, "God God, show! God gives gives you leave leave that you should should go go home home." (Knipperdolling said this with long words.[518]) Then they

513. For a later conception that contemporaries were modern-day versions of biblical characters, see the equation of the "dukes" appointed by John of Leiden with the judges of the ancient Israelites (134r).

514. For Jesus's appointment of his twelve apostles, see Matthew 10:1–4, Mark 3:14–19, Luke 6:13–16. The apostles ("envoys") are also known as disciples ("pupils"), and the former designation refers to the mission Jesus gave them to go spread the "good word" on their own (Matthew 10:5–23, Mark 3:13–15, Luke 9:1–6). Paul, on the other hand, was not appointed by Jesus during his life (famously becoming a Christian only some years after Jesus's crucifixion), but he claimed that whereas Peter had received an apostleship in reference to the Jews, he himself had received from Jesus (post-humously, as it were) the same position in reference to the gentiles (Galatians 2:7–8; see also Romans 1:5, 11:13).

515. Or as we would say, "let the cat out of the bag."

516. This sentence seems to indicate that Knipperdolling's unsuccessful attempt to "inspire" the new apostles was distinct from the benedictions and other hijinks related in the preceding section (97v–101v).

517. For the sense of "curtsy," see note 336. In the present passage, Knipperdolling is clearly referring to which leg is extended in lowering the body.

518. Presumably, Gresbeck means that the words written twice were not actually repeated but pronounced in a drawn-out manner.

sang a song of praise, and each went away home. This happened one day in the city of Münster.[519]

Knipperdolling tries unsuccessfully to make himself king

The next day, they came back up to the marketplace. Knipperdolling went on dancing and raving again, just as he had done [103r] before on the previous day. Knipperdolling sat in the king's place, going and sitting on the king's throne. He wanted to be a king too, and he said to the king, "I should by rights be a king. I made you into a king." When the king saw and heard Knipperdolling say that he should by rights be a king and that he'd made him into a king, the king became angry and went home. Knipperdolling went on acting like a fool. Eventually, the king came back up to the marketplace. Knipperdolling then climbed back down from the throne, and the king went and sat up on the throne. The king then ordered Knipperdolling to keep quiet, and Knipperdolling kept quiet. When Knipperdolling said that he should by rights be a king, and that he'd made him into a king, sitting on the king's throne, Knipperdolling said the real truth, if he'd stuck to it. The common folk looked up and imagined that they should have felt ashamed of themselves because word of their buffoonery had gotten out. But they wouldn't let things run so deep, though things weren't far from that.[520] Then the king said, "Dear brothers and sisters, don't let yourself be affected by what Knipperdolling said, because he isn't in his senses." He said the nicest things [103v] and preached the common folk out of their senses. I can write no more about how they (Knipperdolling and the king) parted. In the end, everyone went back home, and they sang a song of praise.

Knipperdolling gets off lightly

Knipperdolling denounced himself and asked the king for mercy—he didn't know what he had done, the devil had led him astray. The poor people still couldn't notice. For those who by now knew it better had to keep

---

519. Note the vagueness of the chronology. Seemingly, Gresbeck himself isn't very sure about when this event took place.

520. The expression here is a bit obscure, but it seems to mean that while the dispute between the king and Knipperdolling was approaching the point where it would completely undermine their authority, they pulled up short in their dispute before the matter got out of hand.

quiet. The king put Knipperdolling in prison for two or three days, so that he should do penance, wishing to punish him not only for this matter but also for other matters. Also, Knipperdolling would go to work so often that in the end the king didn't really trust Knipperdolling.[521] There were some rebaptizers in the city who would have preferred to have chosen another king. They wanted to have a temporal king and a spiritual king.[522] The king had those who wanted to have this put in prison, so that they would do penance. These were Hollanders and Frisians. If they'd been burghers or landsknechts, the king would have had them executed.

Parody mass

[104r] Now they had another joy in hand.[523] The king had men and women assemble in the cathedral, half in the morning and the other half in the afternoon. Half of the city's women and men came to the cathedral in the morning. The king's master of court[524] was in the cathedral, and he'd had an altar made out of boards and covered this altar with cloths, just like any other altar on which the mass was to be celebrated. So the folk stood and watched what would come of it in the end. The king with his queen came along with his wives and his councilors and servants, and he brought along a fool named Carl. They dressed this fool in vestments, so that he would celebrate the mass. For he was a real fool. This fool used to live with a canon, and he remained in the city on the Friday when they chased out the other folk. So the fool went and stood before the altar, and he celebrated the mass, with all the folk laughing at him. They made offerings to the fool for the mass, and he had a servant, who served him in the mass. When the mass was over, Stutenberent said, "Dear brothers and sisters, all the masses that take place in the world and the mass that the fool celebrated—I consider the one mass to be as holy as the [104v] other. For this reason we

521. The expression "go to work" is presumably an ironic way of saying "engage in tomfoolery."
522. I.e., one for the secular government and one for religious matters. According to Kerssenbrock (*Anabaptistici furoris*, ed. Detmer, 693–94), Knipperdolling asserted that while John of Leiden would continue to be the king "according to the flesh," he was to be the spiritual king.
523. The initial words seem to indicate that the event took place after the events relating to Knipperdolling. The text of the mass that is made fun of seems to be specific to Christmas (see also note 528), and there is evidence that one of the participants may have escaped from the city by January 3, 1535, which would rule out a date in the spring (see also note 527). If this mass does date to Christmas, then perhaps this is confirmation that the preceding narrative about Knipperdolling does date to the fall of 1534 (see also note 502).
524. Tilbeck.

had this fool celebrate the mass, and because we wanted to explain to you what the mass signifies." When the mass was over, the king had the pipes and drums start up, and he fenced with his fencing master in the cathedral with swords, spears, poles, daggers, and halberds. When the fencing was finished, everyone went home.

Repeat performance of the parody

So the other half of the city entered the cathedral, and they too waited for the king, wishing to hear the mass. The same altar was covered in cloths just as it had been before.[525] Eventually, the king arrived very magnificently with his councilors and attendants. The queen also arrived very magnificently with her fellow queens and her councilors and servants. Then came the priests who were to celebrate the mass. There were three of these priests, the one who was to sing the mass, the second who was to sing the Gospel, the third who was to sing the epistle. All three went before the altar and took up the mass, having with them what was appropriate for the mass. The one who sang the mass was a burgher in the city. [105r] His name was Everett Remensnyder.[526] The one who sang the Gospel was named John of Schwerte.[527] The one who sang the epistle was Knipperdolling's servant (his name is unknown to me). So these priests stood up and began to sing

525. The much greater detail given for the mass performed in the afternoon presumably means that Gresbeck himself was present on this occasion.

526. Remensnyder was a minor servant of John of Leiden (see also note 657 for details).

527. The identity of this man seems to confirm that the mass took place in 1534. After his treachery in betraying John of Leiden (74v–75v), Henricus Graes was sent by the prince-bishop to Wesel to infiltrate and betray the Anabaptist circles there (Kerssenbrock, *Anabaptistici furoris*, ed. Detmer, 781), and for this mission the prince-bishop gave him two companions who were to pretend to be his disciples. One of these was John Swerten (as Kerssenbrock calls him), who had departed from the city and left his wife there. An order that the prince-bishop sent to his siege commanders on January 3, 1535, commanded them to preserve the life of this man's wife if she fell into their hands, and this order is taken by Detmer (ibid., 731n1) to be recompense to John for his services. It's possible that this John Swerten escaped from the city immediately after the mass, though the interval until the prince-bishop issued his order seems rather short. According to Kerssenbrock, John Swerten (and the other companion) were supposedly so ignorant of Anabaptist matters that they had to follow Graes's lead in pretending to be his disciples. On the surface, this doesn't seem to fit in very well with the description of someone who less than two weeks earlier had participated in a parody mass. On the other hand, it would certainly have been in the man's interest to conceal from the prince-bishop any such involvement in Anabaptist activities, so we may discount this discrepancy. It seems hard to imagine there were two Johns from Schwerte (a town outside Dortmund, a city to the south of Münster) involved in the Anabaptist events in Münster, so if Gresbeck is correct in naming him as a participant in the mass, this would seem to show that Gresbeck is narrating this mass out of chronological order. Gresbeck includes John among the list of native collaborators (119v).

the mass, singing "Gaudeamus."[528] Father Remensnyder[529] sang "Gloria in excelsis deo," and the common folk responded, singing "Et in terra pax hominibus." Then the epistler sang the epistle, and the gospeller sang the Gospel. Then they sang the "Credo." Father Evert Remensnyder then turned around and preached with vulgar words. At the end, they prayed for the living and the dead,[530] all with unseemly words, and everything that he preached was carried out with vulgarity. When the preaching was over, they made the offering. The king made an offering first along with his queen, and the common folk then made their offerings. They offered every sort of thing that they could get: cats' heads, rats, mice, bats, horse legs, and other unseemly things that they could get.[531] [105v] They offered as shameful things as they could get to the priests. Father Evert Remensnyder stood there and looked at the offerings, as they kissed him on the hand (he'd wound the stole over his hand). There stood the king with his queen and with her fellow wives and the king's councilors and the preachers and Knipperdolling and Tilbeck (he was the sexton[532]) and all the leaders of the rebaptizers. They stood and laughed, watching the great joy that they were carrying on with the mass they were holding. While the offering lasted, all the folk stood and laughed at it, so random were the things they offered, consisting of every sort of beast that they could get. There they chucked cats' heads and cat skins (they'd eaten the cats) and the mice and the rats at each other. When they were chucking the skins, they carried on great joy with this, so there

528. The texts quoted here seem to indicate that this is a Christmas mass. The phrases "Gloria in excelsis deo" and "et in terra pax hominibus" are obviously the antiphon and responsion based on Luke 8:14 (the words spoken by the angels to the shepherds), and the word "Gaudeamus" is probably the introit (opening words) of the nativity mass (in full form, "gaudeamus omnes fideles: salvator noster natus est in mundo": "Let us, all the faithful, rejoice: our savior is born in the world"). (The "Credo" and the "Agnus dei" are sections of the regular mass, that is, the sections of the mass that are included in every mass, as opposed to sections specific to the masses for particular ecclesiastical days.)
529. Gresbeck is being ironic in referring to the mocker with the title "Father" ("paffe" in the German, which is the regular term for a priest).
530. Masses for the dead were another traditional practice rejected by the Anabaptists. See Kerssenbrock, *Anabaptistici furoris*, ed. Detmer, 185, for a statement of Rothman's about his rejection of such masses.
531. The "great tithe" consisted of one-tenth of the major grain crops and was owed to the rector of the church (the man who possessed the ecclesiastical benefice), whereas the "little tithe" consisted of vegetable crops and small animals and was owed to the vicar (the man who was hired by the rector to actually serve as the priest in the church). Hence, it's appropriate for the tithes to be paid to the priest celebrating the service. Tithes were yet another aspect of the traditional church to which the Anabaptists took exception, and presumably the "unseemly things" given as offerings were meant to reflect the Anabaptists' contempt.
532. A sexton (also called a sacristan) is an official put in charge of maintaining a church building and its graveyard. Tilbeck must have held this position for the cathedral, where the parody mass took place.

was great laughter in the cathedral. In this way, they played the fool at the time, throwing cats' heads and cat skins and rats and mice at each other. (In the end, they would certainly have eaten the skin along with the cats, and the mice and rats,[533] and soon enough the king ate [106r] the cats in his court. He had them roasted like a rabbit, having them covered over in sugar a finger thick.) When the offering was finished, the priest went on with the mass and raised up the God.[534] They (the epistler and the gospeller) sat behind him and raised up his vestments, raising them so high that they looked at his backside. At this, all the folk started laughing. When the "Agnus dei" was supposed to be sung, they gave him the "pace."[535] When the priest came and wanted to receive the "pace,"[536] the gospeller turned around and turned his backside to him, and he was supposed to kiss him on his backside. In this way, they played the fool. When the mass was over, he gave the benediction with unseemly words. Once the mass was over, Stutenberent stood and gave a sermon, saying to the common folk why they'd celebrated the mass. He said what the mass signified—all the masses that took place in the world were just as much a [106v] mass as the one that they'd celebrated there. "With all the masses that have taken place in the world they made a disgraceful mockery just as we did with the mass."[537] When everything was finished with the mass, the priests got undressed, since they were clothed just like other priests who were going to celebrate the mass. In this way, they played the fool like this with that mass. Eventually, the king had piping and drumming start up, and he fenced in the middle of the cathedral with his fencing master. All those who could fence had to fence as well. The queen and her fellow wives stood and watched the fencing, as did all the common

533. More indication that this event took place after the tightening of the siege in the fall of 1534 worsened the food situation in the city (people were now forced to eat cats), but well before the dire circumstances of the spring of 1535, when they would have consumed any scrap of food they could get their hands on (including the cat heads and skins and the mice and rats that they had previously disdained).

534. This refers to the late medieval practice by which the celebrant would raise up the consecrated host (taken to be the physical body of Christ) for the entire congregation to see. The Anabaptists of course rejected any such presence in the host and despised what they took to be the idolatry of the traditional mass.

535. At the end of the "agnus dei" section of the mass, the priest would say "pax vobiscum" ("peace be with you") to the congregation, who would then give each other the "kiss of peace." Here the Latin term appears in the German text in a vernacular version of the Italianate form "pace."

536. In regular Catholic practice, the priest remained separate from the congregation and would share the "kiss" only with his assistants in the mass.

537. This sentence was originally written in indirect discourse, but in the Cologne manuscript was rewritten by the original scribe to make it a direct quote.

folk, with great joy taking place there with the fencing and with the piping and drumming. Eventually, the king went home with his wife, having had piping and drumming start up in front of him. He went home to his court, and the common folk went home. This is how they heard the mass in the morning and the afternoon.

Renaming of the city gates

[107r] They gave all the gates in the city new names.[538] The following are the names by which the gates were called before the baptizing came to Münster and the king had the upper hand along with the criminals. There were ten of these gates, and they'd been called this for more than a hundred years and are still called this:

> St. Tilgen's Gate[539]
> Bisping's Gate or the New Work
> Our Dear Lady's Gate
> Jew Fields Gate
> Cross Gate
> New Bridge Gate
> Horst Gate
> St. Maurice's Gate
> St. Servatius's Gate
> St. Ludger's Gate

Other towers and blockhouses around the city kept their names, and these were not changed.

Thus, the king now gave the gates new names, and they follow here in the order that I [107v] wrote the gates above:

538. For a general description of the city gates (as part of the city's defenses), see Kerssenbrock, *Anabaptistici furoris*, ed. Detmer, 19–24. Kerssenbrock refers to the renaming of the gates only in passing (ibid., 774). A confession of December 1534 already gives the new names for four gates (Jew Fields, St. Maurice's, St. Servatius's, and St. Giles's or Tilgen's; see ibid., 774n1). This appears to be further confirmation that for whatever reason, Gresbeck is now relating events from the end of 1534.

539. The name of (A)egidius, a French saint of the late seventh and early eighth century, was variously garbled in the vernacular (the English version "Giles" comes from a French version). In German, the Latin form is used formally, but the Low German version often takes forms like Ilgen and Gilgen. Here, the initial consonant has been dissimilated into "t." This gate is in the southwestern section of the city wall, and Gresbeck gives the remaining gates in the correct order if one goes around the city in a clockwise direction. It's unclear why he starts the list here.

Queen's Gate
Bisping's Gate or New Work
   (This gate kept its name, and this was not changed.)
West Gate
Gold Gate
North Gate
Water Gate
East Gate
Silver Gate
King's Gate
South Gate

Renaming of the city streets

They also named the streets after the gates before the rebaptizing came to Münster and the king had the upper hand in Münster:

St. Tilgen's Street
The Bispinghof or the New Work

This place kept its name, and this was not changed. The Bispinghof [108r] is an asylum,[540] and next to it was the site of St. George's cloister.

Our Dear Lady's Street
Jew Fields Street
Cross Street
In front of[541] the New Bridge Gate (New Bridge Street)
Horst Street
St. Maurice's Street
Salt Street (in front of St. Servatius's Gate)
St. Ludger's Street

The king also gave the streets new names corresponding to those of the gates as he'd ordained for them. The streets follow in the order I set out before:

---

540. For Kerssenbrock's discussion of the Bispinghof asylum, see *Anabaptistici furoris*, ed. Detmer, 61.

541. For the sense of "in front of," see note 120.

Queen's Street
The Bispinghof, etc.
West Street
Gold Street
North Street
Water Street
East Street
[108v] Silver Street
King's Street[542]
South Street

Special placard with alphabet for naming children

The king had the streets named after the gates, and in each street he had a small board hung on which it was written what the street was supposed to be called: "Item.[543] This street is called Gold Street (or Silver Street, and so on)." The other streets kept their names. There were too many of them, and he (John of Leiden) had no plan for them. Whoever in his court called the gates or streets or the cathedral or the cathedral square or any of the churches something other than what he'd ordained had to drink a jar of water. They also had a notice posted in front of every gate, on which was written what the gate was supposed to be called. This was posted in front of all the gates. On this notice was also written the following alphabet:

A a b c d e f g h I k l m n o p q r ſ t v w y z ʒ.

A	a	b	c	d	e	f
Aver	*all*	*blyde*	*connych*	*der*	*elende*	*frolych*
But	all	happy	king	who / the	wretched	happy

---

542. The renaming of Salt Street as King's Street is peculiar in that there already was a street called King's Street (the road leading north from St. Ludger's Gate branches into two, the eastern road being named St. Ludger's Street, which was renamed South Street, and the western road being named King's Street, which it's still called today). Perhaps since Salt Street is the main avenue for approaching the Main Market from outside the city (via St. Servatius's Gate), it was decided to rename this the King's Street as a ceremonial route. It's unclear what happened to the name of the original King's Street. Kerssenbrock (*Anabaptistici furoris*, ed. Detmer, 774) confirms Gresbeck's new names.
543. For the sense of this, see note 393.

g	h	I	k	l	m	n
gevorden	*hoechheyt*	*iunkheit*	*klochheyt*	*luest*	*macht*	*nicht*
become	highness	youth	cleverness	desire	power	not

o	p	q	r	r	ſ	S[544]
op	*provet*	*qvaet*	*ruemet*	*reynne*	*se*	*Set*
on	tests	bad	cleans	pure	they	are

t	v	w	z
truwe	*van*	*wer*	*ʒonciensie*
true	of	defense	they're saints[545]

[109r] This was posted in front of each gate with the alphabet, along with what the gate was supposed to be called. There was also posted a large notice that they'd had printed. Written on it were the provisions that everyone had to adhere to, and whoever didn't adhere to these was to be punished

544. Though in the simple list at the start, the minuscule (lowercase) form of "s" is used, here the form is written in the distinctive majuscule (capital) form.

545. Some points are worth making about this peculiar alphabet. The first "r" is an alternative form of "r" in Gothic handwriting (similar to a cursive "r" in modern English handwriting except that it lacks the vertical stroke on the left). The first "s" is the so-called long "s" (ſ). In medieval orthography, the general (but by no means uniform) tendency was to use this form in non-final position, with "s" used in final position. (This practice was used in English as recently as the late eighteenth century.) The letters "j" and "u" were at this time simply variants of "i" and "v," which explains the absence of these letters. The "w" is a variant of "v," used to represent German sound corresponding to the English "v," with the sounds "f" and "v" being represented with the letter "v." In both his letter from Münster and throughout the Cologne manuscript, Gresbeck shows himself to have a hard time distinguishing when to use "v" or "w," and he confuses the two letters here. The reason for the use of the capital "s" is unclear. One might relate it to the name below if the latter is taken to be the biblical name Seth, but the use of this name here appears inexplicable. The form is probably meant to be the third-person plural of the verb "to be" (Gresbeck uses the forms "sient" and "sien" for this in his literary Low German, but perhaps "set" is the form used by whoever drew up the alphabet). It would seem that to some extent the words chosen are a sort of free association, but towards the end there appears to be something like a sentence. This presumably accounts for the presence of "s" and "z," which were normally just variants for the same sound.

Now for the words associated with the letters. "Aver" could also represent the "over" (the word is the same as the English preposition; for the latter interpretation, see note 558). "Elend" could mean "foreign" as well, and it could also be a noun ("gloom," "foreign country," "exile"), but the word for "f" favors the adjective. The word for "become" can only be the past participle, and not the present indicative. Without context, the word "ruemet" is a bit hard to pin down (it can also mean "withdraw, abandon, evacuate, put away"), but the words around it suggest the meaning "cleans." "Trüüe" can also be a noun ("loyalty"), but the seeming sentence at the end of the alphabet favors the adjectival usage ("true" in the sense of "loyal"). There is a certain amount of confusion about the word for "w." The form here seems to be the word for defense (which would go nicely with the word for "t"), but in the subsequent list the spelling seems to suggest the High German word for "fire." Finally, the last word is actually a running together in speech of the phrase "saints/saintly are they" ("sunt sien se"=High German *sanct sind sie*) (the medial "c" was used mainly for foreign words and was pronounced "ts," and its use to illustrate the third letter via the word for "king" is contrived, since that word normally begins with "k").

depending on how he'd transgressed, a matter of life or death.[546] This text was posted in front of every gate along with the alphabet. The king had the children named according to this alphabet. Whenever a child was born, they had to go to the king and ask him for the name by which the child was to be called. The mother or the father to the child didn't dare give the child its name. The king gave the name according to the alphabet, and the child remained unbaptized. For all the children that were born in the city remained unbaptized until they came of age.[547] Such was the king's intention after he had kept the upper hand.

A	Aver	1st Child's Name
a	all	2nd Child's Name
b	blyde	3rd Child's Name
c	connynch	4th Child's Name
d	der	5th Child's Name
e	elende	6th Child's Name
f	frolych	7th Child's Name [109v]
g	geworden	8th Child's Name
h	hochheyt	9th Child's Name
i	junchheyet	10th Child's Name
k	klochheyt	11th Child's Name
l	luest	12th Child's Name
m	macht	13th Child's Name
n	nycht	14th Child's Name
o	op	15th Child's Name
p	provet	16th Child's Name
q	qvaet	17th Child's Name
r	rumet	18th Child's Name
	reynne	19th Child's Name
ſ	se	20th Child's Name
s	Set	21st Child's Name
t	Truwelos[548]	22nd Child's Name

546. See *Anabaptistici furoris*, ed. Detmer, 763–70, for Kerssenbrock's not entirely reliable version of this royal ordinance, which was issued on January 2, 1535. In his notes, Detmer reproduces a contemporary transcription of the Low German text (the original is lost).

547. It was of course a central tenet of the Anabaptists that baptism could only be undertaken as a conscious act of repentance by a knowing adult.

548. Note that whereas in the alphabet, the relevant form means "trust" (it would seem), the

w	van	23rd Child's Name
v	wever	24th Child's Name
x	x	25th Child's Name
y	y	26th Child's Name
z	Zsyensie[549]	etc.

The naming of children, and the special child of John of Leiden

[110r] This is how the king had the children named according to the alphabet.[550] When the alphabet was finished, he gave the children names after the prophets and the Old Fathers—David, Abraham, Isaac, Israel, Jacob[551] (the old prophets and patriarchs).[552] Some children who were girls the king had named Eva, and some little boys Adam. Many children were born in the city, but those rebaptizers who had many wives got the fewest children of all.[553] The king had fifteen wives, and there was not a one of all the wives who had children by the king. The king had one wife who was fruitful. This wife was Knipperdolling's maid, and she'd previously been married to a landsknecht, who was shot dead.[554] After that the king took her as a wife.

---

corresponding name has acquired a suffix to make it mean "faithless."

549. This entry (written in an abbreviated way through lack of room) is aligned in such a way that it takes the place of the absent entry for "y."

550. Presumably, what Gresbeck means is that the king picked a name beginning with the same letter of the alphabet as the letter that he came to as he went through the order on the printed sheet. It's hard to imagine that he used the words printed on the sheet ("happy" is conceivable, but he could hardly have named a child "the," "on," or "bad"; "king" would likewise seem to be an inappropriate name for a monarch of such contestable legitimacy to give out). Kerssenbrock gives a rather different version of the procedure for giving names. According to him (*Anabaptistici furoris*, ed. Detmer, 659–60), the king assigned the first seven letters of the alphabet to the days of the week ("a" for Monday, "b" for Tuesday, and so on). This version shows no knowledge of the list of the whole alphabet, and is seemingly a garbling of the bizarre but internally logical system laid out by Gresbeck. For instance, why should only the first seven letters be used? See note 558 for further evidence of Kerssenbrock's misunderstanding of the system.

551. Isaac's son was originally named Jacob, but God later changed his name to Israel (Genesis 32:25–29). In the Cologne manuscript, the name "Israel" is heavily marked out; by whom and why is unclear.

552. "Old father" is a German term for "patriarch."

553. Detmer (Kerssenbrock, *Anabaptistici furoris*, ed. Detmer, 626n3) cites a protocol made after the fall of the city by two well-informed boys (aged twelve and fourteen) who gave the following list of the number of wives held by prominent rebels: Rothman, nine; Knipperdolling, two; Henry Krechting, three; Herman Tilbeck, two; Gerard Kibbenbrock, two; Everett (Eberhard) Remensnyder, three; Henry Xanthus, two; Henry Redeker, three; John Redeker, two; Gerard Reining, two; Herman Reining, two; Magnus Kohus, two. (The boys gave further information, but the scribe got tired of writing it all out!)

554. See Kerssenbrock, *Anabaptistici furoris*, ed. Detmer, 618–19, for an anecdote about a

The common people in the city would say that this child ought to belong to the landsknecht, that it didn't belong to the king. The queen was also fruitful when she married John of Leiden (the king).[555] The queen had previously been married to John Mathias [110v] (he made himself out to be a prophet, as I described before[556]). He too was killed, so that this child too didn't belong to the king, except that he was a stepfather to the child.[557] When the child was born, there was great joy in the king's court and throughout the city. The king had the child named Newborn.[558] This child was a girl. It was a prophet's child and a queen's child, and the king was the stepfather,

---

landsknecht who had defected to the city and was staying at Knipperdolling's house. He found out, to his outrage, that John of Leiden, who was also lodging in the house, was sneaking to the bed of a maid at night. This was before the introduction of polygamy, and John was known at the time to have a wife back in Holland. The landsknecht then revealed this in public, and it was in order to prevent any loss of reputation that John and the preachers developed plans for introducing polygamy. This version of the motives for instituting polygamy does not appear in any non-hostile source (i.e., the confessions of captured Anabaptists) and it is refuted by clear evidence that John of Leiden's first marriage in Münster took place long before the introduction of polygamy (see note 206). Perhaps the maid's previous marriage to a landsknecht that Gresbeck mentions here has something to do with the origin of the story in Kerssenbrock. In any event, Kerssenbrock lists John's tenth wife as Knipperdolling's stepdaughter Anna, the daughter of Mathias Hangesbecke, who had the nickname Selenmaker (*Anabaptistici furoris*, ed. Detmer, 658). In two confessions (Niesert, *Münsterische Urkundensammlung*, 178; Cornelius, *Berichte der augenzeugen*, 371), John indicated that when he married Mathias's widow, he was already married to Knipperdolling's "magt" (the same word is used here). The word "magt" basically means an unmarried woman of marriageable age, but can refer specifically to a serving girl. The Latin word that Kerssenbrock uses ("famula") (ibid., 658) signifies the latter only and was presumably chosen as part of the story that John was sleeping with a lowly serving girl (note that Kerssenbrock makes no connection between the girl that John was cavorting with when his peccadillos were revealed by the landsknecht and Anna, whom he mentions only in his later list of the king's wives). Presumably, this lowly sense of the word is not what either John or Gresbeck meant by it.

Kerssenbrock identifies the pregnant wife who was not the queen as Margaret Modersonne, number thirteen in his list of sixteen wives (ibid., 659). Since he otherwise shows himself to be poorly informed about the naming of the children (see note 558), his contradictory evidence about the identity of the second pregnant wife is to be rejected.

555. Mathias's wife was named Diewer. This Frisian name ultimately derives from the Germanic form Dietwarda, which appears in modern Dutch as Dieuwertje and, in truncated form, as Dieuwer. Mathias's wife clearly used the latter version of the name, which is frequently rendered in the Latinized form Divara. See Kobelt-Groch, "Divara of Haarlem," for a not-very-deep discussion of her position as queen. Here "fruitful" means "pregnant."

556. See 1r for the earlier discussion; also 14r–v.

557. According to a confession made by the preacher Dionysius Vinne, John himself claimed not to have "known" Diewer (sexually); see Niesert, *Münsterische Urkundensammlung*, 125.

558. Kerssenbrock seems to have confused the naming of the children according to the alphabetical list with the naming of his wives' children, giving the name to Diewer's daughter Averall and the name Blyda to the other daughter born to a wife of John's (*Anabaptistici furoris*, ed. Detmer, 659). His explanation is that the first was born on a Sunday and the second on a Monday, but this is apparently mere conjecture based on his misconception of the system (see note 550). In any event, whereas the second name is simply the second name on Gresbeck's list, with the first name Kerssenbrock has distorted the first word on the list "aver" into the name "Averall," which he interprets as meaning "über all" ("over everything"). This name is evidently an elaboration of the adverb or preposition in Gresbeck's list along the lines of a phrase associated with the king's pretensions to universal rule (see also note 309).

so that there was great joy in New Israel. The king, he gave a sermon up at the marketplace in the common assembly. He said that such a child had not been born since the birth of God, and there had also not been such a king since the birth of God. The one that God had selected in this way was to be a king over all the world and to be next to God.[559] So the king had the child named Newborn. Thus, I don't know about children of his, even if this man John of Leiden had had ten times more wives than he did (he had the most beautiful wives that there were in the city, noble and non-noble).[560] So the king loved the child a lot and had it named Newborn.

Destruction of the city's churches

[111r] The king gave other names to the cathedral and the old cathedral[561] along with the cathedral square, and all the chapels,[562] and all the churches in the city. The cathedral was called the great stone quarry, the old cathedral the old stone quarry, and the chapels around the cathedral square the small stone quarries, the cathedral square Mt. Zion. St. Lambert's Church was St. Lambert's stone quarry to them, and the Church of Our Dear Lady was a stone quarry, and so on with the names of all the churches throughout the whole city. Whoever called the cathedral or the cathedral square, or any of the churches something else had to drink a jar of water, as I described

559. John was clearly trying to make a dynastic connection between himself and the charismatic Mathias via the child. Obviously, a son of his own by Diewer would have been preferable, but he was making the most of the material he had at hand.

560. This sentence isn't clearly expressed (there's no sign of a problem in the manuscript, and there's nothing self-evidently defective in the syntax). The final explanatory clause about the beauty of his wives presumably means that he must have had sex with them, which suggests that the statement (introduced with the bland conjunction "that," which is used more widely in Low German than in English and is translated here with "even if" with the intent of imposing a more logical flow on the line of thought) about the consequence of his having ten times as many wives is meant to signify something to the effect that it wouldn't have made any difference if he had had many more than his already large numbers of wives, since he was having sex with them as it was and still didn't beget any children. The point is presumably to illustrate the initial statement that the rebaptizers with the most wives had the fewest children: John of Leiden had the most wives of all and yet couldn't produce a single offspring of his own.

561. For Kerssenbrock's discussion of the new and old cathedrals, see *Anabaptistici furoris*, ed. Detmer, 34–37. In the first half of the thirteenth century, a new cathedral was built alongside the old one, each having its own ecclesiastical establishments. In 1377, the old one was finally torn down. The canons of the old cathedral generally shared the facilities of the new one with its canons, but a structure to the north of the new cathedral was built for the use of the former, and this was known as the "old" cathedral (though it was actually newer!).

562. Chapels are small shrines dedicated to a particular saint. Medieval cathedrals tended to have chapels built either directly onto their fabric or nearby.

before.[563] There were seven parish churches in the city of Münster, apart from the cathedral and the old cathedral and the other chapels up at the cathedral square. They destroyed or pulled down all the churches in the city apart from two,[564] and they tore down all the church towers, pulling down all the spires (steeples) of the towers.[565] This was done by a Hollander. His name was Francis and he was an adventurous fool.[566] This idiot Hollander[567] set to it and sawed the spire of the tower underneath at the stonework, sawing apart the columns and leaving two or three columns standing intact. He bored holes into these columns and filled them with gunpowder, then knocked [111v] in a strong plug with a fuse. When the fuse was almost burned up, the gunpowder went off. The pillars then blew apart, giving off a loud noise as if a demi-culverin[568] had been fired. They did this twice to each tower. Eventually, the tower (spire) fell down, but the stonework (base) of the tower remained standing. If things had gone according to their desire, they would have torn these down too along with all the stonework of all the churches.

They first tore down the cathedral and the old cathedral with two towers, and all the chapels that stood around the cathedral.[569] They also destroyed the chapels that stood up at the cathedral square, apart from St. James's Church. This remained standing until the end, and was a parish church.[570]

563. See 108v.

564. See 30v and also note 159 for the start of the destruction of the churches back in April 1534. This procedure seems to have gone on for a long time, and Kerssenbrock (*Anabaptistici furoris*, ed. Detmer, 776) mentions the continued destruction of churches as a means of keeping the inhabitants busy when they were not engaged in strengthening the defenses, specifying that the destruction of the cathedral, which had hitherto been used for public purposes, was undertaken on January 21, 1535.

565. Gresbeck gets himself into a bit of terminological confusion at times, but the sense is clear. The "tower" ("toerne") of the churches consisted of two parts, a permanent square base made of stone and a pyramid shaped spire ("kaep(t)") made of wood that arose from the top of the base (here he also uses the word "spyess" as a synonym for the spire). For the most part, the Anabaptists destroyed the spires, but left the stone bases intact. Sometimes, Gresbeck uses the term "tower" to refer to the entire structure including the steeple and sometimes to just the base without the steeple.

566. Kerssenbrock gives three other names for men who carried out the demolition: the carpenters Everett Kribbe, Derek Trutling, and John Schemme. Trutling at least was a local, as he is attested as demolishing the looms owned by nuns during the disturbances of 1525 (*Anabaptistici furoris*, ed. Detmer, 131).

567. For "clownish Hollander" see note 484.

568. For a discussion of the various sorts of artillery mentioned by Gresbeck, see introduction, section 3.2.

569. The interior of the cathedral had already been vandalized back on February 24, 1534 (Kerssenbrock, *Anabaptistici furoris*, ed. Detmer, 521–23); see 10v.

570. The cathedral wasn't a parish church, and this function was carried out by the neighboring church of St. James. The church served the needs of the ecclesiastics of the cathedral (Kerssenbrock, *Anabaptistici furoris*, ed. Detmer, 46).

But in the end they tore it down too, as you'll hear.[571] Of the bells that were in the cathedral tower, the most and the best remained intact, though they chucked two or three out the window onto the cathedral square.

[112r] They destroyed the Church of Our Dear Lady on the inside. They didn't tear it down, but the spire of the tower was torn down.[572] The bells in the tower remained in it. They placed two demi-culverins[573] up on top of this tower, and inflicted great losses in the camp outside the city. So they shot at the tower from the camp and also hit the church through the roof. Thus, the church remained standing.

They destroyed St. Martin's Church altogether, knocking in the vaulting, so that nothing of the church remains standing apart from the four walls. The spire of the tower was thrown down, and the bells were thrown out of the tower and smashed apart.[574] They also placed up on the tower a demi-culverin with which they shot into the camp, but they didn't inflict as many losses as they did [112v] from the tower of Our Dear Lady. On top of St. Martin's tower, two men were shot dead from the camp.

They also destroyed St. Lambert's Church on the inside, smashing apart everything that was inside.[575] They took the roof (shingling) off the church and left the truss standing. As for the tower on the church, it remained standing. The bells remained intact in the tower, and some bells were shot through from the camp. They had to leave the church standing on account of the tower, in case the tower fell over. On top of this tower they had a lookout who kept watch up there during the day. For this reason, they didn't dare tear down the church, in case the tower fell down. This lookout

571. See 136r.

572. Kerssenbrock remarks on the height of the tower; *Anabaptistici furoris*, ed. Detmer, 54.

573. For a discussion of the various sorts of artillery mentioned by Gresbeck, see introduction, section 3.2.

574. According to Kerssenbrock (*Anabaptistici furoris*, ed. Detmer, 573), the carpenter Trutling was crushed by the premature collapse of this tower, his body being found when the rubble was removed after the capture of the city by the prince-bishop's forces.

575. This is the first (implicit) indication in Gresbeck's account of the Anabaptists' destruction of the churches of the desecration of the internal decoration. Gresbeck restricts himself to the abuse of the physical fabric of the structures themselves (and their use as platforms for guns), paying no attention to the destruction of artwork. Conceivably, it simply had no great meaning to him (cf. Kerssenbrock's heartfelt lamentation of this destruction in *Anabaptistici furoris*, ed. Detmer, 522–23). On the other hand, perhaps Gresbeck wished to steer clear of a subject that wasn't particularly germane to the goals of account and could have reflected badly on him since he was around at the time (the Anabaptists were trying to be overtly offensive in the way they carried out their iconoclasm; for instance, when the cathedral was desecrated back on February 24, 1534, they sawed through a diptych of the Virgin Mary and John the Baptist to use it as the floor cover in a latrine for the guards of the walls (see also note 72) (ibid., 522).

would do great insult to the camp by blowing his horn, and whenever he saw a company of folk who wished to approach the city, [113r] he would blow his horn or strike the assault bell. When the rebaptizers were in an exchange of fire, if they were defeated, they would also strike the assault bell. Then all the rebaptizers would run to the watch post to which each was assigned, and some ran out of the city and rescued the others. Whenever this lookout blew his horn or struck the assault bell, he would stick out a banner in the direction from which the enemy were coming. At night too, there were two watchmen up on this tower, one holding watch before midnight and the other after midnight. Whenever the night watchmen heard something during the night, they struck the assault bell. Then everyone ran to the watch post to which he was assigned. The two night watchmen up on the tower, couldn't know for sure, if there was a secret alarm, that the landsknechts were going to wake them from their sleep.[576] The watchmen up on the tower had a little bell hanging to which a long line was [113v] attached. This line stretched from the tower down to the ground, into a house up at the churchyard of St. Lambert's. These watchmen of the rebaptizers, if they heard something at night around the city, so that they were afraid that the landsknechts were about to fall upon the city, they would run to St. Lambert's Church and tug the little line.[577] Then the little bell would sound, and then the watchman would run and strike the assault bell. Then everyone ran to the watch post to which he was assigned.

576. Here Gresbeck's wry humor seems to have gotten the better of him. At the end of the next paragraph, he uses a reference to the landsknechts "waking them [i.e., the defenders] from their sleep" as a way of making fun of the fact that it was the laxness of the night watch kept by the Anabaptists that led to the capture of the city. Because he uses the same terminology here, he's presumably anticipating the second use of the phrase, but its applicability in the present case is less than self-evident. Seemingly, what he refers to is a situation where those on the ground could detect some secret attempt on the part of the besiegers to take the Anabaptists unawares but the watchers in the tower, who had control of the bell that would summon all the defenders, wouldn't be able to tell for sure what was going on from their lofty perch. In this case, "alarm" signifies not the noise used to give warning of danger but the danger itself that makes the summons necessary.

577. This sentence is badly composed. The initial subject ("these watchmen") is left dangling because it doesn't appear in the main clause. Furthermore, one would take them as the referent of the subject "they" of the intervening "if" clause, but it's clear from the overall sense that "they" refers to the rebaptizers on the ground, who are also the subject of the following main clause. The point is that if anyone on the ground suspected that a secret assault on the city was in the offing, he would pull the line to inform the watchmen in the tower, who would in turn sound the alarm bell to summon everyone to their posts. Seemingly, Gresbeck began the sentence with the intention that it would talk about the reaction of the men in the tower to the ringing of the line, but after the intervening subordinate clauses, he forgot about the start of the sentence and made the men on the ground the subject of the main clause, pushing the reaction of the men in the tower to the next sentence (and in the process shifting to the specific action of the one man who rang the alarm bell in the tower).

The king would often have the assault bell sounded in the city so that everyone would run to his watch post. Then the king walked or rode around the city and observed how many folk he still had on the watch (on the walls). For the company kept getting smaller and not bigger over time. Wherever there was a shortfall in the watch he added folks, taking them from another watch post, imagining that he would defend the city because he would have no shortfall. [114r] But in the end everything was neglect on their part. Clever as they were, the holy folk didn't keep a good watch in the end. The Father slept too long. The godless kept a better watch than the holy folk did, and woke them ungently from their sleep.

They also destroyed St. Ludger's Church on the inside and threw down the roofing of the church. The tower of the church was left standing, and the bells remained in the tower.

They also destroyed St. Egidius's[578] Church and threw down the roofing of the church and also the steeple of the tower.[579] The bells remained intact in the tower.

They also dug around St. Servatius's Church with its tower, so that nothing of it remained intact. They dug up all around the churchyard and carried the earth outside St. Servatius's Gate, making an earthwork out of it.[580] Still, in the end, they threw down St. James's Church.[581]

[114v] They also destroyed all the other churches that were in the city as well as all the monasteries that were in the city, just as they did to the cathedral and the parish churches.

These were the seven main churches along with the cathedral and the old cathedral and all the chapels and all the monasteries. They destroyed them and tore them down so piteously that God may pity it. They dishonored and annihilated them so piteously. God dishonored and annihilated *them* back. They used the stones of and from the churches[582] and the altar

---

578. For the name, see note 539.

579. Whereas previously Gresbeck used the terms "spire" ("spyess") and "pinnacle" ("kaep(t)") as if they were synonyms, here he seems to treat them as separate items. The "pinnacle" is properly the very top of the spire, but for the most part the two terms refer to the whole thing. Here, however, "pinnacle" is used in its proper sense. Even so, one can hardly throw down the spire without at the same time throwing down the pinnacle, so perhaps the present passage simply reflects a hazy conception of the architectural terminology.

580. This removal of earth is mentioned in a confession of December 1534 (Niesert, *Münsterische Urkundensammlung*, 32, 37).

581. For its destruction, see 136r.

582. Presumably, the distinction between stones "of" and ones "from" the churches refers to stonework that forms the physical fabric of the buildings on the one hand and artwork and freestanding

stones and the great stone images and tombstones from the churchyards for building.[583] With them they made the foundations under the earthworks outside the gates, and they also used them to rebuild the gates that had been shot apart. This is how the criminals disgraced the churches, and their intention was to take possession of the whole world and to disgrace and tear down all churches. In the end, however, their regime came to an end.

Articles of the Anabaptists

[115r] One still does find many people in the world who imagine that the rebaptizing was right, as was every action that they carried out in Münster. If that had been right, it would have benefited the lives of many people, noble and non-noble, who risked their lives for its sake. That the rebaptizing is not right is shown by the articles that they undertook after they'd baptized the folk. Those articles that followed after the baptizing were contrary to God and all His saints and contrary to the Christian faith and the entire world.[584] The articles were like this:

1) First, they didn't uphold the Ten Commandments.
2) They chased everyone away from his possessions, his house and home, and they took from the people everything that they had.[585]
   [115v]
3) All goods were to be held in common in the city.
4) They wanted to be free in everything.[586]
5) They wanted to have no government.

monuments inside the churches on the other.

583. The contemptuous use of venerable artistic works symbolizing the power and authority of the traditional church for the strengthening of the defensive works is mentioned by Kerssenbrock, *Anabaptistici furoris*, ed. Detmer, 554.

584. Clearly, these articles are Gresbeck's own (hostile) characterization of what the Anabaptists were up to, not their own. In medieval usage, an "article" signifies the summary of a notion under dispute, whether an academic proposition (like Luther's famous ninety-five theses) or an accusation drawn up against someone under investigation by a judicial authority on the basis of depositions and testimony of witnesses. Here, Gresbeck has somewhat muddled these differing concepts, sometimes presenting (unfavorably) the Anabaptists' own beliefs and sometimes listing "charges" against them.

585. After this article, the following text appears in the Cologne manuscript with the same indentation as before but without a number: "And those who were baptized on the Friday and were compelled to the baptizing also had to bring up their silver and their gold and their money that they had." Gresbeck appears to have thought better of putting this information here, as the text was struck out. At any rate, the same point appears below in a more general form (without reference to the enforced baptisms of February 1534) as article 17.

586. For the sense of this, see Rothman's defense of Anabaptist festivities (92r).

6) They wanted to drive out lords and princes.

7) They raised up false prophets and preachers among themselves, and said God had sent the prophets and preachers.

8) They also didn't hold anything about the sacraments, and they annihilated them.

9) They dishonored churches and monasteries and tore down these.

10) They didn't celebrate holy days, be it Sundays or apostle days.[587]

[116r]

11) They didn't hold the four seasons, and they held one day the same as another, making no distinction among the days.[588] Whether it's Friday or Sunday, they eat meat every day.

12) They lusted after their neighbor's housewife.

13) They took as many wives as they wanted.

14) Their lust was to kill.

15) They betrayed everyone and did them in in terms of their lives and property and everything they had.

16) They (some of them) had their first wives beheaded.

17) Everyone had to bring up all their silver and gold and money. One person did so willingly, the other unwillingly. [116v]

18) They undertook the Word of God and Holy Scripture wrongly, and established them as they themselves wished.

19) The leaders of the rebaptizers established a king and said that God had made him a king.

20) And they were waiting for Christ, who was supposed to descend to earth from heaven and walk with them on the earth for a thousand years.[589]

21) The king with his councilors and preachers made a matrimony[590]

587. Although there were several feast days for the various apostles, the term "apostle day" signified the Feast of Saints Peter and Paul on June 29 in particular. It's unclear why Gresbeck should have singled out this day or the feasts of the apostles in general (as opposed to any other feast days).

588. "Holding" (i.e., celebrating) the four seasons presumably refers to the ceremonies associated with the "Ember Days." These were special days of fasting and prayer on the Wednesday, Friday, and Saturday that followed four dates in the calendar: the first Sunday in Lent (usually late February), Whitsun/Pentecost (usually late June), the Feast of the Exaltation of the Cross (September 14), and St. Lucy's Day (December 13). The placement of these days in the calendar meant that they could be taken to signify the start of the seasons. These celebrations had no biblical authority, and for this reason would no doubt have attracted the disapproval of the Anabaptists.

589. For this description of the millenarian view of the imminent end of the world, see 53r and also note 278.

590. For the sense of "matrimony," see note 203.

among themselves and wouldn't uphold the matrimony that God had ordained. They said that there hadn't been a real marriage in fifteen hundred years, that the Word of God had also been kept in the dark for that long, and that all the folk in the world had lived in heathendom for that long.[591] So they were going to bring forth the Word of God again and establish a new world and increase the world. [117r]

22) Mary had given birth to more children after the birth of Christ, so that Christ had brothers and sisters.[592]

23) And the one man should have as much as the next. This turned out unfairly.[593]

These are the articles that they undertook after they got the upper hand in Münster. There are even more of these articles that have not all been retained in memory.[594] Some rebaptizers who are still alive and escaped when the city was captured and had a share in being the leaders and ruling the game know their system better. So the king set to it with his councilors, prophets, and preachers, so that all property should be held in common so that they got the money from the people, informing the poor people that the one man should have as much as the next. If the one man had as much as the next, then they would be equally rich, and then the

---

591. Kerssenbrock (*Anabaptistici furoris*, ed. Detmer, 631) gives a short list of measures that he attributes to John of Leiden as prophet in the aftermath of the suppression of Mollenhecke's rebellion. Within this, he mentions the teaching that no one had lived in a true marriage since the ascension of Christ because the marriages were contracted in a carnal and not spiritual manner, for the sake of such things as physical appearance, money and wealth, and high birth. For a similar conception, see 46r.

592. Already in antiquity, notions of the purity of the Virgin Mary led to the idea that she was a perpetual virgin who never had sexual relations with her husband Joseph (for the most famous exposition of this doctrine, see Jerome, *Against Helvidius: On the Perpetual Virginity of the Blessed Mary*). By the fourth century, this view had become official doctrine, and has ever since been a firm tenet of both the Catholic and the Orthodox churches. It has to be admitted that the argument flies in the face of all evidence from the New Testament, which on a non-prejudiced reading (i.e., without the a priori assumption of perpetual virginity) can only be taken as providing full evidence of Jesus having siblings of both sexes whom Mary bore to Joseph (Matthew 1:25, 12:46–47, 13:55, 27:56; Mark 3:31, 6:3, 15:40, 16:1; John 2:12, 7:3, 5; Acts 1:14; Galatians 1:19). Given their rejection of the Catholic tradition as a valid source for doctrine when unsupported by scriptural evidence and their insistence upon basing doctrine on a close reading of the Bible, especially the New Testament, it's hardly surprising that the Anabaptists took the scriptural references at face value and rejected the traditional doctrine of the Virgin Mary's perpetual virginity. It should be noted that proponents of magisterial Protestantism like Luther and Zwingli upheld traditional doctrine on this point, and this was one of the issues that led them to reject the more radical line of thought represented by, among others, the Anabaptists. For an earlier reference to this notion among the Anabaptists of Münster, see 77v.

593. Gresbeck says the same thing on 21v.

594. Gresbeck means that he has forgotten any other Anabaptist tenets.

one person no longer had need of the next.⁵⁹⁵ He is a real rebaptizer, they said, who is completely bloodthirsty by nature. To be able to get their way, they wouldn't have left anyone alive in the world, be it emperor or king, duke or count, all the territorial lords, [117v] with no one excepted, noble or non-noble. Their every desire is to kill and to murder. They treat those people who won't give themselves over to the baptizing like a dog. If it's the case that they're willing to give themselves over to the baptizing and adopt their faith, then they treated them as their brothers and sisters. If they won't accept the baptizing and their faith, then they kill these people just like a dog. Much more could be written of this. Everyone can certainly recall—and some certainly know—what sort of life they had in Münster, because the devil was their Father. May everyone protect himself from the Father that the rebaptizers shout to. Their intention was nothing other than to take possession of the entire world and to rule in the world just as they did in Münster. Oh, how they would have done in even more people and starved them to death, just as they did in and outside Münster! Knipperdolling would shout, "One God, one pot, one egg, one cake!" Now, there is one God. Before there would have been one pot and one egg and one cake throughout the entire world, they would have starved many people to death in the world, before the whole world would have become harmonious like this.

Destruction of the city's monasteries

[118r] These are the monasteries that are in the city of Münster that they destroyed, as I described before.⁵⁹⁶

The Convent Across-the-Water⁵⁹⁷ is a nunnery, and these are no-blewomen. It's a parish church. There were three or four nuns in it who remained in the city, and it was a male from Coesfeld who administered the convent.

---

595. This seemingly peculiar statement about one person not needing another is a reflection of the dislike of economic dependence that led to the confiscation of money (see also note 165).
596. It is not clear what Gresbeck thinks he has described before. He has merely alluded to the destruction of the monasteries (114v, 115v, see also 1r, 31r). Does he mean that the procedure for destroying them was the same as the one used in destroying the churches?
597. For Kerssenbrock's general discussion of this convent, see *Anabaptistici furoris*, ed. Detmer, 48–57. The title refers to the fact that it's on the opposite (west) bank of the river Aa from the main city.

At St. Tilgen's[598] there are noblewomen. Three or four nuns remained in it too. The overseer who'd previously been in the convent had four wives and administered it.

St. John's[599] was inhabited by the burghers from Warendorf.[600]

St. George's[601] was inhabited by the burghers from Coesfeld, and Schlachtschap was the leader there.

The Grey Monks[602] was inhabited by the people from Schöppingen[603] and Gildehaus[604] and all sorts of foreign folk.

[118v] Nichting's[605] is a nunnery. It was inhabited by the Hollanders and the Frisians (the criminals) and other foreign folk.[606]

They also occupied the other convents, the sisters'[607] and beguines'[608] houses, and the remaining congregations with the foreign folk who came rushing to the city.

The Brothers' House[609] was inhabited by all sorts of foreign folk and landsknechts.

In this way, they occupied the monasteries throughout the city with the foreign folk who came rushing to the city like this. The people lived in the cells, one with two, three, or four wives, living in this unchaste manner,

---

598. For Kerssenbrock's general discussion of this convent, see *Anabaptistici furoris*, ed. Detmer, 71.

599. For Kerssenbrock's general discussion of this monastery, which belonged to the order of the Teutonic Knights, see *Anabaptistici furoris*, ed. Detmer, 59–61.

600. Gresbeck means that Anabaptists from Warendorf were lodged there.

601. For Kerssenbrock's general discussion of this convent, see *Anabaptistici furoris*, ed. Detmer, 48–57.

602. The term "grey monk" signifies a Franciscan (so called from the color of their habits). For Kerssenbrock's general discussion of this monastery, see *Anabaptistici furoris*, ed. Detmer, 70–71.

603. A town about twenty miles northwest of Münster.

604. A town perhaps fifteen miles north-northwest of Schöppingen.

605. For Kerssenbrock's general discussion of the Nitzing convent (as its proper name was), see *Anabaptistici furoris*, ed. Detmer, 72.

606. Note that in the previous sections, Gresbeck had carefully noted the specific towns that the occupants of the monasteries came from, such towns all being in the vacinity of Münster. Here, Gresbeck notes only the hated Hollanders and Frisians specifically, lumping the people from all other areas under the general designation "foreign folk." Although this may be partially explained by the large numbers of people coming to Münster from local towns (after all, the people from individual towns were numerous enough to occupy a single monastery), it may also be indicative of Gresbeck's general lack of interest in (or at least knowledge about) the broader world outside of the Münsterland.

607. I.e., nuns.

608. For the sense of "beguine," see note 37.

609. For Kerssenbrock's general discussion of the monastery of the Brothers of the Fountain (to use its full name; here Gresbeck uses "frater," the Latin word for "brother"), see *Anabaptistici furoris*, ed. Detmer, 61–63.

and eating and drinking as long as they had something. May everyone now take better care, so that the one person wouldn't run this way and the other one that way.[610] I've certainly seen and heard this much: whenever someone dares to go from his house and leave it standing abandoned, someone else dares to reoccupy it. That's how things went in Münster too. May everyone protect his house better another time.

List of burgher collaborators

[119r] These are the burghers who adhered to the kings and to the Hollanders and the Frisians, so that the criminals held the upper hand for so long in Münster, keeping the common folk under such great duress.

First:

Knipperdolling[611] ——┐
Kibbenbrock[612] ——┘   The two burgher masters of the rebaptizers
Tilbeck[613] (noble[614])
Christian Kerkering[615] (noble)
John Kerkering[616] (bastard, noble)
Henry Redeker[617]
John of Deventer[618]
Herman in den Slotel[619]
Gerard Reynning[620]

---

610. To judge by his subsequent words, Gresbeck means that everybody should stay at home and guard his own property (unlike the burghers of Münster who left the city in July 1534).

611. For Knipperdolling's career, see note 4.

612. For Kibbenbrock's career, see note 14.

613. For Tilbeck's career, see note 62.

614. By "noble" Gresbeck means "patrician" (see introduction, section 3.1).

615. A leading Anabaptist, he served as the president of John of Leiden's board of councilors (Kerssenbrock, *Anabaptistici furoris*, ed. Detmer, 534) and was one of the twelve dukes (130r–132v) appointed right before the capture of the city (ibid., 774). Taken prisoner at the time of the city's capture, he was executed in July 1535. See also Kirchhoff, *Die Täufer in Münster*, 321.

616. One of John of Leiden's building masters (*Baumeister*) (Kerssenbrock, *Anabaptistici furoris*, ed. Detmer, 649).

617. For Redeker's career, see note 105.

618. A member of the city councils of 1533 and 1534, he became one of John of Leiden's building masters (*Baumeister*) (Kerssenbrock, *Anabaptistici furoris*, ed. Detmer, 649). See also Kirchhoff, *Die Täufer in Münster*, 125.

619. One of the deacons (Kerssenbrock, *Anabaptistici furoris*, ed. Detmer, 558). See also Kirchhoff, *Die Täufer in Münster*, 629.

620. Superintendent of the treasury (Kerssenbrock, *Anabaptistici furoris*, ed. Detmer, 562, 584),

Herman Reynning[621]
Albert Wiemhave[622]
Master Henry Rode[623]
Master Til Bussenschutte[624]
Master Jaspar Gelgoter[625]
Bernard Menneken[626]
Magnus Kohuss[627]
Engelbert Eding[628]
Claus Snyder[629, 630] [119v]
Luke Hotmaker
Claus Stype the younger[631]

---

councilor to John of Leiden (ibid., 647). See also Kirchhoff, *Die Täufer in Münster*, 555.

621. Wheat master (Kerssenbrock, *Anabaptistici furoris*, ed. Detmer, 649, 126v). He had two wives (ibid., 626n3). See also Kirchhoff, *Die Täufer in Münster*, 556.

622. Wedemhave in Kerssenbrock. He is attested as objecting vehemently to the proposal to expel the radical preachers and their supporters in November 1533 (Kerssenbrock, *Anabaptistici furoris*, ed. Detmer, 445). See also Kirchhoff, *Die Täufer in Münster*, 730.

623. One of the twelve elders (Kerssenbrock, *Anabaptistici furoris*, ed. Detmer, 576), he was the master of the court for Queen Diewer (ibid., 661). See also Kirchhoff, *Die Täufer in Münster*, 577.

624. Perhaps to be identified with the Til (Tilanus in Kerssenbrock) who served as an artillery officer (Kerssenbrock, *Anabaptistici furoris*, ed. Detmer, 480) and was killed at the time of the city's capture (ibid., 851).

625. Attested as a Lutheran leader in July 1532, he was also attested as an artillery commander for the Anabaptists; see Kirchhoff, *Die Täufer in Münster*, 202, 203.

626. He collected and distributed foodstuffs for the twelve elders (Kerssenbrock, *Anabaptistici furoris*, ed. Detmer, 585) and was wheat master (ibid., 649, 126v). See also Kirchhoff, *Die Täufer in Münster*, 443.

627. Guard of the treasury (Kerssenbrock, *Anabaptistici furoris*, ed. Detmer, 562, 584). He was one of those who abandoned Mollenhecke's uprising and went over to the Anabaptists (ibid., 622; see also note 255 above). He had two wives (ibid., 626n3) and was killed during the capture of the city (ibid., 848). See also Kirchhoff, *Die Täufer in Münster*, 343.

628. Member of the Anabaptist city council elected in February 1534 (Kerssenbrock, *Anabaptistici furoris*, ed. Detmer, 520), he became one of John of Leiden's attendants (ibid., 649) and then one of the twelve dukes. See also Kirchhoff, *Die Täufer in Münster*, 142.

629. This name was scratched out in the Cologne manuscript and doesn't appear in Cornelius's text. He was a prominent supporter of the Anabaptists. He was one of their hostages chosen to guarantee their good behavior in the aftermath of the abortive coup against the Anabaptists in early February 1534 (Kerssenbrock, *Anabaptistici furoris*, ed. Detmer, 498n1; for Gresbeck's account, see 9r). An Anabaptist member of the city council chosen in February 1534 (ibid., 520), he is also attested as one of the leading Anabaptists who occupied the houses abandoned by the canons of the cathedral after they left the city (ibid., 542). See also Kirchhoff, *Die Täufer in Münster*, 633.

630. A number of names are scratched out in this list. It is true that Kerssenbrock would later land himself in a lot of trouble with the city council of Münster for naming local supporters of it whose descendants objected to their being mentioned in his history of the Anabaptist regime (*Anabaptistici furoris*, ed. Detmer, 41–42, 44), but the scratched-out names seem to be of non-entities who aren't otherwise known, so there must be some other reason for omitting them.

631. This name has been struck out in the Cologne manuscript and doesn't appear in Cornelius's text. A dress cutter, he was elected in March 1533 as one of the radical electors whose task was to choose the new city council. Like Nicholas Snyder (whose name was also struck out of Gresbeck's list), he was

Albert Geistehovel[632]
Bernard Picker[633]
William Glasemaker[634]
Herman ter Nate[635]
John Fochke[636]
Herman Fochke[637]
Tony Grotevart[638]
Ernest van den Daemme[639]
John Ernest[640]
John Koning[641]
Ludger Weghake[642]

---

one the Anabaptist hostages chosen to guarantee their good behavior in the aftermath of the abortive coup against the Anabaptists in early February 1534 (Kerssenbrock, *Anabaptistici furoris*, ed. Detmer, 498n1; for Gresbeck's account, see 9r) and as an Anabaptist member of the city council chosen in February 1534 (ibid., 520). See also Kirchhoff, *Die Täufer in Münster*, 668.

632. Member of the Anabaptist city council chosen in February 1534 (Kerssenbrock, *Anabaptistici furoris*, ed. Detmer, 520). He was a baker. See also Kirchhoff, *Die Täufer in Münster*, 201.

633. Member of the Anabaptist city council chosen in February 1534 (Kerssenbrock, *Anabaptistici furoris*, ed. Detmer, 520). See also Kirchhoff, *Die Täufer in Münster*, 515.

634. Another name scratched out in the Cologne manuscript and not present in Cornelius's text. No one of this name is attested in Kerssenbrock, but a Goswin Glasemaker is listed as one of John of Leiden's scribes (*Anabaptistici furoris*, ed. Detmer, 650). See also Kirchhoff, *Die Täufer in Münster*, 218b.

635. Official cobbler by appointment of the twelve elders (Kerssenbrock, *Anabaptistici furoris*, ed. Detmer, 584). See also Kirchhoff, *Die Täufer in Münster*, 475.

636. Attested as a Lutheran leader in July 1532. See Kirchhoff, *Die Täufer in Münster*, 173.

637. Elector for choosing the city council in 1534 (Kerssenbrock, *Anabaptistici furoris*, ed. Detmer, 519). See also Kirchhoff, *Die Täufer in Münster*, 172.

638. Elector for choosing the city council in 1532 (Kerssenbrock, *Anabaptistici furoris*, ed. Detmer, 271) and 1534 (ibid., 519), he was a building master (*Baumeister*) for John of Leiden (ibid., 649). The man's last name should be Grotevader (or the like). See also Kirchhoff, *Die Täufer in Münster*, 231.

639. Another name crossed out of the Cologne manuscript and not in Cornelius's text. The man is attested as one of John of Leiden's royal attendants (Kerssenbrock, *Anabaptistici furoris*, ed. Detmer, 649). See also Kirchhoff, *Die Täufer in Münster*, 116.

640. Another struck-out name. Kerssenbrock knows no one by this name. Apparently, the man's name is John ton Damme (Kirchhoff, *Die Täufer in Münster*, 118), in which case Gresbeck presumably should have called him John van den Damme.

641. One of the prominent Anabaptists arrested on February 9, 1534 (Kerssenbrock, *Anabaptistici furoris*, ed. Detmer, 489n5), he was member of the Anabaptist city council of 1534 (ibid., 520). See also Kirchhoff, *Die Täufer in Münster*, 354.

642. For this man, see Kerssenbrock, *Anabaptistici furoris*, ed. Detmer, 729. He escaped from Münster in 1534 and was released from the prince-bishop's custody after surety was given for his good behavior, but he returned to the city and his guarantors lost their pledges. The only activity during the Anabaptist regime involves a notorious incident that goes unmentioned in Gresbeck's account. Towards the end of his reign, John of Leiden had one of his wives, Elizabeth Wantscherer, executed for wishing to leave his degenerate court. According to Kerssenbrock (*Anabaptistici furoris*, ed. Detmer, 825), the king beheaded her himself, but the confessions of two captured Anabaptists claim that the king had one of his councilors carry out the deed, but this man failed to make a clean job of it, and it was Ludger Wechhacke who removed the head completely (see ibid., 825n1). He soon died during the capture of the city.

Curt Kruse[643]
Jaspar Borcken[644]
Henry Redewech[645]
Everett ter Heege[646]
Kurt Baesscher[647]
Hermanus Faget[648]
Derek Slosseken[649]

643. Another name crossed out in the Cologne manuscript and not in Cornelius's text. Curt is the Low German form of Conrad, and Conrad Cruse was a prominent Anabapist. He was elected by St. Lambert's parish as one of the electors who chose the Anabapist city council in February 1534 (Kerssenbrock, *Anabaptistici furoris*, ed. Detmer, 519) and was appointed as one of the three officials to superintend the compulsory contribution of money decreed under John Mathias (ibid., 562, 584). He then served as John of Leiden's commander-in-chief of infantry (ibid., 650, 663). See also Kirchhoff, *Die Täufer in Münster*, 380.

644. Kirchhoff, *Die Täufer in Münster*, 65, associates this man (under the name "Borchers") with the Jasper Borchardes (Kerssenbrock's form of the name) and his mother Katherine (there's no doubt that the Cologne manuscript has the form "Borken," but final "r" and "n" are easily confused, so perhaps "Borker" was miscopied from the earlier draft). The mother is said to have been banished from Münster for immorality before the Anabaptist takeover (an error was made in Kerssenbrock, *Narrative of the Anabaptist Madness*, ed. Mackay: in Kerssenbrock, *Anabaptistici furoris*, ed. Detmer, 518, "who had been banished" should read "whose mother had been banished"), and both she and her son were noted as Anabaptists, the son having participated in a parody of a Catholic procession in the rural settlement of Hiltrup (ibid.). The son is mentioned in one source among those who took nuns as wives and lived in other people's houses. In the aftermath of the city's capture, mother and son were executed with Everett Remensnyder (who was likewise associated with deriding Catholic ceremonial; see 105r) on July 8, 1535 (ibid., 856).

645. Kerssenbrock apparently knows nothing of this man. Kirchhoff, *Die Täufer in Münster*, 550, 551, mentions one house owned by Else, the widow of John Redeweg, and she was listed as an Anabaptist when the house was registered in 1536. A second house of hers was later claimed by a man in the name of his wife, whose maiden name was Anna Redeweg. Perhaps, our Henry and Anna were the children of John and Else.

646. The queen's chef (Kerssenbrock, *Anabaptistici furoris*, ed. Detmer, 661). See also Kirchhoff, *Die Täufer in Münster*, 257.

647. Kerssenbrock knows of no one with this last name. Perhaps this man is related to the Claus Baesser, who appears nine places lower in the list. Rather mysteriously, Cornelius, *Berichte der augenzeugen*, 167, gives this name as "Cort Bartscherer." Kirchhoff, *Die Täufer in Münster*, 35, 36, notes that Herman Berninck and John Berninck both had the profession of "beard cutter" (*Bartscherer*), and so conceivably they could also have used their profession as their last name. But there's no reason to associate the present "Koert Baesscher" (as Gresbeck gives the name) with either of those two men (or with the Clauwes Bartscherer or Gerdt Bartscherer who are attested as Lutheran troublemakers in 1532; see Kirchhoff, *Die Täufer in Münster*, 18). For what it's worth, the name of John of Leiden's barber is only partially preserved, but his first name was Winold (Kerssenbrock, *Anabaptistici furoris*, ed. Detmer, 649).

648. Another name scratched out in the Cologne manuscript and not appearing in Cornelius's text. The only conceivable name in Kerssenbrock seems to be Herman Foecke, who was chosen as the elector for the Jew Fields parish for the city council election in February 1534 (*Anabaptistici furoris*, ed. Detmer, 519).

649. A participant in a Lutheran attack on the Nitzing convent back in 1525 (Kerssenbrock, *Anabaptistici furoris*, ed. Detmer, 128), he was placed in charge of the city's wagons by the twelve elders (ibid., 585). He was killed during the city's capture (ibid., 850). See also Kirchhoff, *Die Täufer in Münster*, 628.

John Denckher[650]
John Naderman[651]
Henry Lensse[652]
Kurt Boetmester[653]
Big John Boetmester[654]
John of Schweren[655]
Claus Baesser[656] [120r]
Everett Remensnyder[657]
Jost Kalle[658]
Bernard Ruellenar[659]

650. He was chosen as one of the twelve dukes (Kerssenbrock, *Anabaptistici furoris*, ed. Detmer, 774). Kirchhoff, *Die Täufer in Münster*, 484, concerns a peddler who apparently went by the names "Johann Dencker" and "Johann Nordemann." Kirchhoff also indicates that this was the John Naderman whose election as duke Gresbeck relates at length (168v). Yet, since Naderman appears as the next man on Gresbeck's list here, and Kirchhoff, *Die Täufer in Münster*, 120, cites a John Dencker the Elder ("Johan Dencker der Alte"), it certainly seems possible that there are in fact two men in question: John Naderman the duke (listed next) and a separate John Dencker (the man listed under that name by Kirchhoff was apparently described as a heretic and a hangman, so either he or his son seems a suitable candidate for listing here).

651. According to Gresbeck, he was a duke (168v), though there is the possibility that this name is a variant of the preceding one (see previous note).

652. See Kirchhoff, *Die Täufer in Münster*, 395. He is said by one source to have been one of the "soup eaters" who caused disturbance back in 1525 (see 4v). Nothing is known of his activities under the Anabaptist regime.

653. Nothing is known of this man; see Kirchhoff, *Die Täufer in Münster*, 59.

654. Though not scratched out in the Cologne manuscript, the name is omitted in the texts used by Cornelius. There's an "x" drawn in front of it in the Cologne manuscript, which perhaps is connected with the omission.

655. I.e., John of Schwerte (see note 527)? See also Kirchhoff, *Die Täufer in Münster*, 687.

656. Cornelius prints this man's last name as Balsser but in a note gives the alternative Baesser, noting the reading Boesser in manuscript M. Kerssenbrock has no knowledge of this man, but he does mention the name Balser (burgher of Coesfeld mentioned in *Anabaptistici furoris*, ed. Detmer, 469n3), which may have led to the form in Cornelius. Kirchhoff, *Die Täufer in Münster*, 16, has no further information for any of these names.

657. Remensnyder was involved in the death of Gerald Smoker (24v–25r) and participated in the parody mass (105r). He went on to serve as (meat) carver to John of Leiden (Kerssenbrock, *Anabaptistici furoris*, ed. Detmer, 648). He had three wives, including a nun (ibid., 626n3). He hid himself when the city was eventually captured. He would sneak out only to steal food from the landsknechts, but he was discovered on one such escapade and beheaded (ibid., 855–56). See also Kirchhoff, *Die Täufer in Münster*, 559.

658. Cornelius gives the man's last name as Kalle. Either way, the man seems to be unknown to Kerssenbrock. See also Kerssenbrock, *Anabaptistici furoris*, ed. Detmer, 314; he suggests that this man is the Jodocus Calenburg mentioned by Kerssenbrock; ibid., 486.

659. Another scratched-out name not in Cornelius's text. According to Kirchhoff (*Die Täufer in Münster*, 607), this man was also known by the "professional" name Bernard Schomaker, and was listed among a group of citizens of Münster who were being extradited for religious troublemaking in outlying communities and petitioned the city council in November 1532 not to give them up (Kerssenbrock, *Anabaptistici furoris*, ed. Detmer, 279).

Everett Butermaens[660]

John Swertfeger[661]

John Bonttorpt[662]

Bernard Bonttorpt[663]

John Schauerinne[664]

Willebrant Mesmacker[665]

Laurence Maler[666]

John Vienhoff[667]

Hermanus Neyge[668]

Hermanus Neinatel[669]

These are (some of) the burghers in the city of Münster who adhered to the king and the Frisians and Hollanders. Such burghers aren't all written here. They wore the king's livery and were his servants, going to court with the

660. Another scratched-out name not in Cornelius's text. The man is unknown to Kerssenbrock. Kirchhoff, *Die Täufer in Münster*, 367, lists a man of this name as the lessor of a house.

661. John Caterberg the "swertfeger" ("swordsmith," used here as a last name) was a deacon (Kerssenbrock, *Anabaptistici furoris*, ed. Detmer, 558) and duke (ibid., 774). The man apparently also bore the last name tor Heyden (Kirchhoff, *Die Täufer in Münster*, 261; see also Kerssenbrock, *Anabaptistici furoris*, ed. Detmer, 660, 661).

662. John Boentruppe is attested as an apostle (Kerssenbrock, *Anabaptistici furoris*, ed. Detmer, 705). He apparently didn't go on the mission, as he is reported as being killed at the time of the city's capture (ibid., 850). See also Kirchhoff, *Die Täufer in Münster*, 73.

663. Bernard Boentruppe is attested as an elector for choosing the Anabaptist city council in February 1534 (Kerssenbrock, *Anabaptistici furoris*, ed. Detmer, 519). He was put in charge of meat by the twelve elders (ibid., 584) and continued in this post under John of Leiden (ibid., 649). See also Kirchhoff, *Die Täufer in Münster*, 72.

664. Another scratched-out name not in Cornelius's text. The scratching out in this case is very heavy, so that although the given name is clear, there's some uncertainty as to the man's surname. The initial letters "sch" and the ending "inne" are certain. There are probably three letters in between, and the reading given here seems to be correct, but other combinations of "a," "u," "e," and "r" are not inconceivable. In any event, Kerssenbrock records John Schuren as an attendant of John of Leiden (*Anabaptistici furoris*, ed. Detmer, 649), so perhaps the surname here is some variant of that.

665. Nothing else is known of this man; see Kirchhoff, *Die Täufer in Münster*, 449.

666. Cornelius gives this man the name "Mater," but the reading of "l" in place of "t" is certain. Kerssenbrock records no one with such a name. Kirchhoff (*Die Täufer in Münster*, 567) rightly connects this man (despite the false form in Cornelius, which was the only one known to him) with Laurentius Rickwyn, whose profession was painter (Higher German *Mahler*).

667. A John Vlienthoff is attested as a variant for the name of one of the superintendents of tailors in the ordinance of the twelve elders (Kerssenbrock, *Anabaptistici furoris*, ed. Detmer, 584n3). Kirchhoff, *Die Täufer in Münster*, 163, suggests that the form "Vienhoff" could actually signify the name "Wedemhove" (also spelled "Wemhof"), though the only John attested with that name is the baker who had been the husband of the "Wemhof widow" (Kerssenbrock, *Anabaptistici furoris*, ed. Detmer 731).

668. Yet another scratched-out name not in Cornelius's text. The name is unknown to Kerssenbrock.

669. Otherwise attested only as a Lutheran leader in 1532; see Kerssenbrock, *Anabaptistici furoris*, ed. Detmer, 477.

king. These burghers adhered to the king and the Frisians and Hollanders, holding the common folk under such great duress that no one dared to say a word against it. Many is the burgher who would have been glad to see the city given up. These burghers (as well as certain others not listed here whose names aren't retained in memory[670]) were opposed to this and adhered to the king, so that everyone had to keep quiet. Some of these burghers that I listed before are still alive.

Morality play

[120v] So they started up again and carried on a great joyous merriment to while away the time. So the king had the common people summoned to the cathedral. All the common folk, men and women, came to the cathedral, apart from those who had to keep watch on the walls. They wanted to see the great merriment as well as the wonder that was supposed to take place in the cathedral. The king had a stage that was covered with curtains constructed up in the choir in the cathedral, where the high altar stands, with everyone spectating around it. There they put on the play of the rich man and Lazarus.[671] They started up the play and performed, reciting the dialogue to each other. When the rich man conversed with Lazarus and with his words,[672] three pipers with flutes stood below the stage and played a piece with three voices.[673] Then the rich man went on speaking again, and then the pipers went on playing again. The play went on in this way until

670. This parenthetical comment is added in the margin by a different (old) hand in the Cologne manuscript. If this text is legitimate, Gresbeck has once more forgotten names and apparently had no source to jog his memory. Certainly, the phraseology is typical of Gresbeck.

671. The story of the (unnamed) rich man and Lazarus is told in Luke 16:19–31. The rich man ignored the beggar Lazarus in life, and when he is later roasted in the fires of hell, he sees Lazarus being shown around the place by Abraham. The rich man asks their help in putting out the fires that torment him. Abraham replies that the reversal of positions between the rich man and Lazarus is just, and in any event such amelioration was forbidden. The rich man then asks that Lazarus should at least go to his (the rich man's) father's house and warn his brothers of the torment that awaits them if they don't mend their ways. Abraham replies rather unhelpfully (and implausibly) that if they didn't pay any attention to the biblical admonitions, they weren't about to listen to somebody risen from the dead. This edifying tale was a favorite of sixteenth-century religious dramaturgy, both Catholic and Lutheran: see Wailes, *Rich Man and Lazarus*, for a discussion of the ways in which the story was dramatized in ten plays from that century (unfortunately, his introduction doesn't deal with the background of such pieces in late medieval dramaturgy).

672. The word translated here as "words" isn't entirely clear in the manuscript, but such seems to be the reading. The somewhat odd expression here presumably signifies "the words spoken by the character Lazarus." Perhaps the peculiarity of the phrase "with his words" explains why it was omitted in the manuscript from which Cornelius's text derives.

673. "Three voices" presumably means that the pipers didn't play in unison.

the end. Eventually, devils appeared and hauled the rich man off body and soul, carrying him behind the curtains. At this, there was [121r] a great laugh in the cathedral, and they saw great merriment. Oh, how blind had they made the poor people![674] This play was for some people their bread and butter.[675] Some would have preferred to eat something if they'd had anything.[676] But the devils didn't take the rich man away entirely.[677] The rich man would still have converted if he could have received mercy,[678] and so he wanted to escape from the city. The king was informed of this, and he had the rich man hung from a tree up at the cathedral square. This rich man had been the queen's lackey, and he was a Brabanter[679] who'd rushed to the city.

Siege works completed

The king and all the rebaptizers imagined that My Gracious Lord of Münster was going to withdraw from the city in the end.[680] But when they[681] began to make blockhouses,[682] the realm[683] took shape in front of the city, and they wouldn't leave the city (they would capture it first)—as soon as the trench was dug all the way around the city, from one blockhouse to the next, with small blockhouses built in between and a high trench was

674. From his subsequent words, it's clear that by "blindness," Gresbeck means that people allowed themselves to be distracted from their hunger by the entertainment. For similar phrases about entertainment being provided as a substitute for food, see 88v–89r, 90r, 93v.

675. The German phrase ("gesaden und gebraden"=High German *Gesottenes und Gebratenes*) literally signifies boiled and roasted food, but the jingle more broadly designates the "main course." I selected the English expression "bread and butter" to give something of the aural play, even if the literal signification is rather different.

676. Once again, Gresbeck is playing with the conceit that entertainment was taking the place of sustenance, but it was not very filling (see 89r, 93v).

677. More irony, as Gresbeck means the actor who portrayed the rich man.

678. I.e., he wanted pardon from the bishop.

679. I.e, a resident of the Duchy of Brabant. This was in the central part of what is now the Netherlands.

680. Now that Gresbeck's narrative is coming to the starvation of the final stage of the siege, he goes back to the previous fall to relate how the city's desperate situation was brought about by the earlier tightening of the siege.

681. The subject has now shifted to the indeterminate enemy forces.

682. I.e., as part of the tight siege that was instituted in the fall of 1534 in the aftermath of the failure of the second attempt to storm the city.

683. "Realm" ("rych"=High German *Reich*) is the short form of the term "kingdom" (High German *Königreich*) that was used for some reason to describe the no-man's-land between the city and the siegeworks.

[121v] edged with hawthorn,[684] they gave the city up as lost.[685] As soon as the trench was dug around the city, no one could rush into the city or get out of it after that time. All too few were those who made it out of the city across the trench! No more than five or six made it across. After that time, they couldn't get any news (letters) into the city, and they also couldn't get any letters out of the city, so that then the city was lost. They did hold out for a while yet, but they couldn't get anyone in or out.

Escape from the city impossible

So the landsknechts had also manned the trench around the city with a watch at night, and they also kept a watch during the day on horseback and on foot, so that it was pretty much impossible for anyone to get away.

Cattle and other animals confiscated

They still had about two hundred cows in the end. They kept them in the kingdom[686] between the blockhouses and the city. Every captain had to guard them in the kingdom on his day. When the city was first put under siege, they probably still had a good ten or twenty hundred cows. They would guard the cows outside all the gates. One time, the cavalrymen and landsknechts suddenly launched an attack and [122r] took some of the cows away from them (thirty or forty). After that time, they protected the cows better until the end.[687] There were certainly rebaptizers in the city who would have preferred that they'd gotten all of the cows. For no one's situation was improved because of them. But those that the cows belonged to, whether it was a burgher or a woman, these were poor people. The person who had a cow or some other beast, or a dog or a cat, they couldn't keep it

---

684. Hawthorn is a spiky bush, and for this reason these bushes were placed at the edge of the trench as a sort of natural version of barbed wire.

685. The city was first placed under a loose siege in February 1534 (Kerssenbrock, *Anabaptistici furoris*, ed. Detmer, 545–48). In the immediate aftermath of the failure of the second assault on the city on August 31, the decision was taken to surround the city with a continuous line of siegeworks connecting the seven major blockhouses that had been built back in February (ibid., 681–84). This expensive and complicated building operation went on throughout the fall. "They" in the last clause refers to the Anabaptists.

686. See note 683.

687. Apparently, "the end" doesn't signify the capture of the city but the loss of the Anabaptists' ability to feed the cows in the "kingdom" and the resulting slaughter of the cows, which did take place towards the end of the siege (136v).

and it was all taken from them.[688] This is how the criminals (the Hollanders and Frisians) ruled in the city of Münster. They let all this go on—the burghers in the city, Knipperdolling with his fellows.[689]

Man executed for plotting to drive off the cattle

One time, there was a Frisian named Tall Albert.[690] This man was the queen's attendant, and one time he wanted to chase all the cows to the blockhouse, to the landsknechts, so that he would have been taken prisoner and kept his life. The king was informed of this, and he had this Frisian arrested and beheaded him himself. This Frisian wanted to do it out of hunger and woe. Otherwise, he was a real rebaptizer, [122v] just like the king, and the others (his own compatriots[691]) were.

Starvation intensifies

The hunger and woe now became so great that they rushed out of the city and got themselves killed, and some people could no longer walk on account of hunger and began to walk with canes.[692] When the hunger became so great, the king put the people under great duress with the sword. Whoever said a word to the effect that he would be glad to get out of the city or that he would rush from them, he had him put in prison right away and beheaded him right away on the next day. Some people imagined that they would endure, hoping that they would give up, because some people were beginning to die of hunger.[693]

---

688. Gresbeck is rather vague here, but he seems to be speaking of the confiscation of all privately held animals. He's indignant at the injustice of taking away animals from poor people who individually owned only a single one (even a dog or cat).

689. This is another swipe at Knipperdolling and the other local adherents of Anabaptism, whom Gresbeck blames for having failed to look after the interests of the city through their devotion to the foreign Anabaptists. The somewhat incoherent syntax is presumably a reflection of Gresbeck's sputtering indignation.

690. For Kerssenbrock's version of the execution of Albert, which he dates to June 8, 1535, see *Anabaptistici furoris*, ed. Detmer, 821. The fact that it's reported by Gresbeck, who left the city on May 23, strongly suggests that Kerssenbrock's date is too late. In any event, according to a confession of December 6, 1534, the man had been sent to Frisia to fetch supplies, and he was also known as Bonaventure (Cornelius, *Berichte der augenzeugen*, 290). His height was apparently remarkable, as the confession also refers to it. In any event, with this anecdote Gresbeck begins his account of the final stages of the siege.

691. I.e., the hated Frisians.

692. For Kerssenbrock's melodramatic account of the final starvation, see *Anabaptistici furoris*, ed. Detmer, 798–805.

693. Once more there is ambiguity as a result of the shifting referent of the third person plural

Burial of the dead

So the king had a place partitioned off in front of each city gate.[694] Whenever someone died in the city, whether he died of hunger or was shot to death or killed by the landsknechts or the king had him beheaded or did it himself, they buried these people in front of the gate where each one's watch post was. Then the king no [123r] longer wished to bury the dead in the city, and he also wished to execute no more people in the city.[695] But in the end he again executed them in the city, and then he once more buried the dead in the city, up at the cathedral square.

Man betrayed by a friend and executed for plotting treason

There was someone named Claus Northorn, and he was a burgher in the city of Münster.[696] This Claus had written a letter and wanted to send the letter to the blockhouse (to My Gracious Lord of Münster). He'd written in the letter that if My Gracious Lord of Münster would grant him mercy and give him a safe conduct to the blockhouse, so that he could have an interview, Claus would make a plan for the capture of the city of Münster. This man Claus had a companion with him and told this man what he had in mind, saying that he would send a letter out of the city to the blockhouse. Claus imagined that this companion was his good friend and that he would defect with him and help him. Claus's companion set to it and said to the king that Claus had such a plan in hand and would send a letter to the blockhouse and deliver the city to My Gracious Lord. So the king set to it and had Claus arrested. He had him tortured and racked straightaway,

---

pronoun. The starving people hoped to hold out until the Anabaptists gave up. Is Gresbeck here giving his own thoughts at the time?

694. For Kerssenbrock's brief account of the burial of those who starved to death, see *Anabaptistici furoris*, ed. Detmer, 803.

695. Presumably, this suspension of execution was instituted about the time of the relaxation of the prohibitions against merrymaking (87v–94v). One imagines that this would have been around the time that the relief expected to arrive in the late winter and early spring of 1535 failed to materialize. At that time, the regime would have started to lose credibility and perhaps the king and his advisors felt it advisable to adopt a more accommodating attitude. As the situation continued to deteriorate over the course of the spring, however, John of Leiden and his advisors must have felt the need to resume the use of violence to keep the increasingly desperate population in check.

696. In Kerssenbrock's version of this story, the victim's name appears as Nicholas Snider of Nordhorn, and he dates the execution to June 9, 1535 (*Anabaptistici furoris*, ed. Detmer, 823). Again, this date is too late for Gresbeck to have seen it (see also note 690).

so that he had to say to the king what sort of plan [123v] he was undertaking. So Claus told him the plan. The next day, the king set to it, and he convened a common assembly and had Claus hauled up to the cathedral square. The king indicted Claus and cut his head off himself. Someone was standing close by, and this was a burgher in the city. This man took the body and laid it on a bench and then cut it into twelve pieces with a meat cleaver.[697] Then the king had one piece hung in front of each gate, and he had the head stuck out of the cathedral tower on a long pole. Claus's heart and liver were carried home by a Hollander, who boiled and ate it. At that time, the hunger was great in the city, so that they didn't know where to turn. This is how the king busied himself with this man, and how Claus was betrayed by his companion.

Some people given permission to flee the city, and the difficulties of doing so

The king had it said in the preaching that anyone who would be glad to leave the city and wished to have permission should come up to the council hall and have himself enrolled, coming freely and confidently. They would be taken to a gate and then allowed to go. This order was to be valid for three or four days.[698] After that, no one else would be given permission, and if anyone was then found who wanted to leave, they would be killed. Then they came [124r] up to the council hall, men and women and children, and asked for permission. As soon as they asked for permission, they couldn't go back home anymore and had to wait up at the council hall until they were brought to the gate. They first took from the people everything that they had. If they had good clothes on, they had to take these off and they put old clothes on them. Then the king had them brought to the gate, and in this way they walked to the blockhouses. The landsknechts killed all the men for the most part, and they took from the women everything that they had. These they didn't kill. The women remained in the kingdom between the blockhouse and the city until they were let through.[699] The king had the

---

697. Kerssenbrock says that the body was cut into thirteen pieces, presumably including the head in the total.

698. Kerssenbrock refers vaguely to John of Leiden giving permission for people to leave (*Anabaptistici furoris*, ed. Detmer, 805), but says nothing of any deadlines.

699. For the misery of those trapped between the city and the siegeworks, see Kerssenbrock, *Anabaptistici furoris*, ed. Detmer, 805–10. For their ultimate fate, see ibid., 810–19.

household goods of these men and women who were the first to move out of the city on account of hunger fetched from the houses. The king's master of the court[700] went through the city with a wagon, and going to the houses from which they'd left, he brought all the furnishings to one house. This is how they first moved out of the city. This departing lasted till the end. The menfolk defected from the city by night and by day. They were all killed. All the same, they defected from the city, such great hunger did they have in the city. For they much preferred to get themselves killed [124v] than to suffer such great hunger. After this time, there was seldom a time, day or night, that they didn't rush (defect) from the city. No one knew how to escape, particularly those who'd rushed into the city from the camp. They knew full well that they couldn't escape, the one just as much as the other. For they were in dire straits. If they rushed from the city, they would be killed. If they remained in it, they would have to die of hunger. If they rushed from the city without permission, and the king was informed of this, he would have them hung. This was the first time that they rushed from the city like this on account of hunger and woe. The king and his councilors and the leaders (some of them), and also some burghers, had enough to eat—these men didn't run far.[701] The provisions that they had they (the king with his fellowship) had each taken. Those were no humans, given how they made things go on in the city. Between heaven and earth there could be no worse Christians than the king and his retinue or than these rebaptizers.

The aged and the children encouraged to flee

[125r] Soon enough, when the hunger first began to arrive, the king did want all the old women, old men, and children to be gone in good time from the city, so that they would retain all the more provisions.[702] So when they first began to leave the city because of hunger, the king let them leave freely, and he had it said in the preaching that whoever didn't want to endure the hunger and woe should ask for permission. The king would give

700. Tilbeck.
701. See Kerssenbrock, *Anabaptistici furoris*, ed. Detmer, 804, for a similar sentiment, and ibid., 804n1, for plentiful contemporary confirmation that the king and his court had enough to eat amidst the starvation.
702. By mid to late April, it was becoming clear to the besiegers that it was primarily women, children, and old people who were fleeing the city (for evidence, see Kerssenbrock, *Anabaptistici furoris*, ed. Detmer, 805n2).

them travel money for the journey and help them get away by day and by night. At first, the king gave to everyone who wanted to leave five or seven corn cockle white pennies and then let them leave.[703] But in the end he wouldn't give travel money to those who wished to leave. He took from them everything that they had.

Rumored plot to reclaim confiscated property by force

A rumor arose in the city that some burghers and landsknechts would[704] fall upon those who still had enough provisions and food and grab them back. This was reported to the king and the leaders, who'd taken their property. So they had an order issued forbidding anyone to be so bold as to take so much as an egg from someone else—otherwise, he would suffer death. [125v] Didn't they still recall how things had once gone for them when they'd made an uprising when they wished to abolish the matrimony,[705] so that each should take care that things would not go the same for them again?[706] So they had the folk under such duress that they all had to keep quiet. Whoever didn't have couldn't get. Whoever couldn't fast could rush off out of hunger and get himself killed. Whoever had it lucky could survive.

Horsemeat doled out

In this way, they quieted the folk, and they slaughtered some horses, so that they gave a piece of horsemeat for each house. They had the horsemeat taken to the butcher's. The people went there and fetched the meat. The deacons asked everyone how many people there were in each house. They gave a share to each person in accordance with this. They made a list of the houses indicating how many people each person had in his house, and they gave according to this list, having listed each home owner under his name. They did this so that no one should have meat twice.

---

703. For these pennies, see note 101.

704. The word "and" appears before this word. Cornelius hesitantly suggests a lacuna, but the flow of thought seems fine if one simply deletes "and" as a mistake.

705. I.e., Mollenhecke's abortive uprising (47v–51r). The phrase "they'd made" refers to the rebels.

706. The thought is a suggestive question from the Anabaptists to their potential opponents, who are assumed to be the survivors from the previous attempt to overthrow the regime.

Wasteful slaughter of cattle and horses earlier in the siege

[126r] When the city of Münster was first put under siege,[707] they had many horses and cows in the city, so that they couldn't give them all fodder. The hay, straw, and oats began to give out, so that they had to slaughter some of the cows. They weren't able to keep all the horses, either. They set to it and slaughtered one hundred and twenty horses, burying them in the ground with their hides. When they slaughtered the horses, the hunger hadn't yet come to the city. But when the hunger became so great, they remembered those horses, and said what a great loss they'd caused with these horses. They imagined that if they'd salted the horses, they would certainly have lasted for them to the end, when they had to eat horses.

Deacons search for hidden foodstuffs

After this, the deacons went into the houses throughout the city once more and once again conducted a search. Everything in the way of provisions that they could find had to go away with them. Whether it was fat or oil or salt or lard, however meagre or small, they took it from the people. [126v] The king had it proclaimed in the preaching that if someone still had something, he should divide it up among his fellow brothers. Whoever didn't do this wasn't a real Christian. So the king wasn't a true Christian, and neither were the leaders of the rebaptizers. They'd taken everyone's property from them and wouldn't give it back to anyone. The king with his councilors, and the Hollanders and Frisians, and some burghers in Münster—these men would have starved someone to death before they would have given a piece of bread to anyone. And yet they'd taken it from the people!

Officials to oversee wheat and salt appointed

The king appointed wheat masters and salt masters. These were to give fat and salt to the common people who needed this. Those people came and took a little fat or oil or train oil[708] or a piece of suet or salt, and they lived on this for as long as they could.[709] They also gave each person a cup of

707. February 28, 1534.
708. "Train oil" is oil pressed out of fish.
709. A confession of March 30, 1535, already states that only bread and salt remained as food

flour. They had to endure on this for three or four weeks. They starved the folk this way. For the criminals (the leaders) had enough.

Vegetable growing

[127r] The king appointed land masters, and there were four of these land masters in the city. They went into all the plots that there were in the city and divided the plots, assigning a piece of land or two to each home owner depending on how many people there were in each house.[710] There they dug, planting cabbages and turnips and roots, beans and peas. They also gave some people land in front of the gates outside the city, in this way showing each one the bird up in the tree.[711] Whoever had a large plot wasn't allowed to enjoy it himself, not any more than what the land masters had shown them.[712] Each person had to restrict himself to this. They'd also previously undertaken in the city to tear down all the fences (railing) around the plots that there were in the city, so common did they wish to have the plots. The poor people thought that they'd enjoy the land and would live off it. So the poor common people planted and sowed. But the king with his retinue had reaped first, moving in in good time and taking everyone's property from him, and the other common people were supposed to fast after having sowed the vegetable garden. The preachers preached that everyone should live soberly, and they oughtn't [127v] rely so much on the belly god,[713] and they should fast because they oughtn't set their minds on eating and drinking all the time. For they had to endure with the help of God until things got better.

Few survived the city's fall

Of those who were in there and kept their lives there are no more than six or eight who escaped, apart from those who defected from the city

(Kerssenbrock, *Anabaptistici furoris*, ed. Detmer, 780).

710. Presumably, on the basis of the same list of residents used for the distribution of horsemeat in 125v.

711. The last phrase is a proverb that means showing something that could be of use but is impossible to acquire (cf. the similar image in the English expression "a bird in the hand is worth two in the bush").

712. With "had shown," Gresbeck uses the same verb as he did in the proverb about showing the bird in the tree. He actually means "had allotted."

713. The phrase "belly god" is based on Philippians 3:19. For a similar conception, see Knipperdolling's rebuke to the peddler (99r).

at night and got away and those who were taken prisoner in it.[714] In this way, they were all done in. Some people also remained alive when the city of Münster was captured—those who defected from the city on the other side of the city, and those who were secretly hidden in the city by some landsknechts.[715] In this way, they were all dead.[716] Those few who are still alive are still astonished by the regime that took place in the city and that they carried out, which it's impossible to speak of or say. For there was a great punishment from God in the city of Münster.

The stout city of Münster laid low by domestic religious strife

For the city of Münster is a beautiful, great city. There are plenty of beautiful churches in it and monasteries, and it was a city beautiful in terms of houses.[717] It's a strong one, having a double moat around it, with a wall and a high rampart with many towers around the city. During the siege, the rebaptizers made the city firmer than it had been. Outside each gate they had a strong earthwork built, [128r] and they made the wall better around the city, and also the canal a bit better, installing a number of secret loopholes and placing many palisades in the canal around the city, so that the city could hardly be captured by force as long as there were provisions within. If the rebaptizers in the city of Münster had had an upright case in hand, and it had been a war with lords and princes, they would have been praiseworthy given how they defended themselves and how clever they were with plans. For their case was null and void. It was against God and the whole world. This city of Münster is a famous city throughout the whole world, and it was a city rich in terms of merchants and rich burghers

714. Below he notes that John Naderman was one of those who escaped from the far side of the city at the time of its capture (131v). As for the total number of those who escaped, Gresbeck's phrasing seems to imply that the category of those who managed to escape before or during the city's capture was separate from the six or eight already mentioned, but surely he means that the six to eight survivors were the ones who escaped in this way (who else could they have been?).

715. See Gresbeck's comment on 152v that all those Anabaptists who were discovered and taken prisoner at the time of the city's capture were eventually executed.

716. Seemingly just a recapitulation of the same idea expressed above.

717. The early modern editor of the text took exception to this long section on the grounds that its content was repetitious. He drew a line along the side of this page, all of 128r and the section that starts 128v and adds at the start the note "Eandem semper cantilenam canere vitio datur; propterea hec omissa sunt," "Always singing the same song is considered a fault, so this text has been omitted"). As it turned out, whoever copied from this text the manuscript that gave rise to the manuscripts used by Cornelius for his edition mostly ignored the instructions and left out only the section at the top of 128v.

and nobles and the clergy. They maintained themselves magnificently and had good rule in it, except that one burgher was so opposed to another that they couldn't get along.[718] The guilds as well as the common burghers were opposed to the council, and so were the commons against the canons, the one being opposed to the other. All this was first brought about by this priest Stutenberent, the one being opposed to the other. Some people wish to say that it was the fault of the clergy in the city of Münster that the rebaptizing came to the city and so there was such dissension in the city.[719] It was the fault of some burghers, because they [128v] fetched the priest,[720] Stutenberent (Herr[721] Bernard Rothman) into the city. It was Knipperdolling and Kibbenbrock and still others who made a dispute in the city in this way and fetched the priest in. It wasn't the canons and the clergy and the council of Münster that fetched the priest in, and it likewise wasn't them that began the baptizing. It's easy to note whose fault it is. If some of the burghers in Münster had acted as the clergy did, Münster would certainly have remained in Münster. So they were against each other in the city of Münster and wouldn't care about anybody, and nobody was able to hinder them. So God punished them. May God forgive them their sins! Let other cities and burghers have an example in the city of Münster, living harmoniously and giving to God what belongs to God and to the emperor what belongs to the emperor.[722]

Anabaptist leadership becomes temporarily despondent as the hunger worsens

Then the hunger really started—the longer, the more, so that the king and his councilors and all the leaders didn't know how to make it. For the folk wished to escape from the city and couldn't endure the great hunger. The

---

718. For a similar line of thought about dissension in the city, see 3v.

719. For an earlier discussion of who was responsible for the city's problems, see 4v.

720. In addition to the line along the margin to indicate that it was to be omitted along with the preceding two pages, the rest of this paragraph after this point was also written over with hatch-marks and was omitted in the manuscript that lies behind Cornelius's text (unlike the preceding text, which was not omitted as the line indicated it should have been).

721. The German title *Herr* ("lord") is the vernacular version of the Latin honorific *dominus* ("lord"), which was an honorific title used in addressing holders of university degrees.

722. The end of this sentence is, of course, an allusion to Jesus's admonition to render unto Caesar that which is Caesar's and to render unto God that which is God's (Matthew 22:21). In Gresbeck, "Caesar" appears in German spelling ("keysser"), which would then refer not to the Roman emperor of antiquity but to the Holy Roman Emperor.

king had again given permission that whoever would have been glad to get away would be allowed to. He certainly would have preferred them all to be gone out the gate apart from the arms-bearing men. These he wanted to keep in the city. Things wouldn't happen as they would have liked to see. For they did not know how [129r] to make it in the end. When a sermon was being given up at the marketplace, the king sat with his head lying in his hands, and he was always afraid. For he realized what would come of it in the end, that it would come to a bad end. After this time, he would always sit like this with his head in his hands, and he was always afraid. He realized that the relief wouldn't come. It was beginning to come to an end. So the king and his councilors were afraid all the time of an uprising in the city of Münster. The councilors laid down their silver chains and didn't dare to wear them any longer, and the king laid down his golden chains and didn't dare to wear them any longer, either. This lasted for two or three weeks, so that the common folk in the city began to say that they (the king and the councilors) were no longer wearing their chains, and that the king would sit like that with his head in his hands. The king and his councilors were informed that the common folk were going around like this in the city, saying of the king and his councilors that they'd laid down their chains and didn't dare to wear them any longer. So the king had a sermon given up at the marketplace, and he went and sat on his throne. Eventually, the preacher said of the chains that some people were going around and saying of the [129v] king and of the councilors that they'd laid their chains down and didn't dare to wear them any longer. This preacher—his name was Herr Herman Mose,[723] and he was a priest—cursed everyone who mumbled and grumbled against the king and his councilors and all his servants that they didn't dare to wear their chains any longer. Eventually, the king stood up from his throne and he too groused in the sermon before all the folk, saying, "Dear brothers and sisters, some of you go around in the streets and gossip behind my back that I and my councilors have laid down our chains, and some of you go around saying that we're wearing your silver and gold. You should know, dear brothers and sisters, that God has selected me for this. I'll keep myself like this, as well as my councilors and all my servants. For this is no more than an example. They're going to go around in pieces

723. No one of this name appears in Kerssenbrock.

of gold. It had to look different before things became ready.[724] You should also know that you didn't make me a king. It was God who made me into a king. I'll wear the golden chains and I won't ask anybody about this, in contempt of you." Everyone kept quiet and no one dared to say a word against this, so great was the duress under which they kept the folk. Then they started wearing their chains again.

Decision to chose twelve "dukes"

[130r] So the king stood up again and held the folk once more under great duress, and now they had as great duress as at the end. The king took counsel with his councilors, as well as the leaders of the rebaptizers and all the captains, and they wanted to choose twelve dukes. The king and his councilors had it secretly in their hands that they would choose twelve dukes. The king didn't have this shouted out in the preaching, but the councilors and captains told it to one person here and another there, so that talk began to spread among the community throughout the whole city. Some people wouldn't believe it, imagining that they were saying out of buffoonery that twelve dukes would be chosen. So one person believed it and the next didn't, and there was much talk of this in the city of Münster.

Fraudulent selection of the dukes

Eventually, the king had it said in preaching that each brother was to come with his wives and all his household, young and old, to his gate (where each one's watch post was). Twelve dukes were to be chosen,[725] and everyone was to come [130v] at six o'clock in the morning. This is what happened, and everyone came to his gate, each captain with his folk, men and women, young and old.[726] The king had sent one of his councilors or one of his leading servants to each gate. The king's councilor (or servant) was at each

---

724. See 139v for a variant of this somewhat enigmatic expression. Seemingly, the meaning here is related to the English expression, "it's darkest before the dawn." That is, when the outlook was darkest, the king and his councilors took off their insignia of office, but now that things were supposedly "looking up," they would resume wearing their insignia.

725. For Kerssenbrock's account of the selection of the dukes, see *Anabaptistici furoris*, ed. Detmer, 773–76. Gresbeck gives no indication of the meaning of the title "duke," but it was meant quite literally. Kerssenbrock gives a list of all the dukes and the neighboring territories over which they were to rule (ibid., 775–76).

726. Note that a duke is chosen for each gate (so too 133r). In effect, this new method of appointing military commanders was simply a return to the method used for selecting new commanders by gate at the time of John of Leiden's installation as king (54v–55r).

gate with a captain, along with the common folk, and waited for the king. So the king's commander and the captain and a preacher preached there in the meanwhile about these twelve dukes. Eventually, the king's commander said that the men and women should all gather together. Eventually, the commander said, "Dear brothers and sisters, that my lord, the king of the righteous, has had you gather here, this is God's Will. It's God's Will that we're going to choose twelve dukes. So let's pray to God that we may choose someone that God would have a good pleasure[727] in, and that the one that we choose is God's Will, and that we choose someone who serves this purpose, and that he's a good Christian, and that he's perfect in his faith, and that this duke may rule in such a way that God will have a good pleasure in it. For this let us pray to God." So they [131r] fell to their knees and prayed, and they sang a German hymn. Then they stood up again. The king's commander then said that all the men, young and old, should go and stand by themselves over to one side, and that all the womenfolk should be by themselves on one side.[728] This is what they did on both sides. Once the men went and stood by themselves on one side, the king's commander—his name was Bernard Krechting[729]—said, "Dear brothers, now we'll choose someone here among us brothers who knows someone to serve as a duke who's considered a good Christian. This man you are to take up. So we'll pray to God that we won't make a choice unless it's God's Will." Then they once again fell to their knees and prayed to God that they might make a choice that God would have a good pleasure in. (These dukes were all chosen by the king and the councilors before they were gathered together at the gates.[730]) When the prayer was over, the commander said, "Now, dear brothers, God has heard our prayers. Now we'll choose." The commander made the first choice, then the captain, then five or six who also chose. In this way, they chose six or eight from the company, and they wrote down those whom they chose on a list and then cut the names [131v] apart. The king's commander then took these in his hand and said, "Dear brothers, we'll now see whom God will give to us as a duke." The commander took a young boy and took the boy's hat from his head, and then he put the

---

727. For the sense of "good pleasure," see also note 204.

728. The point of the separation is that only the men will participate in the selection of the duke.

729. One of the king's four councilors; Kerssenbrock, *Anabaptistici furoris*, ed. Detmer, 647.

730. Gresbeck's getting ahead of himself. He explains below that he thinks that chicanery was involved in the selection process.

hat in the boy's hand and said, "Look, dear brothers, these names of dukes that have been chosen, I'll place them in this boy's hat, and I'll close the hat tight. The boy will then reach into the hat. Whatever name is on the first slip that the boy grabs in his hand is the duke." This is what happened. The boy reached into the hat and grabbed a slip (a name of one of those who'd been chosen). The commander took the slip from the boy and shouted out the name. This man was the duke. But the commander didn't read the name that the boy had taken out of the hat. He named the one that the king and the councilors had chosen. The commander straightaway took the list out of the hat and threw it away.[731] This is how they chose the duke, and his name was John Naderman.[732] He was a peddler in the city of Münster, and he was a burgher.[733] [132r] He remained alive when the city of Münster was captured. At that time, he defected from the other side of the city, along with some others.[734] When the selection was over, they fell to their knees, and thanked the Father, and sang a German hymn. This duke was chosen in front of the Cross Gate.[735] They made a selection in this way in front of all the gates around the city.

The king greets the new dukes

This duke then cried out and asked, "Dear brothers, now help me thank God and the Father because I'm worthy of God having selected me as a duke, so that I may rule and carry out the Word of God, that this may lead

---

731. Note that Gresbeck merely asserts this chicanery without any evidence to back the claim. How did he know that the procedure was a sham? Is it merely an inference based on the fact that the slips of paper (what he must mean when he says the "list" was thrown away) were immediately disposed of without them being examined by anyone else? He later indicates that the dukes played a key role in maintaining order in the city (133r–134r), so it may be that he assumed that this had been the intention from the start. On the other hand, given the method by which the names from which the duke was to be selected were chosen, it's hardly surprising that the dukes should have been die-hard supporters of the regime, and for this reason one may be somewhat skeptical of Gresbeck's generally unsubstantiated accusation.

732. Oddly enough, this name doesn't appear in Kerssenbrock's list of dukes (*Anabaptistici furoris*, ed. Detmer, 774), but it is recorded in a contemporary list (Cornelius, *Berichte der augenzeugen*, 347). Naderman also appears in Gresbeck's own list of burghers who were notable Anabaptists (119v).

733. Given Gresbeck's generally patriotic attitude towards Münster, and his tendency to shift the blame for events to outsiders (especially the Hollanders and Frisians), it's remarkable that he mentions Naderman's low social status before his status as a burgher. Since Gresbeck at times censures the burghers of Münster who cooperated with the Anabaptists, presumably the order here is meant to disparage Naderman by indicating that even though he was a burgher, he was one of lowly status.

734. The people who escaped in this way were noted above (127v).

735. The letter that Gresbeck dispatched from the city before his departure states that he was stationed at the Cross Gate, which explains why he relates the events there at such length.

to the salvation of my soul, and that God may have a good pleasure in this." So they thanked the Father. The men and the women then gathered together and sang a German hymn. Then they waited for the king again. Eventually, the king came. The common people saw the king opposite and curtsied and bowed to him.[736] The king then stepped down from his horse and had all the men gather together. He asked the commander if they'd made the selection. The commander said yes. [132v] The king asked, "Which is the duke?" The commander and the captain pointed the duke out to the king and named him. The king then gave his hand to the duke, kissed him, and wished him luck. The duke shouted out in thanks to the king. (The king asked his commander and his captain who the duke was, and he asked in a knowing way. The king knew full well who the duke was. In this way, they were tossing the ball back and forth to each other.[737] They were all in cahoots about the buffoonery.) Eventually, the king showed the duke (like all the dukes) what he was to be the duke of. He assigned a gate to each duke, and the dukes were to take care of all the folk that belonged to each gate, men and women, young and old. In this way, the king appointed a duke for each gate, and he appointed a duke for the new blockhouse by the New Bridge Gate. The king also appointed a duke for the sconce[738] that the rebaptizers had made between the wall and the city bulwark, in between St. Ludger's and St. Servatius's Gate.[739] In this way, he manned the city with dukes.

The dukes appoint subordinates

[133r] The king had the dukes chosen by each gate in the way I described above. These dukes took control of the gates. Each duke had all his folk,

---

736. For the terms "curtsy" and "bow," see note 336.

737. Clearly a proverbial way of saying that they were playing out a charade.

738. A sconce was a specially raised up, circular embankment of dirt in which a high trench could be dug. The original purpose of this sort of earthwork was to allow besiegers to shoot down at the defenders in front of the walls from a protected higher position, but the besieged would also raise up similar works to thwart the besiegers. Because the purpose was to ambush the unwary, a common term for such works was a "cat." In English, these fortifications can also be called "roundels," a term which refers to the fact that the works were round-shaped and is similar to the one used by Gresbeck ("ruendell"). The sconce between the two gates was known as "Uldan's Fort" (Kerssenbrock, *Anabaptistici furoris*, ed. Detmer, see 553). For a discussion of these sorts of fortifications with an illustration, see Arnold, *Renaissance at War*, 38–39.

739. In the Cologne manuscript, the phrase "at the Horst Gate" was struck out in favor of the location given here. Kerssenbrock (*Anabaptistici furoris*, ed. Detmer, 554) confirms that Uldan's fort was between St. Ludger's and St. Servatius's Gate. The reason for the confusion is unclear. Although St. Ludger's Gate is in the southern sector of the city and St. Servatius's is in the southeast, the Horst Gate is in the northeast.

men and women, young and old, gather together, each duke in front of his gate. Each duke also carried out a selection, selecting councilors and other attendants.[740] Each duke selected three councilors. Each dismissed all the captains and established a new regime for his gate. Each also appointed a staff. This was no more than a lieutenant under a captain. They also chose a new preacher for each gate. Then the staff appointed a squad master at every gate, and this squad master then established how they were to keep the watch. The duke with his councilors, his staff, and the squad master assigned every one, male and female, to the watch. Each duke defended and manned his gate in this way, so that they imagined that they would defend the city. In this way, the king carried out the plan and selected the twelve dukes, so that they would hold the common folk under duress. They manned the gates all around the city in this way and carried out their buffoonery like this until the end.

The king holds a reception for the dukes

[133v] So the king held a reception and invited all the dukes and councilors as guests, as well as the king's councilors with all their wives and all the king's leading servants. The king held a great banquet with the dukes, the duchesses, the councilors, the viceroy, and the master of the court together with their wives, and with the master of horse, and all the leaders with their wives. The king held a great court with the dukes and the nobles. So, everyone was gathered together there and behaved as if they would carry out their rule for all their lives. Eventually, when the meal was done, they held court and danced, each with his wives. The king held court with the dukes, having invited them as guests, and they ate and drank and were of good cheer. The common folk, meanwhile, were fleeing the city from hunger, and some were beginning to starve.

Regalia of the dukes

Eventually, the king gave each duke a silk cord. Around this cord were bent the best gold pieces that the king had—crowns, angelots, rose nobles, ducats, and gold guilders.[741] The dukes hung this cord from their necks and wore it every day.

---

740. According to Kerssenbrock (*Anabaptistici furoris*, ed. Detmer, 773), each duke had three councilors and twenty-four well-armed attendants.

741. A similar list of coins appears on 56v (see the notes 311–14 for a discussion of where they

Regalia of their staffs

[134r] The king also gave a silk cord to all the staffs (the duke's lieutenants). Around this cord the king bent thick pennies[742] and Joachimstalers,[743] and the one-guilder silver pieces that the king had had struck, and Schreckenbergers[744] and tornos.[745] It was the best silver the king had that he bent onto the silk cords and hung from each one's neck. The staffs wore the silver around their necks every day. Every duke ruled with his staff in front of his gate and kept the common folk under such great duress, so clever was the king with his councilors and leaders in taking control of all the gates in this way and retaining possession of the city all around, so that from that time on there was no one in the city who dared to oppose the king or would have made an uprising. For the king and all the dukes had all the arms-bearing men by their side, so that everyone then had to keep quiet. He would have to either die of hunger in the city or flee out of hunger and get himself killed.

The dukes to save the people as the leaders of the twelve tribes of the Israelites had done

When the king appointed the twelve dukes, he informed the common folk that the relief would come and they would be relieved, just like the children of Israel.[746] They'd chosen twelve dukes, and after that they were relieved.

---

come from).

742. "Thick penny" ("dicke pennige") is the German version of the Latin term *grossus denarius*, which signified a silver coin worth twelve pennies (i.e., one shilling). Several centuries earlier, the term referred to silver coins minted on large planchets as opposed to the very thin coins known as "braceats," but here the term must refer to a coin similar to the tornos (see note 745). The Latin *grossus* is Germanized as *Groschen*, which is presumably what is meant here.

743. The Joachimsthaler was a large coin minted from silver mined since 1518 in the Joachimsthal ("Valley of Joachim") in Bohemia (the word "dollar" is derived from the second half of this compound).

744. The Schreckenberger was a largish silver coin named after the area in Saxony where it was minted.

745. The term "tornos" derives from the Latin name for the French *tournois* (*grossus denarius turnosus* or "large penny from Tours"), a denomination of coin originally minted in Tours. It was worth twelve pennies (i.e., one shilling).

746. Presumably, what the Anabaptists had in mind was the story told in the book of Judges. There, the Israelites earned the anger of God by worshipping Canaanite gods, and God in turn "tests" them (2:22) by subjecting them to defeat at the hands of their enemies. The Israelites duly repent and invoke the aid of God, who responds by setting up leaders called "judges." The title is a Semitic one for "magistrate" in a general sense (equivalent to the Carthaginian "suffetes"), which is rather misleading in the present context because these judges actually served as ad hoc military leaders who arise in times of trouble. In the book, there are six major judges (Othniel, Ehud, Barak, Gideon, Jephthah, Sampson)

This is what the king of Münster also imagined, and he informed the common folk that they too would be relieved in this way. So the poor folk imagined for sure that they would still be relieved.

New plans

[134v] They made every plan that they could think up, and made attempts in every direction with every means that they could think of.[747] The king had an order issued to all the dukes that each duke was to come up to the cathedral square with all his subjects. Each duke was assigned a time when they were to come. One duke came first and another next, until they (all twelve dukes) had all been before the king. This lasted all day.

The dukes present their troops to the king

When the dukes came, the king was sitting behind St. James's Church with his councilors and Stutenberent, and they were sitting on a bench. When one duke came first with his folk, as strong in numbers as he could, the duke went right away before the king in his rank, and his subjects followed him in their ranks. The king and the duke shook hands and gave each other the kiss of peace. The king said to the duke that he should have his folk come together. So the duke had them come together, and they came before the king and the councilors. Then the king said, "Dear brothers, it's my desire and God's will that I've had you gather together here. As it seems to

---

and six minor ones (Shamgar, Tola, Jair, Ibzon, Elon, Abdon), for a total of twelve (which also happens to correspond to the number of tribes). These men then led the Israelites to triumph over their foes, and the applicability of this story to the situation of the Anabaptists is obvious. The regular German translation for this title is *Richter* ("judge"), so the contemporary terminology used by the Anabaptists ("duke") doesn't exactly fit with the notion that the contemporary events were to be a "rehearsal" of the biblical story (presumably, the biblical title was considered inappropriate for the basically military content of the office, and in any event, the "dukes" were actually meant to rule over conquered territories and so needed a proper modern title). For other examples of making contemporaries "assume" the role of biblical characters, see the assassination attempt modeled on Judith (not overtly mentioned by Gresbeck, but see also note 154), and Knipperdolling's attempt to make "new" apostles bearing the names of those of Jesus (102r). See 23v and 35v for other instances of the Anabaptists modeling their behavior after the ancient Israelites.

747. The selection of the new dukes seems rather pointless as Gresbeck relates the aftermath, but in fact the ultimate failure of Anabapist ferment elsewhere to do any good for the besieged is evident only in retrospect. As late as May 1535, an uprising in Amsterdam resulted in a number of executions (see Duke, *Reformation and Revolt in the Low Countries*, 88, with the gruesome woodcut in illustration 1 showing large numbers of bodies of the executed being exposed upside down as a warning), and perhaps Gresbeck's vague notice of planning "in every direction" indicates that there was still hope that some salvation from the city would arise from the Low Countries and the military force organized under the dukes could be used to expedite this relief. If so, nothing was to come of it.

me, dear brothers, [135r] one man is running first and the other next.[748] So you certainly see, dear brothers, that we've been put in dire straits by our enemies, that a siege lies all around us and we're under tight siege, and that we can't move forwards or backwards. You know full well what you promised God, that for His sake you would endure everything God sends to you. It seems to me that you're not upholding for God what you promised to God.[749] So God in turn won't uphold for you the promise that He made to you. For if you uphold for God what you promised to Him, then God will in turn uphold for you the promise that He made to you."

Men pressured into volunteering to continue to fight

Eventually, the king said, "Dear brothers, if there's anyone here among you who would gladly have permission or would gladly be on his way and who doesn't wish to endure the hunger until God relieves us—for I know as a fact that God will relieve us, which I will fast and wait for, and even if I should remain in the city by myself, I will not leave it—if there's anyone present who wishes to be on his way, let him go stand by himself. He'll receive permission, I'll have them taken to the gate." The king went and stood, and he looked around to see if someone did go from the company and stand by himself. [135v] No one was so bold as to dare to go and stand by himself. For there were enough of them standing in the company who would have gladly been on their way, but no one dared to expose himself.[750] For everyone wished to take his chances as to whether he would have wound up dead or alive, and would have preferred to move out of the city. They were afraid that if someone who would have gladly been on his way had exposed himself, the king would have hung or beheaded him. Eventually, the king said to the duke, "Brother, I clearly note that the brothers you have under you wish to stay with us." The duke then said, "For that may the Father have thanks and praise for ever!" Eventually, Stutenberent stood up and gave a sermon, taking something from here and there in Holy Scripture that supported him. Eventually, when the sermon was done, Stutenberent said, "Dear brothers, if you all wish to stay with us and with the Word of

748. Presumably, he means "out of the city."
749. For a similar statement (in the mouths of unnamed preachers) about the promise made to God, see 88v–89r. This is a further reference to the situation in the Book of Judges (see also note 746).
750. Is Gresbeck speaking of himself?

God and to suffer for the sake of God everything that befalls you, hunger and woe, for life or for death, and if, dear brothers, you're minded to do this, then all those who wish to do that, raise up both hands in the air!"[751] All of them then stuck both of their hands up into the air. Then they renewed their promise. With this [136r] the king imagined that no one would rush from the city after this time. But the running began for the first time to take place at a run.[752]

Destruction of St. James's Church

When this sticking up of hands into the air took place, the king said to the duke and to all the folk that they now had to tear down the church. This was St. James's Church.[753] They were to tear down the church up to the last cornice, so that what was to remain standing of the church was the height of a man tall. So the king ordered each duke to assign people there every day to tear down the church. Then the duke went back to his gate with his folk. This was the duke at the Cross Gate. Then all the dukes came before the king and did what the first duke did.[754] Straightaway on the next day, the dukes sent their people, and they began to tear down the church.

Losses suffered guarding the cattle

These twelve dukes stood firm with their councilors and with the staffs and the squad masters, and the king with his councilors and his retinue, holding the common folk under such [136v] great duress and keeping such a tight rein on them that no one dared to speak a "not" right to the end. If one duke was stronger in numbers than another, then when one duke who was not strong was in need, the other duke would come to his assistance. The dukes would protect the cows in the kingdom[755] outside the gates between the blockhouses and the city, and the one duke would help

751. For a similar ploy to shame people into volunteering, see 35r.
752. A bit of a pun.
753. For Kerssenbrock's general discussion, see *Anabaptistici furoris*, ed. Detmer, 46. This was the sole church to have escaped desecration so far (111v).
754. The story related since the bottom of 134v refers to the activities of the duke of the Cross Gate and his subordinates, who happened to be the first to be summoned before the king. The great length of this anecdote compared to the terse notice of the same thing happening to the other dukes confirms the idea that Gresbeck was stationed at the Cross Gate and is describing the events that he saw as a participant (see also note 735).
755. For the "kingdom," see note 683. For the cows, see 121v–122r.

the other protect the cows. They would hold the watch in full armor in the kingdom if they had to protect the cows. When the duke imagined that he'd held the watch in full armor, then they'd gone rushing to the blockhouse and would much rather have eaten something.[756] The landsknechts mostly killed them. The landsknechts would also come running into the kingdom and exchanged fire with the dukes, wishing to take the cows from them. Then they straightaway drove the cows into the city, and they often suffered losses on both sides. Eventually, My Gracious Lord of Münster set to it along with the lords acting in the name of the Empire[757] and brought new blockhouses closer to the city, so that then they couldn't drive the cows out, and then the cows had to stay in the city. Then they slaughtered the cows and ate them.

Starvation worsens

[137r] The hunger in the city now became so great that they died of hunger and defected from the city by night and by day, much preferring to get themselves killed than to die of hunger. Men and women and old, sick people were starving, the young as well as the old, so that they walked with canes because they couldn't walk any longer, so that some of them fell down and died. The common folk used to receive bread from the community (from the bakers), but after this time no one could get bread anymore. At this point, the common folk didn't know how they could feed themselves anymore, or how they could make it. The king with his retinue wouldn't give up the city. They said they'd sooner starve to death than ask men for mercy. The king still had good fasting with (some of) his retinue.[758] These people still had enough to eat, but affliction befell the common folk. So the king wouldn't ask any men for mercy, but only God and the Father. But in the end they would all in fact have asked men for mercy, if they could have gotten mercy. But the door to mercy was closed with the landsknechts when the city was captured.[759]

---

756. Gresbeck's not entirely clear here. Seemingly, he's talking of (presumably isolated) incidents when troops released from duty at the end of a stint of watching the cows made an unsuccessful and apparently unauthorized rush at the siegeworks in search of food.

757. I.e., the neighboring princes who had agreed to help carry on the siege in the aftermath of the failure of the second attempt to storm the city (and the prince-bishop's inability to foot the bill by himself anymore). They were operating in the name of the Holy Roman Empire (hence the expression used here) as members of the Westphalian circle, which had voted to assist the prince-bishop.

758. More of Gresbeck's irony, since he doesn't believe that the king fasted at all.

759. More irony in that phrase "door to mercy" was previously used fairly frequently by the Anabaptists in their (seemingly capricious) decision making about whether or not to execute somebody at

Permission given to those wishing to leave

So the king once more gave permission.[760] Whoever wished to leave the city was to come up to the [137v] council hall. So men and women and children came and asked the king for permission, wishing to go out the gate. The king and his councilors took their clothing off those who asked for permission, and put old clothes back on them, and they had them go to the gate in pairs as if they were going to be hung. The viceroy's[761] servants brought them to the gate, so unworthy did they consider the people who wanted to depart from them and give up the baptizing and return to the heathens. They said that these people were damned body and soul because they wanted to defect from their faith. This departure lasted for eight days in a row. It was ten, twenty, thirty, forty, or fifty people who moved out of the city every day like this. The king then had it said in the preaching that after this time no one would receive permission anymore. If anyone else was found who wanted to receive permission or who wanted to get out by the gate, that person would be killed.

People take desperate measures to get food

Those who now remained in the city fed themselves in a piteous manner, eating every sort of beast on the land or in the water. Anything that was alive they ate. Some people would even say that they ate children.[762] I don't know anything more about how this is. I didn't see it.

People eat inedible things while the Anabaptist leaders have plenty to eat

[138r] They began to eat horses first—the head with the feet, and the liver and the lungs.[763] They ate cats, dogs, mice, rats, great big mussels, frogs, and grass.[764] Greens were their bread. So long as they had salt, this was their

---

their mercy (14v, 18v–19v, 22r, 24v–25r, 79r).

760. For the earlier instance of the king giving permission to leave, see 123v–124v (also, 128v).

761. I.e., Knipperdolling, the executioner.

762. For Kerssenbrock's discussion of the reported eating of babies, see *Anabaptistici furoris*, ed. Detmer, 800–802.

763. The eating of horses is already mentioned in a confession of December 23, 1534 (Kerssenbrock, *Anabaptistici furoris*, ed. Detmer, 73n3).

764. For the eating of animals not normally considered food, see Kerssenbrock, *Anabaptistici furoris*, ed. Detmer, 798–800.

wheat. They also ate ox hides, and they laid old shoes in the malting trough and ate them.[765] So the preachers preached that they should live soberly, that they shouldn't eat so much greens. Did they really have to eat three or four bowls full of greens every day? He[766] also groused that the women were going around in the city crying for bread. Their children were dying, the old people were dying, one dying first, the other next. But the criminal (the king) with his councilors and the leaders, they had enough to eat and let the other folk starve to death. Whoever at that time could steal something from one person or another, they did so—food and dogs and cats. Where they could steal, there they were and ate it. That was their prey. If the king was informed at this time that someone wanted to flee from him, he cut his head off or had him hung from a linden[767] up at the cathedral square.

Children allowed to leave the city

[138v] When the hunger first began to arrive in the city, some people had their children go from the city to the enemy. The landsknechts received the children and took some children with them. The burghers that the rebaptizers drove out of the city by force before and on the Friday wrote to the king and the councilors asking the king to let the children go from the city—they'd look after them at the blockhouses. The king did this, sending the children out of the city. Some burghers who were driven out had also left maidens and old people in their houses to protect the houses for them until they returned. For it wasn't their expectation when they were driven out of the city that they would stay away for so long, but that they would come back to the city in three or four days, as I mentioned before.[768] The burghers also wrote to the old people that they'd left in their houses that the king would let them stroll off. The king did this too and let them stroll off. For the king would have preferred that all the children, all the old people, men and women, would have been gone from the city in good time, as I mentioned before.[769]

765. The process of malting involved placing barley in a container and pouring in water to make it germinate, then removing the barley and stopping the germination. What is going on here is placing the leather of old shoes in such troughs and soaking them in water to soften up the leather to make it at all edible. The eating of leather is mentioned by Kerssenbrock, *Anabaptistici furoris*, ed. Detmer, 800.
766. Seemingly Gresbeck has some specific preacher in mind.
767. See note 130 for why this tree was used.
768. See 12v (see also 40v).
769. See 128v.

Women leave the city, and the king dismisses his junior wives

[139r] So the majority of the womenfolk left the city out of hunger. The king had fifteen wives, and he gave them all permission apart from the queen. He kept only her. He said to the wives that they should each go to their friends to get something to eat, wherever they could.[770] He said to them, "You no doubt see that my power is not great now, so you have to suffer with me until God makes things better. I hope that things will get better soon. God won't abandon his poor little company." Those who had many wives like this did the same, keeping their first wife and letting the other wives leave the city. Of the women who left the city, the landsknechts took for themselves those who were young up at the blockhouse and kept them with them as their wives from then on. The king and those who had so many wives became tired of their beautiful wives and multiplying[771] the world with all these wives. Some rebaptizers would certainly have taken a piece of bread in exchange for a wife, if someone had offered it to them. There's poor holding of court where there's no bread.[772]

A starving man assails the king

[139v] The king didn't know how he would make it anymore, and he didn't know how it would look when things were ready.[773] The common folk rushed from the city in thick numbers now, in thick numbers night and day, whether the king gave permission or not. The hunger put such duress on them that they had to leave the city, or else they would either start raving with hunger or have to die. There was someone in the city named Reneke, who was a gunsmith and had rushed into the city. This man had such great hunger, he leaped at the king and said, "Lord King, I've got to feed!" He snapped his teeth together and acted as if he would bite the king apart or feed on him. The king got himself out of the way and let the gunsmith

---

770. Note that this statement seems to contradict Gresbeck's frequent claim that the king and the other leaders hoarded food for themselves and still had plenty of provisions when the city was captured. On the other hand, there is much evidence that the king continued to have food until the end (see note 701), so perhaps the statement here means simply that even his resources were beginning to feel the pinch, and he had to do a bit of "downsizing" himself.

771. For "multiplying" the world as justification for polygamy, see 38v–39r.

772. Note the use of the same phrase in 93v.

773. See 129v, where John of Leiden uses a similar phrase.

stand there for as long as he wanted. In the end, he was allowed to go away
the way he'd come. He couldn't get anything to eat from the king. This man
was allowed to go along out of the city and get himself killed along with
the others. The king had nothing to spare. But, when the city was taken, he
had surplus enough.[774]

Two ensigns arrested for talking of fleeing the city

The common folk didn't know how they could manage to get out of the city
and be taken prisoner by the landsknechts. For they saw every day before
their own eyes that whoever defected from the city was killed right away.
These [140r] were burghers and landsknechts and all sorts of foreigners,
who would have been glad to get out of the city and to have the city surrendered. So there were two ensigns in the city. These ensigns took counsel one
time. They would have been glad to be out of the city or to have had the
city surrendered. One burgher would go to another, and one landsknecht
to another, if they really trusted each other, and they would speak together
secretly and would have been glad to have had the city surrendered.[775] But
the king and his retinue wouldn't surrender the city. If Knipperdolling had
joined forces with those who would have been glad to surrender the city
and had abandoned the king with his retinue, then some burghers and
landsknechts and other foreigners would have taken their chances[776] one
more time with the king and his retinue and would have done battle with
him one more time and surrendered the city.[777] So one time these two
ensigns were in a house, and they talked of how they would be glad to get
out of the city and to have had the city surrendered. These two ensigns
imagined that they were with good friends and said everything out loud.
Eventually, the others said, "Where will the two of you run? Stay here with
God the Lord. Starve of hunger or get killed, you suffer this for the sake
of God, and in return you'll have life eternal."[778] [140v] The one ensign
answered by saying, "Yeah, good ole life eternal. Having skin full of lice is
also life eternal!" The others remembered the phrase "Yeah, good ole life

774. On the king's surplus, see note 701.
775. Presumably, this is Gresbeck speaking about his own behavior towards the end of the siege.
776. I.e., in risking another rebellion.
777. Note that Gresbeck seems to believe that Knipperdolling still exercised sufficient authority among the locals that they would have followed him in rebelling against the king.
778. For a similar sentiment, see 79v–80r.

eternal. A skin full of lice is also an eternity!" They reported it to the king, and he straightaway had the two ensigns arrested, on account of this phrase.

The ensigns escape from prison, one fleeing the city

So the king had the two ensigns arrested and placed in prison (the cellar; not the city cellar but the cellar underneath the registry[779]).[780] He was going to have them both beheaded, so the ensigns, being sensible landsknechts, broke out of the prison at night and escaped. They got out at the same time, and each went home, to their wives. If they'd remained together, the two of them would have both gotten away.[781] When one of the ensigns came home, he told his wife to hand him the banner from the bedroom.[782] "My lord the king has let me out of prison. We're going to march from the city tonight." His wife gave him the banner from the bedroom, and he then said goodnight to his wife. The ensign went his way, and the ensign's wife went back into their house. This ensign tore the banner from its pole [141r] and stuck it in his sleeve.[783] He then defected from the city, and got away with the banner.[784] The other ensign remained in the city and hid himself. Once day broke, they wanted to check on the prisoners.[785] The two were both gone. The one had defected with the banner, and the other was still hidden in the city. The one ensign was a Hollander, and the other was from Jülich.[786]

---

779. For the registry and the cells underneath that were used to house the accused, see Kerssenbrock, *Anabaptistici furoris*, ed. Detmer, 76.

780. This story is told by Kerssenbrock, *Anabaptistici furoris*, ed. Detmer, 820. According to him, the ensign John of Jülich was arrested because of accusations that he was planning to escape and that he had been spreading talk of sedition. In prison, he plotted to escape with the ensign Christopher of Schoonhoven (a town in south Holland), who had been accused of impiety.

781. The details of the escape and of the wives' involvement are not mentioned by Kerssenbrock.

782. For the importance of the banner in military maneuvering, see note 188. The rather amateurish nature of the military establishment of the Anabaptists seems to be betrayed by the fact that the ensign apparently kept the banner at home.

783. The modern pocket is a comparatively recent development, and in the sixteenth century people often used their puffy sleeves for the purpose of storing things.

784. Gresbeck doesn't explain the ensign's reason for taking the trouble to escape with the banner. Perhaps the ensign thought that possession of it might gain him favor with the besiegers if he was captured. In any event, the commander of the besieging forces wrote a letter to the prince-bishop on April 27, 1535, informing him that on the previous Sunday (April 24) Christopher of Schoonhoven had escaped from the city with a banner and gotten through the siegeworks, but had had to leave the banner in the moat (Kerssenbrock, *Anabaptistici furoris*, ed. Detmer, 820n3).

785. Seemingly, the cells were left unguarded at night.

786. Jülich (the seat of a duchy) is a town about eighty miles southwest of Münster. The Hollander was Christopher of Schoonhoven, and the man from Jülich was named John.

The other ensign is found in the city and executed

In the morning, the king had both the ensigns' wives fetched to the council hall. The king and the councilors asked the two women whether they knew anything about the two ensigns, their husbands, having escaped from prison. They said "No, no." The one wife said, "My husband came home at night and asked me for the banner from the bedroom. He said that my lord the king had let him out of prison, and that they were going to march out of the city right away." The other ensign's wife didn't know what to say. She said that her husband had come home, and she didn't know where he was. This ensign was still in the city. The king conducted a house-to-house search to look for the ensign. Eventually, the king found the ensign in the [141v] house next door to the ensign's, up in the attic. They fetched the ensign out of the house, and the king had him beheaded right away on the next day,[787] while the other ensign got away with the banner. Shortly afterwards, the king had two more landsknechts beheaded. They still had money, and the one had bought something from the other. For this they had to die.[788]

Five men flee the city, and one of them (a burgher) gets separated

So one night, five defected from the city.[789] One was a burgher[790] in the city, and the other four were landsknechts. One of the landsknechts was

787. Kerssenbrock reports that when John of Jülich was captured, they found a banner wrapped up in his sleeve. (The Latin is *in sinu*. I rendered this in my translation of Kerssenbrock as "pocket," but clearly the sleeve was meant.) Since Gresbeck has the man who escaped get away with a banner and this is confirmed by the letter to the prince-bishop, presumably Kerssenbrock (or his source) has confused which ensign had the banner. (Conceivably both ensigns made off with a banner, but why should John have done so if he meant to hide in the city?) In any event, since Kerssenbrock dates the execution to May 11, 1535, and Gresbeck places the execution on the date after John's capture, then given that the escape took place on April 24, John seems to have remained hidden for over two weeks. (Detmer doubts the accuracy of Kerssenbrock's date, presumably because he finds the length of time implied for the concealment unlikely; Kerssenbrock, *Anabaptistici furoris*, ed. Detmer, 820n3).

788. For the suppression of monetary exchange, see note 165.

789. According to Kerssenbrock (*Anabaptistici furoris*, ed. Detmer, 826–27), eight men made the attempt to escape. One would expect that since Gresbeck himself was one of them, he ought to have known how many men he escaped with. On the other hand, since Gresbeck's account only deals with five (himself and his companion plus Little Hans and his two companions), perhaps he decided to dispense with introducing three other men who would play no further role in his narrative and whose disappearance from the story would have to be accounted for.

790. I.e., Gresbeck himself, who uniformly refers to himself in this way for the rest of the account, apart from the very last sentence, in which it's clear that the "I" of the narrator and the burgher are identical (also see note 802 for a mistake on Gresbeck's part in using the first person in connection with himself). It's intriguing that Gresbeck gives absolutely no explanation for his decision to defect. Could his motives for leaving the doomed city have reflected poorly on him?

Little Hans of Longstreet.⁷⁹¹ These five defected on the Sunday after Whit-
suntide,⁷⁹² in the second summer of the siege, and all five kept their lives.
Once the five had gotten out and reached the kingdom⁷⁹³ in between the
blockhouse and the city, they took counsel as to how they might plan to
get through the enemy and across the trench. They reached an agreement
and went to the trench. When they got close to the trench in this way,
they began to crawl. Eventually, Little Hans of Longstreet said, "They're
aware of us," and they crawled back a bit. The burgher then said, "If they're
aware of us, then I won't keep on crawling. I'll head for the Gelders blockhouse."⁷⁹⁴ The burgher said, "If there's anyone who wants to stay with me,
let him follow after me." So one of them stayed with the burgher, and they
[142r] crawled back. Little Hans of Longstreet kept on crawling with the
other two. While they were crawling along, the landsknechts struck up the
changing of the watch, since it was midnight, and as the drums were beating, the landsknechts left the watch and the new watch was about to arrive.
This is how Little Hans of Longstreet got across the trench with the other
two.⁷⁹⁵ By that time, the burgher had crawled back with his companion,
so that he was too far from the trench. While the burgher was crawling
back with his companion, the one lost track of the other. So the burgher
imagined that he'd crawled back to the city. By then, he'd crawled up to the
other side of the trench and was right in the midst of the enemy. He looked

791. In his initial discussion of Little Hans, Kerssenbrock (*Anabaptistici furoris*, ed. Detmer, 825)
refers to him as Hensulus Eckius Langestratius. Presumably this means that the man's full name was
something like Jan (van) Eck van der Langestrate (for Jan/John as his first name, see ibid., 649, where
Kerssenbrock lists Joannes Langstrate among the king's servants, seemingly unaware of the connection
with Little Hans). No other source uses the name (van) Eck, and Little Hans seems to have normally
gone by the geographical name. (In the early modern period, the usage with surnames was fluid. Along
with an inherited name, a man could also have a "secondary" surname based on his own profession or
geographic origin.) The name Langstrate (Longstreet) is not very specific. Seemingly, the expression
"Longstreet" was fairly common in the Low Countries, where roads would develop along the dikes
used there to hold back the sea, such roads being unusually "long" by medieval standards (presumably
because their origin meant that they didn't run into any obstacles over their length). One notable "long
street" ran (and still runs) through northern Brabant, but although there was at least one Anabaptist
from Brabant in Münster (121r), there's no particular reason to associate Little Hans with that area. In
any event, the association of the "long streets" with the Low Countries suggests that Little Hans's family
name was the Dutch "van Eck" rather than the common German name "Eck" (Langstraat seems to be
a moderately common name in Dutch-speaking countries, but Langstrasse isn't a common name for
either places or people in German).
792. May 23, 1535.
793. For the explanation of the term "kingdom," see note 683.
794. The Gelders blockhouse was opposite the Jew Fields Gate and faced west-northwest. It was
the next blockhouse to the south of the Cleves blockhouse, which was opposite the Cross Gate (where
Gresbeck was stationed) and faced northwest.
795. For Kerssenbrock's version of Hans's escape, see note 824.

up and didn't know where he was. He saw the landsknechts standing above him. He crawled back from there and then crawled into the next trench outside the city, not knowing where his companion was. The burgher sat in the trench until it was daylight. He was alive and dead. He didn't know how he could manage to keep his life. If he'd run back to the city, he knew full well that the king would have had him hung or struck his head off. If he went to the landsknechts, they too would kill him. He didn't know which way he would get out.

The burgher surrenders to besieging troops and his life is spared

[142v] When the burgher was sitting like this in the trench and thought one way and another, he eventually said, "Well, then, it's got to be. Now God has to help me and be merciful and compassionate to me." He stood up from the trench and went to the Gelders blockhouse. The landsknechts were standing up in the trench, and they noticed the burgher and shouted to him, "Come here, countryman!"[796] The rebaptizers also saw him and shouted, "Come back!" For they certainly knew him, as he'd defected from the city that night. So the burgher went in to the landsknechts at the Gelders blockhouse. When he was right in their midst, they trained their guns at his body and were going to shoot him. The landsknechts spoke one to another and looked among themselves, and they said that they shouldn't shoot. "We want to take this man prisoner and hear what he'll say." They said, "This is still a young man, we'll leave him his life." The burgher was petrified, so that he was half dead and didn't know what he should say. Eventually, he said, "I ask you, my dear landsknechts, to take me prisoner, because I too was a landsknecht,[797] so that I may be granted an interview and come before the chief captain."[798] The landsknechts said yes, they would take him prisoner. [143r] Then the landsknechts asked

796. The Gelders camp was so named because of the origin of the troops stationed there (Kerssenbrock, *Anabaptistici furoris*, ed. Detmer, 547), but here the term "countryman" ("landesmaen") doesn't indicate that the troops had any reason to imagine that Gresbeck was from their homeland. Rather, the term seems to be a way (presumably polite, or at least neutral) of addressing someone of unknown origin (see a similar address to Gresbeck by another soldier in 151r).

797. There seems to be no evidence that Gresbeck, the young cabinetmaker, had been a landsknecht. Could he be fibbing here? If he had been a landsknecht, he presumably didn't serve for long (and perhaps this service would explain his apparent interest in military affairs).

798. For the sense of "chief captain," see note 293.

the burgher how things stood in the city. He said that there was great woe and hunger in the city, and that if the king was informed about them, he had all those who wished to run from him killed. "So I tried my luck and have come in to you. I ask you to agree to take me prisoner." All the landsknechts then said yes, he should jump up into the trench, and into the ditch they thrust their pikes, which he was supposed to use to clamber up.[799] The burgher did this and jumped into the trench, pulling himself up by the pikes.[800] The trench was a high one, topped with a hawthorn all around.[801] When the burgher came to the hawthorn, he couldn't get over it. So the landsknechts took him by both hands and one foot and pulled him over the hedge. Once the burgher was up in the trench and lying there, he looked up and imagined that the landsknechts were going to hack him to death. The landsknechts then told him to stand up, they wouldn't do anything to him. "What you have on you belongs to us," and they took this from him, down to his shirt. Then they brought him to the captain up at the Gelders blockhouse. The landsknechts said to the captain, "We have a prisoner, a young man. We didn't want to kill him." Then the captain said, "Let him [143v] come here." The burgher came before the captain. The captain said, "You may well thank God that you're here, that they took you prisoner. All those who defected from the city before you, they killed them all." Then the captain had something to eat and drink set before him, and he ate and drank.

The troops find the burgher's companion but fail to find another man (Little Hans of Longstreet)

Once the burgher was up at the blockhouse, and he sat down and drank, the landsknechts stood around him and looked at him. Eventually, the

799. What goes on next might be clearer if one understands that the trench consisted of three parts. In front of the trench proper was a rampart formed by piling up dirt from a ditch dug in front of the rampart. Anyone launching a direct assault on the trench would find this all the more difficult in that they first had to enter the ditch in front and then climb up both the far side of it and the rampart before reaching the main trench occupied by the besiegers, who in the meanwhile could fire down at the impeded attackers. Gresbeck has somewhat confused things in that, up until now, he has used the general term "trench" ("schaensse") to describe the ditch in front, which only in this section receives a distinctive term ("graefft"), with the term "trench" now used properly to describe the actual fortification occupied by the landsknechts.

800. In the late fifteenth century, landsknechts were mostly armed with spears known as pikes, but in the time since then, the use of firearms became increasingly common. Nonetheless, at this time, pikes were still in use.

801. For the use of the hawthorn, see note 684.

burgher said to the landsknechts, "So, my dear landsknechts, I ask you to hear a word from me." The landsknechts said yes, and he said, "I would ask you, as there's still someone else behind me, to agree to take him prisoner too. For he was taken into the city as a prisoner and was stationed up here at the blockhouse as a landsknecht. His name is Little Hans of Nijmwegen." All the landsknechts then said yes, they would take him prisoner, and the captain ordered them to take him prisoner and not kill him. So the landsknechts ran into the kingdom, [144r] and they looked for him and found him. They took this knecht prisoner too and took everything that he had from him too. Then they brought this knecht to the burgher up at the blockhouse, and they gave him something to eat and drink too. Then the captain asked if anyone else had defected with them from the city.[802] They said, yes, Little Hans of Longstreet with two others. Then the landsknechts said, "Provided we catch him, we'll hack him into a hundred pieces."[803] Then the landsknechts ran into the kingdom and looked for Little Hans of Longstreet and the two others, but they couldn't find him. He'd gotten over the trench during the beating of the drums and was gone.[804]

The burgher brought to the commander of the besieging forces

Two lords came riding to the Gelders blockhouse and had the burgher come from the blockhouse. They asked him how things stood in the city. The burgher told the lords the real truth, just as they found out in the end.[805] The lords then ordered the landsknechts to bring the burgher and his companion to My Lord of Overstein[806] as well as the other lords

---

802. In the Cologne manuscript, the text originally read "with us" ("vens"=High German *uns*). The pronoun was crossed out and replaced with the third person plural pronoun "oem." Presumably, Gresbeck had made a slip in referring to himself in the first person.

803. Gresbeck gives no motivation for this vehement hostility towards Hans of Longstreet, which is especially striking after the compassion shown to Gresbeck and his companion. Presumably, Little Hans was himself aware of this attitude, which explains his determination to avoid capture and pass through the lines. See 150v for further suspicions harbored about him by his erstwhile comrades.

804. His escape is related below (146r–v).

805. As an ex-Anabaptist, Gresbeck will continue to be treated with suspicion by the besiegers, and here he wishes to point out that even they would have to admit that when put to the test his credibility would eventually be fully vindicated.

806. By the fall of 1534, after the failure of the second assault on the city, the prince-bishop was unable to continue the siege with his own resources and was forced to seek help from neighboring states, so a conference was called at the city of Koblenz on December 13. There, a number of princes agreed

of the Empire[807] in the place where they had their camp. This is what happened.

The burgher proposes a plan to capture the city

[144v] The captain up at the Gelders blockhouse had a riding horse saddled up along with some landsknechts, and they brought the burgher and his companion to all the lords of the Empire, to My Lord of Overstein and to My Lord of Manderscheid, Count Robert,[808] who would offer his mercy to the burgher in the end, so that he remained alive.[809] All the lords took the burgher by himself and asked about the entire situation in the city. He told them the whole situation—how things were in the city and about how the fortification around the city was in terms of earthworks and gates. There were more prisoners there, and they sent these people along with his companion to Wolbeck.[810] They kept the burgher there and put him in prison. So the burgher sat in prison and made a diagram of all the fortifications and all the earthworks and gates around the city, and he also made a diagram of the whole city. He also scratched a likeness in the ground of the city of Münster, showing where it was captured.[811]

---

to defray the costs of the further prosecution of the siege, but they took over control of the military operations from the prince-bishop, appointing Wirich of Dhaun, Count of Falkenstein, Lord of Overstein, as commander-in-chief of the siege in place of the prince-bishop (Kerssenbrock, *Anabaptistici furoris*, ed. Detmer, 747). The prince-bishop was resentful of having control of the military operations taken from him, and his ill will towards the commander appointed by the princes would later redound to Gresbeck's detriment when he came to be associated in the prince-bishop's mind with Overstein.

807. The lords of the Empire were those lords who were directly subordinate to the Holy Roman Emperor and in this capacity were providing military assistance for the siege.

808. Ruprecht (the regular German equivalent of Robert, though Gresbeck actually uses the French version "Robert") headed one of the three branches into which the family of the counts of Manderscheid (a town in the Rhineland) was divided upon the death of his grandfather back in 1488. Robert was acting here as the war councilor (*Kriegsrat*) of the bishop of Cologne (he's attested as a witness to one of John of Leiden's confessions after the capture of the city); see Cornelius, *Berichte der augenzeugen*, 347, 362.

809. Where the Cologne manuscript reads "my lord of *aüersten*," the two manuscripts used by Cornelius apparently read Monster (i.e., Münster). Because there's no indication in the Cologne manuscript that this form was to be changed, presumably the copyist who drew up the text from which Cornelius's manuscripts were copied made an unconscious slip of the pen by replacing the correct text with the frequent expression "my lord of Münster" (for the same mistake elsewhere, see 150v and also note 852). In any event, the difference is crucial. As Gresbeck goes on to say, whereas he laid his plan out to the commanders of the besieging army, the same plan would be put to the bishop of Münster by Hans of Longstreet—and a major purpose of Gresbeck's account was to win for himself some of the credit for the capture of Münster, which had fallen entirely to the bishop's man, Hans of Longstreet.

810. Wolbeck is a small town to the immediate southeast of Münster.

811. He means that he drew on the ground the plan showing the scheme by which the city was eventually taken. This detail is confirmed in the letter of Wirich of Dhaun (see Cornelius, *Berichte der augenzeugen*, 393), which appears in the appendix as document 4.

The burgher was the very first one to give the lords the plan to capture the city of Münster.[812]

Other defectors from the city executed

Once the rebaptizers saw that the landsknechts had taken the burgher and his companion prisoner, about two hundred defected from the city after them. [145r] Some were taken prisoner, and some were killed. Those who were taken prisoner were taken to Wolbeck and executed there. All too few were those who escaped from there, apart from those who were taken to the city as prisoners.[813] In this way, they were all killed.

The Anabaptists lose strength

A woman came from the city and brought the lords news that they'd chosen another king in the city, and that the king, John of Leiden, was deposed and was no longer king. John of Leiden was not deposed. He'd appointed a lieutenant under him to help him keep the people under duress.[814] It was becoming too much for John of Leiden by himself. This lieutenant is named Bernard Krechting,[815] and he sits by the king in the basket.[816]

---

812. I.e., he claims that he had precedence over Little Hans of Longstreet in suggesting the plan. Kerssenbrock, of course, knows nothing of Gresbeck.

813. The exception seemingly refers to landsknechts like Little Hans of Nijmwegen who were brought into the city involuntarily as prisoners.

814. The idea that there was a new king apparently took some hold among the besiegers. At any rate, in a letter of July 1, 1535 (see appendix, document 3), in which he describes the capture of the city, Justinian of Holtzhausen (an officer) mentions that on the day of the capture the Anabaptist defenders numbered three hundred "sampt dem newen konnig" ("together with the new king"). He gives no name, but presumably he has Krechting in mind. Holtzhausen also mentions the subsequent capture of the "first king," so it seems pretty clear that he does have a change of king in mind, with the previous incumbent remaining in the city. In any event, Krechting would later have cause to regret his transient glory (whatever his exact title), as it earned him a place with John of Leiden and Knipperdolling as the Anabaptist leaders singled out for exemplary public execution (see also note 816).

815. Bernard was the brother of Henry Krechting, another leading Anabaptist (see also note 124). According to the confession he made right after the fall of the city (Cornelius, *Berichte der augenzeugen*, 379), Bernard was first the chaplain of the wife and children of the count of Bentheim. He then became a parish priest (at Gildehaus: Kerssenbrock, *Anabaptistici furoris*, ed. Detmer, 647, 663), but the duke of Gelders's dislike of his (presumably too radical) preaching led him to head for Münster. He claims that for three quarters of a year, he refrained from teaching, but then an unspecified disputation impelled him to be ordained as an Anabaptist preacher. According to Kerssenbrock (ibid., 647), he was one of John of Leiden's four councilors.

816. Gresbeck's referring to the fact that Krechting was gruesomely executed along with John of Leiden and Knipperdolling in January 1536, and their bodies were then exposed in cages raised up outside the tower of St. Lambert's church. The bodies eventually rotted away, but the cages remain there until the present day (the dilapidated originals were replaced with replicas in the nineteenth century). This reference is the latest datable event in Gresbeck's account.

The king had the assault bell struck,[817] so that everyone would run to his watch post, and then the king and his lieutenant would inspect the folk to see how many they still had on the watch. The company of rebaptizers was beginning to grow small, so that they had to be on watch duty every night.[818] All the time, one after another was defecting from the city out of hunger and woe.

This took place during the time when the burgher was in prison, after the time when he defected from the city.[819]

The burgher and some officers inspect the city's defenses

[145v] Eventually, the lords of the Empire had the burgher go to the city one more time at night, and for the journey they gave him a lord of the Empire and two captains, Squire Wilcken and Lenz of Horst. Once they arrived at the city by the moat, the lord of the Empire—he was named Squire Nykede[820] and was outside Münster in the service of My Gracious Lord of Trier[821]—and the two captains and other officers went with the burgher up to the moat. The burgher lowered himself into the water, and then he swam across, crawled through the palisade, and went up on top of the wall. He couldn't make out any of the rebaptizers on watch duty (on the wall). The lord of the Empire and the captains and officers were sitting up on the canal watching the burgher. Eventually, the burgher climbed down from the wall, crawled back through the palisade, swam through the canal, and returned to the lord and the captains. The burgher said that we were now prepared and if the landsknechts had been with us, we would now have captured the city. They then said yes, this was true.[822] The burgher climbed back out

817. For the alarm bell, see 113r–v.
818. The point being that there were now so few available for the night watch that they couldn't take turns (see 87v for night watch duty taking place every third night) and instead everyone had to hold the watch in order for there to be sufficient watchmen. In the event, it would be the lax watch that sealed the city's doom.
819. This sentence appears as an indented comment following the line that marks the end of a section. Seemingly, it's some sort of description of the text rather than an actual part of it (perhaps it would appear as a footnote in a modern text). The early modern editor of the Cologne manuscript took exception to this sort of "meta-narrative," writing a marginal comment that "this writing too is hardly necessary" ("Et hec scriptio minime necessaria").
820. Such seems to be the reading of the Cologne manuscript. Cornelius's text has "Richard."
821. I.e., the bishop of Trier.
822. Once more, Gresbeck is attempting to win credit for the capture of the city. By the officers' own admission, if he had been given the necessary military resources from the start, he could have

of the canal, and they then returned to the blockhouse. Squire Wilcken then said to the burgher that he should [146r] do his best and tell the real truth—My Gracious Lord of Münster would remember him.[823] This is how they inspected the city with the burgher.

The burgher is returned to prison

The burgher returned to the captivity in which he'd sat before, and he walked around free and unrestrained in the place where the prison was and was no longer locked up. All those who'd defected from the city before the burgher and who defected from the city after him were written down under their names in a list, whether they were executed or not.

Little Hans proposes a similar plan for taking the city to the prince-bishop

So the five defected from the city, and all five kept their lives. The burgher was taken prisoner and was saved through intercession. Little Hans of Nijmwegen had been taken to the city as a prisoner by the rebaptizers and was also saved through intercession. Little Hans of Longstreet got across the trench with two others and got away. One of them stayed with Little Hans, and the third man went his own way. As soon as they got across the trench, Little Hans of Longstreet moved with the other man[824] to see Meinard of Hamm in Hamm. This Meinard of Hamm was a captain among the landsknechts. Little Hans of Longstreet took counsel with Meinard of Hamm—if My Gracious Lord of Münster was willing to receive him in mercy and to reward him, [146v] he would deliver the city to the bishop of Münster.[825] Meinard of Hamm set to it along with Little

---

captured the town before Little Hans became involved in the plan at all!

823. Presumably, this is a subtle suggestion that my gracious lord should in fact do precisely this, which he had so far signally failed to do.

824. According to Kerssenbrock (*Anabaptistici furoris*, ed. Detmer, 827), Little Hans's sole companion was Conrad Sobbe, who went his own way once they got to Hamm. Hence, in Kerssenbrock's version of events, Hans acts alone in the subsequent planning. Here, however, Hans's unnamed comrade stays with him throughout the planning stage and plays an active role in leading the assault. Given Kerssenbrock's ignorance of these activities, surely it is more likely that Sobbe is the name of the man who stayed with Hans rather than that of the man who left at Hamm (why would anyone have remembered the latter?), and Kerssenbrock (or a source) has confused the two.

825. For the deliberations of Hans with Meinard (an important military commander), see Kerssenbrock, *Anabaptistici furoris*, ed. Detmer, 827–29. Note that from the start Gresbeck emphasizes the fact that Little Hans was motivated by the desire to enrich himself (in contradiction to Gresbeck's own less pecuniary motives, 156v).

Hans of Longstreet and the other man, and they wrote to My Gracious Lord of Münster that if he'd give a safe conduct to Little Hans of Longstreet and take care of him, they'd come to My Gracious Lord of Münster in the bishopric of Münster and form a plan for winning the city of Münster. So My Gracious Lord of Münster gave a safe conduct to Little Hans and the other man, for them to come. Little Hans of Longstreet then suggested the same plan as the burgher who'd defected with him had done, the burgher who was at the time still sitting in prison.[826] Since the burgher was in jail after previously suggesting the plan to the lords of the Empire, and Little Hans too suggested it, the burgher didn't have anything to say about Little Hans of Longstreet, not knowing where he was.[827] The lords of the Empire wouldn't tell the burgher anything about Little Hans of Longstreet also having suggested the same plan, and the burgher wasn't even informed about Little Hans until the end.

The burgher cooperates with Little Hans in making preparations for the attack on the city

The lords of the Empire and the councilors (some of them) of My Gracious Lord of Münster took counsel and agreed to the plan against the city of Münster. Eventually, they [147r] had the burgher come before them from the prison and then asked him if he knew anything of Little Hans of Longstreet. Then the burgher said no, he would stake his life on it, saying that he'd defected from the city with Little Hans of Longstreet, without the one having talked to the other about it. As for the burgher he'd come to an agreement with the other four to defect from the city. For the burgher wouldn't trust Little Hans of Longstreet because he'd rushed into the city and was the king's attendant.[828] So he wouldn't trust him. After they'd defected from the city, the

---

826. For Kerssenbrock's account of the deliberations about the plan, see *Anabaptistici furoris*, ed. Detmer, 829–32. Overstein's statement that "They [i.e., Gresbeck and Little Hans] came to a complete agreement in every regard just as our prisoner [i.e., Gresbeck] had advised before" (appendix, document 4) appears to confirm Gresbeck's claim to priority.

827. Gresbeck's getting ahead of himself. What he means is that since Little Hans would later propose his plan after Gresbeck had already done so (and was at that time in prison), he would have no idea what Little Hans was up to when he was later asked about him (without being told the reason for the inquiry). This becomes an issue below.

828. Seemingly, what Gresbeck means is that he was willing to actually leave the city with the other men, but he wouldn't discuss the matter in advance because of his distrust of Little Hans of Longstreet. Presumably, he had cautionary stories like the betrayals of Claus Northorn (169r) and of the two ensigns (177r–v) in mind.

one spoke to the other. Eventually, the lords of the Empire and the Münster councilors[829] said to the burgher that he had to ride with Squire Wilcken for a distance of four miles or so.[830] The burgher looked all around, not knowing where he was supposed to go, and he was afraid. Then, someone said to the burgher that he should be at peace, in a period of three or four days he would again be with his lord, Count Robert of Manderscheid.[831] So the burgher rode with Squire Wilcken and Tony Lichtherte (a captain),[832] not having known where he was to go. Eventually, after they went the distance of a half mile or so to the place where they would be, Squire Wilcken asked the burgher if he really didn't know where he was supposed to go. He then said, "Where do you imagine [147v] Little Hans of Longstreet is?" The burgher said, "I don't know where I am or where I'm supposed to go, and I also don't know where Little Hans of Longstreet is, whether he's alive or dead." Then Squire Wilcken said, "Now I'll tell you the real truth. We'll ride to Bevergern,[833] and that's where Little Hans of Longstreet is along with one other man. Little Hans has suggested the same plan as you, so My Gracious Lord of Münster wants to carry out the plan with you two, as do all the lords in the service of the Empire. So we'll ride to Little Hans and prepare whatever's useful for the attack. You're supposed to give advice on this as well." So they came to Bevergern and found Little Hans there with the other man. They made preparations in the form of assault ladders and gangways[834] and everything that was useful for it. Squire Wilcken rode back with Tony Lichtherte to the camp, and Little Hans of Longstreet with his companion and the burgher remained there and prepared everything.

The burgher and Little Hans move closer to Münster

It was Little Hans of Longstreet, his companion, and the burgher, as well as a trench master named Beim,[835] who prepared everything.[836] When

---

829. "Münster councilors" signifies the prince-bishop's rather than the city's.
830. Again, a German mile is much longer than an English one (see note 352).
831. Presumably, "his lord" means only that the man referred to Manderscheid as "my lord."
832. Lichtherte was one of the captains of the original besieging force raised by the prince-bishop (he commanded one of the original blockhouses built in the summer of 1534 after the failure of the first siege, Kerssenbrock, *Anabaptistici furoris*, ed. Detmer, 683). During the final attempt to take the city, he would launch an assault on the walls once the success of the attack within was made known (ibid., 844).
833. Bevergern is a town about twenty-five miles due north of Münster.
834. For crossing the moat.
835. "Trench master" (*Schanzmeister*) signifies the engineer in charge of the fortifications.
836. Kerssenbrock (*Anabaptistici furoris*, ed. Detmer, 832) gives only a cursory mention of the preparations.

everything that was useful for the attack (storming) was ready, Little Hans of Longstreet and the burgher moved to Münster. They moved to a squire's house outside Münster called "Tho Willighege."[837] That is where they were [148r] assigned by Squire Wilcken, and there they awaited Squire Wilcken. They certainly took notice up at the house, and they knew Little Hans of Longstreet because he'd been in the city and had also been stationed outside the city. They didn't know the burgher. So they sent someone from the house to Squire Wilcken on horseback to tell him that he should be aware that Little Hans of Longstreet was there with someone else, and they were from the city. They didn't know up at the house what Little Hans and the burgher had to do. Squire Wilcken returned there on horseback with his lieutenant and had the whole household up at the house informed that they should keep quiet about this, and that no one should be bold enough to say anything about it. Then the lieutenant fetched them from there and brought them to Schönefliet,[838] where they stayed for a day.

Final planning for the attack

A letter came to my lord the cellarer at Schönefliet that Little Hans of Longstreet and the burgher were to come to a village named "Tho Koerde." So they moved to Koerde, which lies a quarter of the way from Münster.[839] All the lords of the Empire and the Münster councilors came there, as did Squire Wilcken and all the commanders of the banners[840] of landsknechts. All the lords took counsel [148v] with Little Hans of Longstreet alone, and not with the burgher.[841] They decided with Little Hans what night they

---

837. Kerssenbrock calls it Willinckhege (thinly Latinized), which he says was a residence of John Stevening. He specifies its location as about a half a mile (i.e., about four English miles) from the city.

838. Schönefliet was a castle built privately in the thirteenth century to the north of Münster on the river Ems, just south of Greven. A later bishop of Münster seized possession of it and gave it to the canons of the cathedral in Münster. During the takeover of the city by the Anabaptists, some canons took refuge there. In the eighteenth century, the canons visited the place increasingly less frequently, and it became a run-down semi-ruin. In 1812, the remains were sold to local businessmen, who over the next few decades removed the stonework of the structure for use as building material until nothing remained of the building.

839. Kerssenbrock says nothing about this location. "Quarter way" must be in reference to the distance from Münster to Schönefliet, and presumably is measured from the city (i.e., since Schönefliet is about five English miles from the city, Koerde was about a mile away; it seems odd to have gone only a quarter of the way from Schönefliet to Münster).

840. For the sense of "banner," see note 457.

841. Note that Little Hans is clearly viewed by the authorities as the main proponent of the plan, and Gresbeck is treated as only a helper (taking care of the equipment, while Hans does the fighting). Gresbeck certainly makes out that he had personally demonstrated the feasibility of the plan by sneak-

would attack the city on, and they agreed with Little Hans about everything. Eventually, Squire Wilcken and Little Hans came from the lords and went before all the commanders. Then Squire Wilcken told all the commanders how the plan was made.[842] Squire Wilcken then said, "Little Hans of Longstreet and the burgher here, they've both made the plan. This is the one that My Gracious Lord of Münster and the lords of the Empire want to carry out."[843] This is what the commanders carried out as well. At this point, the commanders moved out from there, and Little Hans and the burgher remained there until the wagons with the ladders arrived.

Final inspection of the city before the attack

So Little Hans of Longstreet and the burgher went back to the city one more time at night with a captain, Lenz of Horst,[844] and other officers, just as the burgher had done once before. They inspected the city once again, including the moat and the wall, to see if everything there was still in the state that it had been before. The burgher climbed into the canal and measured the canal with a pike to see how wide it was, with Little Hans. They didn't find [149r] any of the rebaptizers holding watch up on the wall, with everything still as it had been. They moved back from there to the blockhouse. Little Hans and the burgher returned to Koerde.

The attack prepared

The wagons with the ladders and gangways came, eight full of ladders and two gangways, and they traveled to the village of Koerde, where Little Hans and the burgher were located. My Gracious Lord of Münster came to terms with the captains and the landsknechts and reached an agreement about the booty when the city was conquered, so that all the landsknechts were satisfied with this and were all willing.[845] Now that the attack was to be

---

ing into the city, but it is conceivable that he was considered an amateur, whereas Hans was thought to have military experience as a veteran landsknecht (and he had been vouched for by Meinard of Hamm). In any event, Kerssenbrock has all the deliberations take place at Willinghege (*Anabaptistici furoris*, ed. Detmer, 830).

842. At first sight, it seems odd to have told them this, rather than what the plan was. Presumably, Gresbeck thinks it was important for the commanders to have been informed of his own role!

843. It's certainly convenient for Gresbeck that in his recollection Wilcken takes the trouble to support his claim to have had a role in proposing the plan without actually giving any details about it!

844. Previously mentioned (145v).

845. In the early modern period, the loyalty of the hired troops was not taken for granted, and their willingness to follow orders was dependent upon their agreement with the terms for distributing the booty.

launched that evening in the night,[846] at eleven o'clock p.m., an order was issued the day before up at all the blockhouses prohibiting all the sutlers from selling wine or beer, so that the landsknechts would not get drunk.[847] When the evening (afternoon) came, they traveled from Koerde with the ladders, to a peasant's farm located right outside Münster. In this way, they set everything in order. [149v] Little Hans of Longstreet went off in advance with his companion to the Cleves blockhouse,[848] and they prepared everything there. The burgher remained with the wagons along with the trench master. When evening came on between nine and ten o'clock, the burgher set out for the Cleves blockhouse with the ladders. There they took the ladders and gangways from the wagons. Peasants were stationed there to carry the gangways and ladders.

The attack begins

So they headed for the city and were going to attack it. The burgher set off in advance, and the peasants followed him with a gangway. Once they came to the city and the moat, the peasants brought the gangway to the moat. Then the peasants went back again. The burgher had Little Hans's companion with him. They tied a line to the gangway, and the burgher tied one end of the line to his body and lowered himself into the canal. He swam across towing the gangway behind him and attached it firmly to the palisade with iron hooks. Then the man who was with the burgher on the canal sent word to [150r] Little Hans that he should come. Little Hans came and walked across the gangway. He'd brought along short ladders and fixed them firmly to the palisade. Little Hans then went and fetched thirty-five landsknechts with captains and officers, and they then crossed over the gangway. All the while, the burgher was standing in the canal and directed them so that they came across. Then Little Hans and his companion headed for the watch, with Little Hans heading for the gate and his companion for the earthwork. They bid them peace with a battle sword and a halberd.[849] In this way, Little

846. June 24, 1535.
847. No doubt the commanders were keenly aware that the first storm of the city had been ruined by the drunken unruliness of one regiment (see also note 180). Sutlers were civilian merchants who accompanied armies and sold provisions (including liquor) to the troops.
848. Opposite the Cross Gate.
849. More of Gresbeck's wry sense of humor, the "bidding of peace" with a kiss being the characteristic Anabaptist greeting (see also note 51).

Hans took possession of the gate and the other man of the earthwork.[850] They then gave a shout, and the whole company of landsknechts launched their attack on the city, with fifty descending upon the gangway where the burgher was standing in the canal. All fifty ran onto the gangway at once, and then the gangway broke apart in the middle, and they were all lying in the canal. They came out of the canal, and the burgher swam back across again. They attacked the earthwork, so that they got across the earthwork, numbering about four hundred at first. Now that Little Hans had control of the gate, he ran into the city with them, leaving the gate open and not manning it with landsknechts. Before the other landsknechts could get across the sconce, the rebaptizers came and slammed the gate shut.[851] Then they couldn't follow.

The burgher remains outside as the attack proceeds

[150v] The burgher came up to My Lord of Overstein at the earthwork, and he was freezing and soaked, since he'd been standing for so long in the water.[852] My Lord of Overstein's attendant then put my lord's Spanish cape[853] around the burgher, since he'd gotten so frozen in the water. For the burgher would certainly have attacked the city at the start, along with Little Hans, but he wasn't allowed to do this because he was still a prisoner, and had no weapon and wasn't equipped with armor.

850. Note that whereas Gresbeck simply sees to the placement of the ladders and gangway, Hans and his comrade pave the way for the full assault by personally leading the daring effort to kill the watchmen.

851. Kerssenbrock gives a rather different account of the breaking of the city's defenses (*Anabaptistici furoris*, ed. Detmer, 835–36). According to him, the troops first filled in the moat with materials that they had brought along themselves (he makes no mention of gangways), and then Longstreet led them up the palisade, at the top of which they killed all the (sleeping) guards they found, apart from one who betrayed the watchword. Longstreet then opened a small postern gate by which the guards had access to the palisade, and through this the troops entered the city by the Cross Gate. Kerssenbrock has all the troops enter at once, and he's quite clear that they entered by a small gate rather than the main one, as Gresbeck suggests. Kerssenbrock doesn't mention the closing of this small gate (ibid., 837), but this event is confirmed in the accounts of Justinian of Holtzhausen and Count Overstein (appendix, documents 3 and 4).

852. Once again, the scribe who transcribed the Cologne manuscript erroneously replaced the title of Overstein with that of Münster (for the earlier instance, see 144v and note 809).

853. A "Spanish cape" was a waist-length cloak (see Grimm, *Deutsches Wörterbuch*, under "Kappe" col. 190; Köhler, *History of Costumes*, 262, with illustration). Such a cloak was a mark of high rank (hence its being remarkable that such a garment would be put on a man as lowly as Gresbeck). When the city of Lübeck wrote a letter to the city of Rostock in 1537 asking their officials to hunt for the missing priest Bernard Rothman, they thought it worthwhile to note in their description of him that he was "generally cloaked in Spanish cape" (see Cornelius, *Berichte der augenzeugen*, 411).

All the landsknechts had no knowledge of him, so that they would have killed him. So Little Hans of Longstreet was in the city with three or four hundred landsknechts, and the gates were slammed shut.[854] The other landsknechts had possession of the earthwork and had thrown open the first gate and let down the drawbridge.[855] My Lord of Overstein was with the burgher in the first gate, and they all hoped to follow the others into the city. When they couldn't follow, the landsknechts shouted that it was one of Little Hans of Longstreet's tricks,[856] and that he'd betrayed them and done in all the captains and officers. When day began to break, the landsknechts had to retreat from the city.[857] Little Hans was with the others in the city, and they didn't know whether Little Hans was alive [151r] or dead along with the captains and officers and the knechts. When they retreated in this way from the city, the women shouted from the city that they should come back and retrieve their big guild, and they sang.[858] A landsknecht came up to the burgher after they retreated from the city, and he asked him, "Countryman, where is your weapon?" He also asked for the watchword. The burgher said, "My weapon is lying in the canal, and the watchword is 'Mother of God,'" and he showed him how wet he was. At the time, the burgher still had the Spanish cape on, so that they couldn't recognize him for sure. Otherwise, they would have killed the burgher.[859] For the landsknechts didn't imagine anything other than that they'd been betrayed, as they had to retreat from the city, and the others

854. Justinian of Holtzhausen has no idea how the gate was closed (appendix, document 3), but Count Overstein states that the rebaptizers' forces seized control of it and shut it (appendix, document 4).

855. The "first gate" must mean the outer gate that was most distant from the city but "first" in terms of approaching the city.

856. Presumably, this distrust relates to whatever action of his led the besieging troops to be so hostile to him at the time of his defection from the city (see 144r and also note 803).

857. I.e., the troops waiting to enter the city once the initial force led by Little Hans had gained control of the gate.

858. The sense of the taunt isn't entirely clear. The word "hense" (High German *Hansa*) could signify an organization of merchants or handworkers engaged in the same trade in a given city. It also signifies the medieval trading association of coastal cities along the Black and North Seas known in English as the Hanseatic League, and a submeaning would signify a "merchant outpost" in a foreign town. Perhaps the word is intended to compare the landsknechts now stuck in the city to merchants who are engaged in (unprofitable?) trade in a distant port and need rescue. Conceivably, it simply means a general "collective" or "society," though it still remains unclear how the troops stuck in the city could be characterized in this way (surely the army as a whole, including those outside, is the "society"). For a rather more verbose version of the women's taunt, see Kerssenbrock, *Anabaptistici furoris*, ed. Detmer, 839.

859. Because he was dressed like a civilian and not a landsknecht.

were inside the city and were killing everyone in the way of rebaptizers that they could get their hands on in the streets.

The city is captured

So Little Hans of Longstreet was in the city with the landsknechts, and the gate was closed and they were locked in the city and couldn't move backwards or forwards. The burgher had said before that they should keep possession of the gate [151v] until the main company of the landsknechts was across the earthwork. They ran ahead into the city, thinking more about the booty than keeping possession of the gate until they knew if they'd won the city or not.[860] For luck hung in the balance for a long time before it could be known whether the city was won or not. The city was won once, then was lost again, then was won again. There were three or four hundred landsknechts in the city, and they killed everyone in the way of menfolk that they found on the streets. The landsknechts too suffered losses. They would say that the landsknechts left one hundred dead as well as these who were shot.[861] If they'd kept possession of the gate as the burgher had said, and gotten all the landsknechts to come across together, then they wouldn't have left one man dead, not one of them would have been shot, and they would have won the city in half an hour. So Little Hans of Longstreet brought the landsknechts into the city, and they battled with the rebaptizers. They chased each other up and down the streets, and fought and shot each other until daylight. They fought a fierce battle up at the cathedral square. There, the rebaptizers suffered great losses, so that the landsknechts then got the upper hand.[862]

---

860. There's no sense of a search for plunder in Gresbeck's account, and it's hard to see how this could have been a consideration when the city was still in the hands of the numerically superior Anabaptists. Rash impetuosity seems a much more likely explanation of the oversight. Nonetheless, in Justinian of Holzhausen's account, a rather uncertain explanation attributed to rumor ("no one knows how this actually happened") for the closing of the postern gate is that the men closed the gate themselves to expedite their plundering (appendix, document 3). Gresbeck must be repeating this absurd rumor.

861. Gresbeck's expression is ambiguous, but presumably he means one hundred dead and wounded.

862. The initial course of the battle in the city went as follows according to Kerssenbrock (*Anabaptistici furoris*, ed. Detmer, 837). The attackers crossed the river Aa, which bisects the city, and made for the cathedral square. They seized the cathedral itself and deprived the defenders of the firearms stored there. The defenders occupied the chapel of St. Michael, which proved to be a sound defensive position against gunfire. The Anabaptists then counterattacked and drove the attacking force back to St. Margaret's Alley. The attackers were hard-pressed there until about half of them managed to sneak out by a side route and then attacked the Anabaptists from an unexpected direction. Believing that

[152r] So the rebaptizers retreated up to St. Michael's Church[863] up at the cathedral square and shot out of it. Eventually, they took a stand up at the market with their wagon fort.[864] The landsknechts had pipes and drums with them in the city and they also had some pennants,[865] so that the king and the rebaptizers imagined that the main company of landsknechts was in the city.[866] The king then made his way out with some rebaptizers and they took possession of St. Tilgen's Gate, while some still remained up at the marketplace.[867] But in the end, first one looked after himself, and then the next.[868] When the king went his way, they hid themselves in the cellars, in corners, so that the landsknechts

the whole city was held by the attackers, the Anabaptists lost heart and fled to the marketplace. As subsequent notes show, there's a certain amount of uncertainty among the sources about the exact course of events that led to the victory of the attacking forces, which makes it all the more surprising that Kirchhoff, "Die Belagerung und Eroberung Münsters," which ostensibly deals with the "siege and conquest of Münster," should dispense with any discussion of these events on the grounds that they're "sufficiently known through the reports of several sources" ("durch die Berichte mehrerer Augenzeugen hinlänglich bekannt").

863. St. Michael's is actually a chapel dedicated to the archangel (Kerssenbrock, *Anabaptistici furoris*, ed. Detmer, 27). Kerssenbrock mentions in connection with the abortive uprising against the Anabaptists in early February of 1534 that in their defensive measures, the Anabaptists occupied the Chapel of St. Michael and the tower of St. Lambert's, which were in close proximity by the main marketplace (ibid., 408). This presumably explains the change in the tradition behind Cornelius's text whereby the reference becomes "St. Lambert's church." Someone must have been offended by the incorrect designation of the chapel in the original text and corrected the phrase to make it refer to the neighboring church.

864. According to Kerssenbrock (*Anabaptistici furoris*, ed. Detmer, 839), the Anabaptists regained their courage at the marketplace, though he has them make a barricade of items found by chance rather than use the abandoned wagon fort as Gresbeck says. In his report of the capture of the city (appendix, document 3), Justinian of Holtzhausen confirms the Anabaptists' stand in the wagon fort.

865. The word for "pennant" ("feneken") is the diminutive of the word for "banner" ("fener"). In any event, these pennants misled the Anabaptists into thinking that they represented a larger number of units than there actually were in the city (see also note 457).

866. This seems to be a reminiscence of the ploy at St. Margaret's Alley that made the Anabaptists break and run earlier (see note 862). According to Kerssenbrock (*Anabaptistici furoris*, ed. Detmer, 840), there was a colloquy at around three a.m. between the attacking landsknechts and envoys from the king, who offered to allow the landsknechts to withdraw from the city. Seemingly, the landsknechts were willing to accept the offer, but the talks broke down over the king's demand that the landsknechts had to disarm before being allowed to leave, a term that they refused to accept as being dishonorable.

867. According to Kerssenbrock, the attackers' spirits revived when an ensign managed to mount the walls and waved a banner from there to summon assistance from outside (*Anabaptistici furoris*, ed. Detmer, 840–41); the king became despondent at the resumption of the fight after the breakdown of the negotiations for the landsknechts' withdrawal, and he then fled to the St. Giles's (i.e., Tilgen's) Gate (ibid., 843).

868. I.e., military discipline broke down, and it was each man for himself. Justinian of Holtzhausen (appendix, document 3) indicates that three hundred men enclosed themselves in the wagon fort with the "new king" (meaning John of Leiden's subordinate Bernard Krechting), and that they surrendered as a body. His account would seem to imply that John of Leiden wasn't there at all, and he betrays no knowledge of the king's departure.

had a winning hand.[869] Then the city was won. The captains had a colloquy with the king and some burghers who'd retreated with him up to the gate. The king and the burghers kept requesting that they be taken prisoner and that the burghers be allowed to go to their houses until My Gracious Lord of Münster came to the city. This was granted by the landsknechts, and then the king came away from the gate with the burghers who were up there with him.[870] Some of the burghers went to their houses, and they put the king and Knipperdolling and some others [152v] in prison.[871] The captains got the keys to all the gates, and they ran to one gate (the Jew Fields Gate) and took possession of it.[872] They then went with the banner and the pipes and drums and stood on the earthwork, shouting that they should come back, the city was won.[873] At this, the landsknechts who were outside the city were still afraid that this was more treachery, since they'd been in the city for so long. Eventually, they kept shouting until all the landsknechts ran to the city, and the cavalrymen dismounted and also ran to the city on foot. They all ran into the city, and running throughout the city, they killed everyone they came across in the way of rebaptizers, apart from Knipperdolling and the king and some burghers who were taken prisoner. These burghers who were taken prisoner were all killed in the end.

869. For the hiding of the Anabaptists, see Kerssenbrock, *Anabaptistici furoris*, ed. Detmer, 846.

870. Kerssenbrock says nothing of the negotiations for the king's surrender, and claims that he was betrayed in his hiding place in the upper floor of the gate by a boy (*Anabaptistici furoris*, ed. Detmer, 843). On the other hand, he does report an agreement to allow the remaining armed Anabaptists up at the marketplace to lay down their arms and leave under truce. When they did so, the truce was broken and they were killed (ibid., 847–48). Justinian of Holtzhausen (see appendix, document 3) merely says that the "first king" (i.e., John of Leiden) and Knipperdolling were captured after the surrender of the main body of Anabaptists in the wagon fort. His lack of detail (John and Knipperdolling were captured under quite different circumstances) suggests that he wasn't very interested in the details of the capture apart from the military events, so no particular inferences should be drawn from his version.

871. For the capture of Knipperdolling, see Kerssenbrock, *Anabaptistici furoris*, ed. Detmer, 852–53. According to Kerssenbrock, this took place two days after the city's capture (Knipperdolling was in hiding), but a letter written by Overstein shows that he was captured at eleven a.m. on the morning when the city was captured (appendix, document 4), which disproves any implication here that Knipperdolling was seized at the time of the king's surrender.

872. Gresbeck has the opening of the gates follow the surrender of the king, who turned them over, but Justinian of Holtzhausen (appendix, document 3) is clear that Little Hans was responsible for re-opening the postern gate. It's hardly surprising that Gresbeck should not want to record this fact given his constant attempt to denigrate Little Hans's achievement precisely for his having failed to keep control of the gate.

873. Kerssenbrock describes the excitement caused in the besiegers outside the city by the announcement that the gate was open (*Anabaptistici furoris*, ed. Detmer, 844–45).

The city is plundered and discovered Anabaptists executed, foodstuffs found

Now they have the city. The landsknechts ran into all the houses throughout the whole city, and they searched for the rebaptizers in the cellars, in the corners, upstairs and downstairs in the houses.[874] They found some more rebaptizers, and [153r] they dragged them out of the houses by the hair and then killed them in the streets, so angry were the landsknechts after having suffered great losses outside the city. There was no mercy with the landsknechts. In some houses they still found butter, cheese, meat, and flour, and in the king's cellar they found five or six vats of wine and one vat with beer, and food enough that the king and all the leaders had no privation yet, because they still had enough to eat, so that some people would say that they would certainly have held the city for a year. The king and his retinue would have certainly held the city for half a year,[875] if not longer. They would also have starved all the common folk to death. When the city was won, some landsknechts said that in vessels they'd found children that were salted, consisting of hands and feet and legs.[876] I can't write anything more about what the truth of this is. I didn't see it. But it certainly is believable that it happened, so great was the hunger that the common man in the city suffered. For the leaders of the rebaptizers said that in good time, if they had nothing more to eat, they would have eaten the old ladies.[877] If they would have eaten fat old wives, they would have had to eat them in good time before [153v] they starved to death. When they were at the end, at the time when the city was captured, the folk were walking so piteously up the streets—women, and some men, and children—that they looked no different than if they'd arisen from the dead out of the grave, and they seemed no different in their face than a death's head. If you saw the rebap-

874. For the search for concealed Anabaptists and their execution upon discovery, see Kerssenbrock, *Anabaptistici furoris*, ed. Detmer, 849–51.

875. The same figure is given in 96v.

876. This unsubstantiated rumor is hardly credible under the circumstances. Apart from any other consideration, it makes no logical sense. Why would starving people still have uneaten preserves? For Kerssenbrock's discussion of the eating of babies, see *Anabaptistici furoris*, ed. Detmer, 800–802.

877. Note that this supposedly bloodthirsty statement from the past is beside the point, as Gresbeck has just indicated that the eating of children would have been the act of the starving commoners rather than the leaders, who he says still had enough to eat. In any event, the words that Gresbeck cites are clearly nothing more than hyperbole, and in this comparatively long discussion of the topic, Gresbeck is just giving vent to his (understandable enough) rancor against the leaders of the Anabaptists.

tizer's head and a death's head, the one looked the same as the other. But there was this much difference between them, that there was still life in the rebaptizer and there was still skin sitting around their head and body. Otherwise, they (some of them) were no different than a dead corpse. As for the fat old women that they would have eaten, as they'd once said, they would have eaten them in good time before they'd starved this way. For the women were starving, so that their skin hung from their bodies as if they had a sack hanging around their bodies, and they were nothing but skin and bones, their hide and liver. This is how ruined the common folk were, having heard for so long the preaching from the apostles and prophets. Oh, Knipperdolling—Knipperdolling and Kibbenbrock and other burghers too—what an opening dance you held! If you hadn't performed the opening dance for the common folk, the Hollanders and the Frisians and the rebaptizers would never have gotten the upper hand in Münster![878] Now, even if you have been punished in body, you still couldn't justify it before God that you've [154r] so betrayed the poor folk and made so many people poor and taken everyone's property from them, and then starved so many people to death, and so many had to die of it, though they had nothing to do with the business. May God be merciful and compassionate to them![879]

Troops dissatisfied with the booty

Now that the city was captured, all goods were plunder, half of the goods and the city and the heavy artillery going to My Gracious Lord, and half of the goods to the landsknechts. So they appointed booty masters. They sold everything that there was in the houses in the way of household furnishings, beds, cans and jars, and they turned it all into money. Whatever each landsknecht had gotten in the way of money and gold and silver they were obliged under their oath to bring to the booty.[880] I can't write any more about whether this is what happened. The landsknechts held five or

878. For the real situation that underlies this imagery of the "opening dance," see 91r. Gresbeck means here that it was the troublemaking of the radically minded local leaders who gave the hated foreign Anabaptists the opportunity to seize control of the city.
879. For God alone can show them mercy (see 46v).
880. I.e., the booty was a sort of community chest in which the soldiery was obligated to deposit every good that they collected. Once these items were converted into cash, each soldier would be entitled to an equal share of the proceeds. Such a system was subject to cheating both through the failure of the soldiers to turn over valuables and through peculation on the part of the officials in charge (the booty masters).

six common assemblies, and each man would have been glad to have his booty. For the booty wasn't distributed as soon as they would have liked. The landsknechts imagined that there'd been five or six tons of gold in the city. When they looked around, the landsknechts didn't get half a ton of gold as their booty. At this, the landsknechts became outraged and clamped the booty masters into irons. For the landsknechts imagined that the booty masters weren't correct in dealing with the booty, because [154v] there ought to have been more gold in the city. There'd been a landsknecht in the city with the rebaptizers, and he was taken prisoner in the city and remained alive, and he came back to the city now that it was captured.[881] This landsknecht said that he knew full well that there was more gold in the city, saying that the king had a great treasure with him consisting of money, silver, and gold. It was while talking drunk that he informed the landsknechts of this. Then the landsknechts first set to work and began to rage. They held a common assembly and had the knecht come to the assembly. They then prepared delegates, and they sent them to the king and had him questioned under torture,[882] so that he would say how much gold there'd been in the city and where the gold now was. They couldn't get information out of the king or find any more gold.[883] Then they came again with the knecht, and he couldn't prove that there was more gold in the city or where the gold now was. The knecht asked for mercy, so the landsknechts shouted that the knecht should be let go. The captains had his head cut off because he'd caused so much outrage among the landsknechts.

Officials tortured by the troops in the vain attempt to find more loot

So the landsknechts once again held a common assembly. They wanted to kill all the booty masters, as well as all the captains, and to plunder the city one more time, and to sell the goods once more. [155r] Once they held the assembly, they had the booty masters come into the center of the assembly and asked them if they did know of more gold. The booty masters said no, they couldn't get more gold together than what amounted to a half ton of

881. Seemingly, after being taken to the city as a captive by the Anabaptists, he either escaped or was allowed to leave.
882. Questioning under torture was a regular practice in contemporary judicial investigation.
883. There's no other evidence for any torturing of the king by the soldiers.

gold, so that each landsknecht got sixteen Emden guilders as booty.[884] So the landsknechts had two of the booty masters racked on the ladder by the hangman, so that they would say where the gold now was.[885] They couldn't get any information out of the booty masters. They didn't know of any gold. But they didn't know how they could make it with the landsknechts. Eventually, the landsknechts took the sixteen Emden guilders. They imagined that they should have gotten more, so they wouldn't leave the city. They wanted to have more from the booty, whether by delivering the city to another lord or by selling the goods one more time and plundering.[886]

The prince-bishop takes possession of the city

Eventually, My Gracious Lord wrote to the city that they should vacate the city for him because they'd certainly always been paid, and they should take their booty and evacuate the city.[887] Otherwise, His Grace would see what he would have to do with the landsknechts. The landsknechts held a common assembly once more, and there they saw that they couldn't get any more from the booty. Then [155v] they moved out of the city as a company. My Gracious Lord of Münster kept two banners[888] of knechts in the city. This is how they vacated the city and moved out of it.

The prince-bishop visits the ex-king

Now that the city was captured, My Gracious Lord of Münster came to the city, three days later.[889] Two banners of knechts moved out to meet him and escorted him into the city. My Gracious Lord straightaway had two blockhouses placed in the city. When My Gracious Lord came to the king, My Gracious Lord said, "Are you a king?" The king is supposed to have answered, "Are you a bishop?" My Gracious Lord then left the king. I can't write any more about how the incident went.

---

884. Emden is a major commercial port to the north at the mouth of the River Elbe, and its currency was used in calculating the landsknechts' pay (see *Anabaptistici furoris*, ed. Detmer, 526, where Kerssenbrock uses the Latinate term "florin" in place of the Germanic "guilder").

885. This torture is confirmed by Kerssenbrock, *Anabaptistici furoris*, ed. Detmer, 857.

886. Presumably, the last two activities would have occurred in the opposite order.

887. Kerssenbrock reproduces the substance of this letter at length (*Anabaptistici furoris*, ed. Detmer, 858).

888. For the sense of "banner," see note 457.

889. For Kerssenbrock's short account of the prince-bishop's brief visit, see *Anabaptistici furoris*, ed. Detmer, 853. According to Kerssenbrock, the visit began on June 28, which would be three days after the capture of the city in the early hours of June 25.

Treatment of the surviving Anabaptists

While the landsknechts were located in the city until they received their boo-ty, they would say that the knechts were being poisoned by the female rebap-tizers. So My Gracious Lord had all the female rebaptizers who were still in the city come up to the cathedral square together.[890] My Gracious Lord took some women, who were the leaders of the female rebaptizers, out of the com-pany. Some of these women were executed. They would not in fact abandon the baptizing and would stand by their faith. They then drove all the other women out of the city.[891] [156r] In the end, they came back to the city,[892] and some moved away to other lands. Some would say that they'd moved to England. My Gracious Lord of Münster was in the city for four or five days,[893] and then he moved out of the city. He had the king, Knipperdolling, and certain others brought from the city to one of his castles, and there they were kept in prison until the time when they were executed.[894] The king and Knipperdolling each had a collar with an iron chain around his neck, and they ran like this beside the horses when they were brought out of the city. I can write nothing of where the queen wound up with her follow wives.[895]

The burgher's final plea

In this way, the plan was made by which the city of Münster was captured. In case the city hadn't been captured in this way, they would have had to wait it out.[896] If, then, the king and all his retainers had not been able to get any further and had held the city to the last man, they would have

890. For Kerssenbrock's short account of the treatment of the women, see *Anabaptistici furoris*, ed. Detmer, 854–55.

891. According to Kerssenbrock, the order of expulsion was issued on July 5, 1535.

892. See Kerssenbrock, *Anabaptistici furoris*, ed. Detmer, 861–62, for the problems caused by the return of women who had fled the city during the final starvation and been pardoned.

893. According to Kerssenbrock (*Anabaptistici furoris*, ed. Detmer, 853), the visit lasted three days.

894. Kerssenbrock (*Anabaptistici furoris*, ed. Detmer, 869) reports that Knipperdolling, Bernard Krechting, and Christian Kerkering were removed from the city to Iburg on July 24. They were trans-ported in separate wagons to prevent them from conversing, and Kerkering was taken out and executed during the journey. The king was kept at Bevergern, and the other two men at Horst, until their exe-cution the following January.

895. At one point (*Anabaptistici furoris*, ed. Detmer, 855), Kerssenbrock claims that the queen was beheaded (he is the only source to assert this; see ibid., 855n2), but elsewhere (ibid., 872) he has John of Leiden speak as if she was still alive after the recapture of the city (and it is hard to imagine that news of her death was withheld from him to spare his feelings).

896. Literally, "await the time." Presumably, Gresbeck means that the besiegers would otherwise have had to wait for the Anabaptists to surrender as a result of starvation.

set the city on fire and burned it to the ground. This was their intention. This is what I've heard they said. So the burgher was the principal person responsible for giving the plan by which the city of Münster was captured, and he suggested it first. Afterwards, Little Hans of Longstreet came, and he then wrote to My Gracious Lord of Münster that if My Gracious Lord of Münster would receive him in mercy, [156v] he'd do his best to win the city of Münster.[897] Little Hans then did his best so that the city of Münster was won, and he also earned mercy. Little Hans of Longstreet said that what he did, the winning of the city, he did for the sake of the innocent money that was in the city.[898] The burgher did not come to the city for the sake of the baptizing, and he likewise did not rush to the city. For he hadn't been to Münster more than once in four years, and he wished to travel home one day. He came to the city just before the Friday,[899] and then remained in the city—he hadn't imagined that the situation would have gone so far astray. So the burgher made the plan, as did Little Hans of Longstreet. What the burgher did he did to keep his life, not to have money or goods, and on top of it he forfeited all his property.[900] So the burgher first thanks God, then all the foreign landsknechts for having taken him prisoner, then My Gracious Lord of Manderscheid, Count Robert, and My Gracious Lord of Overstein, and all the lords of the Empire, and My Gracious Lord of Münster. Next, I thank God that the city of Münster was captured.

Henry Gresbeck, burgher in the city of
Münster, cabinetmaker (a joiner)

897. This and the following sentence were struck out in the Cologne manuscript, and were not copied over in the manuscript that gave rise to Cornelius's text. This is unfortunate, as the last page of the Cologne manuscript is defective, so a certain amount of the text is conjectural. However, most readings are certain, apart from the word discussed in the next note.

898. The word translated as "money" is somewhat uncertain. Only the last letters "–des" remain of the genitive case of this word, which is masculine or neuter singular. The adjective "innocent" ("unschuldigen," literally "blameless, guilt-free") doesn't seem particularly suitable for the word, but it's hard to see what else it could be. Although there was certainly "guilty" money available for plunder in the city, perhaps what Gresbeck has in mind is the plundered property of the supposedly innocent burghers (like himself) who were kept in thrall by the Anabaptists. In any event, a reference to Little Hans's supposed cupidity fits in perfectly with Gresbeck's claim right below that he had no desire for monetary gain in suggesting the plan.

899. According to the letter that Gresbeck sent from the city (see appendix, document 2), he had hoped to return home (wherever that was) from the city within fourteen days, so apparently he went to the city less than two weeks before the forced conversions of February 27, after which he was no longer able to leave (or so he claims).

900. Apparently, his contribution to the city's capture was not thought to be sufficiently meritorious to prevent his property from being forfeited to the prince-bishop by right of conquest.

Appendix

Document 1

Letter of Henricus Graes to the inhabitants of Münster, January 1(?), 1535

> This is the text of the letter that the treacherous preacher Henricus Graes sent back to Münster after making off with the Anabaptists' secrets and money (Gresbeck, 77r). For the original German, see Stupperich, *Die Schriften B. Rothmanns*, 429. Now that he is out of harm's way, Graes comes close to taunting his erstwhile comrades.

God grant us all His spirit out of mercy and mild compassion, so that we may know the path of righteousness, amen. Dear inhabitants! Since the situation has turned out that God has opened my eyes so that I've seen the false, poisoned collapse of the business that's being carried on now in Münster, and God has therefore conveyed me out of the city as a mirror so that everyone may see himself reflected in me, that all the business that's now being conducted in Münster is a fraud, accordingly, it's my humble prayer that you will finally open your eyes—it's high time!—and see of your business that it's clearly contrary to God and His Holy Word. The previous prophets have all been prophets just like me, so that you poor, stupid people can't recognize that in its entirety what you're engaged in is fraud and deception. I know for sure that if you would yet convert and shun the ungodly business, you will all remain in possession of life. With this, be commended to God! For greater recognition, so that you may believe what's written, I've impressed my signet underneath, which is known to you.

Document 2

Letter of Master Henry the Cabinetmaker to His Lords

> This is the text of the letter that Gresbeck tried to sneak out
> of the city in the late spring of 1535. Its preservation in the
> Landesarchiv in Münster presumably indicates that the letter
> had been intercepted by the besieging forces and turned over
> to the prince-bishop. The German was first published in Cor-
> nelius, *Berichte der augenzeugen*, 322–24.

My poor service,[1] which my poor self is capable of!

My dear, honorable squires, as I, your poor servant, Master Henry the cabinetmaker, went from you by your leave, I was going to be with you again
in fourteen days. Unfortunately, that is not what happened. I remained in
Münster for the sake of my poor mother, and for the sake of the poor possessions that I had in Münster.[2] I hadn't imagined that things would go so
far in Münster. I got a housewife whom your Worships certainly know, as
I'm told by your miller Bernard, who's also in Münster.

Also, my dear squires, I stayed with my wife at her mother and brother's residence. If I hadn't done this, a foreigner would have lived there or
they would have torn it down and burned it, so I had to remain in Münster.[3] For they say all of that was godless property. If I hadn't lived there, that
would all have been torn down, and I would have forfeited all my property.

Also, my dear squires and your dear mother, I am asking you to write
for me and to request of My Gracious Lord of Münster that I may receive
mercy so that I can rush out and rush to one of the blockhouses. My dear
squires, your dear mother told me the truth before: "Master Henry, if you

---

1. This phrase is a late medieval/early modern form of greeting suitable for a subordinate addressing his superior(s).

2. Gresbeck's mother was a widow named Margaret. In the aftermath of the city's conquest, she
abjured Anabaptism and retained possession of her house, which she left to her son Henry because of
the merit he earned in the city's capture (presumably meaning that he got the house rather than his
brother?) upon her death in 1542. For such details as are known about her, see Kirchhoff, *Die Täufer
in Münster*, 223.

3. Gresbeck's new wife was of surprisingly high social status (see also note 7 below), and her
property would be subject to plunder by the Anabaptists if left unguarded (for property taken from
the homes of rich people, see Gresbeck, 57v, Kerssenbrock, *Anabaptistici furosis*, ed. Detmer, 542–43).

go to Münster, you'll get yourself baptized too." For she told me the truth. I wouldn't believe it. My dear squires, I request of you for God's sake that if I've angered you, you'll forgive me this. For I've certainly been your poor dear servant, and I am asking to be your poor servant, as I live.

Also, my dear squires, I can't hold out with my wife any longer, because in the next days I must either die of hunger or rush out and get myself killed.[4] So I am asking you not to forget me. For we poor burghers who remained there on the Friday were forced to it there and couldn't avoid it. For I've never had any guilt in this, as Your Worships certainly know.[5]

Also, my dear squires, I hope that I'll attain mercy from my wife's mother and brothers. [v] Her family is that of the Clevorns: the blessed [i.e., deceased][6] Albert Clevorn's daughter, her brothers named William and Albert Clevorn and Lord Christian Clevorn, and her mother, Clevorn's wife.[7] If I should have mercy from My Gracious Lord and from you, I ask that you write and make the request for me. Otherwise, I have no idea how I shall get away. My dear squires, do try your best in this! I urgently make this request of you. My service for all time, no more than a thousand good nights! Because of my distraught heart, I can't write any more. If I live to see the day when I may come to you, then you'll certainly learn everything. My dear squires, I request for God's sake that you do remember me to My Gracious Lord if possible. All my good friends will have good nights! Whether I live or die, may God help us all!

---

4. For a similar expression, see Gresbeck, 124r, 137r.

5. What he means is no guilt in the Anabaptist enterprise. But how would the squires have any knowledge of what he was up to in the city? Presumably, he means that they would know that he'd shown no interest in it in the earlier period and could extrapolate from that.

6. I.e., deceased.

7. Kerssenbrock lists an Albert Clevorn among the patrician magistrates who successfully administered the city in the days before the Anabaptists (*Anabaptistici furosis*, ed. Detmer, 393), and Albert Clevorn is also listed among the members of the first city council after the city's recapture, which was appointed by the prince-bishop in 1536 (ibid., 889). That Gresbeck should have married a woman connected with this family is at first sight surprising. The patrician families had ambitions to associate themselves with the knighthood of the bishopric, and once the knights began to reject intermarriage with them in the early fifteenth century, the patricians restricted themselves to marriages within their social circle, generally disdaining intermarriage with the notables of towns around Münster and with the non-patrician families of the city's ruling class (Lahrkamp, *Deutches Patriziat,* 197). Hence, it would normally be out of the question for the daughter of a patrician family to marry a man of such comparatively low status as Gresbeck. Undoubtedly, the unexpected marriage is to be explained with the supposition that his future wife was one of the women left behind by rich families to guard their property when the menfolk opposed to Anabaptism withdrew or were forced out of the city in February 1534 (Gresbeck, 40v; cf. 12v).

Also, my dear squires, I have my watch post opposite the Cleves blockhouse outside the city of Münster, by the Cross Gate. I can certainly be
called to there in the evening or the light of day, and call "Hans of Brilen"
and not "Master Henry Carpenter." Otherwise, they'll notice in the city,
and then I'd surely be done in. I would rush out as soon as I can. My dear
squires, do try your best in this! I will be your servant for as long as I live.

Master Henry, carpenter in Münster
Remember me!

Document 3

Justinian of Holzhausen's Account of the Capture of Münster

(Written on July 1, 1535)

> Justinian of Holzhausen was an officer in the besieging army.
> The excerpt here comes from a much longer letter written by
> him to the city council of Frankfurt. For the original German,
> see Cornelius, *Berichte der augenzeugen*, 361–67 (the excerpt is
> on 364–67).

[364] For the sake of capturing the city, we kept a captured cabinetmaker
from Münster for about four or five weeks. He reported, depicted, and
showed in the earth how the city is equipped on the outside with defenses,
especially in the place where he did watch duty.[8] Upon this information
and report of his and with trust in him, we decided to inspect the city in the
reported place.[9] Although it was decided among us to persevere in this until
the arrival of us (the military councilors), the confirmed bishop made the
plan through another prisoner[10] [365] who was also familiar with the place,
ordered gangways and other gear helpful for the purpose,[11] and in our ab-

---

8. For Gresbeck's account of his sketch of the city's defenses, see 144v.
9. For the initial investigation of the city's defenses, see 145v–146r.
10. I.e., Little Hans of Longstreet.
11. For the construction of the gear, see 147v. The gangways must have struck everybody's imagination, as they are mentioned both here in the Gresbeck passage and in Overstein's report (appendix,

sence decided with the commander together with the captains to undertake the matter and put it to the test. Therefore, on St. John's Day,[12] towards evening around eleven or twelve o'clock, they were sent with everything. Our prisoner was in the forefront together with the bishop's informant,[13] and our man swam across the outer canal, which is about thirty feet wide, and he towed across the gangway, which was tied to his body by a long line, and fixed it firmly in place.[14] Then, sixteen men ordered to do so followed him over the gangway, and pulled down the iron stakes in the canal. This took place by the Cross Gate between two great walls. They got over the wall onto the great sconce raised up with earth, and on it and directly under it they stabbed the sleeping watchmen to death, two on their guns, the others in their beds in the guardhouses. Meanwhile, the other knechts who had been waiting here secretly headed off. These men followed.[15] Right away, the first men then took possession of the small door that was in the city door and remained open unlocked all night. Once forty to fifty men got across the gangway, it broke apart.[16] The knechts rushed to the wall that our knechts had possession of, and there they fixed the ladders in place (though they were a bit too short). About five hundred got on top and then into the city, with four banners and their captains.[17] In the city, these men began to engage the enemy, as they were now headed for the shouting, the longer the stronger, and in the city they pressed and stabbed and shot each other hither and yon, up and down, around the squares and streets. In the meanwhile, the little door up on the wall was closed again.[18] No one knows how it actually closed, except that some people would say that our own knechts did it, with the intention that they could then plunder all the more at leisure.[19] The pursuing in the city lasted until towards daylight at around six

document 4).

12. June 24.

13. Note how clearly Little Hans is associated with the prince-bishop, while Gresbeck is considered by the officers of the besieging army as "their man." This distinction would explain why the prince-bishop chose to give all the credit for proposing and carrying out the plan for the city's capture to Little Hans alone.

14. For Gresbeck's escapade with the gangway, see 149v–150r.

15. This and the preceding sentence are not entirely clear, but apparently Justinian means that while the sixteen men first mounted the walls and killed the guards, the remainder of the attack force waited and then followed once surprise was assured.

16. Gresbeck, 150r, puts at thirty-four the number who got across before the gangway collapsed.

17. For the significance of "banners," see main text, note 457.

18. For Gresbeck's discussion of the closing of the postern gate, see Gresbeck, 150r.

19. This rumor is clearly ridiculous. No one in his right mind would intentionally trap himself

o'clock, without anyone being able to get in or out. At that point, the confirmed bishop's informant came with the chief lieutenant and some knechts [366] and reopened the little door, although the main body, which was still outside the city, couldn't know whether they were defeated or not. As soon as day broke, they were also shot at from their encampment on the other sconce, so that they had to fall back completely, all the way to a small group that included the main captain[20] and Lord George Weiss and Marx Hessen, the Trier military councilor,[21] who were staying in an old trench close up to the city and waiting for what God would grant. In the meanwhile, an ensign with some of our knechts came back on top of the wall. Our knechts fell upon an exit close by the same wall and shoved the gate open, so that they lowered the drawbridge. At this point, the main captain and the main body rushed in, killed any men that defended themselves. Up to about three hundred, including the new king,[22] enclosed themselves within a wagon fort with their artillery up at the cathedral square.[23] They asked for mercy. Mercy was proclaimed to them, and with white batons they were expelled from the territory across the sea.[24] Otherwise, none of the women or children perished, provided that they didn't defend themselves. Thus, it was by the especial grace of God and not through the skill of the soldiery that the city was conquered. For when the first gangway broke apart and the little door was closed, the knechts who were in the city and gave more thought to plunder and theft than defense would never have conquered the city. For those who were capable of arms bearing were still up to eight hundred strong, which could hardly have been anticipated, even with the

in an enemy-held city with an eye to improving his chances of plundering without interference before the perilous task of defeating the enemy has even begun, much less been achieved. The way in which Justinian repeats the rumor shows that he has no particular faith in it and is merely repeating it as the only known explanation for the failure of the attackers to retain possession of the door. Carelessness in the heat of battle is much more likely to be the real explanation. After all, no one had expected the door to be open, so no provision had been made about seizing it (and presumably the importance of keeping it open did not occur to anyone as they rushed into the city). In any event, Gresbeck accepted this explanation (151v).

20. For "main captain," see main text, note 293.

21. *Kriegsrat.*

22. For the mistaken report that when Bernard Krechting was appointed as a subordinate to John of Leiden, he actually replaced him as king, see Gresbeck, 145r.

23. For Gresbeck's account of the final battle by the wagon fort, see Gresbeck, 152r.

24. Presumably, this is the source of Gresbeck's uncertain report that the expelled women went to England (156r).

report of all the prisoners who'd previously gotten out.[25] They also captured the first king[26] and Knipperdolling, and the bishop put them in prison. The location of Stutenberent, their leading privy councilor, still remains hidden.[27] They are still being likewise found and stabbed.[28] Little money in gold was found—so little that the bishop, to whom belonged half of it, threatened not to pay the landsknechts from it—although it's known that there was a lot there. Where it has gone, God knows.[29] They say that the people in Münster buried it before this time . . .

Document 4

Count Wirich of Falkenstein's Account of the Capture of Münster

(Written on November 6, 1535)

> This excerpt comes from a long report to the bishops of Mainz, Cologne, and Trier and the princes of Jülich, Hesse, and Nassau (the rulers who took over the besieging army in the fall of 1534) that was written by the commander of the besieging forces and his military councilors some months after the capture. For the German text, see Cornelius, *Berichte der augenzeugen*, 383–98 (excerpt on 393–98).

[393] Around this time, two of them—the one being Little Hans of Longstreet and the other called Master Henry Grossbeck, cabinetmaker and burgher in Münster—betook themselves from the city one night (Trinity Sunday[30]), though one without the knowledge of the other. Little Hans of Longstreet was previously a trench master outside the city and defected

---

25. I.e., captured escapees from the city.

26. Again, this refers to the mistaken idea that John of Leiden had been replaced as king by his subordinate Krechting. Hence, the phrase "first king" must signify John.

27. He was never found.

28. That is, a week after the city's capture, hidden Anabaptists were still being discovered (and executed).

29. For the affair of the landsknechts' dissatisfaction with the booty and their attempt to track down the supposedly hidden gold, see Gresbeck, 154r–155r.

30. Trinity Sunday is the first Sunday after Pentecost, and Pentecost is the fiftieth day after Easter. Since Easter fell on March 28 in 1535, Pentecost was Monday, May 17, with the following Sunday being May 23.

to it, becoming the king's attendant. But with assistance and knowledge, as we think, this man Little Hans got through the ditch and then all the way to Hamm, where he kept himself for a while, unbeknownst to us.[31] The other, however, Master Henry the cabinetmaker, was captured towards daylight and delivered to me (the commander).[32] In order to save his life, this man described every situation in the city and also how the fortifications are laid out all around, and then, at our request, the artillery, walls, and gate through which he supposed it to be possible to get in most skillfully, thoroughly drawing clearly in the earth as a model how the right gate is defended.[33] When we noted the skillfulness and it pleased us, we had this gate and canal inspected at night in the presence of him and one of our men together with military councilors and certain captains, and at once he swam across the first ditch all the way to the palisade fence on the wall.[34]

Upon this inspection, we took counsel with him according to all urgency, and as soon as the night, which at that time was quite short and light, got somewhat darker,[35] we decided to put the plan to the test with the help of God. In the meanwhile, we were informed that Little Hans of Longstreet was at Hamm, and as soon as we learned this, we ordered him to wait so that we could question him, just like our prisoner, about a sure situation for conquering the city. [394] There comes to us other information, that Little Hans obtained a hearing with My Gracious Lord of Münster to offer certain good plans, and for this reason Your Princely Graces gave him a free and totally sure safe conduct for body and life.

When Little Hans got the safe conduct from Your Princely Graces and was negotiating with Your Princely Graces, we stopped our undertaking with him.

Upon this, we reached an agreement, at the request of Their Princely Grace, with the councilors about having Little Hans and our captive cabinetmaker come together in order to hear the plans of both of them at the same time. They came to a complete agreement in every regard just as our

31. For Gresbeck's account of Little Hans's escape to Hamm, see Gresbeck, 146r.

32. As in Justinian of Holtzhausen's account, Gresbeck is clearly associated with the officers of the besieging army, while Little Hans is the prince-bishop's man.

33. For Gresbeck's account of his sketch of the city's defenses, see Gresbeck, 144v.

34. For the initial investigation of the city's defenses, see Gresbeck, 145v–146r.

35. Since the Julian calendar was running ten days ahead of the solar calendar in the sixteenth century, the summer solstice would have fallen on about June 11 by the calendar, so the nights would only have started getting longer after that date (and the actual assault took place nearly two weeks later).

prisoner had advised before.[36] Upon this previously suggested plan the confirmed bishop ordered the preparation of all the gear that was helpful for it.
When all equipment was in hand, and the night was somewhat darker,[37] an
agreement about the day and hour for undertaking this was to be made . . .

At this point, during our absence, the councilors of the confirmed
bishop of Münster reached an agreement with the commander together
with the [395] captains in the blockhouses about the day and hour for conquering the city, which was fulfilled with the help of God, as follows . . .

After this, the common man[38] was warned and admonished on St.
John's Day[39] to prepare themselves in full armor in their blockhouses and to
stay sober,[40] and when night came on, between ten and eleven, they moved
out for the designated Cross Gate.

When enough men were gathered, there was over the outermost canal
an arranged gangway, over which our captive cabinetmaker swam with a
line that was attached to the gangway tied around his body and positioned
correctly. First, some knechts with short weapons were ordered across, who
secretly got through the stick fence and, on the wall as far as the sconce,
stabbed to death the watch that was on it. Some more men followed them,
and the gangway broke apart under them.[41] Those who got across it found
the small door in the gate open and took possession of the gate. The rest of
our knechts rushed with the assault ladders to the sconce and one helped
the other up it on the spears and hafted axes, so that in a short time up to
about five hundred knechts with some captains and ensigns got on top of
the sconce and into the city. Now that they dropped in in squads, and the
people in the city were on the move, a strong squad in the city came to the
rebaptizers by the Cross Gate, they fell upon our knechts, few of whom

36. This passage confirms Gresbeck's claims (144v, 146v) to have been as instrumental in formu-
lating the plan for the city as Little Hans was.
37. The attack on June 24 by the calendar actually took place on Gregorian July 4. In point of
fact, the night on that date would have been only about eight minutes longer than it had been on the
solstice, so the additional darkness was minimal.
38. I.e., common soldiers.
39. June 24. This day was theoretically associated with the solstice (or at least the start of summer), but due to the Julian calendar running ahead of the solar calendar, the solstice had taken place
about seven days earlier.
40. No doubt the debacle of the first storm on the city that was caused by drunkenness was very
much on the commanders' minds (see main text, note 180). Gresbeck, 149r, notes the prohibition
against selling liquor to the troops.
41. For Gresbeck's escapade with the gangway, see Gresbeck, 149v–150r.

[396] at that time perished by this, and thrust them out, kept possession of the gate and slammed it closed, so that no more of our men could get in and the rest could not get out.[42] Meanwhile, they chased each other up one street and down the next, and forced each other all over the place, with hostile shouting and crying. In this engagement, some knechts of ours perished. This engagement in and outside the city continued until the second hour in the day.[43] During this, it happened that our men in the city opened the Jew Fields Gate, the one next to the Cross Gate, which was most weakly defended. Through it, I (the commander) came in with the main body of our army. Now that the people in the city were for the most part overcome, the rest enclosed themselves together within a wagon fort up at the marketplace, wishing to put themselves on the defensive there. When they noticed that they were too weak, however, they pleaded for the mercy of sparing their lives, which was granted to them after a council was held, and they were immediately expelled from the city and territory. During this negotiation, the king John of Leiden and Knipperdolling were found and seized. The king was presented to me (the commander) by a landsknecht, but he was extorted back by Wilcken and the knechts and brought and delivered to the Münster councilors. After the city was conquered in this way through the assistance of God, the confirmed bishop moved in on the Monday after St. John's Day.[44] The aforementioned Wilcken, together with some captains, rode to meet His Princely Grace, carrying with him the king's crown on his hand and his sword, presenting these to the confirmed bishop of Münster as booty. . . .

[397] . . . Straightaway, the confirmed bishop reenlisted three banners to occupy the city with.

In these days, everything in the way of household goods that there still was in the houses was listed by the booty masters, three of whom were appointed by each banner. Those who had withdrawn[45] were granted leave to buy back their property. If they were not present, and in the case of those

42. Note that Overstein attributes the capture of the postern gate to a counterattack by the Anabaptists rather than to carelessness on Little Hans's part (see Gresbeck, 150v, for a rather different version of this event).
43. On July 5 (the relevant date by the Gregorian calendar), the sun rises in Münster around 4:15 a.m. (standard time), so the second hour of the day would have started around 5:15 a.m.
44. June 28.
45. I.e., those who had fled the Anabaptist regime and were not held culpable for their behavior.

who were dead, everyone was permitted to buy; at any rate the resident natives of the territory were. Whatever was sold in this way was all brought to a common booty, and one half of the whole booty was distributed to our much mentioned Gracious Lord and the other half to knechts and captains, apart from us (the commander) and the military councilors.

All captured guns, large and small, were retained by the confirmed bishop of Münster . . .

Works Cited

Albrecht, Thorsten, et al. *Das Königreich der Täufer: Reformation und Herrschaft in Münster.* Münster: Stadtmuseum Münster, 2000.

Arnold, Thomas. *The Renaissance at War.* London: Cassel & Co., 2001.

Arthur, Anthony. *The Tailor-King: The Rise and Fall of the Anabaptist Kingdom of Munster.* New York: St. Martin's Press, 1999.

Backus, Irena. *Reformation Readings of the Apocalypse: Geneva, Zurich, and Wittenberg.* New York: Oxford University Press, 2000.

Baumann, Reinhard. *Landsknechte: Ihre Geschichte und Kultur vom späten Mittelalter bis zum Dreißigjährigen Krieg.* Munich: Verlag C. H. Beck, 1994.

Black, Jeremy. *European Warfare, 1494–1660.* London: Routledge, 2002.

Blau, Friedrich. *Die Deutschen Landsknechte: Ein Kulturbild.* 3rd ed. Vienna: Phaidon Akademische Verlagsgesellschaft Athenaion, 1985.

Blickle, Peter. *The Revolution of 1525: The German Peasants War from a New Perspective.* Translated by Thomas A. Brady Jr. and H. C. Erik Midelfort. New York: Johns Hopkins University Press, 1981.

Cohn, Norman. *Pursuit of the Millennium.* Rev. ed. Oxford: Oxford University Press, 1973.

Cornelius, Carl Adolf. *Berichte der augenzeugen über das münsterische wiedertäuferreich.* Münster: Druck und Verlag der Theissing'schen Buchhandlung, 1853.

Corrsin, Stephen D. *Sword Dancing in Europe: A History.* London: Hisarlik Press, 1997.

De Bakker, Willem, Michael Driedger, and James Stayer. *Bernhard Rothmann and the Reformation in Münster, 1530–35.* Kitchener, ON: Pandora Press, 2009.

Deppermann, Klaus. *Melchior Hoffman.* Translated by Malcolm Wren and edited by Benjamin Drewery. Edinburgh: T. & T. Clarke, 1987.

Duffy, Christopher. *Siege Warfare: The Fortress in the Early Modern World, 1494–1660*. London: Routledge & Kegan Paul, 1979.

Duffy, Eamon. *The Stripping of the Altars: Traditional Religion in England ca. 1400–ca. 1580*. 2nd ed. New Haven: Yale University Press, 2005.

Duke, Alastair. *Reformation and Revolt in the Low Countries*. London: Hambledon Press, 1990.

Egg, Erich. "From Mariagnano to the Thirty Years' War 1515–1648." In *Guns: An Illustrated History of Artillery*, edited by Joseph Jobé, 37–54. New York: Crescent Books, 1979.

Goertz, Hans-Jürgen. "Radical Religiosity in the German Reformation." In *A Companion to the Reformation Word*, edited by R. Po-Chia Hsia, 70–85. Oxford: Blackwell Publishing, 2006.

Grimm, Jacob, and Wilhelm Grimm. *Deutsches Wörterbuch*. 1854. Reprint edition, Munich: Taschenbuch Verlag, 1999.

Hamilton, Alastair. *The Apocryphal Apocalypse: The Reception of the Second Book of Esdras (4 Ezra) from the Renaissance to the Enlightenment*. Oxford: Clarendon Press, 1999.

Haude, Sigrun. *In the Shadow of "Savage Wolves": Anabaptist Münster and the German Reformation during the 1530s*. Boston: Humanities Press, 2000.

HRG = Handwörterbuch zur deutschen Rechtsgeschichte. Edited by Albrecht Cordes et al. 2nd ed. Berlin: E. Schmidt, 2004.

Hsia, R. Po-Chia. *Society and Religion in Münster, 1535–1618*. New Haven: Yale University Press, 1984.

———, ed. *A Companion to the Reformation World*. Oxford: Blackwell Publishing, 2004.

Huebert Hecht, Linda A. "Hille Feicken of Sneak." In *Profiles of Anabaptist Women: Sixteenth-Century Reforming Pioneers*, edited by C. Arnold Snyder and Linda A. Huebert Hecht, 288–97. Waterloo, ON: Wilfrid Laurier University Press, 1996.

Kerssenbrock, Hermann von. *Anabaptistici furoris: Monasterium inclitam westphaliae metropolim evertentis; historica narratio*. 2 vols. Edited by Heinrich Detmer. Münster: Druck und Verlag der Theissing'schen Buchhandlung, 1899–1900.

Kirchhoff, Karl-Heinz. "Die Belagerung und Eroberung Münsters 1534–35." *Westfälische Zeitschrift* 112 (1962): 77–170.

———. "Die Endzeiterwartung der Täufergemeinde zu Münster 1534–35." *Jahrbuch des Vereins für Westfälische Kirchengeschichte* 78 (1985): 19–42.

————. *Die Täufer in Münster 1534–35: Untersuchungen zum Umfang und zur Sozialstruktur der Bewegung.* Münster: Aschendorffsche Verlagsbuchhandlung, 1973.

Klaassen, Walter. *Living at the End of Ages: Apocalyptic Expectation in the Radical Reformation.* Lanham, MD: University Press of America, 1992.

Klötzer, Ralf. *Die Täuferschaft von Münster: Stadtreformation und Welterneuerung.* Münster: Aschendorff, 1992.

————. "The Melchiorites and Münster." In *A Companion to Anabaptism and Spiritualism, 1521–1700,* edited by John D. Roth and James M. Stayer, 217–56. Leiden, NL: Brill, 2007.

Kobelt-Groch, Marion. "Divara of Haarlem." In *Profiles of Anabaptist Women: Sixteenth-Century Reforming Pioneers,* edited by C. Arnold Snyder and Linda A. Huebert Hecht, 298–304. Waterloo, ON: Wilfrid Laurier University Press, 1996.

Köhler, Carl. *History of Costume.* Edited and augmented by Emma von Sichart, translated by Alexander K. Dallas. London: G. G. Harap, 1928.

Lahrkamp, Helmut. "Das Patriziat in Münster." In *Deutsches Patriziat, 1430–1740,* edited by Hellmuth Rössler, 195–207. Limburg an der Lahn: C. A. Starke Verlag, 1968.

Lübben, August. *Niederdeutsche Grammatik nebst Chrestomathie und Glossar.* 1882. Reprint edition, Osnabrück: Otto Zeller Verlag, 1970.

Lutterbach, Hubertus. *Der Weg in das Täuferreich von Münster: Ein Ringen um die heilige Stadt.* Münster: Dialogverlag, 2006.

MacCulloch, Diarmaid. *Reformation: Europe's House Divided 1490–1700.* London: Allen Lane, 2003.

Mackay, Christopher S. *Narrative of the Anabaptist Madness: The Overthrow of Münster, the Famous Metropolis of Westphalia.* Leiden, NL: Brill, 2007.

Mellink, A. F. *De Wederdopers in de Noordelijke Nederlanden.* Groningen, NL: J. B. Wolters, 1954.

Miller, John. *Landsknecht Soldier: 1486–1560.* Oxford: Osprey Publishing, 1976.

Niesert, Joseph. *Münsterische Urkundensammlung.* Coesfeld: Bernard Wittneven, 1826.

Oberman, Heiko A. *Luther: Man between God and the Devil.* Translated by Eileen Walliser-Schwartzbart. New Haven, CT: Yale University Press, 1989.

Oman, Charles. *A History of the Art of War in the Sixteenth Century.* New York: E. P. Dutton & Co., 1937.

Pater, Calvin Augustine. *Karlstadt as the Father of the Baptist Movements: The Emergence of Lay Protestantism.* Toronto, ON: University of Toronto Press, 1984.

Pertz, Georg Heinrich. "Handschrift der herzoglichen Bibliothek zu Meiningen." *Archiv für Gesellschaft für Ältere Deutsche Geschichtskunde* 8 (1843): 671–74.

Petersen, Rodney. *Preaching in the Last Days: The Theme of the "Two Witnesses" in the Sixteenth and Seventeenth Centuries.* New York: Oxford University Press, 1993.

Pirckheimer, Willibald. *Opera politica, historica, philologica et epistolica.* 1610. Reprint, edited by Melchior Goldast. Hildeheim: Georg Olm Verlag, 1969.

Redlich, Fritz. *The German Military Enterpriser and His Work Force: A Study in European Economic and Social History.* Wiesbaden: Franz Steiner Verlag, 1964.

Richards, John. *Landsknecht Soldiers: 1486–1560.* Oxford: Osprey Publishing, 2002.

Roth, John D., and James M. Stayer, eds. *A Companion to Anabaptism and Spiritualism, 1521–1700.* Leiden, NL: Brill, 2007.

Schiller, Karl Christian, and August Lübben. *Mittelniederdeutsches Wörterbuch.* 1875–81. Reprint, Wiesbaden: M. Sändig, 1969.

Scott, Tom. "The Peasants' War." In *A Companion to the Reformation Word*, edited by R. Po-Chia Hsia, 56–69. Oxford: Blackwell Publishing, 2006.

Snyder, C. Arnold, and Linda A. Huebert Hecht, eds. *Profiles of Anabaptist Women: Sixteenth-Century Reforming Pioneers.* Waterloo, ON: Wilfrid Laurier Press, 1996.

Stayer, James M. *Anabaptists and the Sword.* New edition including "Reflections and Retractions." Eugene, OR: Wipf and Stock Publishers, 2002.

———. *The German Peasants' War and Anabaptist Community of Goods.* Montreal: McGill-Queen's University Press, 1991.

Strauss, Gerald. *Manifestations of Discontent on the Eve of the Reformation.* Bloomington: Indiana University Press, 1971.

Stupperich, Robert. *Die Schriften B. Rothmanns.* Münster in Westfalen: Aschendorffsche Verlagsbuchhandlung, 1970.

Wailes, Stephen D. *The Rich Man and Lazarus on the Reformation Stage: A Contribution to the Social History of German Drama.* Selingsgrove, PA: Susquehanna University Press; London: Associated University Presses, 1997.

Williams, George Huntston. *The Radical Reformation.* 3rd ed. Sixteenth Century Essays and Studies 15. Kirksville, MO: Sixteenth Century Journal Publishers [Truman State University Press], 1992.

Index

"n" following a page number indicates a note on that page; plates (pl.) are located between pages 150 and 151.

Index of Scripture References

"n" following a page number indicates a note on that page.

About the Author

Christopher S. Mackay has a doctorate in classical philology from Harvard University (1994). Full professor in the Department of History and Classics at the University of Alberta, he has published books on a wide range of topics: *Ancient Rome: A Military And Political History* (2005, 2007), *Malleus Maleficarum: Latin Text and English Translation* (2006, 2012), *Narrative of the Anabaptist Madness* (2007), *Breakdown of the Roman Republic* (2009, 2012), and *Hammer of Witches* (2009). He also translated and adapted Michel Launey, *An Introduction to Classical Nahuatl* (2011).